Best American Short Plays Series

THE
BEST
AMERICAN
SHORT
PLAYS
1995–1997

Best American Short Plays Series

THE
BEST
AMERICAN
SHORT
PLAYS
1995–1997

edited by

HOWARD STEIN
and
GLENN YOUNG

GARDEN CITY, NEW YORK

Copyright © 1997 by Applause Theatre Book Publishers
All Rights Reserved
Published in New York, by Applause Theatre Books

Manufactured in the United States of America

ISBN 1-56865-701-3

CONTENTS 1995–96

CONTENTS 1996–97

THE BEST AMERICAN SHORT PLAYS 1995–1996

To Marianne and Priscilla

INTRODUCTION

Home and the family have been major subjects for the American playwright for the better part of this century. Ben Brantley, daily theater critic for *The New York Times*, defines a bona fide classic family play as "a work that conveys the mystical, cannibalistic pull of family ties even as they unravel." This description aptly sums up Brantley's reaction to *Buried Child* by Sam Shepard, and could as well fit Eugene O'Neill's *Long Day's Journey Into Night*. However, it is less appropriate a description for the family plays that overran Broadway and the American theater from 1920 to 1960, which include *They Knew What They Wanted*, *The Little Foxes*, *Awake and Sing*, *Holiday*, *All My Sons*, *Death of a Salesman*, *Glass Menagerie*, *Cat On A Hot Tin Roof*, *Dark At The Top Of The Stairs*, *Picnic*, and finally, in 1959, *A Raisin In The Sun*. Nevertheless, these plays and their concentration on the American Family gave energy, muscle, and stamina to the development of the nation's theater. Indeed, the entire culture was always alluding to Home and the Family through songs and novels, as well as through plays: "Home Is Where The Heart Is"; "Show Me The Way To Go Home"; "Home, Home On The Range"; "You Can't Go Home Again"; *The Long Voyage Home*; and finally *Home*, by Samm-Art Williams.

The theater reflected and illuminated society's preoccupation. But where classical plays such as *The Oresteia* used the family to dramatize the subject of Justice, where *Hamlet* and *King Lear* used the family to dramatize the scope of the human spirit, and where Molière's comedies used the family to dramatize "Lord, what fools we mortals be," American plays used the family to present familiar situations and problems that pervaded American society. Conflicts between parents and children, husbands and wives, and sisters and brothers brought to light family dilemmas that cut across social, economic, and psychological barriers, revealing and representing what was close to "home" in the American family. The American family was thus both glorified and unmasked.

With a few significant exceptions (Lanford Wilson, Neil Simon, and A.R. Gurney), American family drama was forever changed with the 1960 production of Edward Albee's *The American Dream*. This short play exploded the myth of the American family, causing the subject of Home to be treated in an entirely new fashion. Kopit's *Oh, Dad, Poor Dad, etc.* and David Rabe's *Sticks and Bones*, plays that appeared in New York City within a few years of Albee's, were satiric in tone, surreal in treatment, and severe in their attitude toward family life. Nevertheless, fascination with the topic of Family has continued, even if, perhaps, with less intensity. For example, in the summer of 1995, the McCarter Theater in Princeton organized a series of short plays for Random Acts, their new-works festival under the guidance of Emily Mann, Artistic Director, and Janice Paran, Dramaturg and Supervisor. Paran assigned the subject "Home" to the playwrights, all of whom were commissioned to write for the festival. Two of those plays are included in this volume: *Home Section*, by Janusz Glowacki and *The Sandalwood Box*, by Mac Wellman.

Since the 1960s, however, interest has shifted from the American family to America itself. Inspired by the Vietnam War and the Civil Rights Movement, playwrights inundated the theater with plays dealing with the past, present, and future of America. Listen to the titles: *America Hurrah, God Bless, 1776, 1492, Indians, U.S., We Bombed In New Haven, Blues For Mister Charlie, Viet Rock, MacBird*...the list goes on. Playwrights today continue to explore the nation as a whole, rather than the individual families that comprise it. In this year's volume of *The Best American Short Plays*, we have included a comic narrative in one act called *The Original Last Wish Baby*, by William Seebring, which attacks American culture, values, and attitudes. One scene ridicules the conventional talk show by having a pundit say, "The phenomenon speaks directly to who we are as a nation." Although the line is written in a mocking tone, the content is all too familiar.

Cassandra Medley's *Dearborn Heights* is a very different play from Seebring's satire. Copyrighted in 1995, the drama takes place in Michigan in 1951, and deals with the hypocritical, damaging, and humiliating treatment of American blacks by American whites. Medley then takes the story one step further to show how that abuse can tear the black community apart by causing American blacks to turn on each other. The subject is especially appropriate for 1996 America. Jonathan Levy's *Old Blues* also harks back to another time, the time of the old college try and old college ties and the romanticism of college singing groups. But, like *Dearborn Heights*, this play is haunted by an off-stage presence. In *Dearborn Heights* that presence is the unseen white customers in the cafe, whose stares and glares grow into an ominous, smothering cloud of disapproval. In *Old Blues*, the dead companion, who has died with his boots on as a charter member of the group, represents the values of the anachronistic nature of the group he left behind. The plays indirectly direct themselves to present-day America.

Lavonne Mueller, in her *American Dreamers*, writes about a fictional encounter in 1962 during which Carl Sandburg joins forces with Marilyn Monroe to consider the present and future of America and its dreams. Mueller's imaginative and inventive rendering of two American icons meeting under extraordinary conditions (she used a similar device in *Little Victories*, where Susan B. Anthony joins forces with Joan of Arc) allows her to express, through them, her concern for this nation. Michael Feingold, on the other hand, uses the playwrighting techniques of the past to shed light not only on the conventions of nineteenth-century playmaking, but also on the narrow minds of the twentieth-century playgoer. Feingold does not confine his sharp bites to America, by any means.

Perhaps the most telling subject among the plays in this volume is that of faith, the nation's most critical and crucial issue, especially faith in love. Paul Selig's *Mystery School* portrays three women struggling with belief as a source of immediate, as well as eternal, salvation; as a means of dealing with both the present and the future. Allan Knee's *The St. Valentine's Day Massacre* would appear to be a conventional drama of two lovers, or ex-lovers, in a "same time next year" ritual. But, in the course of their exchange, Kenny recognizes unbearable signs in Sherry—as he says with a note of alarm, "I get the feeling you don't believe in love anymore, either." While teaching at Columbia, I met one day with our master teacher of Directing, Liviu Ciulei, who startled me by announcing that he had confronted his students that very morning and concluded that they didn't believe in love. I tried, unsuccessfully, to calm him down. Later that day, I called our youngest son, Josh, age 36, and asked him if he thought his generation believed in love. His answer was, "My generation, Dad, can't afford love. They can afford big cars, long trips, international vacations, state of the art stereo equipment, but they can't afford love."

Monroe, in *American Dreamers*, claims that with her devotion and passion for the President, "This love is going to save the world." Not the lovers, not the community, not the nation, not the hemisphere, but the world. Ed, in *Degas, C'est Moi*, calls out, ". . . are Edgar Degas and I not united by our shared humanity? By our common need for love?" *Fitting Rooms* opens with a conversation between two female friends of long standing, about marriage and happiness, the central issue being the changing nature of love. Their faith in what love can accomplish has eroded to the point of collapse. But, by the end of the play, it is clear that for these two women, and for the others in the fitting rooms next to them, the only fitting room, the ultimate fitting room, is love. While *Degas, C'est Moi*, and *St. Valentine's Day Massacre* both deal with youthful love, John Ford Noonan's *When It Comes Early* deals with aging love. Although the play has flashes of the vigor and vitality of the couple's early love, the bulk of the story concentrates on the human, generous, and compassionate nature of their aging love, as both life and love begin to disintegrate before their eyes. The scope is considerable, but the message is clear: love may not conquer all, but we are nothing without it.

> Of all the things America has lost
> It's faith in love it misses most.

When this volume appears in bookstores, I will be approaching my seventy-fifth birthday. Time to stop and concentrate on my wife, my children, and my grandchildren...maybe golf. I am especially grateful to Glenn Young for having given me the opportunity to co-edit with him the last six volumes, and I wish *The Best American Short Plays*, under his discerning stewardship, a long and fruitful life. And to you, the readers, at the risk of sounding like Kate Smith, thanks for listening.

Howard Stein
September, 1996

Susan Cinoman

FITTING ROOMS

SUSAN CINOMAN

Fitting Rooms was first seen at the Ensemble Studio Theatre, and later at Naked Angels under the direction of Jane Hoffman. Other plays by Susan Cinoman, including *Sweet Sand*, *Temple Beautiful*, and *Gin and Bitters*, were also presented at EST. A full production of one-acts titled *Cinoman and Rebeck*, were presented by the Miranda Theatre Company at Alice's Fourth Floor in New York City and received critical acclaim.

Susan Cinoman began as an actress and sketch comedy writer in Philadelphia with her all female comedy group, "The Soubrettes," with whom she recorded the song "Bimbo Rap." She has gone on to be included in the Maxwell Anderson Playwrights Series at the Rich Forum in Stamford, Connecticut, and is an active member of the Miranda Theatre Company and the Theatre Artists Workshop of Westport. Her first musical, *Out of the Blues*, which she wrote with composer Joe Goodrich, is currently being produced by the Miranda Theatre Company. Her latest full length play, *Love and Class in Connecticut*, is forthcoming. Cinoman lives in the aforementioned Connecticut with her husband and her two daughters.

A tony boutique on Philadelphia's Rittenhouse Square. The clothing is elegant and chic with a few bizarre and hideous originals that are there to appeal to some of the clientele. The three pairs of women change clothes in three separate fitting rooms. The action switches quickly from one dressing room to another.

MARIEL: My husband would kill me if I bought this dress.

LINDA: You're kidding.

MARIEL: Well, no. I mean, I don't think he would literally kill me. But I know he wouldn't be very happy.

LINDA: Well, who cares about that.

MARIEL: That's true.

LINDA: I mean it's not as if he makes you happy.

MARIEL: But can anyone really make anyone else happy?

LINDA: What do you mean?

MARIEL: I mean don't you have to make yourself happy.

LINDA: I guess that's true. All the more reason for you to buy the dress.

MARIEL: You don't care what any man thinks about you, do you?

LINDA: No.

MARIEL: How do you manage that?

LINDA: I think about other things.

MARIEL: Like what?

LINDA: Like your marriage. Pamela's marriage. All your marriages.

MARIEL: But how does that do it for you?

LINDA: I don't know really. Between that and work I'm busy.

[*Light change to* RISSA *and* KATE.]

RISSA: Did you want to try that on, Mrs. Oliver?

KATE: Yes. Thank you, Rissa.

RISSA: That's a good color for you.

KATE: It is?

RISSA: Definitely.

KATE: How can you tell?

RISSA: How can I tell?

KATE: Yes. How do you know?

RISSA: You're a Winter.

KATE: What am I?

RISSA: A Winter. I'm a Summer. My most beautiful colors are red and yellow. Now that color would look good on me, but not great. It would make the green tones in my skin come out. But, if I wanted to look beautiful I wouldn't wear that color, but you would. Because you're cold. Very cold.

KATE: Do you have this dress in red or yellow?

RISSA: Yes. But, you won't look as beautiful in it. Remember? Cold. Winter?

KATE: Yes, that's right.

RISSA: Sure.

KATE: Then I guess I'll try this on. In this color.

RISSA: That seems to be the way to go.

KATE: Uh-huh.

RISSA: This is going very well.

KATE: Mmm.

RISSA: For you.

[*Light change to* MARIEL *and* LINDA.]

MARIEL: I think I look like an eel in this.

LINDA: I love it on you.

MARIEL: I don't think Gary will.

LINDA: Gary.

MARIEL: He is my husband.

LINDA: But not your father.

MARIEL: But he'll say it's too tight.

LINDA: So? What will he do? Ground you?

MARIEL: It's easy for you to say.

LINDA: Yes. It is.

MARIEL: I'm just trying to do the right thing.

LINDA: It's not a moral issue. It's just rayon.

MARIEL: I mean I'm trying to be a good partner.

LINDA: But it's your wardrobe.

MARIEL: But I'm his wife.

LINDA: But it's your body.

MARIEL: But it's his charge card.

LINDA: But it's your signature.

MARIEL: It's so hard to know what to wear.

LINDA: Look, wearing clothes is just like anything else. It seems really important to you how you look. But, basically after the first minute that someone sees you they pay no attention, anyway. So, you might as well do what you want to do.

MARIEL: That doesn't make me feel better.

LINDA: Is that my function? Am I here to make you feel better?

MARIEL: As my friend, yes.

LINDA: Is that what friends are for?

MARIEL: Among other things.

LINDA: You never make me feel better.

MARIEL: But that's not within my power.

LINDA: But it's in mine for you.

MARIEL: Yes.

LINDA: And why is that?

MARIEL: Because you're the independent one.

LINDA: So?

MARIEL: So, I'm the dependent one.

LINDA: OK . . .

MARIEL: And the dependent one can't make the independent one feel better.

LINDA: Then what can the dependent one do for the independent one?

MARIEL: You mean after the independent one makes the dependent one feel better?

LINDA: Yes. What does the independent one get to feel?

MARIEL: Superior.

LINDA: I see.

MARIEL: But not better. Only the independent one has the power there.

LINDA: So, if I make you feel better and persuade you that you don't look like an eel, then I get to feel superior.

MARIEL: Yes.

LINDA: You don't look like an eel.

MARIEL: Really?

LINDA: Absolutely.

MARIEL: Now, I feel better. Will you ask the salesgirl if they have this a size smaller?

[KAHINE *and* TIA *enter. They are very young and thin, dressed in tight tops and denim skirts or jeans with lots of black touches, maybe all black, red lipstick.*]

KAHINE: Where are the prom dresses?

TIA: Oh cool, Ka. Look at this one.

KAHINE: That's more your type of thing.

TIA: But . . . it goes with your hair.

KAHINE: My hair's gonna be burgundy, I told you that.

TIA: Well, I forgot. Like, have me arrested or something. Is Suzanne Vega gay?

KAHINE: Probably.

TIA: All the cool people seem to be gay. Don't you think?

KAHINE: Cool boots.

TIA: They're not very retro.

KAHINE: So?

TIA: So . . . I thought that was what you liked.

KAHINE: Retro is going out.

TIA: You're kidding?

KAHINE: I'm dead serious.

TIA: Wow.

KAHINE: What's coming in is Eco. Like, plants and animals.

TIA: Really?

KAHINE: Yeah. All different species. They say it's because of the Berlin Wall.

TIA: What Berlin Wall?

KAHINE: You know, the one that fell.

TIA: Are the Berlin Wall and The Iron Curtain the same thing?

KAHINE: Tia, one's a wall and one's a curtain.

TIA: Oh.

KAHINE: They can't be the same thing.

TIA: So, where are we having the prom? Did the committee decide it?

KAHINE: Tatou.

TIA: Cool.

KAHINE: Of course, Danielle didn't even know where it was.

TIA: Danielle is an asshole.

KAHINE: Please. Who isn't?

TIA: You. You're not.

KAHINE: Well.

TIA: Am I?

KAHINE: No. You're not. But you will be if you try that scanky thing on.

[*Change to* LINDA *and* MARIEL.]

LINDA: I don't see the sales girl.

MARIEL: Do you like the back of this?

LINDA: Yes. I told you to buy it.

MARIEL: Don't get hostile, please.

LINDA: Mariel, I'd like to go have lunch.

MARIEL: You sound just like Gary.

LINDA: No, I don't.

MARIEL: You do. He doesn't understand that it takes me time to make a decision. He doesn't understand that I get anxiety when I'm rushed. He likes me to feel anxiety.

LINDA: I don't like you to feel anxiety.

MARIEL: You must because you're rushing me.

LINDA: I'm sorry.

MARIEL: I told you that it might take some time to find the right dress.

LINDA: I know.

MARIEL: I told you that I'd wait for you to finish work so I didn't feel rushed.

LINDA: You're right.

MARIEL: And then you rush me anyway.

LINDA: You're right. I'm sorry.

MARIEL: You are?

LINDA: I'm deeply sorry.

MARIEL: You're my best friend.

LINDA: I know.

MARIEL: You're the only one I can talk to.

LINDA: I know.

MARIEL: If it wasn't for you I'd just stay at home and wait for Gary.

LINDA: I know. I know.

MARIEL: It's no picnic having a rich husband, you know.

LINDA: I'm sure it's very difficult for you.

MARIEL: You don't really think it's difficult.

LINDA: Sure, I do.

MARIEL: No, you don't. You don't know what it's like to have to be enthusiastic over someone else's accomplishments all day long.

LINDA: No . . .

MARIEL: And to have to be the perennial hostess, and to have to sexually service someone even when you don't feel like it just to know that you can have breakfast the next morning.

LINDA: Jesus, Mariel . . .

MARIEL: Well, it's true.

LINDA: Then why do it?

MARIEL: Do what?

LINDA: Why be a well paid minion if it makes you so miserable?

MARIEL: Well . . . because . . .

LINDA: Yes?

MARIEL: Because what's the alternative?

LINDA: The alternative . . .

MARIEL: Isn't the alternative . . . to be you?

[*Change to* RISSA *and* KATE.]

RISSA: I think I like this one better.

KATE: I . . . I appreciate all your time, Rissa . . .

RISSA: No problem. I mean your welcome, Mrs. Oliver. You know, I hate when people say thank you, and people say back to them, "No problem." Like, you didn't say, "Is this a problem," to which I would answer, "No problem." You said, "I appreciate that," to which I answer, "you're welcome." You know what I mean?

KATE: I do.

RISSA: I know. You know a lot of that I picked up from you, Mrs. Oliver.

KATE: What?

RISSA: You know, the right way to be. You come in, you look nice, you talk enough, but not too loud. In my neighborhood everybody screams. And the grammar. I mean you could break your neck tripping over the G's that get dropped all up and down Ninth Street. Not that I inspire to be an intellectual snob. But, someday I'd like to own this business. Someday I'll be finished at Drexel . . . I . . . are you OK, Mrs. Oliver?

KATE: Actually I'm having a little trouble with the zipper.

RISSA: Here . . . let me . . .

KATE: Oh, thank you . . . I appreciate that . . .

RISSA: Now, wait . . . see, this is an Osaki . . . see, this is a challenge here . . . it's a tiny little thing here in the zipper, like something that they use in lasers. You know the Japanese.

KATE: Yes.

RISSA: Fusing fashion and high tech. You know how they do that.

KATE: Well, thank you.

RISSA: No problem.

KATE: What do you think?

RISSA: It's a great winter color for you.

KATE: Really?

RISSA: Rich, but not overly rich. Youthful. Perfect. What exactly were you looking for?

KATE: A dress to meet my daughter in.

RISSA: What? You never met your daughter before?

KATE: Oh . . . I . . .

RISSA: Mrs. Oliver? Are you OK?

KATE: I'm sorry.

RISSA: Don't be sorry. You just went a little white there. Maybe you'd want to be trying this stuff on by yourself.

KATE: No, that's all right, I . . .

RISSA: I'm just picking something up here. I'm very funny that way. About people. And their feelings.

KATE: I'm a little nervous these days.

RISSA: You know, I thought that on Thursday. When you came in Thursday.

KATE: What?

RISSA: I thought, Mrs. Oliver seems nervous today. Or, not nervous exactly . . . uptight.

KATE: Really?

RISSA: I swear to God. I made a mental note of it.

KATE: About me?

RISSA: Well, you're my customer, Mrs. Oliver. And, I mean, you know, I read about you in the paper all the time, and your benefits that you give and all, and you always come back in here. It's very important to us. To me. It's important, and not just because of money.

KATE: No?

RISSA: Well . . . it's because of money, because it would be good to have money, and so someone is naturally interested in money, but, for me . . . it's you. Because of your . . . carriage.

KATE: I don't know.

RISSA: It's just, I admire that in you. Because, me, in my field, the fashion field, you know, I may not exactly be Donna Karan at the moment, but I noticed that all the buyers I've met, like, the real ones, like, from Nan Duskin, they all have this carriage, too. Like, well, if I were crude, like my ex-boyfriend, I'd say, like, they all have a stick up their ass, but I don't mean it like that. I mean, they have a way, like they're regal, or anchoring the national news, or something.

KATE: I don't know.

RISSA: I love it on you. I do.

KATE: Well, you've been right before.

RISSA: It's my job. And also discretion. I can keep a secret like no-body's business. You wouldn't believe what I know about my customers.

KATE: Really.

RISSA: No one you would know. Well, there is one.

KATE: You know something about someone I know.

RISSA: I shouldn't say.

KATE: No. Of course.

RISSA: But, if I did tell you, then you could tell me anything you wanted, really, because you'd have one on me. Because, if it ever got out about this person who, only I would know about this, although I didn't necessarily hear it from her . . . well, any chances I have to own this business would be gone.

KATE: You probably shouldn't say.

RISSA: No. But, I will if you want me to . . .

[*Change to* LINDA *and* MARIEL.]

LINDA: Mariel . . . stop crying . . .

MARIEL: I can't . . . I can't.

LINDA: Mariel . . . we're in a fitting room.

MARIEL: I just can't go on with my life like this. It's so empty. I'm such a nothing.

LINDA: Look . . . aside from how our lower bodies look in these mirrors there's really nothing wrong with either of our lives.

MARIEL: That's easy for you to say.

LINDA: Yes, it is.

MARIEL: You're a strong person. You were prepared for misery.

LINDA: Oh?

MARIEL: Ever since high school you knew you could never be

happy. I mean, you would never read a book unless you were sure the author killed herself.

LINDA: You're a strong person, too.

MARIEL: I thought that if Gary and I got married everything would fall together for me.

LINDA: You did?

MARIEL: Well, no. But, I didn't know what else to do.

LINDA: You've been a child your whole life, Mariel.

MARIEL: At least I wasn't afraid to fall in love.

LINDA: I wasn't afraid to fall in love.

MARIEL: You still are. This one's not smart enough. That one's not good enough in bed.

LINDA: Those are the facts, Mariel.

MARIEL: I truly loved Gary when I married him.

LINDA: And look at all it's done for you.

MARIEL: What am I going to do? I can't even stand for him to touch me.

LINDA: I tried to warn you.

MARIEL: And I have nowhere to go.

LINDA: You can always come and live with me.

MARIEL: And be your wife?

LINDA: What does that mean?

MARIEL: Isn't that what you want? To have someone make your life nice for you the way Gary wants me to do that for him.

LINDA: That's ridiculous.

MARIEL: No, it isn't. You'd love to have someone cook for you and nurture you and make you feel like the big cheese.

LINDA: Is that a crime?

MARIEL: Well, it won't be me. I'm through earning my keep as a good girl.

LINDA: I'm sure I didn't ask you.

MARIEL: But, you want it. You want me to cook for you.

LINDA: Mariel, do you have some strange desire to cook for me?

MARIEL: I don't have the desire to cook for anyone.

LINDA: But you have the desire to poison someone.

MARIEL: Yes.

LINDA: Who?

MARIEL: You. And Gary.

LINDA: So, now the truth is out.

MARIEL: I guess it is.

LINDA: You completely resent me because you believe that I am superior to you. In taste, intellect, and lifestyle.

MARIEL: That's not the truth. The truth is I'm tired of being pushed around by powermongers.

LINDA: Oh. Well, in either case I think you'd better hurry and pay for that dress. We have lunch reservations.

[*Light change to* RISSA *and* KATE.]

RISSA: So, how old were you when you gave her up for adoption?

KATE: I was quite a bit older than you might imagine an unwed mother being.

RISSA: So, you were unwed.

KATE: I was only unwed to the child's father.

RISSA: But to Mr. Oliver you were . . .

KATE: Wed.

RISSA: Whoa.

KATE: And now he's gone. And there are no children.

RISSA: And you haven't seen her for all these years?

KATE: No.

RISSA: Didn't you wonder about her?

KATE: Sometimes I wondered. Sometimes I was obsessed. And sometimes I didn't think about her at all.

RISSA: Wow.

KATE: I probably shouldn't have told you this.

RISSA: Oh, no. It's good. Because, you know, I can help you find the right outfit.

KATE: Oh. So, now you don't think this is right?

RISSA: Well, I thought it was. Like, for a party. But to meet your daughter who you gave up for adoption, I don't think so.

KATE: It's too . . .

RISSA: Green. You need to wear something pink now, I would say. Yeah . . . I have the perfect dress . . .

KATE: Why do you say pink.

RISSA: Well, pink . . . It's soft, feminine. It'll make her feel more sorry for you. You want her to feel sorry for you because she's probably really pissed off right now.

KATE: Actually, she doesn't know yet.

RISSA: You didn't get in touch with her.

KATE: Not yet.

RISSA: Were you planning on just showing up at her doorstep and saying, like, hi, I'm your new Mom, how do you like my dress?

KATE: I hadn't thought it through, really.

RISSA: Try this. If you were my biological mother that's what I'd want you to wear.

KATE: Really?

RISSA: Yes.

KATE: You're very kind, Rissa.

RISSA: Me? Please, I'm a businesswoman.

KATE: You're a real person.

RISSA: Is that such an honor?

KATE: You really listen.

RISSA: I like my ladies to look good.

KATE: What about you? Do you have a close relationship to your mother?

RISSA: My mother? My mother is a saint.

KATE: That's nice.

RISSA: So, I completely take her for granted.

KATE: But, you love her.

RISSA: She's my mother.

KATE: She gave you life.

RISSA: But, I don't remember that.

KATE: Oh.

RISSA: You know how it is. Your mother. You need her when you're sick, or you got dumped, or you're broke, or some tragedy, event, or another. And, like, when everything is great for you you pretend your mother is, like, Sophia Loren, or somebody amazing like that, who would take you to the Cannes Film Festival. And she takes it from you 'cause she can still remember when you were cute, and you made her like a woodcut of your dog or something.

KATE: Oh, I see.

RISSA: Yeah, but you don't necessarily care that she had all this pain when you were born. I mean, you feel bad, but for the most part that's her problem.

KATE: Uh huh.

RISSA: If it had been up to you, you probably would have stayed where you were.

KATE: Right.

RISSA: So how did you find your daughter?

KATE: I just looked up her number. I always knew where she was.

RISSA: And all this time you never tried to reach her.

KATE: No.

RISSA: So, how come you want to now?

KATE: I don't know really.

RISSA: Well . . . I should stop asking so many questions anyway. People aren't supposed to be so interested in each other. You know.

KATE: I don't mind.

RISSA: It's just that, I don't know, for as far back as I can remember I always liked knowing other people's business.

KATE: I just hope she likes me, that's all.

RISSA: Yeah. What if you don't like her.

KATE: What?

RISSA: I mean what if she turns out to be nothing like you imagined, like, what if she's wild, or rude, or even dumb, or something.

KATE: I don't think so.

RISSA: You never know.

KATE: I really don't think so.

RISSA: So, what kind of relationship do you think you'll have with her?

KATE: What do you mean?

RISSA: I mean, are you gonna spend holidays with her, stuff like that?

KATE: I don't know.

RISSA: You're going to introduce her to your friends, kind of like bring her into society?

KATE: Well . . . I imagine that those aspects of her life are already defined.

RISSA: Oh. Is that what you imagine?

[*Light change to* TIA *and* KAHINE.]

TIA: I sent white light to my mother and father last night because they are going down the Nile.

KAHINE: Going down the Nile's not dangerous.

TIA: But they were going in, like, a gondola. It was my mother's whole thing.

KAHINE: Your mother's cool.

TIA: I hope they don't die or something.

KAHINE: My father might be coming to see my apartment this weekend.

TIA: Uh-huh. Has he ever seen it before?

KAHINE: No. But I sent him a picture of it.

TIA: When was the last time you saw him?

KAHINE: Umm . . . I think it was right after I burned down the dorm.

TIA: That was a while ago.

KAHINE: Yeah. But he calls a lot.

TIA: Well, he got you a great apartment.

KAHINE: What do you think of this?

TIA: I can't believe my parents are making me live with them again this year. I'm, like, the only one at school who doesn't have their own place. Why, because I'm sixteen? Well, too bad, too bad.

KAHINE: Tia! Tia! I asked you what you thought of these on me? I'm wearing these pants to show you and you're not looking at me. Why can't you look at me when I show you something?!

TIA: Kahine, Kahine . . . calm down . . . I'm looking at them. They look great. OK? Are you OK?

KAHINE: OK. I hate it when you do that.

TIA: I'm sorry.

KAHINE: I hate it when I ask you something, and you go right on to the next thing.

TIA: OK. I'm sorry.

KAHINE: I hate that.

TIA: I won't do it again.

KAHINE: Do you think these make me look fat?

TIA: Not at all.

KAHINE: 'Cause my dance teacher told me I looked fat.

TIA: That's bullshit.

KAHINE: I don't look fat?

TIA: Not at all.

KAHINE: Do I look good in them?

TIA: Excellent.

KAHINE: You sure?

TIA: Yes.

KAHINE: You swear?

TIA: Yes.

KAHINE: Even the lace?

TIA: They're perfect.

KAHINE: 'Cause they're really expensive.

TIA: So what?

KAHINE: Well . . .

TIA: You look beautiful in them, and William will think so, too!

KAHINE: OK. [*She takes them off.*]

TIA: What are you going to do?

KAHINE: I'm going to steal them.

   [*Light change to* MARIEL *and* LINDA.]

MARIEL: Are you trying to tell me that you're a lesbian.

LINDA: I'm not trying to tell you anything. You're the one who's crying and telling me you can't go on.

MARIEL: With the marriage. Not go on in general. You're the depressed one. You're the pessimistic one.

LINDA: I'm not depressed.

MARIEL: Well, you're pessimistic.

LINDA: Yes. But I'm not unhappy about it.

MARIEL: So, why must you control me?

LINDA: Someone must.

MARIEL: Maybe you're really in love with me.

LINDA: Mariel . . . you are very confused.

MARIEL: Are you implying that I'm in love with you?

LINDA: I'm not implying anything.

MARIEL: Is that why I'm so dependent on your opinions?

LINDA: I don't know.

MARIEL: Is that why you could always make me lose my confidence?

LINDA: What confidence?

MARIEL: Is that why I got so jealous when you slept with Pamela's husband?

LINDA: I didn't know that made you jealous.

MARIEL: Well, it did somehow.

LINDA: You never told me that.

MARIEL: You spent all that time talking about Pamela. And her husband. And I thought . . . what's wrong with my husband?

LINDA: You were jealous because I didn't sleep with Gary?

MARIEL: Maybe.

LINDA: Oh, God.

MARIEL: Why? Did you sleep with Gary?

LINDA: Mariel . . .

MARIEL: Did you?

LINDA: What would you care if I did? You just said you can't stand him.

MARIEL: You did, didn't you?

LINDA: I thought we were trying to figure out if you were in love with me.

MARIEL: Oh, you must really think that I'm an idiot.

LINDA: No. I don't.

MARIEL: After all these years. Is that why you left your high pow-
ered job to come shopping with me, today? Because you feel
guilty?

LINDA: I don't feel guilty.

MARIEL: Well, you wouldn't. You and your big important job.

LINDA: Oh. And now you're jealous of my job.

MARIEL: No, I'm not. I don't even know what it is.

LINDA: I'm a judge. I'm the youngest city judge to ever sit on the
bench. There. Are you jealous, now?

MARIEL: You're very mean.

LINDA: Mariel, for once I'd like to have a conversation with you that
doesn't involve men or clothes. For once, after being friends
with you for eighteen years, I'd like to be acknowledged by you
for my work, and I'd like you to stop using me as the mirror for
all of your neuroses.

MARIEL: Is that what I do? I thought I was looking up to you.

LINDA: It's a use job.

MARIEL: I think you're the user.

LINDA: I don't think so. "Linda, how does this look on me? Linda,
do I look fat in this?"

[*Fast change to* RISSA *and* KATE.]

RISSA: That's the dress for a mother.

KATE: You're certain I don't look fat?

[*Fast change to* TIA *and* KAHINE.]

TIA: Kahine. Don't do it.

KAHINE: Why not? Do they make me look fat?

TIA: No. Just don't take them!

KAHINE: But, I want to.

TIA: I don't want you to.

KAHINE: Why not?

TIA: Look . . . they cost two hundred dollars!

KAHINE: So?

TIA: So, that's a lot to steal.

KAHINE: So?

TIA: God, Kahine, I feel like we're on an ABC "After School Special." Don't steal the fucking pants, OK?

KAHINE: Fuck you, Tia! Don't be such a pussy for a change!

TIA: Don't be such a psycho case for a change.

KAHINE: I'm not a psycho case.

TIA: Oh, right, Kahine.

KAHINE: You think I'm a psycho case all of a sudden?

TIA: No, not all of a sudden.

KAHINE: Oh! You always thought I was a psycho case!

TIA: Well, Kahine, when you came into Modern with your wrists slashed, and bandaged with my old Danskins,™ then I had a clue.

KAHINE: You were crying in Modern.

TIA: I know!

KAHINE: I thought you really cared about me.

TIA: I did.

KAHINE: You didn't.

TIA: Yes, I did. But I still thought you were crazy.

KAHINE: You are shallow.

TIA: No, I'm not.

KAHINE: I thought we were both deep, but you are not deep.

TIA: Yes, I am. I'm deep.

KAHINE: You are not. You're shallow.

TIA: Kahine, I'm sorry. I don't want you to steal the pants. I don't want to get caught stealing. My mother shops in this store.

KAHINE: Your fucking shallow mother.

TIA: My mother is not shallow.

KAHINE: Your mother is an asshole.

TIA: At least I have one.

KAHINE: Did you think that saying that was going to make me not steal these pants?

[*Change to* RISSA *and* KATE.]

KATE: Well, I really needed to tell someone this. I'm glad you got it out of me.

RISSA: Well . . .

KATE: And I trust you. Maybe it's your earthiness. I don't know.

RISSA: My earthiness? You think I'm earthy?

KATE: You know. Your street sense. In many ways I've been very sheltered.

RISSA: Street sense? Do I sound like I come from the streets?

KATE: I don't mean it as an insult.

RISSA: Do you mean it as a compliment?

KATE: I mean it as an observation. I've never talked to anyone about this before.

RISSA: So, now you're talking to a salesgirl in a boutique.

KATE: But I think of you as more than that.

RISSA: But don't. 'Cause I'm proud of what I do.

KATE: I don't mean to patronize.

RISSA: But you should. You're a patron.

KATE: Look, I . . .

RISSA: No . . . it's my fault. I just watch alot of talk shows . . . I get this mixed up with that.

KATE: I would like to know what you think.

RISSA: Yeah?

KATE: Yes. What do you think she might want from me?

RISSA: Well . . . who doesn't fantasize about coming from money.

KATE: Does one?

RISSA: And having a fairy godmother come along and buy her her own store, and all. I mean, I fantasized that about you, and I'm not even your long lost daughter.

KATE: Is that something you want.

RISSA: It's why my mom plays the lottery.

KATE: Your own place.

RISSA: I'm not your daughter, am I?

KATE: You?

RISSA: Am I? Is that what you've been trying to tell me? Is that why you want to know what I think? You weren't really that interested in the secret that I told you about Damaris Warren and her affair with that archbishop, were you?

KATE: Well, yes, I was.

RISSA: I think you've been trying to tell me this for a long time haven't you, Mrs. Oliver? I always knew there was something between us. And you know how I'm always so interested in your parties, and how I wanted to please you when I made those lace collars for you? And how I look up to you. I mean, there's always been something there, hasn't there?

[KAHINE'S *frantic voice cuts through the action.*]

KAHINE: Hey . . . hey, salesgirl!

RISSA: Uh-oh.

KAHINE: Look . . . I'm taking these pants with me? Did you hear me?

[MARIEL *and* LINDA *come out of their dressing room.*]

RISSA: Hey honey, just calm down, OK?

KAHINE: I'm taking these pants. And I'm not paying for them. What are you going to do?

RISSA: Those are leggings.

KAHINE: What?

RISSA: Those are leggings. Not pants.

KAHINE: Do they come with a top?

RISSA: Yes . . .

KAHINE: Well, I'm taking that, too.

TIA: Kahine, stop. You're going to get in a lot of trouble.

KAHINE: Don't start crying again, Tia.

MARIEL: That little girl looks insane.

LINDA: Dear, why don't you just calm down and stop screaming. We're in a very nice store.

KAHINE: Why don't I just kill myself? That's what you want, isn't it, Tia?

TIA: Kahine, you're my best friend. I just didn't want to get in trouble.

KAHINE: I hate you and your shallow world.

RISSA: Little girl, give me those leggings or I'm going to beat the shit out of you.

KAHINE: Go ahead.

[*She pulls a silverpoint pen out of her pocket.*]

TIA: That's my silverpoint! Did you take that from my bag, Kahine?

KAHINE: Yes! I liked it, so I took it.

TIA: You dropped out of art 'cause you were bored doing silverpoint, and then you stole my silverpoint!

KAHINE: I liked it.

TIA: Give it back! And give back the leggings!

KATE: I should really go, Rissa dear. Is there a back entrance?

RISSA: One second, Mrs. Oliver.

MARIEL: I know how you feel little girl.

KAHINE: You don't know anything about this. This is between me and my enemy.

TIA: I'm not your enemy.

KAHINE: My traitor!

TIA: I'm not a traitor! Stop saying bad things about me!

KAHINE: Stop crying, traitor!

TIA: I didn't do anything. I just told her not to steal the pants. Leggings.

KATE: I really have to go. If something should happen here it wouldn't be good for me . . . I mean . . .

RISSA: I don't think anyone should move right now, Mrs. Oliver.

MARIEL: Give me that little knife now. You could hurt yourself.

KAHINE: It's not a knife. It's a silverpoint. It's used for drawing.

MARIEL: But it's sharp. I don't want you to hurt yourself.

KAHINE: Why not?

MARIEL: Because . . . you're cute.

TIA: I always thought you were cute. I always thought you were cuter than me!

MARIEL: Just try to calm down. Poor thing.

LINDA: Mariel . . . why don't you let the store handle this?

MARIEL: Who's the store?

RISSA: I'm the store. But, if you can calm this kid down and get her out of here, fine.

LINDA: I really don't think she's going to hurt herself with that ball-point pen, or whatever it is.

[KAHINE, *realizing she has lost some impact, grabs a pair of scissors near the cash register.*]

RISSA: Shit.

KATE: This is awful.

RISSA: This is what kids are like sometimes, Mrs. Oliver. You gotta be prepared for anything. You know?

KATE: But, I'm not good in these sorts of situations. I mean, what's the protocol?

RISSA: There is no protocol when children are involved. It's all about survival.

KATE: Oh, my . . .

LINDA: Keep your distance, Mariel.

MARIEL: No.

[KAHINE *starts to lose her balance. She grabs her stomach and gets shakier.*]

TIA: She only ate ketchup and water for lunch. And for dinner she drinks a Slimfast milkshake. And then she has a cigarette 'cause she wants to be a dancer, and I keep telling her to eat, but I have to do homework, and my Mom makes me get off the phone by ten, and there's only so much I can do for her 'cause she already tried to kill herself twice, and her stupid boyfriend William is an arsonist! There, and if you think I'm a traitor then now I am one, but it's only because I love you, and you're so fucked up.

MARIEL: She's probably all malnourished and everything.

LINDA: Oh, God.

KAHINE: Don't call my father.

TIA: Your father?

KAHINE: You better not call him.

TIA: I can't, he's in Tokyo or someplace.

MARIEL: I'm sure your father loves you very much.

KAHINE: How would you know?

MARIEL: Men always love their daughters. It's their wives they have problems with.

KAHINE: I just don't want him to be called.

MARIEL: Well, we're going to have to call him.

RISSA: You're going to call Japan on my phone?

MARIEL: I'll use my card.

RISSA: Fuck it. Just call direct. Where's he staying, and if you don't tell us I'll turn those scissors around and cut all the perm out of your head.

TIA: I remember! He's at the Tokyo Sheraton!

KAHINE: Marriot.

MARIEL: Yes, Operator, how do I place an overseas call to Japan? . . . I do?

RISSA: What?

MARIEL: Can you believe in this day and age I have to wait for an open line?

RISSA: See that, Mrs. Oliver? And we had trouble with that Osaki zipper! Even the Japanese have their problems. Mrs. Oliver?

[*She is gone.*]

LINDA: This is an excellent way to lose customers.

RISSA: Yeah. It is.

[KAHINE *stumbles.*]

TIA: Here! I've got them! I've got the scissors.

RISSA: Give me the phone. I'm calling the police.

LINDA: Good. Now, let's get out of here.

TIA: Please, don't call the police.

MARIEL: Please. I'm waiting for the overseas operator.

[KAHINE *passes out.*]

LINDA: Oh, for God's sake.

TIA: See? I told you she doesn't eat anything!

RISSA: Well, sit her the hell down. I've got a hoagie.

TIA: Kahine . . . you've got to eat some of the ladie's hoagie!

LINDA: Look . . . I've got to get back to work. Are you coming out to lunch with me?

MARIEL: I don't think so.

LINDA: What are you going to do, stay here by the phone for this child?

MARIEL: Yes. For the moment.

LINDA: Mariel . . . this not the ASPCA.

MARIEL: I want to do this.

LINDA: But we have lunch plans.

MARIEL: Not anymore. I don't feel like lunch.

LINDA: Oh? What do you feel like?

MARIEL: I feel like . . . getting divorced. And having a baby.

LINDA: That's rational.

MARIEL: I know I don't feel like sitting somewhere and clamoring for your attention.

LINDA: Is that what you think you do?

MARIEL: Yes. I clamor.

LINDA: And what do I do?

MARIEL: You divvy out. You divvy out. And I clamor.

LINDA: Well, then . . . Can I call you?

MARIEL: Can you?

LINDA: Should I? I mean, can I call you, or how do you want to leave this, Mariel? I mean are we leaving this, Mariel? Because I don't really think I could do without this . . . without your friendship . . . Oh . . . what am I saying? I'll just be at work, and you can call me if you want to. Do you think you'll want to?

MARIEL: Yes. I think I'll want to.

LINDA: Well, good then. Then, I'll wait. To hear from you.

[LINDA *exits.*]

RISSA: OK? You're all right now?

KAHINE: That was a good hoagie.

RISSA: Yeah?

KAHINE: Uh-huh.

RISSA: Well, I get the meats down on Ninth Street. But I think the magic is in the olive oil. You can get anything down there. Detergent, cannolis, anything you need.

TIA: We'll have to go there sometime, right Kahine? We love to shop.

KAHINE: OK.

TIA: Kahine, you don't really think I'm shallow, do you? Like you said? 'Cause I would just die if you thought I was shallow.

KAHINE: No.

TIA: Kahine's my best friend. That's why I get so worried when she's starving.

RISSA: I can understand that.

MARIEL: Oh . . . hello . . . They're going to put me through. Do you want to talk to your father?

KAHINE: Me?

MARIEL: Would you like me to? To explain the situation? I can tell him that you were furious and hysterical. And that you needed to be understood. And listened to. And taken seriously, but by him in particular. That your rather frenetic behavior was a last ditch effort to get his attention, but that luckily you have a lot of support, and that you appreciate that support very much. Shall I tell him all of that?

KAHINE: No.

MARIEL: Well, what if I just give you a ride home, then. I have a driver.

KAHINE: That's cool.

TIA: That is so cool.

MARIEL: Hello? Oh no, operator. You can just cancel that call.

RISSA: There, now. Everybody's OK. And you all have nice outfits. So there can't be anything to get so upset about, right?

TIA: Right.

RISSA: Right. So . . . sometimes things get a little crazy when you're trying on clothes. It just does it to you, sometimes. So, what are you gonna do?

END OF PLAY

Mlada Imaginaire
adapted from the French by Michael Feingold

SCRIBE'S PARADOX, OR
THE MECHANICAL RABBIT

MICHAEL FEINGOLD

Michael Feingold has worked in the theatre for more than twenty years as a critic, playwright, translator, lyricist, director, dramaturg and literary manager. A graduate of Columbia University and the Yale School of Drama, he is best known as the chief theatre critic for *The Village Voice*. His column has won him a Guggenheim Fellowship and the American Book Awards' Walter Lowenfels Prize in criticism.

Feingold's alternate career in the theatre itself began in 1970, when he was named Literary Manager of the newly formed Yale Repertory Theatre, a post he held for seven years. For YRT he directed numerous staged readings, wrote and/or directed children's shows with student actors (including such future luminaries as Meryl Streep, Sigourney Weaver, Chris Durang, and Albert Innaurato), and provided translations for many of the Rep's most significant productions, including the Brecht/Weill *Rise and Fall of Mahagonny*, *Little Mahagonny*, and *Happy End*; Molière's *Bourgeois Gentleman*; Diderot's *Rameau's Nephew*; Ibsen's *When We Dead Awaken*; and the Dostoyevsky/Camus *Possessed*, staged by Andrzej Wajda. He subsequently became Literary Director of the Guthrie Theater in Minneapolis, followed by a stint as Literary Manager of the American Repertory Theatre in Cambridge, Massachusettes.

In New York, he has directed for the American Place Theatre, Circle Rep, Manhattan Theatre Club, and the WPA theatre, among others. His translations have been heard in many of the above theatres, as well as at La Mama, the Public Theatre, Theatre Ubu, the Classic Stage Company, and on Broadway (*Happy End* with Meryl Streep and Christopher Lloyd, and the recent *Three Penny Opera* starring Sting and Maureen McGovern). His translations of opera, light opera, and songs by composers from Offenbach and Schumann to Penderecki have been heard at the Santa Fe, San Francisco, and Los Angeles opera houses, and in many concert halls.

Currently, Feingold teaches classic drama to playwriting students at New York University's Tisch School of the Arts, and a course in collaboration for directing and dramaturgy students at

Columbia University's Hammerstein Center. His new translation of *The Firebugs* by Max Frisch was done at the Guthrie Theatre in Minneapolis, Minnesota in August 1995, and *When Ladies Battle*, his translation of the Scribe play, was produced by the Pearl Theatre, off-Broadway, in January 1996.

CHARACTERS

ORFIN   A playwright
A FEMALE THEATREGOER
A PROFESSOR
MADAME DU CAMP   An actress
RANDEAU   A stage director

SCENE: *Paris. The lobby of the Theatre des Somnambules, where* ORFIN'S *latest play is running.*

TIME: *1895. Just after a performance.*

FEMALE THEATREGOER: [*Coming out of the auditorium and approaching* ORFIN.] Excuse me, but aren't you Monsieur Orfin?

ORFIN: Are you a debt collector?

FEMALE THEATREGOER: What an idea! Of course not!

ORFIN: In that case, I am Orfin, at your service.

FEMALE THEATREGOER: I thought so! Your play is very good. I enjoyed it immensely.

ORFIN: Thank you. I hope you will tell all your friends.

FEMALE THEATREGOER: I will, but—[*Looking around cautiously, lowering her voice.*]—it is not well made.

ORFIN: I beg your pardon?

FEMALE THEATREGOER: Your play is not a well-made play.

ORFIN: [*Somewhat nettled.*] It was made well enough for you to enjoy it.

FEMALE THEATREGOER: Oh, you know what I mean.

ORFIN: I'm not at all sure.

FEMALE THEATREGOER: It isn't well constructed.

ORFIN: Ah, you mean like the plays of Monsieur Scribe and Monsieur Sardou?

FEMALE THEATREGOER: Yes, exactly. There is no central figure trapped between two untenable choices. There is no clever antagonist to counter each of the central figure's attempts to escape from this situation.

ORFIN: No quid pro quo, you mean?

FEMALE THEATREGOER: That is precisely what I mean. For instance, take *A Glass of Water*—

ORFIN: I'm not thirsty, thank you.

FEMALE THEATREGOER: Oh, don't be silly. I mean Monsieur Scribe's famous play of that name.

ORFIN: Ah, yes. *The Glass of Water*. And what about it?

FEMALE THEATREGOER: Each of the characters is in one of these untenable dilemmas. Each move brings one side or the other up against a countermove. The exposition is all in the first act, the climax in the third, the resolution in the fifth.

ORFIN: Yes, Monsieur Scribe is very clever about these things.

FEMALE THEATREGOER: But your play has no such structure.

ORFIN: Dear lady, my play is in one scene. Under the circumstances, it could hardly resolve in its fifth act.

FEMALE THEATREGOER: But it could follow a pattern of rising action. It could have an untenable dilemma, and a series of quid pro quo maneuvers.

ORFIN: I find my temper rising in lieu of the action; your demands make talking to you an untenable dilemma. If you go on in this manner, my maneuver will simply be to walk away.

FEMALE THEATREGOER: But I am only an innocent audience member who wants to know more.

ORFIN: Your attitude suggests to me that you lost your innocence long ago. [*She gasps.*] Aesthetically speaking, I mean.

PROFESSOR: [*Coming up to them.*] Madame, is this man bothering you?

ORFIN: On the contrary: The lady is doing her best to bother me.

PROFESSOR: I warn you, sir, if you insult her again, you will have to deal with me.

ORFIN: And who, may I ask, will I then be dealing with?

PROFESSOR: [*Bowing.*] I am Kaltfisch, Professor of Aesthetics at the University of Lyon.

ORFIN: May I suggest, Professor, that Lyon's aesthetics need considerably more reforming than mine.

PROFESSOR: Sir, if your aesthetics include harassing innocent women in theatre lobbies—

ORFIN: You came in late, Professor. I am the author of the play being presented here. The lady is harassing me about my lack of structural sense.

PROFESSOR: [*Clasping his hands.*] My dear fellow, can you ever forgive me! Your play is simply splendid!

FEMALE THEATREGOER: [*Perturbed.*] But Professor—

PROFESSOR: [*Ignoring the interruption.*] You do away with all these antiquated hoodoos about "structure." No contrivance, no manipulation, no elaborately rigged-up system of alliances and counter-alliances—just a person who does something and its consequences. That is drama at its purest. None of the nonsense of Scribe, Sardou, Dumas fils, Augier, Feuillet, and so forth.

ORFIN: I appreciate your enthusiasm, Professor, but I hope you will let me put in a word in defense of my colleagues. My own approach is different from theirs—this is a changing world we live in—but I admire and even enjoy their contrivances, as you call them. I love to watch the little machines whirl and click into place as these not-quite believable characters maneuver their way from one situation to another. You are quite right to say that it is not the living drama, which is what I prefer, but it is the pattern of drama, and we are all beholden to the pattern, so we must respect it.

MADAME DU CAMP: [*Sweeping up, grandly dressed.*] Orfy, my love, we've been looking for you all over the theatre.

ORFIN: Jeanne, please let me introduce—

FEMALE THEATREGOER: Oh, Madame, what a magnificent performance!

MADAME DU CAMP: Thank you.

FEMALE THEATREGOER: [*Extending her program to be signed.*] You are the most wonderful actress of our century! That red dress! And the way you looked at him when he accused you of infidelity with the chauffeur!

MADAME DU CAMP: [*Laughing as she signs program with an elaborate flourish.*] Oh, well, Duse will probably find some even more cunning way of doing that in the Italian version. [*To* ORFIN.] Remember her in the confession scene of *The Princess of Baghdad*? With the little boy? That was divine!

ORFIN: [*Imitating Duse folding the child's hands over his heart.*] I remember. "I have been faithful! I swear it! *Lo giuro!*" It was brilliant... though not half so brilliant as you, my dear.

MADAME DU CAMP: Well, you'll have to write me something brilliant like that to do in your next. Which had better be soon, Orfy. That's why I've been trying to find you. We're taking this play off. It's not going to run. The new one must be ready in five weeks.

ORFIN: But everyone loves you in this! I love you in this! You've never been more wonderful. And this is the most original thing I've ever written.

MADAME DU CAMP: Oh, Orfy, don't be banal. I mean— [*Looking at* PROFESSOR *and* FEMALE THEATREGOER.] —you'll forgive my saying this in front of your relatives from the country, but—this play doesn't give me a chance. I only get one costume change, I only have two entrances. I don't get an exit because the curtain comes down for intermission with me still onstage—

ORFIN: [*Testily.*] Talk to Randeau about that. I told him you should exit before it came down.

MADAME DU CAMP: Oh, Orfy, honey, that isn't the point. I have no big scenes!

ORFIN: No big scenes! What about the confrontation scene! This woman has just been telling you how wonderful you were in it.

MADAME DU CAMP: I'm wonderful, I know, but the scene has no "build." I need to feel that roller-coaster of motion sweeping me along. I can do my part, but there's nothing hanging over my head, no extra push. You look back at the classics, sweetie. Look at Scribe—

ORFIN: Scribe! You want me to write like Scribe!

MADAME DU CAMP: Well, I'll tell you, he never wrote a woman a weak role. I come out there in *When Ladies Battle*, or *Adrienne Lecouvreur*, and I know exactly what's going on. I have something I want, I have a secret I must conceal, I have an enemy whose maneuvers against me are all announced openly, step by step, so that I can take steps to counter them, I get three or four costume changes, the audience sees me go from happy to sad to hysterical in an instant, and every scene has a strong entrance, a crushing last line, and one or two laughs. Now how can you top that?

ORFIN: [*Through clenched teeth.*] In *Adrienne Lecouvreur* you have to die by sniffing poisoned violets. How can I take that seriously?

MADAME DU CAMP: Well, it doesn't have to be Scribe. In those days they all knew how to do it. Take Augier for instance, *Olympia's Marriage*—

ORFIN: In *Olympia's Marriage* the elderly judge rescues his son from marriage to the ex-courtesan by shooting you, I mean her. It's absurd. A Paris audience would laugh it off the stage today.

MADAME DU CAMP: I don't know, I've been thinking of reviving it— it's very popular in America just now.

ORFIN: America! We're talking about civilization here, not the savage tribes.

MADAME DU CAMP: Wait till you see my Act III wedding dress. And Randeau's worked out something spectacular for my death scene.

ORFIN: [*Bitterly.*] So this is my fate! To be replaced by a mechanical rabbit from fifty years ago!

MADAME DU CAMP: Oh, don't take it so hard, my cabbage. I want to do your next one immediately after. The Augier revival is just to give you time to write it. And practice the old pattern a little. We want you to write a play that's really well made, so everyone will love it. We know you can do it.

ORFIN: Yes, but do I want to? The world's not well-made. Those plays are old, artificial postures.

MADAME DU CAMP: [Laughing.] Yes, darling. That's why we love them. Reality is depressing—more so every year. People come to the theatre for escape. They need artifice—the more artificial the better.

ORFIN: Why am I always at your mercy this way?

MADAME DU CAMP: [Simply.] You adore me.

ORFIN: Yes. And your husband owns the theatre.

MADAME DU CAMP: Oh, hush. Don't talk about my husband, or these people will suspect some kind of marital intrigue. [Looking at PROFESSOR and FEMALE THEATREGOER, who have been watching with rapt attention.] Who are they, anyway?

PROFESSOR: [Bowing.] Kaltfisch, University of Lyon.

MADAME DU CAMP: Oh, Professor! How lovely to see you. Goodness, in this flurry I almost forgot all about our appointment. Has the Augier family approved our terms?

PROFESSOR: [Touching his breast pocket.] I have the contract here, Madame, whenever you are ready.

ORFIN: [Agog.] You praise my new aesthetic, and then you negotiate for Augier, most hackneyed of the old "well-made" playwrights?

PROFESSOR: The old must be given its chance, Monsieur, before the new sweeps it away.

FEMALE THEATREGOER: [Who has edged over to MADAME DU CAMP.] I can't tell you how excited I am! I saw Rejane play Olympia when I was a little girl. To think of seeing you in it now!

MADAME DU CAMP: [Joshing.] It will make you feel like a little girl all over again. [*They laugh together.*] Would you like a tour of our theatre? Come, I'll show you around. Come, Professor.

PROFESSOR: With pleasure.

[*They go off, leaving* ORFIN *alone in the now deserted lobby. Pause. Then* RANDEAU, *the director, comes up to him.*]

RANDEAU: Don't be downhearted.

ORFIN: Any special reason why not?

RANDEAU: You've triumphed. Everyone is talking about your play.

ORFIN: But, apparently, no one is coming to see it.

RANDEAU: That's all right. Let them come and see Augier for a while. They all know the terms have changed. The old tricks have been exposed as tricks. In the future, plays like yours will be enjoyed as plays. And the old plays will be enjoyed the way you and I enjoy them, for the pleasure of their trickery.

ORFIN: You make the future sound very just.

RANDEAU: It's a blind sort of justice, true, but in art it's the only kind we get. Anyway, you won't lose money by this.

ORFIN: I won't.

RANDEAU: I need someone to adapt the Augier script. His tricks are a little staler than Scribe's.

ORFIN: Won't the Professor object?

RANDEAU: You don't think professors ever really know their subject, do you? Come on, let's go for a drink and I'll tell you what I want done. We can go to that new place in Montmartre, where the painters hang out—the Lapin Agile.

ORFIN: All right, we'll go to the Lively Rabbit and try to wake up the mechanical one.

RANDEAU: That's the spirit! You'll write a well-made play yet.

ORFIN: [*Looking back to where* MADAME DU CAMP *has exited as he follows* RANDEAU *out.*] I already have. [*He exits dramatically.*]

CURTAIN

Janusz Glowacki

Translated by
Zuza Glowacka

HOME SECTION

JANUSZ GLOWACKI

Janusz Glowacki was born in Poland and graduated from Warsaw University. He has since worked as a playwright, screenwriter, novelist, short story writer, and essayist, and is the author of seven plays, ten books, six screenplays, and four produced movies, one of which, *Hunting Flies*, was directed by Andrzej Wajda.

In August 1980, during the strike in Gdansk shipyard which resulted in the birth of Solidarity, Janusz Glowacki spent time with the striking workers. From that experience he wrote the novel *Give Us This Day*. The novel, censored in Poland, was published underground in 1981 and all around the world soon after.

In December 1981, Mr. Glowacki was attending the opening of his play *Cinders* at the Royal Court Theatre in London. While he was there, martial law was declared in Poland. He decided not to return to his country and instead moved to New York. In 1984, *Cinders* was produced by Joseph Papp at the New York Shakespeare Festival and received Premio Molliere's Award as the best production of 1986 for its Buenos Aires appearance.

This was followed by the tragi-comedy *Fortinbras Gets Drunk* (1986), a macabre retelling of Hamlet from the Norwegian point of view, and critically acclaimed *Hunting Cockroaches*. The latter was produced at the Manhattan Theatre Club in 1987 (starring Dianne Wiest and Ron Silver, and directed by Arthur Penn), at the Mark Taper Forum (starring Swoosie Kurtz and Malcolm McDowell), and by more than fifty other professional theatres across the U.S. It was cited by the American Theatre Critics Association as an Outstanding New Play in 1986, and received the Hollywood Drama Logue Critics Award. *Time Magazine*, among others, named the play as one of the ten best of the year.

His latest play, *Antigone In New York*, was produced at Arena Stage in Washington, D.C., in 1993. *Time Magazine* called it, too, one of the best ten plays of the year. The play was awarded Grand Prix at the Wroclaw Biennale of Contemporary Polish Plays in 1994.

Janusz Glowacki is the recipient of the National Endowment for the Arts Playwriting Fellowship, the Guggenheim Fellowship, Jurzykowski Foundation and Drama League of New York Playwriting Award.

CHARACTERS

WITEK

OLEK

PLAYWRIGHT

The stage is dark. The sound of Chopin's "Grand Polonaise in A Flat" is heard. A light turns on. The music fades. The stage setting is that of a typical living room on Fifth Avenue. Arm chairs, two Tiffany lamps, a sofa, a Persian rug, coffee table, etc. The stage is divided in two by two expensive doors which are closed at the moment. On stage right there is an entrance which connects the living room to the remaining rooms in the apartment. At this time, there aren't any people on stage. From backstage we hear loud noises of furniture being moved around, and men's voices.

WITEK: [*Offstage.*] Drop it here . . .

OLEK: [*Offstage.*] Move it here . . .

[*An extremely loud crash followed by cursing is heard. Two renovating men enter the stage. They are carrying painting materials and a ladder. The first man, WITEK, is talkative; the second, OLEK, is a big man, and is in a philosophical mood which is the usual case when a person is hungover. The third member of the crew is presently working in the maid's room; he is not seen on stage. They are all Polish immigrants. The specialty of Polish-Americans is renovating apartments, as the Korean specialty is running grocery stores. WITEK and OLEK are very professionally preparing the living room to be painted. They are stacking things in the middle of the room, covering with a white sheet, and putting some sheets on the floor. Afterwards, they begin their painting job. From the moment they entered the stage they have been talking continually.*]

OLEK: So you did it?

WITEK: I did it

OLEK: You put it on.

WITEK: I put it on.

OLEK: I wouldn't have put it on if I were you.

WITEK: Why not?

OLEK: It's a mortal sin, the Pope made that perfectly clear.

WITEK: I put it on.

OLEK: And...?

WITEK: And then she told me to put on another one.

OLEK: Why?

WITEK: Just in case.

OLEK: Did you do it?

WITEK: Absolutely not.

OLEK: You were absolutely right.

WITEK: Actually, I only had one.

OLEK: Thank God. And...?

WITEK: And nothing. I put on my clothes and left. Watch it! You're spilling the paint.

[*From backstage, a loud noise is heard, as though a heavy object was just dropped. The noise comes from the room in which the third worker is moving furniture.*]

WITEK: [*Yells in his direction.*] What the fuck are you doing!

OLEK: What the fuck did they send us this guy for?

WITEK: It was Maciek's idea.

OLEK: Why? So I can share my money with this asshole.

WITEK: I told you, he used to be famous in Poland, Maciek liked one of his plays.

OLEK: What was it called?

WITEK: Uhhhh... *Skating On Thin Ice*. No. Wait. *A Polar Bear in Warsaw*. No. *Good-Bye Gulak*. No. *Hello Prague*. No... Something.

OLEK: I don't like playwrights myself. One day I went to a bar in Poland, met a playwright, and before I knew it, I was sentenced to three years in prison.

WITEK: He doesn't write for the police. He writes for the theater.

OLEK: Same thing! Witek, you are an experienced man.

WITEK: Sure. I've been working six years on this stuff.

OLEK: That's what I mean. So what do you think? Can women grow back their hair.

WITEK: What do you mean?

OLEK: [*Pointing.*] On the head.

WITEK: Never heard anything about it.

OLEK: Me neither. God, I'm tired... I worked my ass off. This is the fifth room today.

WITEK: Only three left.

OLEK: Three rooms. Shit!

WITEK: [*Proudly.*] This is not Brooklyn, this is Fifth Avenue. Two rooms left and the maid's room.

OLEK: What's a maid's room?

[*Again a crash is heard from backstage.*]

WITEK: That's the one, the playwright is fucking up. [*With a nostalgic smile.*] Olek?

OLEK: What?

WITEK: Is your father dead?

OLEK: Alive, why?

WITEK: Where is he?

OLEK: Where is he supposed to be? In Zelazowa Wola, of course.

WITEK: [*Deeply moved.*] Olek?

OLEK: What?

WITEK: Did your father ever dream?

OLEK: About what?

WITEK: About you, his son Olek, renovating five bedroom apartments on Fifth Avenue. In New York City?

OLEK: My father wanted me to be a pianist.

WITEK: Pianist?

OLEK: Pianist. All of the fathers in our neighborhood wanted their sons to become pianists.

WITEK: Why?

OLEK: Because one man from Zelazowa Wola made a lot of money with the help of his piano.

WITEK: What's his name?

OLEK: Chopin.

WITEK: Yah, I heard of him, but I also heard that the money he made wasn't good for shit. He lived with some old French bitch, and fucked her for food.

OLEK: [*Surprised.*] Really? My father never mentioned that.

WITEK: Hey Olek! what the fuck you doing?

OLEK: Anyway, I wasn't very good at the piano. [*Looking at the wall.*] Don't worry, I'll fix it . . .

WITEK: We should roll up this carpet.

OLEK: Why the fuck roll it? It looks like shit.

WITEK: Because it's a Persian.

OLEK: So what?

WITEK: A Persian has to look like shit, that's its quality. One Russian told me that he and his grandmother used to work fucking up new carpets to make them look like authentic Persian shit. They stomped on the carpet non-stop all day, and got three dollars per hour, each, for stomping.

OLEK: There is no shit in the world I would stomp on for three dollars an hour. [*Pointing to his head.*] And when a woman falls in love?

WITEK: What?

OLEK: Doesn't it grow back then?

WITEK: Oh, I don't know . . .

OLEK: Me, neither.

[*From backstage an even louder noise, like that of a book shelf crashing against the ground is heard.*]

OLEK: The bookcase.

WITEK: No, I think it's that big Picasso.

OLEK: Aha . . . This playwright of yours.

WITEK: What?

OLEK: I don't trust him.

WITEK: You said that already.

OLEK: I'm not talking about him being a squealer right now, it's just that objects don't get along very well with him.

WITEK: Naa, he's just sloppy, has two left hands.

OLEK: That's not what I mean.

WITEK: So what do you mean?

OLEK: There was this woman.

WITEK: What woman?

OLEK: In Zelazowa Wola.

WITEK: A pianist?

OLEK: No, whatever she touched fell apart, like my new chair. And then it turned out that she was Lisbonian.

WITEK: You mean, lesbian.

OLEK: That's what I said. You can deceive a man but a chair, forget it. [*Pointing backstage.*] And he is pro-condoms.

WITEK: I'm pro, too.

OLEK: You're a different story. Besides, you had only one, and he carries the whole pack in his pocket.

WITEK: How do you know? Did you search his pockets?

OLEK: Of course. If I don't trust someone I search his pocket.

WITEK: You are a thief.

OLEK: I didn't take them. I only put holes in them.

WITEK: Why?

OLEK: To save his soul . . . with a nail. He should be grateful.

WITEK: Olek, if I ever catch you touching my condoms . . .

OLEK: Fine, but you'll go to hell. [OLEK *is taking a painting down from the wall. A huge hole is seen.*]
    Aha, you see . . . ?

WITEK: What?

OLEK: A hole.

WITEK: So what? There probably was a safe here.

OLEK: Maybe yes, maybe no.

[*Again a terrible noise from backstage.*]

WITEK: Maciek said they almost produced his play on Broadway. You know, something about Russia being ruled by the Mafia, who are the communists who used to shoot workers.

OLEK: But they are not shooting workers any more.

WITEK: But they could start shooting any time. And they promised him that immediately after they start shooting, his play will be reconsidered.

OLEK: But they're already shooting in Chechnya.

WITEK: But Chechnya doesn't count. On the legs, yes.

OLEK: What?

WITEK: Yes. It grows back on the legs.

OLEK: Ahhh . . . I'm not talking about the legs. I only wanna know about the head.

[*Again a noise is heard.*]

WITEK: Motherfucker! He did it again. Have you got any paper?

OLEK: Only this. [*He takes out from his pocket a book, hands it to* WITEK.]

WITEK: [*Reads it.*] "How To Seduce a Stewardess." [*He tears off the cover of the book, and a few pages, slaps it on the wall, and paints over it. The cover slowly slips off of the wall.*]

WITEK: I should spit on it first. [*Glues the cover to the wall.*]

OLEK: I'm sure that if Chopin was born 100 years later and came to America he would have been a big hit.

[*Helps him with the gluing.*]

OLEK: It's much easier to make it here as a pianist than as a construction worker. Because when you play the piano nobody hears your accent.

WITEK: When Maciek came here six years ago, he didn't speak a word of English and had five dollars in his pocket. And now, you see how beautifully he speaks; everybody thinks he was born in Brooklyn. [*He finishes fixing the hole.*] And now put some paint on it, but be careful.

OLEK: [*Painting the newspaper.*] Aha!

WITEK: Maciek has become a very important person. A week ago I met two guys at his apartment, both in white suits, black shirts, white ties, black socks, white shoes, black hats, Rolexes, and on every finger they had a golden ring. WASPs from the Upper East Side. And you know what they were talking about?

OLEK: What?

WITEK: That the quality of food on the Concord has gotten worse.

OLEK: Has it?

WITEK: How the fuck I should know. I don't fly the Concord. And you know who I met later in the hallway?

OLEK: Who?

WITEK: My wife, Kasia.

OLEK: Your wife?

WITEK: Yeah.

OLEK: I thought she left you.

WITEK: Of course. Do you really think she is stupid enough to stay with me? Maciek introduced her to the most sophisticated millionaires. She is one of them, now.

OLEK: Did you talk to her?

WITEK: [*Proud of his wife.*] Do you really think she is stupid enough to talk to me? She drives a Jaguar, all thanks to Maciek.

OLEK: When did she leave you?

WITEK: A year ago. It's all because of my fucking mother. You know, every night after dinner, she locked Kasia up in the room. And this one time she forgot. And the bitch ran away. But, she loved me. Like crazy. Especially when I came to take her from Poland. I mean, I told her I had a penthouse with a doorman . . .

OLEK: Why did you say that?

WITEK: Why? Why? Because I loved her. She wouldn't have married me without a doorman.

OLEK: Maybe she found out you are gay.

WITEK: What? Me? Gay?

OLEK: Well, you did fuck me.

WITEK: Well . . . well, it was a misunderstanding. We talked about it already. I was sure you were gay. I just wanted to be nice. You are the one who started with that thing.

OLEK: Only because they told me in Warsaw that all men in New York are gay, so . . . I wanted to fit in. I didn't want you to think that I am stupid or anything . . . You know what?

WITEK: What?

OLEK: A week ago I met a woman, Zosia. She has beautiful bowed legs like iron arches. She can strangle a dog with these legs.

WITEK: Does she live in Greenpoint, somewhere between McGuinnes and Manhattan Avenue, and have blond hair?

OLEK: No. On Calyer Street and she is bald like an American eagle. And all female from Zakopane are bald. Her mother, her grandmother, two cows. It's because of Lenin.

WITEK: Why?

OLEK: I don't know why.

WITEK: Aha. Give this spot one more touch.

OLEK: And she never asked me to wear this [*Pointing to his crotch.*]

WITEK: No?

OLEK: No?

WITEK: What if she got pregnant.

OLEK: Just yesterday, I asked her about that.

WITEK: And what?

OLEK: [*Smiling, proud of Zosia.*] She said that she would drown herself in the Hudson River.

WITEK: This is the kind of women I like.

OLEK: And she really takes care of men. When I sleep at her house she always puts two glasses next to my bed: one full, in case I am thirsty, and one empty in case I'm not. Here are some photos of her. [*He shows the pictures to* WITEK.] Here she is wearing a hat, and here she is bald.

WITEK: I like her better with the hat. Okay, lets start the other room. [OLEK *opens the door to another room and bumps into something unusual. We notice two legs of a man who hanged himself.*]

OLEK: I think I should marry her.

WITEK: So, do it.

OLEK: Shit.

WITEK: What?

OLEK: Her mother. She will never accept me. [*With no emotion at all.*] Someone is hanging here.

WITEK: I can see. Why won't she accept you?

[*They continue talking, scrutinizing the body.*]

OLEK: You know, her mom was once on TV and she is such a snob. But Zosia is completely different. What do you think? Who is he?

WITEK: How the fuck am I supposed to know.

OLEK: They showed her mother on "Primetime" as the only woman horse-carriage driver in Central Park.

WITEK: Oh, yeah. I remember that.

OLEK: [*Sadly.*] You see ? You see? She's famous.

WITEK: But they only put her on because she whipped her horse to death.

OLEK: [*Proudly.*] You see? She is strong . . . What do you think? Is he Polish?

WITEK: Nah

OLEK: Jewish?

WITEK: Nah.

OLEK: Mexican?

WITEK: Why Mexican? He's got blond hair.

OLEK: I'm just talking. It helps me think.

WITEK: Anyway, what's the difference?

OLEK: It's a big difference. Yesterday in Greenpoint, they beat up this Indian—but by mistake. They thought he was a gypsy.

WITEK: Uh huh.

OLEK: But then they explained everything to him, and he completely understood. He said he would have done the same thing. [*Pointing to the body.*] How'd he get in here.

WITEK: Because look at the way he's dressed. Clean collar, silk tie, and polished shoes... Of course the doorman was going to let him in. I told you you have to dress better. In New York, do you know what is the most important thing?

OLEK: What?

WITEK: Shoes.

OLEK: Shoes?

WITEK: Shoes. Maciek said people here only look at two things: the shoes and the teeth.

OLEK: Yeah, you're right. He's got nice shoes. Maybe I can borrow them when I go to Zosia's tonight.

WITEK: Why do you think he did it?

OLEK: This Mexican?

WITEK: He's not Mexican.

OLEK: I know... Maybe his feet were hurting him. Once my feet hurt me so bad, I would have done anything to get off them.

WITEK: Oh, shut up. You know. If we don't paint the whole apartment we won't get paid.

OLEK: I know. I know. I know. Fuck it. There's no fucking justice in this world.

WITEK: I know.

OLEK: I know, I've got it.

WITEK: What?

OLEK: I'll search his pockets.

WITEK: Don't do it.

OLEK: [*Gets down on his knees, crosses himself, gets up and starts searching the dead man's pockets.*] This is the duty of any one who finds a hanging man. I heard about a man who hanged himself with $5,000 dollars in his pocket...that's not him...[*Sadly.*] One works hard, one gives his whole heart away to his painting job, and this asshole has the right to just walk in here and hang himself. Free fucking country.

WITEK: Shut up. Let me think.

OLEK: In Zelazowa Wola, if someone felt like hanging himself he would go home quietly, would put the rope around his neck, kick the chair and that's it! This is what you have a home for.

WITEK: [*Reflecting.*] You know, Olek, renovating is like fucking a tiger. A lot of fun, but scary.

OLEK: You really fucked a tiger?

WITEK: I'm just speaking metaphorically. Jesus Christ, do I have to explain everything to you? Sometimes talking to you makes me want to hang myself, too.

OLEK: Don't do it. Look. [*He opens and closes his hands into fists.*]

WITEK: So what?

OLEK: [*Pointing to the body.*] He can't do it.

[*Noises offstage.*]

OLEK: I don't get why that fucking playwright doesn't just go back to Poland.

WITEK: Actually, I heard his grandmother on his ex-wife's side was half Jewish.

OLEK: [*Understanding.*] Ahhh...Poor bastard...So, this is why he's screwed. I can't believe it. [OLEK *grabs a bucket and his paints and ignoring the corpse, enters another room.*]

WITEK: What do you think you're doing?

OLEK: [*Offstage.*] I'm painting. I'm a working man, I won't let any hanging man disturb me.

WITEK: So how are you going to paint the ceiling? He will be covered with paint.

OLEK: [*Reenters.*] I've got it. Let's take him down, put him in the room we've already painted, and afterwards hang him back again. That way, everybody will think he hanged himself after we painted.

WITEK: Are you crazy? You are supposed to be Catholic.

OLEK: You're right. The police could find out. Better not touch the body.

[*Enter* PLAYWRIGHT: *tired, dirty, with paint all over his clothes and body. He's carrying a thick copy of* The New York Times *under his arm. He does not notice the hanging body.*]

WITEK: [*Pointing at the* PLAYWRIGHT.] Look!

OLEK: What? You don't like him, but he's brilliant. I always say that one should hang out with people on certain level. He got the solution.

WITEK: You don't like him. But he's a good playwright. He's already got a solution.

OLEK: What?

WITEK: Of course. We'll cover him [*Points to the hanging body.*] with the *Times*, then paint the ceiling, then take the paper off and we'll be done. [*Reaches his hand out to the playwright.*] Give it to me.

PLAYWRIGHT: [*Slightly confused.*] It has the Home section. [*He then notices the body and stares with a stoned look on his face.*] Oh my God. He's got nice shoes.

[*Chopin's "Grand Polonaise in A Flat" is heard.*]

WITEK: What's that?

[*Everybody listens to the music in silence.*]

OLEK: Chopin's "Grand Polonaise in A Flat." I'm playing.

BLACKOUT

THE END

David Ives

DEGAS, C'EST MOI

DAVID IVES

David Ives was born in Chicago and educated at Northwestern University and Yale School of Drama. A 1995 Guggenheim Fellow in playwriting, he is probably best known for *All In the Timing* an evening of one-act comedies first produced by Primary Stages in New York and subsequently in Chicago, San Francisco, Seattle, Dallas, Philadelphia, Washington, St. Louis, Berlin, Vienna, and Sydney, among many other places here and abroad. *All In The Timing* was awarded an Outer Critics Circle Award for playwriting, was nominated for a Drama Desk Award for best play, was included in *The Best Short Plays of 1993–94*, and was the most-performed play nationally (except for Shakespeare productions) in the 1995–96 season. Other plays by David Ives include: *Don Juan In Chicago*; *Ancient History*; *The Land of Cockaigne*; the short plays *English Made Simple*; *Seven Menus*; *Foreplay or the Art of the Fugue*; *Mere Mortals*; *Long Ago and Far Away*; and an opera, *The Secret Garden*, which premiered at the Pennsylvania Opera Theatre. Two other of his short plays, *Sure Thing* and *The Universal Language*, have been included in the *Best Short Plays* series.

This play is for Martha, of course.

SETTING: ED, *on a bed. Morning light. A grey wall behind him.*

ED: I decide to be Degas for a day. Edgar Degas. Why Degas? Why not Degas? Pourquoi pas Degas? Maybe it's the creamy white light spreading on my walls this morning...

[Creamy white light spreads on the wall.]

Maybe it's the prismatic bars of color on the ceiling...

[Prismatic bars appear at the top of the wall.]

Maybe it's all the cheap French wine I've been drinking...
[He finds a wine bottle in his bed.] But yes, today I will be Degas! It's true, I don't know much about Degas.

[SLIDE: Degas is projected on the wall.]

Dead, French, impressionist painter of ballerinas...

[SLIDE: A Degas dance scene.]

...jockeys...

[SLIDE: A Degas racetrack scene.]

...and ummm...

[SLIDE: Nothing.]

...that kind of thing. And granted, I'm not French, dead, or a painter of any kind. And yet—are Edgar Degas and I not united by our shared humanity?

[SLIDE of Degas, again.]

By our common need for love?

[SLIDE: Doisneau's photo, "The Kiss."]

Coffee?

[SLIDE: A cup of coffee.]

Deodorant?

[SLIDE: A naked armpit that disappears as DORIS *enters.]*

DORIS: Oh God, oh God, oh God. Have you seen my glasses?

ED: Doris breaks in on my speculations.

DORIS: I can't find my glasses.

ED: Doris, I say to Doris, I'm going to be Degas today.

DORIS: He's gonna kill me if I'm late again.

ED: Doris doesn't see the brilliance of the idea.

DORIS: This is a tragedy.

ED: Doris—I am Degas!

DORIS: Don't forget the dry cleaning.

[DORIS *kisses him, and exits.*]

ED: Alas, poor Doris. Distracted by the banal, as usual. No matter. I start my day and brush my teeth as Degas.

[ED *hops out of bed and produces a green toothbrush. The bed disappears.*]

Wow! This is wonderful! In the bathroom, everything seems different, yet nothing has changed. The very sink seems transfigured. The porcelain pullulates with possibilities. And will you look at the light on that green plastic! The bristles are disgusting, but the light is fantastic!

[*We hear the sound of shower running.*]

In the shower, it feels strange, lathering an immortal. What's even stranger, the immortal is lathering back. How did I become such a genius? I, who flunked wood shop in high school? Was it my traumatic childhood?

[*SLIDE: A boy of five.*]

My lost pencil box?

[*SLIDE: A pencil box, marked, "Lost Pencil Box."*]

Uncle Stosh's unfortunate party trick with the parakeet?

[*SLIDE: A Parakeet.*]

That parakeet helped make me what I am. I'm great. I'm brilliant. My name will live forever! [*He considers that a second.*]
No. It's too big. Too big. And I'm hungry.

[*SLIDE: Two fried eggs. Sound of frying.* ED *shakes a frying pan.*]

Frying my eggs I get fascinated by the lustrous yellow of the yolks, the burnt sienna around the edges... Something burning? My muffin. [*Produces a completely blackened muffin.*] Being Degas is going to take some practice. [*Tosses the muffin away.*] I go out into the world with dry cleaning.

[*He grabs some clothing as we hear city noises, cars honking, etc. The light changes and a SLIDE of a city skyline appears.*]

O glorious polychromatic city, saturated with light! Gone the dreary daily deja vu. Today—Degas vu.

[*A* CAR DRIVER *enters at a run, holding a steering wheel, headed right for* ED. *Loud car horn and screeching brakes heard as* ED *dodges aside.*]

ED: Idiot!

DRIVER: Moron! Watch where you're going!

ED: Jerk! Do you know who you almost killed?

DRIVER: Asshole!

[DRIVER *exits.*]

ED: Another couple of inches and the world would've lost a hundred masterpieces.

[DRY CLEANER *enters, writing on a pad.*]

DRY CLEANER: What can I do for you, honey?

ED: At the dry cleaners I notice something strange...

DRY CLEANER: [*Taking the dry cleaning.*] One shirt, one skirt, one jacket.

ED: My dry cleaner acts exactly the same.

DRY CLEANER: You know you need some serious reweaving.

ED: Madame, I would love to capture you in charcoal.

DRY CLEANER: My husband already caught me in puce. [*Tears a sheet off the pad.*] After five. [THE DRY CLEANER *gives the slip to* ED, *and exits with the clothing.*]

ED: Not a flutter. Then, on the corner, the newsguy tries to sell me my paper just like always.

[NEWSGUY *enters*.]

NEWSGUY: Daily Noose?

ED: Have you got anything en Francaise?

NEWSGUY: Let's see, I got *Le Mot, Le Monde, Le Reve, Le Chat, La Chasse, Le Mystere, Les Mamelles,* and the *Nouvel Observateur.*

ED: I'll take the *News.*

NEWSGUY: Change.

[*He flips an invisible coin, which* ED *"catches," then the* NEWSGUY *exits*.]

ED: Still not a blink of recognition. Then as I head down Broadway, people pass me by without a second glance. Or a third, or a fourth.

[PEOPLE *enter and pass him*.]

I might as well be invisible. I, Edgar Degas!

[*More* PEOPLE *pass him*.]

And then I realize with a shock: it makes no difference to be Degas. I could be anyone!

[*More* PEOPLE *pass him*.]

And yet... And yet maybe the other Degas walked this invisibly through Paris.

[*SLIDE: A Degas street scene of Paris, as we hear a French accordion and the clip-clopping of horses*.]

Bumped into by the bourgeoisie on the upper Left Bank...

[*A* PEDESTRIAN *bumps into him as a* WORKER *enters carrying a crate loaded with cabbages*.]

Shouted at by workers at the Key Food de Montparnasse...

WORKER: Watcha back, watcha back!

[WORKER *exits.*]

ED: Cursed by the less fortunate.

[HOMELESS PERSON *enters.*]

HOMELESS PERSON: Fuck you. Fuck you.

ED: There's a kind of comfort in this.

HOMELESS PERSON: Fuck you.

ED: Completely anonymous, I'm free to appreciate the grey blur of pigeons...

[*SLIDE: Flying pigeons.*]

The impasto at *Ray's Pizza*...

[*SLIDE: Pizza window.*]

The chiaroscuro of the M-11 bus.

[*SLIDE: A city bus. An* UNEMPLOYMENT WORKER *enters.*]

UNEMPLOYMENT WORKER: Next!

ED: My delicious anonymity continues at Unemployment.

[*Accordion and horses stop as a sign descends which says, "Line Forms Here."*]

UNEMPLOYMENT WORKER: Sign your claim at the bottom, please.

ED: Do you notice the name I signed in the bottom right corner?

UNEMPLOYMENT WORKER: Edgar Day-hass. Edgar Deejis. Edgar Deggis. Edgar De Gas. Edgar De What?

ED: Edgar Degas. And—?

UNEMPLOYMENT WORKER: And—this name at the bottom does not match the name at the top of the form.

ED: No, no, no, no...

UNEMPLOYMENT WORKER: Are you not the same as the person at the top of the form?

ED: I am a person at the top of my form. I am Edgar. Degas.

UNEMPLOYMENT WORKER: The dead French painter?

ED: The same.

UNEMPLOYMENT WORKER: Next!

[UNEMPLOYMENT WORKER *exits and the sign goes away*.]

ED: Recalling my painterly interest in racetracks, I stop off at OTB.

[*SLIDE: A Degas Racetrack scene, as another sign descends which also says, "Line Forms Here."* OTB WORKER *enters*.]

OTB WORKER: Next!

ED: I would like to put ten francs on Windmill.

OTB WORKER: Oh mais oui, monsieur.

ED: Windmill—I say to him—because the jockey wears brilliant silks of crimson and gold. Windmill—I tell the man—because her sable flanks flash like lightning in the field.

OTB WORKER: [*Handing over the betting slip*.] Windmill—

ED: —he says to me—

OTB WORKER: —always comes in last.

ED: And Windmill does. But who cares? [*Tears up the betting slip*.] I'm Degas!

[OTB WORKER *exits and the sign goes away. SLIDE: the City Library*.]

Oh. The library. Maybe I should look myself up.
[*A Sign descends: "Silence." A* LIBRARIAN *enters*.]

Excuse me. Have you got anything on Degas?

LIBRARIAN: The crassly conservative counterfeminist patriarchal pedophile painter?

ED: No, the colorist who chronicled his age and continues to inspire through posters, postcards and T-shirts.

LIBRARIAN: Section D, aisle 2.

[LIBRARIAN *exits*.]

ED: Who needs the carping of critics, the lies of biographers? I know who I am. Famished by creativity, I stop at Twin Donut.

[*SLIDE: A donut, as two tables appear. A* YOUNG WOMAN *sits at one, writing in a journal.* ED *sits at the other.*]

TWIN DONUT WORKER: [*Enters with a plate.*] Vanilla cruller?

ED: Ici! And some drawing paper, please.

[DONUT WORKER *hands him a napkin.*]

ED: [*Cont'd.*] There I am, scribbling a priceless doodle on my napkin when I notice someone staring at me.

[*The* YOUNG WOMAN *stops writing and, pausing for thought, looks at* ED.]

ED: [*Cont'd.*] A young woman writing in a journal. Has she recognized me? She smiles slightly. Yes. She knows I am Degas. Not only that. [*He looks again.*] She loves Degas. That one look has redeemed all my years of effort. My work has given meaning to someone's life. Should I seduce her? It would be traditional.

[*A schmaltzy-romantic violin is heard.*]

YOUNG WOMAN: [*Writing.*] "April six. Twin Donut. Just saw Edgar Degas two tables over. So he likes vanilla crullers too! Suddenly this day is glorious and memorable. Would love to lie in bed all afternoon and make love with Degas..."

ED: But no. I'd only cast her off, break her heart. Not to mention what it would do to Doris.

YOUNG WOMAN: "Dwayne would kill me."

ED: But isn't it my duty as an artist to seduce this girl? Experience life to the fullest...?

YOUNG WOMAN: Adieu.

ED: Adieu.

[YOUNG WOMAN *exits and the tables disappear. Afternoon light. Street sounds and a SLIDE of a city street again.*]

ED: On Fifth Avenue, a mysterious figure passes me, leading a Doberman. Or vice versa.

[*A* FIGURE *in a raincoat, hat and sunglasses, holding a stiffened leash, as if a dog were on it, crosses.*]

ED: [*Cont'd.*] Somebody famous. But who? Woody Allen? Kissinger? Roseanne? Then other things distract me. Money...

[*SLIDE: A dollar bill.*]

Job...
[*SLIDE: The want ads.*]

Athlete's foot...
[*SLIDE: A naked foot.*]

But wait a minute. Whoa, whoa, whoa! For a picosecond there, I forgot: I am Degas!

[*SLIDE: Photo of Degas. A* HOT DOG VENDOR *enters.*]

HOT DOG VENDOR: Hot dog! Hot dog! Hot dog!

ED: The labor of hanging onto one's identity amidst the daily dreck.

HOT DOG VENDOR: You got a pretzel here!

ED: It's too much.

HOT DOG VENDOR: Good Humor! Good Humor!

[*Empty picture frames descend, as the* VENDOR *exits and a* MUSEUM GUARD *enters.*]

ED: At the museum, I tour the rooms of my work. Amazing how much I accomplished—even without television.

[*SLIDE: A Degas self-portrait.*]

A self-portrait. Not a great likeness, maybe. But so full of... what?... feeling. I stare into my fathomless eyes.

[*A* MUSEUMGOER *enters and stands beside him looking at the self-portrait.*]

MUSEUMGOER: Mmm.

ED: Mmmmmmm.

MUSEUMGOER: Bit smudgy, isn't it?

ED: "Smudgy?"

MUSEUMGOER: This area in here.

ED: Yeah, but what about this area over here?   .

MUSEUMGOER: No, but this area here. Something not quite realized.

ED: Okay. So I had an off day.

MUSEUMGOER: Off day?

ED: Not all my work was perfect.

MUSEUMGOER: Indeed. Indeed...

[THE MUSEUMGOER *slips away.*]

ED: Philistine. Probably headed for Van Gogh. To kneel in adora-
tion at the sunflowers—of course. Vincent. "Vince," we called
him. What a jerk.

[*SLIDE: "Woman with Chrysanthemums."*]

   What's this... "Woman with Chrysanthemums." Ah, yes.
A personal favorite. God, when I remember that morning over
a century ago—can it be that long now?—when this was an
empty canvas and I stood in front it paralyzed by its whiteness.
Then I reached for my brush... [*He produces a paint-
brush.*]... and it all crystallized. I saw it all. This pensive
woman, oblivious of the transcendent burst of color right at her
shoulder. The natural exuberance of the flowers—alongside her
human sorrow. Yes. Yes! Our blindness to the beautiful! Our in-
sensibility to the splendor right there within our reach! When
I finished, I was exalted. Will I ever have a day that inspired
again...?

MUSEUM GUARD: Step back, please.

ED: Excuse me?

MUSEUM GUARD: You have to step back, sir. You're too close to the
painting.

ED: I'm too close to this painting...?

MUSEUM GUARD: Do you copy?

ED: No, I don't copy.

MUSEUM GUARD: Sir?

ED: I step back.

[*He does so, and the SLIDE fades out and the picture frames fly up out of sight. The* GUARD *exits.*]

But the glow of my exaltation stays with me all the way to the Akropolis Diner...

[*Two tables again.* DORIS *enters.*]

DORIS: Oh God, oh God, oh God.

ED: ... where Doris meets me for dinner.

DORIS: What a day.

ED: What a fabulous day. Epic!

DORIS: Six hours of xeroxing.

ED: No, but listen. Degas. Remember?

DORIS: Degas...?

ED: I've been Degas all day. Since morning.

DORIS: The toilets erupted again. The women's room was like Vesuvius.

ED: I am Degas.

[WAITER *enters.*]

WAITER: What do you need, my friends?

ED: Cherie?

DORIS: Alka Seltzer.

WAITER: One Bromo.

DORIS: Make it a double.

WAITER: And you, sir?

ED: I'll have a Reubens.

WAITER: We got a Rube! [*Exits.*]

DORIS: They said they were going to fix those toilets last week.

ED: As Doris dilates on toilets, I begin to feel Degas slip away a little . . .

DORIS: Waiter!

ED: . . . like a second skin I'm shedding . . .

DORIS: Waiter!

ED: . . . leaving nothing behind.

DORIS: Where is that guy?

ED: Then I see a man at another table, staring at me. Looking at me with such pity in his eyes. Such unalloyed human sympathy.

DORIS: At least I found my glasses.

ED: Then I realize.

DORIS: They were in my purse all the time.

ED: The man is Renoir.

DORIS: [*Holding up her glasses.*] See?

ED: By now, Degas is completely gone.

[*Light changes to night light, the rear wall darkens to black, as* ED *and* DORIS *rise from the tables, and the tables disappear.*]

ED: [*Cont'd.*] Doris and I walk home in silence.

[DORIS *exits.* ED *is alone, as the lights darken further around him, to a single spot.*]

ED: [*Cont'd.*] People say they have a voice inside their heads. The voice that tells themselves the story of their lives. Now I'm walking up the street, now I'm taking out my key, is there a meaning to all this, who's that person on the stairway coming down, now I'm putting my key in the door, now I do this, now I do that. The facts of our lives. Yes, I too have always had a voice like that in my head. But now, tonight, no one is listening. That presence that always listened in the back of my mind is no longer there, listening in. Nor is there a presence behind that presence listening in. Nor a presence behind that, nor behind that, nor behind that. All the way back to the back of my mind, no one is listening in. The story of my life is going on unwatched. Unheard. I am alone.

[*The bed reappears.* ED *sprawls on it, his forearm over his eyes.*]

I find myself upstairs, sprawled on the bed while Doris runs the bathwater. Degas is dust. All my glory, all my fame, all my achievements are utterly forgotten. Immortality? A cruel joke. I have done nothing. Absolutely nothing ...
[*A light comes up on* DORIS, *drying herself with a towel.*]

Then I find myself looking through the doorway into the bathroom and I see Doris standing naked with her foot up on the edge of the old lion-footed tub, drying herself. The overhead light is dim, but Doris is fluorescent—radiant—luminous—with pinks and lavenders and vermillions playing over her skin. The frayed towel she's wrapped in gleams like a rose. She turns and looks back at me and smiles.
[DORIS *turns and looks over her shoulder at* ED.]

DORIS: Bon soir, Degas.

ED: Degas? Who needs him?

[*He holds his hand out to her across the intervening space, and she holds hers out to him.*]

Lights fade

THE END

Allan Knee

THE ST. VALENTINE'S DAY MASSACRE

ALLAN KNEE

Allan Knee wrote the award-winning adaptation of *Around the World In Eighty Days*, which was chosen last summer by Theaterworks/USA for New York City's free summer theater. His other plays include *Shmulnik's Waltz* (Jewish Rep), *The Lost Boys* (American Repertory Theater, Cambridge), *Second Avenue* (Manhattan Puchline), *The Minister's Black Veil* (Playwright's Horizons), *Santa Anita '42* (Chelsea Theater at the Brooklyn Academy of Music), and the Broadway musical, *Late Nite Comic*. His one-act play, *Christmas Eve On Orchard Street*, was included in *Best American Short Plays of 1990*. For television he wrote the four-part PBS series of Nathaniel Hawthorne's *The Scarlett Letter* and *A Gorey Halloween*, based on the characters of Edward Gorey. His film, *Journey*, won a Cine Eagle at the Washington Film Festival. His current projects include a musical adaptation of *Little Women* (with Alison Hubbard and Kim Oler) and an original musical *Dancing On The Rooftops* (with Jon Marans and Daniel Levine). He is a graduate of the Yale School of Drama.

SETTING: *A cafe in some part of town. February 14. A man and a woman in their early 30s confront one another. The man, KENNY, is enthusiastic as he takes off his coat, sets down a package. The woman, SHERYL, stylish, is more wary. They are both in an emotional, edgy state.*

KENNY: Sheryl, I almost didn't recognize you. You look so—

SHERYL: Terrific?

KENNY: Yes! I can't get over it. The ensemble. The suit, the hair. You've got such—

SHERYL: Style?

KENNY: Style! Yes! This must have been a fantastic year for you. My God, no more fatigue boots—no more army surplus!

SHERYL: Well, look at you. No more pin-striped suits? wing-tipped shoes?

KENNY: Don't be fooled by appearances. This is a very, very studied look. [*Holding out his arm.*] Feel this. Go on—feel it.

SHERYL: I'm really not interested in your body.

KENNY: Feel it, Sheryl.

[*She feels his leg with a finger—makes a sour face.*]

KENNY: [*Cont'd.*] My personal trainer is very enthusiastic about my progress.

SHERYL: You have a personal trainer?

KENNY: Actually, I have two—one for the upper part of the body— one for the lower.

SHERYL: I can only stay 15 minutes. I can't waste a whole afternoon.

KENNY: You're not still pissed at me, are you? Surely, you've forgiven me?

SHERYL: For being an asshole? Yes, I've forgiven you for that.

KENNY: Good. I've forgiven you, too.

SHERYL: What have you forgiven me for?

KENNY: Let's see. Lack of insight—peevishness—small mindedness—

SHERYL: I'm going. [*She gets up.*]

KENNY: [*Stopping her.*] It's a joke. I admit there were misunderstandings! And, more than once, I was a little bit at fault.

SHERYL: A little bit?

KENNY: I'm not perfect. But you have to admit I'm pretty close to it. Now, sit down. Please. Finish your drink at least.

[*She sits back down.*]

KENNY: [*Cont'd.*] What we're doing I think Valentine himself would have been proud of. It's clearly something he would have done if he had had the opportunity. And maybe he did, who knows— maybe he met his girl over drinks, overlooking the park. Valentine was a great sentimentalist.

SHERYL: Like you.

KENNY: I don't mind the comparison. In fact, I rather like it. Shall I tell you about St. Valentine?

SHERYL: Let me see if I remember what you told me last year. He was misunderstood by the church, ill-treated by his peers, abused by his parents, and martyred by society.

KENNY: And why? Why I ask you? Why did this misfortune happen?

SHERYL: Because he was an unfaithful, irresponsible bastard!

KENNY: No, Sheryl, you're wrong again. If Valentine had any failings—it was being too faithful. Too caring. He loved too much.

SHERYL: They martyr people for loving too much?

KENNY: That is the number one cause of martyrdom in the Western world. Read your church history. The good die young. Listen to your Billy Joel. Cruel, nasty men live long lives and die peacefully in their sleep. The good suffer ignominies, premature baldness, constipation, IRS audits, and wet dreams. Say what you want about me, Sheryl, but don't mock Valentine. He was a defender of the faith. He died for love. And no one dies for love anymore. I get the feeling you don't believe in love anymore, either.

SHERYL: Not really.

KENNY: Something sour you on it?

SHERYL: Someone.

KENNY: Present company excluded of course?

SHERYL: Kenny, can we stop this crap right now? When I agreed to meet with you once a year, I agreed to it because I thought it'd be fun—quirky, perhaps—at least somehow it'd be interesting. But, it hasn't been interesting, it's not been quirky, and it's never been fun.

KENNY: Well, not for you maybe, but I've had a hell of a good time.

SHERYL: I'm sick and tired of warring with you.

KENNY: Then I surrender.

SHERYL: No, you don't surrender. You have to win all the time.

KENNY: Everyone likes a little victory. Don't you?

SHERYL: I'm not about winning or losing. I've changed.

KENNY: Obviously. You reek of confidence now—you have an aura of magnificence about you. The clothes, the hair. You exude the odor of the first floor of Bloomingdale's. So, talk to me. Tell me what's going on.

SHERYL: I went to a psychic.

KENNY: [*Surprised.*] You went to a fortune teller?

SHERYL: No, Kenny, I went to a psychic—who advised me to stop seeing you.

KENNY: But you don't see me.

SHERYL: [*Mounting anger.*] For three years, six months, and four days I saw you. We lived together for more than two of those years. We shared the same bathroom, Kenny. I gave you the best three years of my life.

KENNY: And you want them back now?

SHERYL: Yes! Yes, I do! Can you give them back to me?

KENNY: I'm not holding on to them.

SHERYL: Bullshit!

KENNY: Maybe a few memories.

SHERYL: Rupert advised me to reverse everything I was doing.

KENNY: Rupert?

SHERYL: The pyschic. He advised me to make a long list of my activities—the things I did, the places I went, my behavioral patterns. So I did. I voted Republican. I started eating meat. I changed my way of dressing. And I took a job with Drexel Burnham.

KENNY: The brokerage house? I thought they were all behind bars—or living in Argentina.

SHERYL: They started up again.

KENNY: Incredible.

SHERYL: They're just the ones that got caught, that's all.

KENNY: Oh, so they're more to be pitied than censured? You're endorsing dishonesty, Sheryl.

SHERYL: It's the way of the world.

KENNY: And you've jumped on the bandwagon? Congratulations. What do you do at Drexel?

SHERYL: I'm a stockbroker.

KENNY: [*Cries out.*] I don't believe it! A stockbroker? Tell me you turn the switch on the electric chair, but don't tell me you sell stocks! What happened to your passion for the people?

SHERYL: [*Bites out.*] It died! Like a lot of things die! You give up you go on! You see the futility of things! I'm a stockbroker! And a good one! You don't like it? Tough shit!

KENNY: Forgive me. I'm just so happy to see you.

SHERYL: This is how you express your happiness?

KENNY: Your skin looks terrific. Like crystal.

SHERYL: I had a chemical peel.

KENNY: That must have taken real guts.

SHERYL: The skin's still a little raw.

KENNY: Looks great. Sheryl, did you know that birds pick their life-long mates on St. Valentine's Day?

SHERYL: How do they know it's St. Valentine's Day?

KENNY: They check with Audubon—I don't know. Instinct, perhaps. So, you're a stockbroker?

SHERYL: Yes.

KENNY: Happy?

SHERYL: Most of the time.

KENNY: Making money?

SHERYL: Enough.

KENNY: Getting laid? Forget that question. [*He laughs nervously, stops.*] Are you getting laid? You look so sexually satisfied.

SHERYL: I am.

KENNY: You're not being promiscuous, I hope?

SHERYL: Kenny, you look tired, old and worn. You're spending your days at the gym trying to change your body image. But, unfortunately, you're still a very shabby, flabby man!

KENNY: God, I miss you. I miss someone who could talk to me like that. Put me in my place—smack me around—

SHERYL: I never smacked you. Though often enough I wanted to.

KENNY: Would you like to smack me, now? You can, you know. Give me a good old-fashioned smack. Go on, Sheryl. Let me have it.

[*She smacks him—surprisingly hard.*]

KENNY: [*Cont'd.*] You obviously still love me.

SHERYL: I'm over you, Kenny.

KENNY: So, why did you come today?

SHERYL: To tell you I've met someone.

KENNY: Someone you like?

SHERYL: Enormously.

KENNY: Is it a man?

SHERYL: Yes.

KENNY: You're sleeping with him?

SHERYL: This is 1995, Kenny.

KENNY: So, you're not sleeping with him?

SHERYL: I've got to be going.

KENNY: [*Calls.*] You want to handle my account?

SHERYL: No.

KENNY: Sheryl—

SHERYL: Go elsewhere. Go to Merrill Lynch.

KENNY: I hate Merrill Lynch. What's he look like?

SHERYL: Who?

KENNY: Your boyfriend.

SHERYL: A cross between Al Pacino and Mel Gibson.

KENNY: That short, huh? I hope he's wealthy.

SHERYL: Millions.

KENNY: I'm sure he's conservative?

SHERYL: Democrat.

KENNY: Virile?

SHERYL: He shaves twice a day.

KENNY: Romantic?

SHERYL: Kenny, go find some 18-year-old co-ed who still believes in St. Valentine's Day—because I don't! And I think we should stop this!

KENNY: Stop what?

SHERYL: Meeting. Year after year. It's getting us nowhere.

KENNY: We were once lovers! When your father died I held you in my arms for a week—

SHERYL: People break up all the time and that's the end of it. They don't set up meetings once a year to carry on some inane tradition.

KENNY: Inane? This is the most important day of the year for me! I was like a child waking up this morning! "Valentine's Day!" I cried out. "It's Valentine's Day!" I danced out of bed!

SHERYL: Don't you get it, Kenny—I don't love you anymore? I'm not interested in you. You're just a man with a lot of worn-out opinions.

KENNY: [*He goes to her and puts his hands affectionately on hers. His voice soft and intimate.*] I hate myself.

SHERYL: Please, stop this.

KENNY: I look in the mirror every morning and think what an ugly bastard I am.

SHERYL: Please take your hands off of me.

KENNY: I can't.

SHERYL: Kenny, please—

KENNY: They seem to be stuck to you. Must be some sort of chemical acid on your clothes.

SHERYL: [*Pulling away*.] I'm not amused.

KENNY: Sheryl, I have a confession.

SHERYL: What is it?

KENNY: "I get no kick from champagne, mere alcohol—"

SHERYL: Stop it—please stop it.

KENNY: Are you really seeing someone?

SHERYL: I told you I was.

KENNY: Where'd you meet him?

SHERYL: At Drexel.

KENNY: He's a broker?

SHERYL: A client.

KENNY: You're fucking a client?

SHERYL: Yes.

KENNY: Isn't that unethical?

SHERYL: Not in the brokerage business! [*She starts to leave.*] Have a wonderful life, Kenny. Nice seeing you again.

KENNY: [*Calls desperately.*] Sheryl—I'm dying!

SHERYL: [*Turns, stunned.*] What?

KENNY: I didn't want to tell you.

SHERYL: You're dying?

KENNY: That's why I look so lousy.

SHERYL: Don't kid about something like this.

KENNY: I'm not kidding.

SHERYL: What are you dying of?

KENNY: I don't want to upset you.

SHERYL: Is it AIDS?

KENNY: Worse.

SHERYL: What?

KENNY: Diaper rash. An advanced case.

SHERYL: Goddam you, you make fun of everything!

KENNY: Itch all night—

SHERYL: Nothing is sacred to you.

KENNY: [*Strong.*] Everything is sacred to me! Life is sacred to me! Love is sacred to me! You are sacred to me! St. Valentine is sacred to me!

SHERYL: St. Valentine is a made-up saint!

KENNY: A made-up saint? Says who?

SHERYL: Says everyone. He's a fraud—like you.

KENNY: I'm a fraud, am I?

SHERYL: Face up to it, Kenny! We don't mix well. We're like oil and water. It doesn't work for us!

KENNY: Because you're a stubborn, spoiled, inhibited bitch.

SHERYL: I am not inhibited! I may be spoiled—I may be stubborn at times—but I have a very alive body!

KENNY: Miss Frigidaire!

SHERYL: That is amusing—that is really amusing, Kenny, coming from a 34-year-old, adolescent boy scout whose idea of being kinky is making love in his shredded underwear!

KENNY: You found my shredded underwear irresistible.

SHERYL: The truth is, I found your shredded Fruit-Of-The-Looms® disgusting.

KENNY: You said I reminded you of Tom Cruise.

SHERYL: And I hate Tom Cruise!

KENNY: You said *Born On The 4th of July* was your favorite movie.

SHERYL: I lied! I found it indulgent and tiresome! I don't want this anymore! I stopped wanting this four years ago! I can still see you crawling in bed with me in your long johns and smelly socks, reading your dirty little books—your how-to manuals—setting out like some demented sex therapist to find my G-spot, when all I wanted from you was some genuine passion. I wanted to lose myself in you. I wanted wild, filthy conversation.

KENNY: You wanted me to talk dirty to you?

SHERYL: Yes!

KENNY: This is amazing! This is really amazing, Sheryl! It's what I wanted to do! I wanted to talk filth to you! I used to fantasize about you constantly, everywhere. Once, at a Passover seder, I imagined I was Elijah and entered the room wrapped only in a sheet, and while everyone was blessing the matzoh, I took you on the table before my folks, my cousins, my aunts. Talk about passion, filth, blasphemy!

SHERYL: Kenny, please!

KENNY: I couldn't go to a museum without imagining every nude was you—

SHERYL: Stop!

KENNY: I'd ravish you—

SHERYL: Kenny!

KENNY: And, I wouldn't let up even if you shouted—

SHERYL: Enough!

KENNY: I'd keep at it! I'd come at you again and again.

SHERYL: This is madness.

KENNY: Wild, vile words would pour out of me. And I'd stand over you like a collosus with my penis unsheathed and I'd howl—

SHERYL: Stop.

KENNY: —and make all sorts of noises while you'd be screaming—

SHERYL: Give it to me hard!

KENNY: Yes!

SHERYL: Ravish me!

KENNY: Bite me!

SHERYL: Hurt me!

KENNY: Yes!

SHERYL: Screw me!

KENNY: Oh, God, yes!

SHERYL: Don't stop!

KENNY: No!

SHERYL: Kenny!

KENNY: I'd do it eight—nine times in a night!

SHERYL: More!

KENNY: Tigers do it 16 times in a three-hour span!

SHERYL: Oh, my tiger!

KENNY: [*Growls.*] My Sheryl.

SHERYL: Kenny!

KENNY: Sheryl!

SHERYL: Kenny!

KENNY: Sheryllll!

SHERYL: [*Overlapping.*] Kenneeee!

[*They both cry out in ecstasy. Gradually, they come to themselves, embarrassed.* SHERYL *straightens herself.*]

SHERYL: [*Cont'd.*] I've got to go.

KENNY: I know. It's late for me, too. I'll pay the check.

SHERYL: You can't afford it.

KENNY: I can afford it.

SHERYL: Look, let's not stand on ceremonies. If you're broke—

KENNY: I'm not broke.

SHERYL: You're obviously out of work.

KENNY: Who said I'm out of work?

SHERYL: You said—

KENNY: I've got a job with a law firm.

SHERYL: As what?

KENNY: A lawyer.

SHERYL: Bullshit! A lawyer? Since when?

KENNY: Last June.

SHERYL: You finally passed the bar? I don't believe it.

KENNY: Third time lucky.

SHERYL: But the clothes?

KENNY: It's dress-down day at the company.

SHERYL: Dress-down? You're kidding?

KENNY: No.

SHERYL: We tried it at Drexel, dressing down—the clients went crazy. They thought the bottom was falling out of the market.

KENNY: It takes a little getting used to. But people come around.

SHERYL: Do they?

KENNY: You know what? Getting together with you—once a year, one day a year, a few hours, a few minutes even—is the sanest thing I do.

SHERYL: [*She gets up.*] I've really got to go now.

[*When she hesitates,* KENNY *suddenly senses he could have her back, but all he says is.*]

KENNY: Me too . . .

SHERYL: [*She stops, looks at him.*] Next year I pick the place.

KENNY: You really getting married?

SHERYL: I'm thinking of it.

KENNY: No matter what—this day is ours.

SHERYL: The last two devotees of St. Valentine. [*She starts away again.*]

KENNY: [*Calls.*] Sheryl?

SHERYL: Yes?

KENNY: I love you.

SHERYL: You really fantasized all that about me?

KENNY: I still do. I wish—

SHERYL: [*Stopping him.*] Kenny, please. Bye.

KENNY: Bye.

[*They do not move.*]

THE END

Jonathan Levy

OLD BLUES

For Mary

JONATHAN LEVY

Jonathan Levy received his B.A. from Harvard University, and his M.A. and Ph.D. from Columbia University. He has had over thirty plays and libretti for adults and children produced at the Brooklyn Academy of Music, Alice Tully Hall, Phoenix Theatre, Manhattan Theatre Club, American Shakespeare Festival, in Stratford, Connecticut, the Eugene O'Neill Playwrights Conference, and Playwrights Horizons, to name a few. His play *Charlie The Chicken* was included in *The Best Short Plays of 1983*.

From 1973 through 1978, he was the playwright in residence at the Manhattan Theatre Club, and then acted as their Literary Advisor from 1982 through 1984. He was a member of the National Endowment for the Arts Theatre Policy Panel, and was Co-Chairman of Theatre For Youth from 1979 through 1981.

Presently, Dr. Levy is a Distinguished Teaching Professor in Education at SUNY Stony Brook, a professor in Harvard's Graduate School of Education, and a Chief Examiner in Theatre Arts for the International Baccalaureate.

In the past, he has taught at Brandeis University, Columbia College, University of California at Berkley, Bennington College, the Lincoln Center Institute, and the Juilliard School of Music, among others. In 1996 he was named Outstanding Theatre Teacher in American Higher Education by the Association for Theatre in Higher Education (ATHE).

CHARACTERS

CHRIS   Gray brush cut, gray, ravaged, boyish face. Thin, Archibald Cox bow tie. Top tenor.

EDDIE   The host. Small, enthusiastic. Lead.

BROOKS   A dandy. Styled hair. Baritone.

RICHARD   A Resident in Surgery. White hospital trousers, and a big parka, gray-green with Orlon fur, trimmed in road construction orange.

SETTING: EDDIE'S *apartment in the East sixties. Quite bare. A bar with a bowl of cheese dip and potato chips on it.*

TIME: *Winter, 1975.*

The stage is dark. Sound of a pitch pipe being blown. A throat cleared. The pitch pipe is blown again. Three voices—two tenors and a baritone—singing.

VOICES: As the blackbird in the spring
'Neath the willow tree
Sat and piped I heard him sing
Singing Aura Lee.
Aura Lee, Aura Lee,
Maid with golden hair
Sunshine came along with thee
And swallows in the air.

[*Lights up slowly on* CHRIS, EDDIE, *and* BROOKS *singing. They end. Long pause.*]

BROOKS: I thought it was pretty tactless of the minister to keep going on about Bill being convivial. Everybody knows convivial means drunk.

EDDIE: Old Billy. Son of a bitch.

BROOKS: It's going to happen to us all, and you can't ask for it quicker than Old Bill. One minute dictating behind your desk. The next, dead on the floor. [*He goes toward the kitchen.*] You want a beer, Eddie?

EDDIE: Sure.

[*Exit* BROOKS *to the kitchen.*]

EDDIE: [*Cont'd.*] Here today . . .

[CHRIS *walks on humming.*]

BROOKS: [*O.S.*] Where do you keep the church keys?

EDDIE: Betsy took them. Every last one we had in the house.

BROOKS: [*O.S.*] Does she collect them or what?

EDDIE: Spite. Pure spite. All the light bulbs too. You figure it. Use the can opener.

BROOKS: [*O.S.*] That's ridiculous.

EDDIE: You're telling me. I live here. [*Pause.*] You're lucky, Chris. Count yourself lucky you never got married.

[CHRIS *turns, gives him a baleful stare and walks off humming. Enter* BROOKS *with two beers.*]

BROOKS: Boy, those kids got big. That boy of his, what's his name . . .

CHRIS: Scott.

BROOKS: Right. Scottie. He's bigger than I am. So's the girl, for that matter . . .

CHRIS: Helen.

[*He walks off humming.*]

EDDIE: Why do they let them keep the coffin open? That really ticked me off. Why do they do it? It's barbaric.

BROOKS: That's the way Ann wanted it.

EDDIE: So what? Who ever listened to her before? That big red face, in with the lilies. The goddamn choir singing flat.

BROOKS: It took eight men to lift him.

EDDIE: I'm going to be buried in my Whiff tie. I wrote it into the will. My Pi Eta cuff links, my Bronze Star, and my Whiff tie.

CHRIS: [*After a pause.*] I'm going to be cremated.

BROOKS: [*After a pause.*] Let's sing something.

CHRIS: [*Beginning "Mood Indigo."*]
You ain't been blue, no—oo how . . .

EDDIE: O God, Chris. "Mood Indigo."

[CHRIS *sings the walking bass line. It is way out of his range, but it gives some idea of how Bill sang it.*]

EDDIE: Christ, I miss him. Especially in the second chorus. He was so . . .

BROOKS: Convivial.

EDDIE: Companionable. That's a word, isn't it, Chris? You're the English major.

CHRIS: It's a word. It used to be a word.

[*He walks off singing "Since You Got that Mood Indigo," the walking bass line.*]

EDDIE: Listen to that. You know, when we were all singing the melody, the words, you know what Bill was singing? Bum bum bum bum. [*Pause.*] I can't help thinking he could have gotten more out of life.

CHRIS: You know what the tenor's singing when you're singing the words? [*Very high and white.*] Wah wah. Wah wah. Wah wah. [*Ad lib.*]

BROOKS: [*Under the singing.*] Who's the new guy, Eddie?

EDDIE: A nephew of old Charlie Taylor's. An ex-Whiff. Charlie says he sings up a storm. I told Charlie, what the hell, we may as well listen to him. Of course the kid is thrilled.

BROOKS: Just as a point of information, Eddie: Who is old Charlie Taylor?

EDDIE: You remember. Redheaded second tenor from Hotchkiss. Took out Bob McKay's sister Junior Year.

BROOKS: Margie. The dirty blond with the bangs. God, I had the hots for that girl.

CHRIS: [*After a pause.*] Micky. Micky McKay. Short for Michele.

BROOKS: Micky McKay. What the hell ever happened to Micky McKay?

EDDIE: Probably became a nurse. She always did have good hands, right, Brooks? You ought to know.

BROOKS: [*After a pause.*] Probably a grandmother by now.

EDDIE: Right. Probably a swinging grandmother.

BROOKS: With little gray whiskers and a five handicap. And *very* cheery. I took her to the Princeton Game Senior Year. She had on a six-foot Yale scarf and one of those wooly Scotch hats with a pom-pom.

CHRIS: No you didn't.

BROOKS: What, Chris?

CHRIS: You took Nell Ellsworth. Dingo Cullen took Micky McKay.

BROOKS: Jesus, I think he's right.

CHRIS: I am right. Just don't ask me what happened last Thursday.

EDDIE: Who did I take, Chris?

CHRIS: You didn't have a date. You drank half a bottle of bourbon and puked all over the Calhoun Common.

EDDIE: What a memory.

CHRIS: Particularly since I drank the other half of the bottle.

BROOKS: What a sketch he was, that Dingo Cullen. Whipped it out at a Wellesley mixer and peed into the rhododendrons. Then he turned to all and sundry and said "When you got to go you got to go." That's the way he got the name Dingo.

CHRIS: [*After a pause.*] You're thinking of Big Dick Welles. [*Pause.*] Dingo Cullen was a microbiologist. [*Pause.*] And what he said was: "Time and tide wait for no man."

EDDIE: You know something, Chris? You were wasted as an English major. You should have been a History major.

CHRIS: [*After a pause.*] Let's sing something.

BROOKS: I'm going to get another beer.

[*He goes into the kitchen.*]

EDDIE: Hey, Brooks. Your liver doesn't care what you pour down there. Beer's as bad as booze if you drink enough of it. You keep drinking past forty, the front of your brain starts coming out through your nose.

BROOKS: [*O.S.*] Eat me, Eddie.

EDDIE: Up yours with a meathook, Brooks.

CHRIS: Boys, boys.

[CHRIS *takes out his pitch pipe and plays a note. He begins to sing.* EDDIE *joins in. Then* BROOKS *comes in from the kitchen with a beer and joins them.*]

THE THREE: Graceful and easy
I said to Mandy
Nothing is too good for you.
I said to Mandy
When she was handy
Nothing is too good for you.

EDDIE: So where is our bass?

CHRIS: "In de cold, cold ground..."

EDDIE: Don't be morbid, Chris. I meant the kid.

CHRIS: Do you know what morbid means, Eddie?

EDDIE: Tell me, Chris. You're the English major.

CHRIS: It means having to do with death. The dead. Eddie, if I didn't think continually about the dead I wouldn't have a friend in the world. [*Pause.*] Present company excepted.

BROOKS: I think that's the most I've heard Chris say at one time in ten years.

CHRIS: What's there to say.

[*He walks off, not humming. Pause.*]

EDDIE: Guess who walked into the bank the other day. Al Thomas.

BROOKS: Old Al Thomas?

EDDIE: You remember Al Thomas. Fat second bass from Indiana or Ohio or somewhere.

CHRIS: [*After a long pause.*] Terre Haute. [*He sits.*]

EDDIE: He must have made a bundle. Set up four trusts of two hundred thou apiece for his grandchildren. I tried to put him into tax-frees but he said "I'm not worried about the taxes, Eddie. Forget about the taxes. The Government has been good to me and I'm not out to screw the government."

BROOKS: I don't believe it.

EDDIE: It's true. He was something big in Aerospace.

BROOKS: I don't believe anyone in our class has grandchildren. Cassie's still in kindergarten.

CHRIS: You were always retarded, Brooks.

BROOKS: When I went back for the tenth, all those married guys with their broods and their mortgages, they envied the shit out of me. I felt like a boy. They'd all gone to seed, fat, they looked fifty... And I was playing a lot of golf at the time, and I kept up my tan. They all had these wagons, half a block long, littered with old juice containers and parts of dolls and collapsible cribs, and I still had the red MG. I drove away from there, I tell you, I felt like a king.

EDDIE: Boy. That red MG. What ever happened to the old MG, Brooks?

BROOKS: Scrap.

EDDIE: You should have told me, Brooks. I would have bought it from you. For old time's sake.

EDDIE: Chris, do you remember Spring Trip Junior Year?

CHRIS: Like the back of my hand.

BROOKS: We went South. Williamsburg. Charleston.

EDDIE: Atlanta.

CHRIS: Talahassee. Fort Lauderdale.

EDDIE: You got in in Fort Lauderdale, didn't you, Brooksie?

BROOKS: No. But I got bare tit in Palm Beach. [*Pause.*] Or am I wrong, Chris? [*Pause.*] It seems like yesterday.

CHRIS: I loved those trips. The concerts. And the receptions out-doors. Those old alums pushing drinks on you, begging for an-other song. And you always knew, whatever horror show you put on, the bus was leaving the next morning and you could drink a bottle of beer or two in your seat and sleep.

EDDIE: I never did figure out how you slept through the Saint Mark's bridge game, Chris.

CHRIS: Leave the mess where it lay.

BROOKS: Little girl from Florida State or some goddamn place. Her hair loose and a corsage pinned to her shoulder. Looked like but-ter wouldn't melt in her mouth. First time I danced with her, though, I knew she was hot to trot. [*Pause.*] Madge wants to go back to school.

EDDIE: That'll teach you to rob the cradle.

BROOKS: To be a psychiatric social worker or some damn thing. I put my foot down. If we needed the money, I said, it would be a different story. But we don't and we've got two kids under seven and damn it they need their mother. Ask anybody.

EDDIE: Betsy's into martial arts. So I'm told.

BROOKS: Of course we could use the money. Who couldn't use a lit-tle extra money? But the kids come first.

CHRIS: You know what I miss most? The dancing. The waltzes. Why doesn't anybody waltz any more?

BROOKS: They do, Chris. It's coming back.

CHRIS: Not in time.

EDDIE: It's true, though. You know what Petey wants for his birth-day? A dinner jacket. I swear, I can't believe it. At his age, we were lucky to get Ed Junior into clean jeans.

BROOKS: How's he doing, Eddie?

EDDIE: Ed? Great. Just great. It just takes these kids a while to find their feet these days. I personally think it's a healthy thing.

CHRIS: Why doesn't anyone wear tails any more?

BROOKS: Nobody did then. Except the Glee Club.

CHRIS: I did. All the time.

BROOKS: Rarely to class, Chris.

CHRIS: I rarely got to class, Brooks.

EDDIE: [*To* CHRIS.] I always remember you in tails. Nobody wore tails the way you did. With your blond hair slicked back and your patent leather pumps. And that crazy opera cape. You always looked like something out of a Fred Astaire movie.

[*Pause.* CHRIS *turns, goes to the bar and begins to pour himself a drink.*]

BROOKS: Uh uh, Chris. That's a no-no.

[CHRIS *holds up a bottle of tonic water.*]

CHRIS: Eau de quinine. Zero proof. I may be plucky, but I'm not crazy.

[*The doorbell rings.*]

EDDIE: O.K.

[EDDIE *goes to the door and opens it. Enter* RICHARD.]

RICHARD: Sorry I'm late. All hell was breaking loose at the hospital.

EDDIE: That's O.K. No sweat.

CHRIS: We're not going any place.

EDDIE: Let me get your coat. I'm Eddie. We talked on the phone.

RICHARD: I remember.

EDDIE: This is Brooks. Chris. This is Charlie Taylor's nephew.

RICHARD: Richard Crewes.

EDDIE: Ex-Whiff.

[EDDIE *takes his coat.* RICHARD *is wearing hospital whites and has a beeper attached to his belt.*]

EDDIE: [*Cont'd.*] I'll hang it up.

BROOKS: When were you in New Haven?

RICHARD: I got out in '70.

BROOKS: Med School?

RICHARD: College. I was '74 in Med School.

CHRIS: A child, Eddie. They sent us a child.

EDDIE: You're killing us with those numbers, Richard.

RICHARD: Freud said there's no such thing as a joke.

BROOKS: Are you going into psychiatry, Dick?

RICHARD: No. Neurosurgery. I've given it a lot of thought. The hours are pretty regular. The money's terrific. And I've got really good hand-eye coordination.

[*Pause.* CHRIS *nods, then walks off humming.*]

BROOKS: Where did you go to Med School, Dick? Yale?

RICHARD: No. Harvard.

EDDIE: [*Returning.*] That's a word we don't mention much around here, fella.

[RICHARD *looks at him, then crosses to the dip and potato chips and eats hungrily.*]

RICHARD: Excuse me. I'm on my dinner break.

EDDIE: I could make you a sandwich. I think there's some bread in the house. And stuff. It may be a little old.

BROOKS: I saw that bread, Dick. You don't want it.

RICHARD: This is swell.

BROOKS: What about a brew?

RICHARD: A what?

EDDIE: A beer.

RICHARD: I'd better not. I haven't had much sleep this week and I'm afraid it would knock me on my ass. Have you got a soft drink? Coke? Gingerale? Anything. Water would be fine. [*He continues eating.*]

EDDIE: I'll look.

[*He crosses to the kitchen.* RICHARD *eats.*]

BROOKS: Med School. That's some grind, isn't it?

RICHARD: Not so bad. Unless I've blocked it out.

BROOKS: I've heard the first two years are a bitch. Eighteen hours a day, seven days a week. Make you memorize all the muscles of the eye.

CHRIS: Trick you into drinking urine.

RICHARD: What?

CHRIS: My father was a doctor. He was full of Med School stories.

RICHARD: Maybe then. Not now. The Dark Ages are over.

BROOKS: Still, they must keep you pretty busy. Can't leave you much time for singing.

RICHARD: Actually, I spend most of my spare time backpacking. We're into backpacking.

BROOKS: Who? You and Charlie Taylor?

RICHARD: No. Corinne and I. The girl I live with.

BROOKS: Your fiancée?

RICHARD: No. The girl I live with.

[*Pause. To* CHRIS, *who is humming.*]

RICHARD: [*Cont'd.*] Excuse me for asking, but have you been that color long?

CHRIS: All my life.

RICHARD: I mean the, uh, pallor.

[CHRIS *crosses to a mirror, studies himself in it, then crosses back to* RICHARD.]

CHRIS: Inherited. All the men in my family have porcelain skin.

[*Enter* EDDIE *with a Coke and more beer.*]

RICHARD: Do me a favor, will you . . .

CHRIS: Chris.

RICHARD: Chris. Get your blood pressure checked.

[CHRIS *crosses to a chair and sits.*]

CHRIS: That's a cheery note. Makes a man want to burst into song.

EDDIE: [*Entering with more dip.*] Hey. Hey, Richard. The ground rules here are absolutely no shop. And, believe me, you better stick to them unless you want Brooks here to start boring the shit out of you with talk of high adventure in the bond business. [*Pause.*] Here's your Coke.

RICHARD: Thanks. [*Of the dip.*] This is terrific. What's in it?

EDDIE: I don't know. It's left over from the old regime.

RICHARD: It's very tasty. [*He drinks.*]

BROOKS: Eddie probably told you, Dick. We lost our bass last week after—what?—twenty years together...

EDDIE: More. Twenty-five. Six.

CHRIS: Six.

BROOKS: Keeled over in his office with a massive coronary.

CHRIS: Listen to this, Richard. It'll interest you.

BROOKS: His wife and another couple came to pick him up for a Cuban meal.

EDDIE: Bill was into Cuban food in the fifties. Way before it became an in thing. Old Bill.

CHRIS: Always a pace setter.

BROOKS: Found him stone dead on the carpet. Like a beached whale, Ann said. It was quite a shock for her. You can imagine, Dick.

CHRIS: Let's make some music while the rest of us are still around. [*He takes out his pitch pipe.*]

RICHARD: Chris, look, I'm sorry I opened my mouth. It's just that I'm at the hospital all day it's hard to change gears.

CHRIS: That's all right. I envy your earnestness. I really do.

BROOKS: Hey, Chris.

[*He crosses to him.*]

CHRIS: Let's sing, for Christ's sake.

EDDIE: What do you know, Richard?

RICHARD: Name it.

EDDIE: We don't do a lot of modern stuff—show tunes and all that. We do more traditional music.

BROOKS: More classically oriented.

EDDIE: Do you know "My Cutie's Due on the Two Two Two?"

RICHARD: For sure. I know all the oldies. My roommate had me down as some kind of freak.

EDDIE: A freak?

RICHARD: It's his word. He was into entomology. Spiders. He kept them in a shoe box in his dresser. So who was he to talk?

EDDIE: Why don't we start with something slow to sort of get tuned up. You game for "Slow Motion," Richard?

RICHARD: Sure. [*Vocalizing.*] When big brown bears go woof,
Ah me,
When big brown bears go woof.

CHRIS: We usually take it a half-step down. Out of respect to my failing prowess.

RICHARD: Fine with me.

ALL: Slow motion time,
Jes' idle a trifle
Happy, content with
Slow motion time.
Folks often say
"You're crazy, you're lazy,"
They don't know, they won't go,
Slow motion time.
Dawdle all the day,
Yawn the hours away,
I'se sleepy, so tired,
Time for me to lay right down and
Relax myself,
Don't look 'round,

Jes' lie down,
Indolent, somnolent,
Slow motion time.

BROOKS: Hey. That's not bad.

EDDIE: That's good. Nice legato, Richard.

RICHARD: Thanks. [*Looks at his watch.*] You want to try the other one?

EDDIE: Sure. Just let me lubricate the old pipes. [*He takes a long swallow of beer.*]

CHRIS: We do this one in the original key.

BROOKS: We've been doing this so long together we probably put in lot of stuff that isn't strictly in the music.

RICHARD: That's O.K. I'll follow.

[CHRIS *blows his pitch pipe again. They sing. The three older men do movements—eye movements, hand movements, business with their drinks, etc.* RICHARD *stands still and sings. He sings much better than they do.*]

ALL: My cutie's due on the two two two
She'll be coming through on the big choo choo
She's been away for months
But I haven't cheated once
Stayed home nights
I didn't dance
Wasn't taking any chance
Didn't flirt
Though it hurt

RICHARD: Just couldn't do my little cutie dirt

ALL: The days are long, the nights are black
But I just know that she'll be back
Cause I love her and she loves me
So say, hey hey hey
Don't say there ain't no Santa Claus
I know goddamn well there is because
My cutie's due on the two two two
Today.

EDDIE: Hey. Pretty good blend.

CHRIS: [*To* RICHARD.] Comfortable for you?

RICHARD: Sure.

BROOKS: You want to try some of the, uh, moves this next time through, Dick?

RICHARD: Fine with me.

CHRIS: I'll give you your note.

RICHARD: Don't need it.

EDDIE: Well, I need a note.

[CHRIS *gives the notes.*]

ALL: Bright college years with pleasure rife
The shortest, gladdest years of life
How swiftly are ye gliding by
O why does time so swiftly fly?
The seasons come, the seasons go
The earth is green or white with snow
But time and change can naught avail

RICHARD: [*Solo.*] To break those friendships formed at Yale

ALL: In after years should troubles rise
To cloud the blue of summer skies
How bright will seem through mem'ry's haze
Those happy, golden bygone days
So drink her down with Mory's Ale
For God, for country and for Yale
My cutie's due on the two two two
Today.

[*During the phrase "Mory's Ale,"* RICHARD'S *beeper starts beeping.*]

RICHARD: [*Over the end of the song.*] Excuse me, Eddie. Eddie, where's the phone?

EDDIE: In the bedroom. In through there.

RICHARD: Thanks. [*Exit* RICHARD *into the bedroom.*]

BROOKS: [*After a pause.*] What do you think?

CHRIS: He's good.

EDDIE: I think he's terrific.

BROOKS: Not to speak ill of the dead, but he's a hell of a lot better than Bill. Billy had the range, the low notes, but he always sounded as if he had to clear his throat.

EDDIE: That was the booze. Many's the night I've seen him put away half a bottle of Scotch before dinner.

CHRIS: Every night of his life, God bless him.

BROOKS: My only question is, does he have the feeling? The spirit? He seemed a little ... reserved.

EDDIE: Brooks, for crying out loud, that was his first time through. He's young. He'll get it.

BROOKS: Chris?

CHRIS: Fine with me.

BROOKS: Then it's unanimous. I don't think we have to bother with the urn and the black balls and all that.

[*Pause. Re-enter* RICHARD.]

BROOKS: Tell him, Eddie.

EDDIE: Congratulations.

RICHARD: For what?

EDDIE: You're our new bass. Unanimous. No abstentions.

RICHARD: Thanks. I appreciate it. I really do.

BROOKS: It's not a decision we came to lightly, Dick.

RICHARD: I'm sure it wasn't. Eddie, where's my coat?

EDDIE: We sometimes sing at a little gin mill midtown. At lunchtime. They have entertainment Tuesdays and Fridays. Usually Dixieland but sometimes it's us. They get a lot of the advertising crowd. No pay, but free lunch and all the booze you can hoist.

BROOKS: You can call in sick those afternoons.

RICHARD: That sounds swell, Eddie. Look. Where's my coat? I've got a sick woman on my hands.

EDDIE: Well, why didn't you say so? [*He goes to the closet.*] We rehearse. Wednesday nights at different houses. The person whose house it is supplies the refreshments. Not that we'd expect you to take a turn yet, seeing as how you're not established.

BROOKS: Next Wednesday chez Brooks. What do you drink, Dick? Dubonnet? Campari? You name it, I've got it.

RICHARD: Listen. I'm not sure yet about Wednesday. I'll call you.

EDDIE: [*Holding the coat.*] Why aren't you sure?

RICHARD: I have to be on call nights. I never know till the last minute.

EDDIE: That's not what you said on the phone.

RICHARD: Things change.

EDDIE: Sometimes you have emergencies.

RICHARD: Right. Look, I've really got to go.

BROOKS: We sing at private parties too. Always lots of unattached chicks.

RICHARD: Give me my coat, Eddie.

CHRIS: You don't like us much, do you, Richard? You think we're ridiculous.

RICHARD: No. Not at all. It's been terrific. Only, to be frank, I didn't realize it was going to be a regular thing.

EDDIE: A regular thing? Goddamn it, that's the whole point.

RICHARD: I'm sorry, Eddie.

EDDIE: I'll bet you are.

RICHARD: Please, can I just have my coat?

EDDIE: No.

RICHARD: What?

EDDIE: Don't worry. The wounded and dying can get along without you for two minutes.

RICHARD: Brooks, would you please ask him...

EDDIE: You come in here, you come highly recommended by a man, by Charlie Taylor, a man who's been my friend since before you were born. You come into my house, my home, you won't drink with us, you wolf down all the cheese dip...

RICHARD: This is ridiculous.

EDDIE: I don't give a flying fuck about the cheese dip. There's more where that came from don't you worry. But it's indicative. I'm talking about manners, Doctor. Simple, goddamn manners.

BROOKS: Give the boy his coat, Eddie.

EDDIE: I will. In a minute. I don't want his coat. I wouldn't be caught dead on skid row in a shitty coat like this.

RICHARD: Give me my coat, Eddie. I don't want to hurt you.

EDDIE: Doctor, you have hurt me. To the quick. Do you know where that is?

RICHARD: Eddie...

EDDIE: You know Yale turned down my kid? Turned him down flat. Didn't even put him on the waiting list. And he is a wonderful kid. I practically went down on my knees to the Dean. I told him there have been four generations of Knoxes at Yale. Not captains of anything, not Phi Beta Kappas, not the stars. You probably wouldn't notice them while they were there, but they turned into useful goddamn people. Who coughed up for the Class Fund even when the Market was shot to hell, who denied themselves. Not selfish people. I tell you, I went up for the Harvard Game this year and I looked at the young people around me in the stands and it could have been...N.Y.U. So what I'm saying is, Doctor—and I hope I'm not talking out of turn—what I'm saying is, they really lost something at that place these past years. And manners is only part of it. Here's your stupid coat. [*He gives* RICHARD *the coat and walks off.*] Go cure your patient.

BROOKS: Dick, look, I'm sorry. The thing with his son broke his heart.

EDDIE: No it didn't. It broke his grandfather's heart. It made me furious.

BROOKS: Don't take it personally.

RICHARD: Believe me, gentlemen, I won't. [*Exit* RICHARD.]

EDDIE: [*After a pause.*] Didn't even thank me for the Coke. Look. I'm sorry. A real horror show, right? But I swear to God, fellas ...

BROOKS: What, Eddie?

EDDIE: Shit, I don't know.

BROOKS: Want a brew?

EDDIE: No,` thanks.

BROOKS: [*After a pause.*] I'm going to take off, Eddie. It's late.

EDDIE: Hey, Chris?

CHRIS: Present.

EDDIE: Chris, sing something, will you, for crying out loud?

CHRIS: Sure, Eddie. If you like. What?

EDDIE: I don't know. Anything. You're the only one of us who ever had a real voice anyway.

[*Pause.* CHRIS *crosses to the bar, pours himself a drink from the tonic bottle, turns, and sings to* EDDIE.]

CHRIS: Mavourneen, mavourneen
Sure one kiss would be no sin,
For I love you, ayalh,
Your poor slave is Barney O'Flynn.

[*Pause. Lights down slowly. Blackout.*]

THE END

Cassandra Medley

DEARBORN HEIGHTS

CHARACTERS

GRACE   A very light-skinned African-American woman in her late 20's, early 30's. She is thin and rather "slight." She carries a studied "air" of self-conscious "refinement" and speaks with a soft, lilting Tennessee accent. She is dressed in the "dress up" style of the early 1950s. A close-fitting hat is banded around the top of her head, perhaps with a bit of a small veil attached. She wears summer net gloves, stockings with the seams down the back, 50's style high heels, a "smart summer suit" of the mass-produced variety based on "high fashion." Her pocket book, which usually dangles from her wrist, is resting in her lap.

CLARE   Dark-skinned African-American woman, same age as GRACE. Rather hefty with a deliberate "commanding" bravado that disguises her vulnerability underneath.

SETTING: *A "homestyle" diner in Dearborn Heights.*

TIME: *A mid-Summer Day, 1951*

GRACE *is seated at restaurant table. The table is draped in checkered cloth, napkin dispenser, a tiny vase with a single plastic flower stem. It should give the feeling of a "homestyle" restaurant-diner. Several shopping bags and packages surround* GRACE *underneath the table. She takes out a large, folded newspaper article from her purse, admires it. The Andrews Sisters' "I'll Be Seeing You in Apple Blossom Time" plays in background, coming from an unseen juke box.* GRACE *is clearly waiting for someone, as she sips the lemon coke in front of her. A basket of fresh bread has been already placed before her. There is a second table setting with a second lemon coke placed across from* GRACE. *She should appear to be glancing out of an imaginary window. A few more beats and then suddenly her face lights up and she waves to someone unseen. She quickly folds her newspaper, returns it to her purse and waits. Sound of a* DOOR

CASSANDRA MEDLEY

Cassandra Medley's plays include, *Ms. Mae*, one of several individual sketches which comprise the Off-Broadway musical, *A...My Name Is Alice*, which received the 1984 Outer Drama Critics Circle Award, and is still touring regional theatres and Europe. Other plays include, *Ma Rose*, *Waking Women*, *By the Still Waters*, and *Terrain*, all presented and produced throughout the U.S. For her screenplay, *Ma Rose*, Cassandra was awarded the Walt Disney Screenwriting Fellowship, in 1990. She is also the recipient of the 1986 New York Foundation for the Arts Grant, and a New York State Council on the Arts Grant for 1987, was a 1989 finalist for the Susan Smith Blackburn Award in Playwriting, won the 1990 National Endowment for the Arts Grant in Playwriting, the 1995 New Professional Theatre Award and the 1995 Marily Simpson Award. She teaches playwriting at Sarah Lawrence College and Columbia University and has also served as guest artist at the University of Iowa Playwrights Workshop.

CHIME jingling. Enter CLARE, *dark-skinned Black woman, same age as* GRACE *and dressed in the same style.* CLARE *faces the audience.* GRACE *waves as though through a window and gestures.* CLARE *turns, crosses to the table with her shopping bags in tow.*

CLARE: [*Fanning her perspiration.*] Whew! If it ain't hot as all-get out, out there.

[*Smiling* GRACE *helps* CLARE *with the packages which they tuck underneath their seats.*]

GRACE: Oh, you should feel "Knoxville" you think this is aggravating! I thought moving to Michigan was my release from "the fiery furnace," I see I was mistaken . . . truth is I done pulled off my shoes ha . . . I'm [*Whispering.*] "in my stocking feet."

CLARE: Ha. Well, I'm 'bout to pull mine off right behind you girl. Got a bunion that's "sounding off" like a bugle at the V-E Day parade!

GRACE: [*Gazing around.*] Ain't this a sweet place?

CLARE: [*Glancing around.*] Well . . . yeah . . . I guess . . . I mean, why is it . . . well . . . empty?

GRACE: Chile, I come here everytime I come to Dearborn shopping.

CLARE: Oh?

GRACE: Copied their way of doing "tuna salad" . . .

CLARE: Where's the waitress hiding out? [*Looking around for a beat, she then smiles and gives a brief friendly nod to an unseen waitress in the distance.*] Oh . . . good . . .

GRACE: [*Indicating the drinks on the table.*] See? Got us our lemon cokes.

CLARE: [*Still staring out, puzzled.*] Y'see that?

GRACE: I been here couple times, trust me. I promise she won't be as slow as that salesgal in the "Lingerie Department."

CLARE: [*Distracted.*] Ummm? Don't mind me, girl, I just . . . well when a place is empty makes me "jittery" . . . [*She "cackles" with a wave of her hand.*] . . . Starts me to wonder "what am I gonna be spending my money on? Funny food or something . . . ?"

[*Sound of a* DOOR CHIME *jingling.*]

GRACE: Ha . . . your turn to be the "stranger" and have me show "you" a new place! . . . See? Here come a couple of people . . .

CLARE: Oh! Wonderful! [*Settling into her seat, relaxing, buttering her bread.*] I am ready to "chow"—my stomach is about to "mutiny."

GRACE: [*Pause.*] Well what happened? What did I miss?

CLARE: Humph! The "so and so" of ah Floor Manager finally decided to put in a appearance . . .

GRACE: [*Glancing at her watch.*] Girl, I was wondering if I should have the waitress hold the table. I started to go back 'cross the street to check on you . . . wondered how long they'd keep you waiting.

[CLARE *stops and reaches down into her packages. She pulls out a box and reveals a pair of long white evening gloves. She salutes* GRACE *"army" style.*]

CLARE: "Mission accomplished" under enemy fire.

GRACE: [*Impressed.*] Well!

CLARE: I tole you if I waited there long enough and held out for that store manager . . .

GRACE: [*Overlapping.*] And they finally let you exchange them for the right fit?

CLARE: That's right! Boils me how they try and treat "us" when we shop in these suburbs . . .

GRACE: Well, I'm impressed . . .

CLARE: They up there trying to tell me they "can't exchange my gloves cause they was purchased in the De-troit Montgomery Wards and not this here Dearborn Heights branch of Montgomery . . ."

GRACE: [*Overlapping.*] . . . Wards.

CLARE: Yeah, you heard they "crap!" That's all it was! "Crap."

GRACE: [*Glancing at the menu.*] . . . You gonna have fries . . . or you still on your diet . . . ?

CLARE: [*Putting on one of the formal gloves as she speaks.*] I just explained to them with a smile on my face [*She illustrates "smile."*] that fine, "I will make sure to write *The Chronicale*, Michigan's largest Negro newspaper, and to tell all my church members to make sure not to shop at Montgomery Wards period."

GRACE: That did it, huh?

CLARE: And I tole him, I say, "You know Wards got no business putting better quality merchandise in the Dearborn stores then they got in the Detroit stores ANWAY" . . . like we "enjoy" driving out all this way into the suburbs just to get us decent . . .

GRACE: Well it's so "pretty" out this way . . . but no—you right . . . you right . . .

CLARE: [*Pauses, shrugs.*] I guess they just figured, "Let's just get this colored bitch out the way, what the hell."

GRACE: Nunno! No! What you did was . . . y'know . . . I admire . . . I mean . . . anything large or small that we do for the "Race" . . .

CLARE: [*Carefully packing the gloves back in their box, then taking up her menu.*] Dearborn is a very long way to come to shop if you don't drive . . .

GRACE: Is it? [*Pause.*] . . . Driving out here with you was nice, but I like the bus . . . I don't mind . . . [*Stiffly smiling.*]

The DOOR CHIME sounds again as other unseen customers enter.]

CLARE: [*Smiling.*] Ha. [*Pause.*] That is one "sharp" hat you got . . been meaning to tell you all morning . . .

GRACE: [*Touching her hat, smiling.*] Oh, I collect hats, I love hats . . . thank you . . . you so sweet . . . didn't know if I should wear it just for shopping.

CLARE: It's gorgeous on you girl! If you "got it" why not "flaunt it."

GRACE: People . . . well . . . don't want folks to think one is you know . . . [*She makes a silent gesture to indicate "stuck on oneself."*] . . . people can think things you know . . .

CLARE: [*Placing her hand on top of GRACE'S hand.*] Girl . . . when that Moving Van pulled up and you and your husband got out . . . and next thing I know there you are out there putting in rose bushes along ya driveway, and I thought to myself, "thank you,

Jesus" ' . . . cause, see, we on our street are "vigilant" . . . the last thing we want is a bunch of "sorry," shiftless Colored Folk "ruining" what we all trying to build!

GRACE: Didn't mean for two months to go by 'fore I came over.

CLARE: You're a little on the "shy side" ain't ya?

GRACE: [*Smiles.*] My husband teases me . . . I thought you maybe thought . . . took it for granted I was . . . you know . . . [*She makes a gesture to indicate "stuck up."*]

CLARE: [*Smiling, waving off suggestion.*] Childe, pal-lease! Okay, now the question is do I have the "BLT" dripping in mayo or . . .

GRACE: Oh, and "by the by" . . . they delivering me and O.Z.'s new television set tomorrow . . .

CLARE: Well, ah right!

GRACE: [*Pauses, rather uncertain.*] Well, yeah . . . I think I'm gonna "miss" the radio . . .

CLARE: Now you can keep up with that crazy "Lucy" every week . . .

GRACE: Something, well, I dunno, something "cultivated" 'bout the radio.

CLARE: Chile, last night, "Lucy" dyed her hair jet black, would you believe, and "Desi" got hisself on this "quiz show" he had no business fooling with . . . oh, they had me "in stiches" so I nearly choked to death! . . . "Cultivated" . . . [*Pause.*] You got such a . . . "sweet" way with words. I been admiring all morning how you . . .

GRACE: Some Negroes get excellent educations down South contrary to what you might hear 'bout us!

CLARE: 'Course you gotta be "word-fancy" if you gonna qualify as "telephone operator." [*Graciously.*] Oh, we must order something extra special, you're my first new girlfriend to celebrate!

[GRACE *offers a toast with her coke.*]

CLARE: [*Cont'd.*] I'm living right next door to "one of the first five Negro women to be hired by the phone company." I tole my Momma 'bout it.

GRACE: Ah, ain't you sweet! Ain't you the sweetest thing!

CLARE: Well, the whole entire street is proud! My goodness! [*Pause.*] You make sure you preserve that pic-ture they had of you in the "Chronicale" for your children. [*Pause, staring at her.*] 'Bout time some Negro women got hired to do something more worthwhile than that ole "mop and pail" stuff I be doing up at the Hospital!

[*They toast with their lemon cokes. Pause.*]

CLARE: [*Cont'd.*] I tell you, here I am living right next door to a Negro Pioneer!

GRACE: Truth be told, when I went for the interview my hands were shaking so . . . I could barely hear my voice.

CLARE: Who cares? For the very first time in De-troit, whenever we call "directory assistance" it could be one of five new Negro operators . . . could be you . . . don't worry . . . if I recognize your voice I won't "chat" . . . I know how to act as opposed to "some" of our people . . .

GRACE: [*Graciously.*] Well, now, you got something to be proud of yourself now . . . standing up for yourself like that! . . . Whew! That's what I luv 'bout being up North! Back down in Knoxville you wouldn't dare . . . they don't even allow us to try the clothes on, just have to take your chances . . . and you don't dare return it if it don't fit . . .

CLARE: Well, I am proud to say I've never been "South" of Dayton, Ohio, where I'm from.

GRACE: [*Glancing over the menu.*] This being our first shopping trip together and a day of celebration . . . I say we "sin" and have hot fudge sundays . . .

[*The DOOR CHIME sounds again as other unseen customers enter.*]

CLARE: Let's see the pic-ture.

GRACE: Well, I dunno . . . I mean . . .

CLARE: Naw-naw . . . don't you carry it 'round with ya? I would, you couldn't stop me from showing it 'round if it was "me" . . .

GRACE: We don't want folks accusing me of the "sin of pride," now do we?

CLARE: So how's your hubby liking driving for the Bus Company? 'Course, my Clyde's got "lifetime" job security at Chryslers . . .

[GRACE *takes out a folded newsprint photo from her purse and hands it over to* CLARE.]

CLARE: [*Cont'd. Reading from the paper.*] "July 23, 1952" . . . 'Course, I have my own copy back at the house.

GRACE: Ain't you the sweetest thing! [*Pause.*]

CLARE: Some Colored folks might think I was causing too much of a "rucus" over a pair of gloves . . .

GRACE: Girl, you don't know me! [*Laughing.*] . . . Wait till you get to know me better . . . I admire "spunk," "grit" as we call it back down home.

CLARE: Well, like you say . . . our very first "girls day out" . . . didn't wanna embarrass you.

GRACE: The first of many!

[*They toast.*]

CLARE: Folks keep staring at us, Grace . . . don't look . . .

[GRACE *on reflex reaches her hand to her hat to make sure it's on right.* DOOR CHIME *sounds.* CLARE *slowly gazes around. The* DOOR CHIME *jingles as more unseen patrons enter. There is the soft sound of murmuring.*]

CLARE: [*Cont'd.*] Act like nothing's wrong.

GRACE: What is wrong?

CLARE: Oh, gawd . . .

GRACE: What?

CLARE: Oh, mercy.

GRACE: What is it?

CLARE: Oh, Jesus, my Jesus . . . don't stare! Sorry, but . . . don't let 'em know we know.

GRACE: What? What do we know?

CLARE: Girl, you made a mistake in coming to this place . . .

GRACE: You don't mean . . .

CLARE: That's right, that's the ticket alright . . .

GRACE: But . . .

CLARE: Everybody else is being served over there, over there . . . over there . . .

GRACE: But they served me: they always serve . . .

[*Embarrassed pause between the two women.*]

CLARE: Well! [*Pause.*] I guess they realize now that they "took a few things for granted" didn't they?

GRACE: Oh, God.

CLARE: You had them "fooled."

GRACE: Gawd!

CLARE: Now they realize you—

GRACE: Don't "say" it—

CLARE: Ain't the shade they "assumed" you was.

GRACE: Jesus in Heaven.

CLARE: We better call on somebody.

GRACE: [*Mortified.*] Clare, I'm so . . . I'm so . . .

CLARE: Nunno, don't get up. Don't let 'em think "we know."

GRACE: Least down South they got . . . we got "signs" up.

CLARE: Well, I never been down South, couldn't drag me down South.

GRACE: I'm still not used to dealing with up "here" . . . the signals to go by . . . that waitress has always been so nice to me . . . how could I be so stupid . . .

CLARE: KEEP YOUR SEAT . . . keep your face in the menu for the time being . . . [*Pause.*] . . . We came here to have "lunch" and by-golly have lunch is what we gonna "have." They'll have to serve us or throw us out! [*Pause.*] Now then . . .

[CLARE *reaches into her bag and pulls out a ribboned broach the size of a small badge. She hands it to* GRACE.]

CLARE: [*Cont'd.*] . . . "The Southwest Detroit Ladies Cavaliers" wants to welcome you as a new member!

[GRACE *distractedly waves off broach.*]

GRACE: Shouldn't we just get up and go . . .

CLARE: [*Reaching down.*] Don't look around . . . pretend nothing's wrong. [*Smiling self-consciously.*] . . . now, uh, the "grapevine" tells me you being, uh . . . shall we say "approached" by the "Metropolitan Ladies of Triumph" . . .

GRACE: Well . . . they have, you know . . . uh . . .

CLARE: Oh, I know, they "after ya" right? They always scrounging 'round for "new blood" like "gnats at a picnic" . . . not that I'm bragging but they ain't the Ladies Club for a Colored Woman of "quality" . . . believe me . . .

GRACE: Look, why cause a whole lotta fuss? Let's just . . .

CLARE: Keep smiling so they don't know we're upset . . . hate it when Colored People don't know how to keep their dignity in public . . .

GRACE: I am so so embarrassed. [*Pause.*] How do you tell up North where "we" can go and can't go?

CLARE: Grace, you gotta learn the difference 'tween De-troit and the suburbs—Detroit and Dearborn, Dearborn and Detroit . . . me being President of Cavaliers means I can, you know, "guide" you more easily than they can in "Ladies of Triumph." [*Pause.*] Relax . . . lean back, let 'em know we ain't to be "budged" and we ain't to be "bothered!" Now, then. [*Pause.*] Every year we "Cavaliers" happen to raise more than "Ladies of Triumph" do for the NAACP . . . why, "they" was so "low-class" they held they "Annual Fashion Show" at the "Y." "We" at least rent the Elks Lodge over on Livernois and 9 Mile . . .

GRACE: "Up North" was supposed to be so 'easy' . . . come to find out it's even more complicated . . .

CLARE: You just gotta fine-tune your sense of place! Look for other Negroes, and if you don't sense 'em there, then they don't want us there. Feel out the air around you! . . . We sponsor this "Gospel Jubillee" in the Spring that'll send you to Heaven and back . . .

GRACE: Down South it is clearly marked . . . please, please pardon me . . .

CLARE: It is very unusual for any "newcomer" to get a "unanimous" vote from our membership.

GRACE: I shoulda sensed something . . . no wonder everybody's sitting so spread out away from this table . . . Lord, the "cook" is peering out at us from the kitchen . . .!

CLARE: Let him! . . . see when "we" shop in these here suburbs we gotta be armour plated inside girl . . . Don't let "them" push us around . . . That's the spirit of a Lady in "Cavaliers" . . . [*Pause.*] Plus, as an added bonus I'll teach you how to drive . . . guarantee you'll pass "the road test" . . . and don't you dare ask me to accept no fee! [*She guffaws softly.*]

GRACE: My man's the, you know, the basic "Ole-fashioned" Southern type . . . he prefers to do the driving in our—

CLARE: Chile, you up North now! We the "New Negro" women up here! . . . [*Leaning in on her and softly poking her.*] I can tell ya want to . . . tell the truth . . . ain't you tempted by just a itty-bitty bit of independence?

GRACE: Thing of it is, they know me here! . . . The waitress is "Mattie" over there . . . told me all 'bout her "bunions" . . . even promised me the recipe for "chicken-a-la-king" . . .

CLARE: "Mattie," huh? Ooough! If I just had it "in" me to "lay her out" to her face!

GRACE: Clare, please . . .

CLARE: I'm not blaming you—don't think that, you made a honest mistake . . . but, see now this is the very reason why you need to join us "Cavaliers."

GRACE: [*Graciously smiling.*] . . . To tell the truth, very soon I'm gonna be in need of the "restroom facilities" . . . or otherwise I'd be all for sitting this out . . . [*Pause.*] 'Sides, [*Smiling.*] I seriously doubt if I'm gonna be able to, you know, "receive" the proper "impression" of Cavaliers—I don't think your Club Members want me to be famished in the process . . .

CLARE: Ha. [*Pause.*] Sweetness . . . [*Pause.*] Let us leave this minute! Please—please pardon me!

GRACE: Nunno, I'm the one got us into this—

CLARE: Nunno . . . "last" thing I want is for you to be put through . . . you know . . . stress and strain and, and "devil-made" conniptions 'cause of "yours truly" . . . please . . .

GRACE: Nunno . . . it's "my fault" . . . but, we'll just take our stomachs and our business to where we can get respect AND so we can concentrate . . . ha . . .

CLARE: Fine . . . All we need to do is just "maneuver" out of this here with some lil bit of "dignity" . . .

GRACE: Just follow me to the door . . .

CLARE: Don't panic . . . worst thing is to panic . . . compose your face 'fore you get up . . .

GRACE: Everybody's eyeing us . . . oh, Gawd . . . The longer we sit here it's just more awful!

CLARE: I will not give them the "satisfaction" of seeing me panic . . . think they gonna "run me out" oh, naw! Get up when I'm good and ready, "my time, not they time" . . . Grace, control yourself!

GRACE: All their eyes trained on us!

CLARE: My dear, just gimme one second . . . Don't come unstuck . . . you are not "down South," now. Just keep a steady hand till I get my shoes on . . .

GRACE: Fine—fine. Long as we don't get into no more monkey business foolishness, let's go.

CLARE: Wha kinda "business," excuse me?

GRACE: Clare . . . please . . .

CLARE: Please "explain" that last remark . . . calmly compose your face, and then we will rise and get out of here.

GRACE: [*Pause.*] There is no need for you to "order" me around in such fashion.

CLARE: [*Taking a long gulp from her glass.*] Sons-of-bitches! [*To* GRACE.] Excuse me, pardon me.

GRACE: Nunno, under the circumstances I'd say the same 'cept I got too much of the "church woman" in me.

[*They pat each other's hands in mutual comfort.*]

CLARE: I'll sit here as long as I can stand it—ain't gonna run me off like no "whipped mongrel!"

GRACE: Thing of it is, they don't . . . they don't snarl at us . . . or yell at us, or attack in the same way they do down home.

CLARE: No, I will not just "fold my tent" and like a lamb, "bleet" all the way home . . . Oh, it gauls me . . . but, they ain't gonna break me . . . !

GRACE: Pardon me, but there is no need to make the situation any worse.

CLARE: I'm the "dark" one that's gotta get past their stares, walk through to that door over there!

GRACE: Now, hold up Clare Henderson . . . just 'cause I'm light don't mean I'm not feeling the same as your feeling!

CLARE: [Overlapping.] Take it easy . . . nobody's saying nothing 'bout your—

GRACE: Well, what are you saying?

CLARE: Well, who you calling a "monkey?"

GRACE: Now, wait a minute here! We are not gonna lower ourselves to such a "level," now are we?

CLARE: Look, if the "boot" fits then march in it!

GRACE: [Pauses, then.] Well! Trouble is "your kind" gets so . . .

CLARE: So?

GRACE: "Wound-up."

CLARE: [Folding her arms.] Here we go! I knew you'd get to it sooner or later . . . the "darker" we come, the more we embarrass you, huh?

GRACE: Look, I'm the one they treated so nice "before."

CLARE: Before me.

GRACE: Before!

CLARE: You wouldn't be treated like a leper "now" if I wasn't sitting up here, would ya?

GRACE: You think it's easy? D'you think it's easy being taken for granted as "one thing" then facing the "flip" look when . . .

CLARE: Then you knew they was "taking it for granted," yet you lead me in here!

GRACE: [*Putting on her gloves, grabbing her packages to leave.*] I made an honest mistake. I'm "new" in this here city, if you have the "decency" to recall.

CLARE: I got the "decency to recall" that soon as you and your high yella Clark Gable "wannabe" husband moved on the block you've had your noses tipped in clouds, so high and mighty! [*Pause.*] Oh, yeah, anything to lord yaselfs over the whole entire street! The Block votes to get all new "look alike" Lamp Lighter Front Porch Lamps in front of each and every house, like in the white suburbs. But, naw—naw! You and your husband gotta do something "fancier," something more "high toned"—just a tad one step above the rest.

GRACE: Humph! . . . Why don't you get yourself a "telescope" out of one of them Sears catalogues so you can keep your "busybody" nose better in everybody's business? A neighbor can't "sneeze" and you report it to everyone!

CLARE: [*Pauses . . . Studies* GRACE *with contempt.*] And to think you had me "groveling" . . . at your feet to . . . [*She snatches up the club brooch.*] . . . oh, all them "begged" me to take you out, show you shopping . . . lunch you as "our treat" . . . but I tole 'em, I said, "I wonder if she's not too siddity, too "high-toned" and stuck up for us."

GRACE: You are so damn "pushy" who would want to "join?" [*Reaches for her bags under the table.*]

CLARE: Damn, you red-bone, "high yella," "lemon meringues" always the first to be hired to the best jobs . . . always flaunting ya color, and every other Negro fawning over ya'!

GRACE: That's right! "Vanilla" still beats out "chocolate" any day!

CLARE: Every night probably get down on ya damn knees and pray, "thank you, Jesus, for making me light, bright and almost white."

[*A pause, then.*]

GRACE: Is that what you would do in my place?

CLARE: [*Stunned a little, but struggles to hide it.*] I tole the Cavaliers you had no intentions of joining us anyway . . . [*She starts putting on her gloves.*] . . . Or do you think it entirely "escapes" me that the Ladies of Triumph all happen to be just about as "pale" as they can find 'em?

GRACE: [*Remains stock still.*] Nobody's telling me I ain't a dedicated Negro woman, same as you!

CLARE: Ha! . . . "dedicated!" [*Mocking* GRACE.] "Lez go, lez go, 'fore we cause mo' trouble . . ." You can't wait to go "shuffling" out of here with your tail between you legs . . . [*Pause.*] So your lil "diner" friends have "let you down" . . . well, "ta-ta" . . . [CLARE *gestures dismissively to* GRACE.]

GRACE: Hell with you, I'll sit as long as I want to!

CLARE: Fact is, the rest of "us" . . . don't want y'all "high tone types" . . . don't need ya . . .

GRACE: Oh, you want us, you crave us . . . don't blame us if you fawn all over us . . .

CLARE: Y'all don't have no real idea what real "color" feels like.

GRACE: And you do? . . . You, and the way you just had to "throw your weight around" in that store 'bout those "gloves" . . . not the principle of the thing I minded, but you had to be so loud, so "pronounced" about it . . .

CLARE: I? I was "standing up for something!" [*Gesturing with her gloved hand.*] But, of course, you got treated way, way more "courteous" by the salesgal . . . Guess you thought I didn't notice?

GRACE: I noticed that the other Colored shoppers were "cringing," but, of course, you thought you were "displaying" your courage in front of each and every damn body . . .

CLARE: [*Cooly lights a cigarette and studies* GRACE.] What's it like being "accepted" everywhere you go?

GRACE: And what the hell is that supposed to mean?

CLARE: Taken for "granted" as just a . . . you know . . . "normal," everyday, "pretty woman" . . . what's it feel like?

GRACE: Don't you dare start "toying with me" . . .

CLARE: Since I'm so "bossy," and "nosey," I'm gonna be sure and tell the "whole block" . . .

[CLARE *pauses, smiling with a sardonic expression on her face.* GRACE *rises to leave.*]

GRACE: [*Mocking expression.*] You are such a "small-minded" woman.

CLARE: Why, sure not as sharp as you, girl. After all, as you say yourself, "they know you here," right? What's it been like? Lemme guess . . . here you ain't been in De-troit two months and ya already staked out a "nice" friendly, "homestyle diner" in Dearborn Heights where you "treat" yourself to cool, restful summer lunches . . . [*Pause.*] Tell me, what's it been like, Grace, so I can tell the whole street!

GRACE: No, hold up . . . ! It . . . has never been my intention that I was . . .

CLARE: What's that? Sorry, I'm too "simple-minded . . ."

[GRACE'S *face contorts in sudden shock and pain. She drops her head in silence. A long beat. Suddenly a tight smile crosses* GRACE'S *face.*]

GRACE: Don't try and pull that outlandish crap on me.

CLARE: So she does her passing on a "shopping spree" to the suburbs, now don't that beat all!

GRACE: You the one who would want to wouldn't ya? . . . not me.

CLARE: How many afternoons do ya treat yaself to "make believing" you a white "heifer?"

GRACE: Wouldn't you just like to know . . . wouldn't you just like to be able to "dress yaself" in my dreams?!

CLARE: Thank God I was born with some real "paint" on my bones, and not no poor "in-between!" Lease way's when folks "see" me they know what side of the fence I'm looking back from!

GRACE: "Fence!?" Oh, and don't you just wish you could "open the gate!" Don't try and tell me you don't just wish you could scrub even just a "layer" of that . . .

CLARE: [*She is visibly trembling, but softly taunting* GRACE.] And we all know how ya got that "shade" of grey.

GRACE: . . . a layer of that "dirt color" down the drain. [*She is trem-*

bling.] Don't care how much "face cream" and lipstick you put on . . .

CLARE: [*Trembling and smiling a fierce vicious smile.*] Generations of "poon-tag" raped and put out on the market . . .

GRACE: . . . and "rouge" and . . . and eye-shadow, and "Nu-nile" gloss on that nappy, hot-combed head, you still ain't gonna be close to being . . .

CLARE: [*Hurt, but taunting.*] The real "true" woman you get to be everytime you "escape" . . . right? Right? And you thank God you can "escape" . . . don't cha! Don't cha!

GRACE: [*Nodding.*] Absolutely . . . Abso . . . [*Realizing what she's saying, she cringes, drops her head.*]

[*Suddenly there is a ground swell of sound. The unseen* WHITE PATRONS *begin* BANGING TABLEWARE AGAINST GLASSWARE *to protest* GRACE *and* CLARE'S *presence. They both look up startled.*]

CLARE: [*Softly, grabbing* GRACE'S *hand.*] Don't turn around Grace . . . don't let them see your fear . . .

GRACE: But what if they . . . if they grab us . . . if they punch us . . .

CLARE: They too "gen-teel" for that . . . we're just "women" and it's just two of us . . . they won't go too far. [CLARE *lifts her glass and shouts out loud, facing the audience.*] Well, I got a lemon Coke out of it, nothing you can do about that can ya'!! Smash the glass, but you can't take the Coke back!!

UNSEEN VOICE: Get on back to De-troit where you niggers belong!

[GRACE *takes a long sweeping look at the audience, she stares at* CLARE *as they gather their packages.*]

GRACE: Oh, it "gauls me . . ." oh, it "gauls me."

CLARE: [*Softly smiling.*] Welcome to the "Motor Capital of the World."

[*They rise together. They stare out at the audience as they clutch each other's arms and hold their heads high. They take slow steps towards the audience. Soft "CACKLING" from an unseen "crowd" can be heard in background. They take slow dignified steps towards the audience. They "cross" a lighted boundary, the* DOOR CHIME *"sounds,"* TRAFFIC NOISE, *they are standing face front to the audi-*

ence with the impression that they are now outside the diner. They still clutch each other for a few moments, then pull away.]

CLARE: [*Cont'd. Panting.*] Feels like I'm a icicle all over.

GRACE: My heart's racing . . . racing.

CLARE: Lemme just stop shaking . . . ha . . .

GRACE: My heart's pounding . . .

CLARE: [*Suddenly checks her packages.*] Did we get everything, Grace? . . . *Quickly counting her packages. Pause. Frantically.*] Whew! . . . We made it . . . ha . . . one day we'll tell our kids how we stood up to the crackers one summer day in Dearborn Heights!

[*It is obvious they are too embarrassed to look each other in the face.*]

GRACE: [*Pause, then.*] To think all that ugly could come out of my mouth . . .

CLARE: All that trash I was talking . . . please . . . don't see how you could ever "pardon" me . . .

[GRACE *tries to answer, cannot.*]

CLARE: [*Cont'd., soft.*] Did I have all the Colored cringing back at Montgomery Wards?

GRACE: [*Turning to her.*] Nunno . . . you stood up for . . .

CLARE: [*Overlapping.*] . . . No, you were right . . . I embarrassed everybody . . .

GRACE: Colored Rights!

CLARE: I was so—so loud and bodacious . . . tell me true now . . .

GRACE: What could I say to you that you could possibly believe after today? [*Staring out in a daze.*] They . . . they . . . got to see the . . . "base" side of us, that's what gets to me.

CLARE: [*Pause.*] You left me standing there at the counter, I must have been behaving pretty awful.

GRACE: [*Pause.*] Clare . . . [*Pause.*] understand something . . . I may have "crossed" the Mason-Dixon line, but it's still in me . . . Even when I take the long ride out here on the bus, just to go past all the lovely homes and gardens? Still can't even bring myself to take a seat, sit "up front" even though I know we're "allowed" to up North, here . . . and I can't even tell my husband that.

[*They both smile to each other a moment.*]

CLARE: Know what we need? [*Pause.*] We need ta "shop" all this outta our system . . . calm our nerves . . . haha . . . Okay Hudson's, here we come . . . gonna get me some new patten-leather heels right now! Where'd I park m'car? I'm so frazzled . . .

[CLARE *begins to move off*, GRACE *stops her with her voice.*]

GRACE: First time I went there I really didn't "think" of it as "passing" . . . [*Pause.*] But then again, didn't I? And then the next time . . . and then the next . . .

CLARE: Don't start "unraveling" nothing! . . . Leave where it lays, forget it took place, come on . . .

GRACE: But . . . truth be told . . . when I really deep down think about it . . .

CLARE: [*Smiling.*] Oh, to hell with the "truth" . . . thinking too much frays the nerves, don't you know that?

GRACE: Clare . . . ! [*Pause.*] Everytime we meet up, "today" is gonna be "behind" our eyes our . . . smiles . . . our "hellos."

[GRACE *grabs* CLARE'S *hand for a moment as they still look away. Embarrassed,* CLARE *pats* GRACE'S *hand, gently pulls off and "brightens."*]

CLARE: Now, we gonna get the car, get back cross the line to Detroit and get us some food in us 'fore we faint from this heat . . .

GRACE: Will I tell O.Z. about today, I wonder? Will you tell Clyde?

CLARE: I always say it's a wise woman who charts a clear course 'tween women's business and men's.

GRACE: Now, if I join up with Cavaliers you'll probably think—

CLARE: No, I will not.

GRACE: I'm feeling obliged in some way . . .

CLARE: No, you mistake . . . I DON'T INTEND TO "THINK" ABOUT IT EVER . . . [*Pause.*] I guess I "push against" folks . . . so I don't break . . . [*Pause.*] Never let nothing BREAK ME . . . I JUST—I JUST [*Pause. Studies* GRACE, *then.*] . . . I say we "toss" this whole day in the pile marked "never happened" and stop feeding on it, period . . .

GRACE: It's not just gonna dissolve away.

CLARE: Don't fool yaself . . . pieces fall away bit by bit, 'till finally it's just a haze of a recollection way, way back . . . then, presto, it never happened.

GRACE: [*Pause.*] Wonder if one day we might end up "real buddies?" . . .

CLARE: [*Pause. Smiling.*] Could be dangerous to your home life. [*Pause, smiles.*] . . . For one thing, you just might end up learning how to drive.

GRACE: [*Giggling.*] Ha. [*Then, she suddenly turns somber.*] . . . "Toss it back and forget it ever happened . . . ?"

[*Pause. They stare off in different directions.* GRACE *removes her sunglasses from her purse, puts them on.* CLARE *takes out her compact, check's her face.*]

CLARE: [*Her face is a smiling "mask."*] I already have . . .

GRACE: [*Pause, then.*] "Dearborn Heights."

Fade out.

END OF PLAY

Lavonne Mueller

AMERICAN DREAMERS

LAVONNE MUELLER

Lavonne Mueller is currently New Plays Editor of Applause Books. Her play, *Letters to a Daughter From Prison*, about Nehru and his daughter, Indira, was produced at the First International Festival of the Arts in New York City and went on to tour in India. Her play, *Violent Peace*, was produced in London in 1992 and was the "Critics Choice" in *Time Out Magazine*. Her play, *Little Victories*, was produced in Tokyo by Theatre Classic Productions and directed by Riho Mitachi. Her play, *The Only Woman General*, was produced in New York City and went on to the Edinburgh Festival, where it was "Pick of the Fringe" by the Scotland critics. She was awarded the Roger Stevens Playwriting Award, which she received at the Kennedy Center in Washington, D.C., in 1992. She is a Woodrow Wilson Scholar, a Lila Wallace Reader's Digest Writing Fellow, and has received a Guggenheim Grant, a Rockefeller Grant, three National Endowment for the Arts Grants, a Fulbright to Argentina, an Asian Culture Council Grant to Calcutta, India, and a U.S. Friendship Commission Grant to Japan. Her plays have been published by Dramatist Play Service, Samuel French, Applause Books, Performing Arts Journal, Theatre Communication Group, Heinemann Books, and Baker's Plays. Her textbook, *Creative Writing*, published by Doubleday and The National Textbook Company, is used by students around the world. She has been an Arts America speaker for the USIS (United States Information Service) in India, Finland, Romania, Japan, Yugoslavia, and Norway. She was recently a Fulbright Fellow to Jordan and received a National Endowment for the Humanities grant to do research in Paris during the summer of 1995.

CHARACTERS

MARILYN MONROE   age 36
CARL SANDBURG   virgorous 70-plus

TIME: *August 1, 1962, 11:30 pm*
PLACE: *A hotel suite in Washington, D.C.*

AT RISE: We see MARILYN *sitting before a Russian samovar. Next to the samovar are colorful folk-painted cups with the letter "C" on them. There are five phones scattered throughout the room. A large saucer-like bulging disk is on the wall over the head of the bed. From the window we can see the Capitol Building.* MARILYN *is wearing a black dress with pearls. Her blond hair is up in a twist. We see* MARILYN *look at her watch impatiently. Then she goes to the phone and calls downstairs to the hotel desk.*

MARILYN: This is 508. I'm expecting a Mr. Sandburg. [*A beat.*] Are you sure? [*A beat.*] You can't miss him. He's muscular with bushy white hair. [*As she is waiting for the desk to look for Sandburg, she walks to the window and admires the view of the Capitol Building. Then, into the phone.*] You have two fat men with bushy white hair? No, I don't see why I should talk to them. They're not Sandburg, I guarantee you. But thanks, anyway.

    [*She hangs up. She goes to the window and stares out again. Then she looks at her watch. She goes to the table and picks up her pen and doodles on a piece of paper. Then she goes to the door and looks both ways down the hall. She goes to the phone.*]

    [*Into the phone.*] This is room 508 again. I'm still waiting for Mr. Sandburg. He should have been here an hour ago. He's never late. I'm the one who should be late. [*A beat.*] Yes...yes...yes...that's right. Bushy white hair. He's probably carrying Schopenhauer. [*A beat.*] Over by the main door? Go grab him. I'll wait.

    [*She swings her foot impatiently, then examines the very high spike heels she is wearing. She squints at the heels, then kicks them off*

and walks to the sofa where there is a shoe box on the sofa. She takes out a pair of very conservative pumps with one-inch heels. She puts them on.]

[*Rattles into the phone without taking a breath.*] Yes. I'm still here. Wonderful. Let me talk to him. [*A beat.*] Carl? Of all times for you to be late. I have so much to tell you. I figured your poetry reading ran over time at the White House? Right? Just hurry on up... [*She opens the door just a crack as she holds the phone. Into the phone.*] What? [*A beat.*] Who are you? [*A beat.*] Otis Sprague? [*A beat.*] You have a lot of muscles and thick white hair? Please put the Desk back on the phone. [*A beat.*] Desk? I don't want a Sprague. [*A beat.*] Yes...yes...I know I asked for muscular.

[*We see* CARL *come in the partially opened door. He puts his guitar inside by the door. He stands by the door only partially seen. His hair is combed back very smoothly and he is wearing a tux. He stands listening to* MARILYN.]

MARILYN: [*Cont'd.*] The man I want is bushy. With tufts of cactus spiking out over his forehead. Worse than Robert Frost. Worse than Albert Sweitzer, even. You'd never know he writes poetry. He looks like a drifter.

CARL: I am a drifter.

MARILYN: [*Looks at* CARL *and smiles. Into phone.*] Never mind. I've found him. [*She hangs up.*]

CARL: Poor Mr. Sprague. Did he know for one shining moment he was talking to Marilyn Monroe?

MARILYN: You'll be glad to know I'm not the same Marilyn.

CARL: What's wrong with America is not Marilyn Monroe.

MARILYN: Not Carl Sandburg, either. But America only needs one of us. [*A beat.*] Did you see Him?

CARL: I saw Her. [*A beat.*] Like the tux?

MARILYN: Frankly, no.

CARL: She did. [*A beat.*] Poets can be sex objects, too. Except for her, I was wasted tonight at the White House on a lot of cranky old senators.

MARILYN: You look like a wai...

[CARL *cuts her off and they both say "waiter" together.*]

CARL: Have you fallen into platitudes?

MARILYN: I've always liked waiters.

CARL: When's the last time you married one?

MARILYN: Carl, please sit down. I want to hear all about your poetry reading. And tonight...we don't have loads of time like we usually do.

CARL: [*Clears his throat and reads formally from a paper he takes out of his jacket.*]
When Lincoln makes love
there's only bread.
Ink and blood run down his chin
the juice of a failure.
His dead
take away the butter.

MARILYN: I wrote that.

CARL: Just passed it off as my own. [*A beat.*] They loved it.

MARILYN: I guess after being my poetry teacher all these months, you're entitled.

CARL: I'm really here to get you to run off with me.

MARILYN: Playing John Wayne?

CARL: I've always wanted to rescue Marilyn Monroe.

MARILYN: Oh, for heaven sakes, I'm perfectly all right. I wanted you to come by tonight so you could see how successful your student is.

CARL: My students don't usually wind up in government.

MARILYN: All those books you got me to read...the poems I've written for you...our long conversations. How could He resist me after that?

CARL: True love, huh?

MARILYN: This love is going to save the world.

CARL: [*Rolls his eyes mockingly and sits at a table*.] Right now, let's save Carl. I need tea. With brandy in it. [*A beat*.] A samovar?

MARILYN: From an admirer.

CARL: [*Holds up his cup*.] Folk Art?

MARILYN: Another admirer.

CARL: Cups with two ears?

MARILYN: No two ears are the same.

CARL: [*A beat as he watches her put the cup under the samovar spout*.] Don't tell me you're going to pour?

[*She abruptly puts the cup down without pouring tea in it and gets a silver shaker.*]

CARL: [*Looking around.*] Five phones?

MARILYN: I have fans, you know. [*She holds up the cocktail shaker.*] Do you want sugar ... milk ... ?

CARL: Brandy.

MARILYN: All I got is a shaker of Daiquiris.

CARL: Shaker on in.

MARILYN: One lump or two?

CARL: The usual.

[MARILYN *pours the daiquiri into his cup and then she adds a quick flip of tea from the samovar and stirs.*]

MARILYN: [*Pours daiquiris into her own cup and stirs.*] I measure my life in boozy spoons.

CARL: "In the room the women come and go...."

MARILYN: "...speaking of Michelangelo." [*She drinks the contents of her cup.*]

CARL: So you're still on T. S. Eliot?

MARILYN: I'm not still on Eliot. Eliot's still on me.

CARL: You remembered.

MARILYN: When Eliot finishes a poem, he's just another reader. [*A beat.*] After a man is elected, he's just another voter.

CARL: And after a lover loves?

MARILYN: That's the way I feel about my movies. When I looked at *Let's Make Love* the other night while I was waiting around for somebody...

CARL: You seem to be waiting around for people these days.

MARILYN: I didn't know who the girl was in that movie.

CARL: [*Singing to the tune of "Billy Boy" as he strums the guitar.*]
Don't you want to be a poet
Norma Jean, Norma Jean?
Don't you want to leave the rot
charmin Norma?
It wouldn't be a thrill
to sell out for caviar and dill
you're a smart girl who oughta leave the lo...t.

MARILYN: Are you making a statement about my acting?

CARL: [*He looks at her and smiles.*] You're my golden sun.

[*A beat as she looks curiously at him.*]

CARL: Colette's mother always said that to her.

MARILYN: I have to admit, nobody's ever loved me like a mother. Especially not my mother. [*A beat.*] You know, Yves Montand is flat footed.

CARL: No, I didn't know that.

MARILYN: He has a hell of a time buying shoes.

CARL: I didn't know that.

MARILYN: Sometimes I walk round and round in this room just like in Van Gogh's prison pictures. [*A beat.*] I've only waited for two people in my life. Him...and Abe. [*A beat.*] You're my Abraham Lincoln.

CARL: I'll warn you, I'm not too old fashioned when it comes to women.

MARILYN: Neither was Lincoln.

CARL: You're the first person who understands that.

MARILYN: I could have been his wife.

CARL: Hidden away in the White House? You could have been him.

MARILYN: They both had blisters on their eyes. From crying when little Willie died.

CARL: Did you read that in my book?

MARILYN: In mine. I've lost children.

CARL: We've all lost children.

MARILYN: Can you believe She bleaches her arm hairs? [*A beat.*] Was she wearing a silly pill box?

CARL: Isn't pill box a military installation?

MARILYN: Her hat.

CARL: Looks a little Mao-ist, don't you think?

MARILYN: Did she put her little cultivated hand on yours...while she cooed about your...meter? [*She says "meter" like "Peter."*]

CARL: Wasn't she nice to poor old Frost? When he lost his way at the Inauguration...his papers flying all around his head?

MARILYN: Have more tea.

CARL: No thanks.

MARILYN: You're being petulant.

CARL: A new vocabulary word. From Mr. Wonderful?

MARILYN: Actually, I picked it up from Yves Montand.

CARL: No flat language he...

MARILYN: Don't tell me you're jealous of Yves Montand, too?

CARL: I'm jealous of everybody.

MARILYN: Are you trying to be theatrical to show the error in being theatrical?

CARL: Marilyn...oh, Marilyn, I'm trying very hard not to fall in love with you.

MARILYN: That's not much of a compliment.

CARL: Do you want a compliment?

MARILYN: Try one.

CARL: You're as real to me as Lincoln.

MARILYN: What else?

CARL: It's your turn.

MARILYN: I like your hair.

CARL: I like yours.

MARILYN: They're putting our mops all over the covers of books and magazines.

CARL: The public always imitates what we find the most silly about ourselves.

MARILYN: I have only one regret—one more than Piaf who regretted nothing. [*A beat.*] Just once, I want to spread my brains at the same time I spread my thighs.

CARL: What about the literary husband you've left? I would think he did it.

MARILYN: [*Grabs* CARL's *guitar and sings.*]
What does the writer
have under his pen.
ha-wang
ha-wang . . .

CARL: What about your new love?

MARILYN: He can't do both at the same time.

CARL: Pretty scary for a man to take on different ends of a woman all at once.

MARILYN: All my husbands hang pictures of me on the wall—groin high.

CARL: And I wouldn't?

MARILYN: You'd have my little verses attached.

CARL: Never mind. I'm old enough to be your grandfather.

MARILYN: That excites me.

CARL: Time is on the side of my pen.

MARILYN: Your poems excite me.

CARL: But I tend goats.

MARILYN: [*Fondly.*] Yah.

CARL: I smell of fly repellent, pine tar, Lysol. I wear hoof trimmers in my back pocket.

MARILYN: You have a wife.

CARL: My wife has me.

MARILYN: Do you know why I like you?

CARL: I'm photographed all the time.

MARILYN: We both have dirt under our fingernails. [*Looking at her fingernails.*] The orphanage still clings to its roots.

CARL: The family's an orphan.

MARILYN: But only one person can serve the time.

CARL: When I was a kid, I had to clean all the manure from the shed. There were bells on the handle of my shovel. When the bells didn't ring, my father ran out and boxed my ears. [*A beat.*] I got a love of music that way.

MARILYN: There were no bells on my mops and pails. You know more than anybody—I'm boring.

CARL: America doesn't think so.

MARILYN: You mean fans?

CARL: I have fans, too. They aren't so bad.

MARILYN: But you know what they want.

CARL: Not my body parts.

MARILYN: You can have the hidden me.

CARL: Joe wouldn't like it.

MARILYN: Joe? Joe! You and your love of baseball.

CARL: It's the poet's game. You can do a lot of writing between innings.

MARILYN: Joe gets so bored in the winter.

CARL: Winding up a pitch is just as fine a thing as sliding in for a rime. And don't forget Hemingway.

MARILYN: "I'd like to take the great DiMaggio fishing. They say his father's a fisherman."

CARL: *The Old Man and the Sea.*

MARILYN: Joe would rather fish around in my mouth. [*Opens her mouth.*] Under all these caps, I'm Dracula. [*A beat.*] The man who was the kindest to me was a dentist.

CARL: Goats never disappoint me, either.

MARILYN: He had his hands in my mouth. Up to his knuckles. Yet he never...never...enjoyed it. [*A beat.*] Some of the caps come out. See if you can find them.

CARL: Goats are the poor man's cow.

MARILYN: That impresses me.

CARL: Their teats don't have to be large.

MARILYN: Well, aren't they lucky. [*A beat.*] Go on. Find the ones that move.

CARL: You can get a quart of milk a day if you're careful. [*He puts two fingers in her mouth.*]

MARILYN: Feels good.

CARL: Your teeth are solid. [*He takes his fingers away.*] What did the good dentist say when he first looked into the mouth of Marilyn Monroe?

MARILYN: He...gasped. Like this. [*She makes a sigh of disgust.*]

CARL: Over a few cavities?

MARILYN: There was the stench.

CARL: [*He puts two fingers from both his hands and opens her mouth.*] Your tongue was covered with sticky film. Bacteria lined the root ends. Enamel, the hardest substance made by the body, was tortured by scum. Rancid food and acids sheathed the nodes and flaps of tissue. You opened to him—acid, water, dirty enzymes, filthy cell hairs, sticky mucus. [*He lets her mouth close.*]

MARILYN: He hadn't expected it. When I knew him better, he said the smell was as foul as dead bodies dragged into the Los Angeles Morgue where he worked as a student.

CARL: When he cleaned away all the foul, he said: "Now your lovers can kiss you."

MARILYN: And I said . . . "now I have to let them."

CARL: There's a scar on your neck.

MARILYN: It's from nobody famous. [A beat.] I'm really trying not to be so affectionate toward scripts.

CARL: When I start to write, I bring on to the page all my friends, my loves, my hates. Then I get absorbed and slowly these people and things leave. And then even I leave. [A beat.] There's a scar on your wrist.

MARILYN: From somebody famous. [A beat.] I love the way you pull that off—especially in your poem, Chicago.

CARL: You really do read me.

MARILYN: I read you 'cause your city doesn't look up my dress.

CARL: Oh, it looks up your dress, all right.

MARILYN: And because you write about ordinary people.

CARL: There are no ordinary people.

MARILYN: How do you do it?

CARL: The way you say . . . "Joe".

MARILYN: [Says steamily.] Joe . . . Joe.

CARL: There. See what you've written.

MARILYN: The audience has to discover the thing you hold back. The audience has to take away the mystery. [A beat.] Joe . . . no . . .

CARL: Be your own enemy. Fight against what's wrong in your art.

MARILYN: I think so much about the imaginary characters I play— their problems, their joys—that I doubt the living.

CARL: Neither one of us ever wanted to be real people. [A beat.] Please, let your hair down.

MARILYN: He prefers a twist.

CARL: Well, that's what counts.

MARILYN: [*Takes out her hair pins and lets her hair fall down.*] He likes it this way in bed.

CARL: Is the bed good?

MARILYN: In what way?

CARL: All the way.

MARILYN: [*She sits on the bed.*] He's efficient.

CARL: Can't be too much fun for you.

MARILYN: He's decisive.

CARL: Do you respond likewise?

MARILYN: Carl, don't make fun of me.

CARL: You're making fun of you.

MARILYN: This affects the world.

CARL: Weren't Picasso's guitars more intense than his people?

MARILYN: I'm talking about the President of the United States.

CARL: Just met him. [*A beat.*] Come away with me. Tonight.

[*A silent beat.*]

MARILYN: I'm helping Him.

CARL: He's using you.

MARILYN: I'm using Him.

CARL: So, now you're the woman behind the throne?

MARILYN: The woman beside the throne.

CARL: A woman's already there, Marilyn.

MARILYN: He doesn't love her.

CARL: He loves you?

MARILYN: At first, He wanted other women when he had me. Usually He likes more than one of us at the same time.

CARL: [*Strums his guitar and chant-sings.*]
Little lusts have lesser lusts

upon their groins to urge them;
lesser lusts have smaller lusts
and so ad infinitum.

MARILYN: Don't make fun. Lust is expensive.

CARL: You only think that 'cause you give it away. [*He takes a coin from his pocket.*] A penny can buy you anything.

MARILYN: [*Takes the penny.*] So . . . you learned to love Lincoln from a penny, too.

CARL: Wild mountain goats are able to stand on a space no bigger than that. [*He takes the penny back and holds it out.*]

MARILYN: Do you think we could ever fill a space so big?

CARL: Sure. [*A beat.*] Cling to me. Like Darwin on the back of those huge tortoises in the Galapagos islands.

[CARL *moves her to his back. She gets on his back and he takes her piggy-back around the room.*]

MARILYN: [*Singing on his back to the tune of "Billy Boy."*]
Is a lady on your back
farmer Carl, farmer Carl?
Is a lady on your back
far . . . mer Ca . . . rl?

CARL: [*Singing.*] There's a lassie on my chassie
                 trying hard to get my sassy . . .

[CARL *and* MARILYN *fall happily onto the bed.*]

CARL: My age. My idiotic poetic age. [*A beat.*] Do you still put your panties in the refrigerator?

MARILYN: Keeps them cool in the summertime.

CARL: I saw *The Seven Year Itch.*

MARILYN: Oh, you read me, too.

CARL: Are the "cool" panties on, now?

MARILYN: I hate it when you talk like that.

CARL: You mean like a man?

MARILYN: I mean like a fan.

CARL: There. We've rimed together. And that's all I ever wanted.

MARILYN: [*She pulls away from him and stands.*] Do you think you're the only one who resists me? [*A beat.*] Think this lamp lusts after me? [*She throws the lamp on the floor.*] Think this table wants me in bed? [*She throws the end-table against the wall.*] See those props? I've learned about orphans from them. [*A beat.*] I'd look outside . . . longing . . . licking the window pane.

CARL: You watched the bugs on the floor. Wondering if you could be that strong.

MARILYN: They kept bright lights on all night at the orphanage. My shadow was a giant against the wall. I couldn't believe it was me.

CARL: You were already on the screen.

MARILYN: I unbuttoned dreaming.

CARL: The good disadvantage.

MARILYN: When I was twelve and got my first period, I screamed to the walls: I'm learning to think.

CARL: Thinking starts the blood. [*A beat.*] I began to bleed playing the strings on my first guitar.

MARILYN: It's about my time of the month . . . my blood is beginning to run.

CARL: It's your attachment to common life.

MARILYN: Yes, I can spot the common orphan anywhere.

CARL: Turn me loose in a field, and I can find a goat.

MARILYN: I used to go to Times Square. Stand against a building. And look for orphans. Cheaters. Trying to pass themselves off. Trying to act like they had plenty of room growing up. When I know the beds in any orphanage are so close together you can't walk between them. So close together you can stir them with a stick. Beds with metal bars like a circus cage. I stood in those beds to change. Clothes hang a different way on me. [*A beat.*] Of all the painters you've shown me, it's Rembrandt I like best. His little mangy dogs. Those lost dogs he puts on his canvas for the common people. Stray dogs follow orphans—skulking after little girls with dirty hair . . . little girls in eyes filmed with red haw like a hunting dog. [*A beat.*] I ate dried apples for breakfast, dried apples for lunch. And drank a quart of water and swelled for dinner.

CARL: My first poems were naming horses. Purple Rose. Timber Line. Road Salt. Smartweed. My first guitar was made from a big fat seed box and some fence wire. My art came from the same place as the hoe. How more alike can we be?

MARILYN: I had long curls that bounced around like sea anemones.

CARL: In the Orphanage?

MARILYN: Yes.

CARL: They cut them off.

MARILYN: Yes.

CARL: You screamed.

MARILYN: I could see my bald shadow on the wall.

CARL: You kept the curly scraps.

MARILYN: Oh, yes. And sewed them into my pillow.

CARL: Don't regret hair.

MARILYN: Those little curls could think for themselves without any regard for my head.

CARL: Be thankful their martyrdom is over.

MARILYN: Have you got a knife?

CARL: I always carry one for peeling apples.

MARILYN: Like Frost?

CARL: You're still with Eliot, remember?

MARILYN: Give me the knife.

CARL: Take back Frost.

MARILYN: You mean—take back both of him?

CARL: One will do.

MARILYN: A person who can sing is two people. Give me the knife.

CARL: I'm the one who has to think of endings.

MARILYN: I'm dreaming in Ibsen. I'm dreaming in Proust.

CARL: I can't bear the fact that other people write.

MARILYN: Acting can be as satisfying as murder.

CARL: It's that long silence of the blank white sheet of paper that hates life and laughter. I fear its mysterious forces breathing against my hand.

MARILYN: Give me the knife.

CARL: My mother cut out all my shirts with a butcher knife.

MARILYN: Your mother was large, with feet as big as footballs.

CARL: I twisted myself some homemade spurs out of piano wire. I wrote poetry on a piece of paper nailed on the back of my walking cultivator.

MARILYN: You were Zola. Using two quarts of ink a year.

CARL: I had cramps in my hands from cheese making.

MARILYN: Give me the knife.

CARL: I take time paring an apple. That's real writing.

[CARL *takes the penknife from his back pocket and slowly hands it to* MARILYN. *She takes the knife and begins stabbing a pillow on the bed and bright yellow brassy feathers pop out of the pillow and fall everywhere.*]

MARILYN: My curls. From the orphanage. [*She looks down at the feathers and begins to sort tenderly through the feathers.*] All my sweet lost children. You little raw pulps that were my babies. I love every one of you. [*Abruptly.*] Isn't well made fiction wonderful?

CARL: Fiction holds the world together. [CARL *gets his guitar and sings.*]
On top of sweet Marilyn
all covered with glitter,
she keeps right on singing
about her life's litter.

MARILYN: [*Singing.*] Her voice is so mournful...

CARL: [*Singing.*] ... with sobs and with tears...

MARILYN: [*Singing.*] Marilyn's been cashing in on the orphanage...

CARL: [*Singing.*] ... for the past 36 years.

CARL & MARILYN: [*Singing.*] On top of ole Carl all covered with bells...

CARL: [*Singing.*] He's been bagging his poverty...

MARILYN: [*Singing.*] Cause poverty sells.

[*They embrace, laughing.*
    MARILYN *suddenly pulls away from* CARL.]

MARILYN: You know he's deformed.

CARL: Your President?

MARILYN: Yes.

CARL: What about all the swimming and football games?

MARILYN: Those things don't happen as often as you think.

CARL: Are you trying to enlist my sympathy?

MARILYN: He hates sympathy.

CARL: Even from you?

MARILYN: Daily enemas. Salt water boils. Migraines. He vomits all the time from the pain.

CARL: It must have been a big help having once been married to a baseball player.

MARILYN: Joe always walks around with his elbow in a bucket of ice.

CARL: All his sprained ankles... sore arms...

MARILYN: I like the look of pain. It's real.

CARL: And your new Mr. Wonderful has all that glamorous agony.

MARILYN: He feels so awful, half the time he won't even let me touch him.

CARL: How do you manage that?

MARILYN: I try to touch him when he's not paying attention.

CARL: I can't imagine a man not paying attention.

MARILYN: When he's ... deep in conversation.

CARL: So he does talk to you?

MARILYN: He told me to put a lump of sugar behind my teeth and drink tea through it, Russian style.

CARL: Affairs of State.

MARILYN: I'm reading a book on diseases of the mouth.

CARL: For all the times he's impotent?

MARILYN: If sex were successful 99.9 percent of the time, there would still be 2 limp dicks every day. [*A beat.*] Believe me, he asks my opinion on things.

CARL: Castro?

MARILYN: I told him to have a list ready of some good Cuban doctors living in Miami.

CARL: In case he bombed the hell out of a lot of Cuban civilians.

MARILYN: It would be humane.

CARL: Sounds like hard-core strategy to me.

MARILYN: Just the old battle between grace and liberty, between St. Augustine and St. Thomas.

CARL: Maybe you ought to read more poems and less religion. Your man is a poet, after all. Short phrases. Alliteration. "We stand in a new Frontier—Frontier of perils, promises ...

MARILYN: I've got Byron.

CARL: Was that his choice?

MARILYN: It was your choice. Our first lunch. At the Algonquin. Remember? You said you admired a poet who fought for his convictions.

CARL: Did you read Byron right after our lunch?

MARILYN: War didn't interest me.

CARL: You hadn't been politicized then?

[*A beat.*]

CARL: [*Cont'd.*] What are these terrible rumors? These ugly insinuations? [*A beat.*] Let me take you away from here.

MARILYN: You'd take me away from my best role.

[*The phone rings. She answers the phone.*]

MARILYN: [*Into the phone.*] Hello . . . [*A beat.*] It's arrived? Good. Bring it upstairs. I don't want to be disturbed; just leave it by the door. Thanks.

CARL: How long are you planning to stay in Washington?

MARILYN: As long as he wants me.

CARL: So you're making a little nest here?

MARILYN: That's a cliché, isn't it?

CARL: Aren't you living one?

MARILYN: Damnit, Carl, I'm trying to be my own actress.

CARL: Very profound.

MARILYN: I'm not one Marilyn Monroe all the time.

CARL: Maybe one is all he wants.

MARILYN: Then acting will be my oldest profession.

[*A beat.*]

CARL: He's no Lincoln, for godsakes.

MARILYN: I know . . . He's not that thin.

CARL: A little paunch, is it?

MARILYN: He loves Milky Ways.

CARL: Cosmic, even when he eats?

MARILYN: He hides them in the dresser under his socks.

CARL: In the Chester Arthur Chester Drawers?

MARILYN: His wife has him on a diet all the time.

CARL: And you wouldn't?

MARILYN: Why would I want to do that?

CARL: You'd be responsible for him, wouldn't you?

MARILYN: He's got Secret Service men for that.

CARL: You'd turn over control to strangers?

MARILYN: Of course it's true—he can't afford any extra weight on his back. I told him, if I wanted to assassinate him, I'd aim a rifle full of heavy duty chocolate at his head.

CARL: You told him that?

MARILYN: I told him that and he said . . . never tell my enemies.

CARL: And are there enemies out there who want to get him?

MARILYN: Everybody in the world loves our Man. *Lass' sie nach Berlin kommen!*

CARL: Wrong country.

MARILYN: Right fanaticism.

CARL: You do have potential for politics.

[*She hears a thud by the door and goes to open it. There is a rocking chair covered with brown butcher paper. She pulls it inside the room and shuts the door. She excitedly unwraps the package to reveal a sturdy wooden rocking chair.*]

CARL: His?

MARILYN: A very good imitation.

CARL: Like Monet in those pink plastic frames at the dimestore,

MARILYN: Do you go to dimestores?

CARL: You see the best paintings there.

MARILYN: I never thought of the Mona Lisa as great. 'Cause it was always on chocolate boxes when I was a kid. Then when I grew up and saw it at the Louvre in Paris . . . I said, "What do you know. I've been gobbling up art all this time."

CARL: [*Touching the rocking chair.*] I've seen the original.

MARILYN: I guess I can take it off my income tax.

[*A silent beat. Then* CARL *puts the paper back over the rocking chair.*]

CARL: I came here to take you home.

MARILYN: If I had a home, Carl, you could take me there.

CARL: Stay with us on the farm.

MARILYN: Forever?

CARL: There's that Italian director who wants you for his next film in a couple of months.

MARILYN: I don't speak Italian.

CARL: You don't have to.

MARILYN: Who could dub my voice?

CARL: Rome.

MARILYN: Be serious.

CARL: We'll feed you goat cheese for two months. Then put you on a plane for Italy. You'll cross the ocean at night and see the Great Dipper and the Little Bear outside your oval window. All the stars and the rest of the Orion will swirl around you, a harvest of glittering new fans.

MARILYN: But you'll be down on the ground—silent and far away from me.

CARL: And lamenting my age.

[*A silent beat.*]

MARILYN: I can't leave Washington. [*She takes the paper off the rocking chair.*]

CARL: I'm going back to Illinois on the train. At 5A.M. [*A beat.*] Come with me. We'll ride together through our America. Grain dust and acres of yellow wheat blowing at our backs. We'll stick our heads out the window and let our famous hair stream out behind us. [*A beat.*] We need the sympathy of mountain peaks and bluff grass. [*A beat.*] We'll reach out and touch rocks as red as new bricks. Eat wild grapes right from the vine. American dreamers—that's us. Come with me. Let's sing to the wild artichokes and bull thistles. Let's wave at the ponds and sloughs. Smell the moss roses. Wish on the prairie mud. American Dreamers. It's what we do best.

[*A silent beat.*]

MARILYN: I can't.

CARL: Why not?

MARILYN: He needs me.

CARL: So do I? Who will keep me honest?

MARILYN: Who will keep him honest?

CARL: You're in a "B" movie, my friend.

MARILYN: He has a file-cabinet marked "lies."

CARL: Have you given up poetic reasoning?

[*A beat. She goes to the rocking chair, picks it up, and puts it on the center of the bed.*]

MARILYN: "Sir Lancelot...thou are the goodlyest person that ever came among knights..."

CARL: Thomas Malory.

MARILYN: You gave him to me.

CARL: Undercover work for Mr. President is not what I call poetry.

MARILYN: I call Mr. President...Doc.

CARL: As in Papa Doc?

MARILYN: As in "lover Doc."

CARL: His divinity ails him.

MARILYN: Just like my divinity ails me. [*A beat.*] You can't expect him to get ordinary relief.

CARL: Are you putting the scrotum around the man?

MARILYN: Once...before we did it in his official bedroom...he took a short swim. I sat at one end of the White House Pool. And every time he swam down to me, he grabbed a breast.

CARL: Presidential foreplay. Ask not what your breasts can do for you; ask what your breasts can do for your country.

MARILYN: Of course I was holding his daiquiri.

CARL: Did you say anything through this foreplay?

MARILYN: Yes. But I had to time myself. I'd go: "Why do we have Jupiter missiles in Turkey?" Lap one. Breast one. "Those missiles are useless and out of date." Lap two. Breast two. "How can we make demands on Cuba with stuff like that?" Lap three. Both breasts.

CARL: How do you know about Turkey?

MARILYN: I've got a loyal fan in Istanbul.

CARL: Do you ever get any answers beside this pool?

MARILYN: No. But talking politics is exciting.

CARL: Dirty.

MARILYN: Yah.

CARL: And how is the loving after a swim?

MARILYN: Pro forma.

CARL: That's all?

MARILYN: Church songs came over the orphanage wall. I'm his religion.

CARL: I believe his mother already gave him one.

MARILYN: Mom wears a large Crucifix in her belt. Like a missionary.

CARL: She walks among Pagans.

MARILYN: When the pain gets bad, he curses God. If he were an atheist, he couldn't. So, his Mother can take credit for that.

CARL: And you? What do you take credit for?

MARILYN: When he's at the peak of his pleasure, he forgets his back pain. Being in me is like being in Church. Incense . . . the chalice held on high . . . two Hosts on the paten . . . *Deo Gracias* . . . final calm. I assure you, if he could screw me all the time, he wouldn't have to go to Mass.

CARL: Well, you've done wonders for Paula and me.

MARILYN: Really?

CARL: You've sparked my old garden tools.

MARILYN: Oh, tell me.

CARL: I put her down like a fat fragrant peony. The bed is chocolaty fudge dirt. She bucks and weaves. I'm a sun-hot trellis and, oh, what pollination we do make.

[*A silent beat.*]

MARILYN: I did all that?

CARL: Yep.

MARILYN: Sounds almost as good as what Doc and I call our summits.

CARL: Summits?

MARILYN: I gulp down a lot of pills. We don't have much time to make out—before I get comatose. Soon as he pulls out of me, he puts his finger down my throat and forces everything up.

CARL: The way he gestures...jabbing the air with one forefinger. Now I know where that finger's been.

MARILYN: He said he learned how to deal with international crises from me. [*A beat.*] Of course...the longer we wait...the more "Crisis." He likes to feel my pulse. A reminder that time is measured. In a dark way. If he doesn't vomit me, the anonymous constancy of my heart beats will turn into silence and blindness.

CARL: Is this exciting for you?

MARILYN: I never climax, if that's what you mean.

CARL: Why not?

MARILYN: He'd view that as retaliation.

[*Silent beat. Suddenly, the saucer-sized disc over her bed beings to sputter and glow in sparks of yellow.*]

CARL: What in the world is that?

MARILYN: A false alarm. [*A beat.*] When he enters the bedroom up above mine, it turns red. Then I know he'll be here in twenty minutes.

CARL: I suppose he swings down on a rope to your room like Tarzan.

[CARL *goes to look at the disk as it sputters.*]

MARILYN: Once it went bonkers like that when we were making love.

CARL: Some monster trying to bless you, no doubt. [*He looks at the trailing wire. He follows a fine wire that goes to the window and outside the window and upward. He opens the window to look at the wire going up.*]

MARILYN: Don't open the window. You'll let all the hot air come in. It's bad for Doc's sinuses.

[CARL *closes the window. He takes a small pocket wrench out of his tux pocket and goes to the sputtering disk. He tinkers. Then he gives a solid rap to the disk with his wrench. The disc stops sputtering.*]

MARILYN: How did you fix it?

CARL: [*Shaking wrench at her.*] Unlike you, I retaliate.

[*A silent beat as she stares at him.*]

CARL: Somebody in Chicago told me a pretty harsh rumor about your "man."

MARILYN: Who?

CARL: A real estate agent with one foot in Las Vegas. His kid is studying poetry at the University of Chicago. All three of us had lunch at Walgreens Drugstore on State Street last week.

MARILYN: Walgreens?

CARL: He takes my grass roots seriously.

MARILYN: So, what did he tell you?

CARL: Your "Doc" is hooked up with the Mafia.

MARILYN: Is that suppose to shock me?

CARL: And when a person implicates him ... that person disappears.

MARILYN: You ought to eat in better places.

CARL: I had to recite two narrative poems and a couplet over the oilcloth counter just to get that lunch paid for.

MARILYN: Are you still mooching free meals?

CARL: I don't enjoy my food when I have to pay for it.

MARILYN: What does some salesman in remote Chicago know about anything.

CARL: The 2nd City.

MARILYN: You're prejudiced.

CARL: When it comes to Chicago, it's good business for me to be prejudiced.

MARILYN: I wish you'd never written that poem.

CARL: If you're in search of thugs, consult Milton.

MARILYN: I consult Shakespeare. The White House copy.

CARL: I hate Shakespeare.

MARILYN: You and Tolstoy. Mad cause the Bard didn't make heroes out of farmers.

CARL: Are you making heroes out of the Mafia?

MARILYN: They're just another political party.

CARL: I don't think it's legal for any party to bump off annoying constituents.

MARILYN: Is that what the salesman in remote Chicago is saying?

CARL: Ever read Hans Andersen's "Little Mermaid?" For love... she exchanged her fish tail for a woman's legs. Then found herself walking on needles and burning coals.

MARILYN: [*Picks up a book and extends it toward him.*] I stick to Clausewitz.

CARL: [*Takes book and read the title.*] *Philosophy of War.* [*A beat.*] The White House copy?

MARILYN: 20th Century Fox's copy.

[*One of the phones rings.* MARILYN *picks it up.*]

MARILYN: [*Into phone.*] 508 ... Look, I'm busy. Carl's here. You know all about him. Carl Sandburg. I told you last week, this is the night he's reading for the U. S. Senators and then he was coming by the hotel to see me and I don't have too much time with him 'cause I'm on call and pretty soon I'll have to...yes... but...I know you're busy, too. But...yes...yes...oh, ok.
[*She hands the phone to* CARL.] He wants to speak to you.

CARL: Who?

thighs as she smiles and parades in front of the rocking chair. Then she throws the hip-waders back under the bed.]

CARL: Giving away a few secrets in this envelope?

MARILYN: [*She goes back to looking at the world map still holding the pin.*] Look for yourself. I'll tell you one thing, I'll never play pinball with Nicky again. He always puts the machine on top of his shoes and uses his belly to win a game. Now, do you think that's fair?

CARL: [*Looking at the brown envelope hesitantly.*] I don't know if I want to see this.

MARILYN: Afraid to get involved?

CARL: Afraid to be a traitor.

MARILYN: You think I'm a traitor?

CARL: Giving Nikita information that your love-Doc screams out when he arches in passion?

MARILYN: Doc comes so fast, he wouldn't have time to scream out the first word of a top secret.

[CARL *gingerly opens the envelope slowly.*]

CARL: It's a calendar.

MARILYN: Recognize me?

CARL: [*Flips through calendar pages.*] These are the "papers" for Nikita!

MARILYN: You'll find a courier envelope in one of those dresser drawers—under my drawers.

[*She sticks the map pin saying "Moscow" on the world map.*
        CARL *goes to the map.*]

MARILYN: I have "calendars" where all these pins are.

[*The phone rings.* MARILYN *picks it up.*]

MARILYN: [*Into phone.*] 508. Yes. Speaking. I got the cups. I'm drinking out of them right now. [*She motions* CARL *to give her the cup.*] How's Raul? Good. I'm glad you both like it. I'm sending the same "papers" to Nikita... I'm sorry Esso and Texaco pulled

MARILYN: Nikita. [*Silent pause.*] Khrushchev.

[*As* CARL *is talking to Nikita,* MARILYN *goes to the closet and r*
out a large world map with pins. She takes a pin from the mar
of the map and holds it as she studies the map.]

CARL: [*Into phone.*] Sandburg. [*Listening.*] Yes, I wrote that...y
wrote that, too. I didn't know you were fond of poetry...n
rally I realize the great poets are Russian—like Pushkin...
write poetry? [*Listening to Khrushchev read his original p*
Hmmmmmmmm, good cadence. Good riming. A few pu
passages on the last part, Nikita. [*Listening.*] No, that's not
italistic propaganda. "Purple mountains majesty" is capital
propaganda. Yes...yes...I read Frost. And Robert Ser
[*Listening.*] Oh, you must mean Harriet Monroe?...You n
Marilyn Monroe. "When Lincoln makes love/there's
bread."...Yes, of course, I'm quite familiar with that p
You quoted it at the Soviet Trade Exhibition in Havana in
It makes you determined to have good relations with the
Well, that's the power of poetry. I'll give you back to the p
ess.

MARILYN: [*Into the phone.*] My Nikita Mariquita. When will
you again? Not for a whole month? Yes...yes...of course
disappointed...but you're going to Cuba, right? Yes...y
I know you'll make time for me. Yes, I'm drinking tea fr
right now. You stole it from Gromyko? Well, it's beau
Yes...yes, I've got the papers. Right here. [*She points to*
the mattress for CARL *to get them, but he looks under the bed in*
CARL *comes out from under the bed with two hip-waders whi*
holds up against him.] Yes...yes, you'll send a courier for th
Right. I understand. They'll be ready. [*She motions* CARL *t*
under the mattress. He abruptly drops the hip-waders on the floo
pulls out a brown envelope from under the mattress and holds
to her.] I'm holding right now. Of course I'll be ca
I'm not going to let anybody intercept them. Keep your s
on, Nicky. [*She hangs up. Happily slapping at the rocking c*
Dah!

[*She picks up the hip-waders and puts them sexily up again*

out of your country. We can talk about that when I see you. Yes . . . I'm looking forward to our visit. I want to see everything on your beautiful island. See you then. Adios, Fidel. [*She hangs up and slaps the rocking chair saying "ole!"*]

[*As* MARILYN *is speaking,* CARL *opens the dresser drawer and he picks up an official envelope with Russian lettering on it. A pair of black lace panties are stuck to the envelope.*]

CARL: Castro?

MARILYN: [*Holds up cup and points to "C."*] He says the "C" isn't for Castro. It stands for "Communism."

CARL: I believe Hoover calls it "Commonism."

MARILYN: I don't know why Doc doesn't get rid of him. Hoover can't even pronounce things right.

CARL: Maybe because your Doc is on the Index.

MARILYN: Everybody's on the Index. If they started rounding up all Hoover's suspicious people, you'd need Madison Square Garden to hold them.

[CARL *puts the calendar in the courier envelope and puts the panties back in the drawer.*]

MARILYN: Oh, what the hell. Nicky likes my poetry. [MARILYN *goes to the dresser and takes the panties back out and puts them in the courier envelope with the calendar, licks the envelope, and then lifts off the mirror above the dresser and pulls down a mailbox lid and drops the courier envelope down the chute.*]

CARL: Your own Russian mailbox?

MARILYN: Ambassador Dobrynin is on the first floor.

[MARILYN *puts the mirror back on the wall above the dresser. She looks in the mirror.*]

MARILYN: I look like hell.

CARL: [*He makes a foot gesture at the space under the bed.*] Hip-waders?

MARILYN: You know how water sports turn him on. [*A beat.*] I'm afraid I got some bad news for Doc tonight. I keep hearing from Poco that some missiles are going up in San Cristobal.

CARL: Surely he knows.

MARILYN: Doc wants Castro out. But, he thinks Castro can't last. I know better. Fidel can last. [*A beat.*] I'll send a plane to Cuba to take some high altitude pictures.

CARL: Just remember: No bird soars too high... if it soars with its own wings.

[*Phone rings.*]

MARILYN: You answer it.

[CARL *hesitates.*]

MARILYN: Go on.

[MARILYN *goes to the rocking chair on the bed, takes it off and puts it on the floor. She sits in it.*]

CARL: [*Into phone.*] Monroe. [*He listens.*] Just a minute please. [*Handing her the phone.*] It's George Bundy.

MARILYN: Take a message.

[CARL *stares at* MARILYN *helplessly as she continues to stare at the rocking chair.*]

CARL: [*To* MARILYN.] The Presidential Assistant for National Security.

[MARILYN *rocks without answering.*]

CARL: [*Into phone.*] Miss Monroe has her hands full right now. Can I relay a message to her? [*Listens. To* MARILYN.] He wants your opinion on a possible Denfense Condition #2.

MARILYN: I have to talk to Sweeney. Tactical Air Command. I'll call him back tomorrow.

CARL: She needs another day. [*Listens.*] Thank you. [*He hangs up.*] He hasn't received the "films."

[*She points under the mattress for* CARL *to get another calendar which he does and then he automatically gets a brown envelope from the drawer.*]

CARL: You'd think he could get his own.

MARILYN: They're scarce. [*A beat.*] Mail it behind the Picasso.

[CARL *goes to the painting and moves it aside. He pulls down a mail-box lid and puts in the brown envelope.*]

MARILYN: I'm trying to invent a new position. [*She stands and looks at the rocking chair. Then she motions to* CARL *to sit in the rocking chair.*] Sit.

[CARL *sits in the rocking chair.*]

MARILYN: Sit tall.

[CARL *sits tall.*
     She straddles him on the rocking chair, one leg on each side, facing him.]

MARILYN: Nope. Too much pressure on his piriformis muscles.

[*She stands. A beat. Then she moves* CARL*'s legs apart and sits between his legs, her back to him.*]

MARILYN: Too heavy on his lumbar curve.

[*She stands. She now sits, straddling the arms of the rocking chair, one leg over each arm as she faces him.*]

MARILYN: I've decided on something called the Sacral Rock. [*A beat.*] Now . . . just tip over to the left.

[*She gently helps* CARL *tip to the left, all the way over so that she and the rocking chair and* CARL *go over on one side.*]

MARILYN: Keep your back up against the slats. Rock . . . rock . . .

[*They fumble, roll around, and end up laughing and flinging themselves on their back looking at the ceiling. After a beat, all five phones ring. Marilyn gets up, gathers all the phone receivers like a bouquet.*]

MARILYN: [*Into all the phones.*] Room 508.
     [*She listens to all five telephones by her ear. Into phone #1.*] Commander Thomas Power? [*Listens. Then.*] Five Cuban launcher sites. [*She jerks the plug of this phone out of the wall and tosses the phone aside.*]
     [*Into phone #2.*] The C-S-B-F? Oh, the Catholic Service Bureau of Florida. [*Listens. Then.*] Spread the rumor in Cuba that parents will lose the rights of paternity over their kids to

the Cuban State. Patria Potestas. [*She yanks the plug of phone #2 out of the wall and tosses the phone aside.*]

[*Into phone #3.*] Mr. Bush? [*Listens. Then.*] They've positioned tactical nuclear battlefield rockets for use against invasion forces. [*She yanks the plug of phone #3 out of the wall and tosses the phone aside.*]

[*Into phone #4.*] Le May? [*Listens. Then.*] Twenty SS-4 M-R-B-Ms able to send megaton-yield warheads as far as Washington. [*She yanks the plug of phone #4 out of the wall and tosses the phone aside.*]

[*Into phone #5.*] Third Marine Corps of the Western Hemisphere? [*She listens. Then.*] I want an arsenal of small vessels and yachts—non governmental—ready at all times in the direction of the Cuban coastline. [*She yanks out the plug of phone #5 and tosses the phone aside.*]

[*A beat.*] Thank God they all have calendars.

CARL: Doesn't the President do anything himself?

MARILYN: He uses the best people for what he wants done. Smart leadership is dumb leadership.

CARL: You should definitely attend cabinet meetings.

MARILYN: When I walk into a room, personalities change. That's why Doc doesn't attend a lot of important conferences. Even strong people can make recommendations on the basis of what either one of us might want to hear. [*A beat.*] But it torments him that he can't delegate being a Daddy.

CARL: I would think Miss Pill Box does everything.

MARILYN: She can't be Him. [*A beat.*] The power of being a Father is almost more than he can bare. [*A beat.*] Give me my shoe.

CARL: [*He looks in his pockets and brings out a yo-yo.*] I can do "around the world" with my yo-yo.

MARILYN: [*She takes the yo-yo from him and tosses it aside.*] My shoe.

[CARL *takes a shoe off her foot.*]

MARILYN: [*She points to the map with her shoe heel.*] Doc believes in winnable nuclear war.

CARL: Don't say that. I have daughters.

MARILYN: People are always so curious about what it's like to be dead. It's surprising considering how easy it is to imagine. What's it like to be Nikita or Fidel or Doc, that's the real mystery. But to be dead ... I only close my eyes and "picture" things and places around me. [*She closes her eyes.*] I picture ... the bed as nothing. The closet door ... is nothing. The air-conditioner ... is nothing. They're all nothing to me, as real as the light picking up their rays. I've fallen into enough darkness to know my mortal limits. [MARILYN *stands and goes to the map and sweeps away the pins on the map with her arm.*]

I can even imagine the world dead. [*A beat.*] Cut a notch in the windpipe of United States ... to relax the muscles binding the organ sack. [*She slashes at the United States with her shoe heel and bits of paper fly.*] Slide my index and forefingers under the hide of Moscow, letting out the carnal stink of grass and sage. [*She slashes at Moscow with her shoe and bits of paper from the map fall away.*] Saw down the belly of China, Africa, South America—toward the genitals of Europe. [*She slashes at China, Africa, South America and Europe and bits of paper fall from the map.*] I part the cavity and expose the bloodless gray-green organs of the sea.

CARL: You'd never clean a carcass.

MARILYN: I'll cut out Washington, D.C. The heart. And keep it for myself. [*She wipes off the imaginary blood from her shoe and puts it back on.*]

CARL: Taking only the "heart" is poaching.

MARILYN: You saw *The Misfits*?

CARL: That's why you'd never cut up the world.

MARILYN: The world's not a beautiful wild horse.

CARL: Some of it is.

MARILYN: I'm playing against type.

CARL: Then come to Illinois with me. Play farmer.

MARILYN: I want to play Falstaff. That will convince critics once and for all that I don't have to be Marilyn.

CARL: Be Falstaff in Illinois. [*He goes to the map.*] There's survival in

Illinois. Invention and imagination in the rest of the country, too. And in the world. In the darkest tunnel of Pennsylvania, a poem exists. [*He tries to slap the torn paper back on the map.*] If we go into the bowels of Moscow or Africa, we'll find the lines of a Greco face. [*Trying to slap the torn pieces of the map back on.*] The solid black mud of China or South America is Homer, blind but writing away. [*He slaps the torn pieces of the map back on.*]

MARILYN: I want the one performance that will kill all the other ones.

CARL: Come to Illinois. Everybody knows that Illinois is half a day away from half of the USA. We'll sit next to purple corn flowers and wild pink prairie roses without so much as calling them beautiful.

[*Silent beat as she looks at* CARL. *She is shaking her head "no".*]

MARILYN: Help me get ready. [*A beat.*] Help me get ready for Him. [CARL *goes to the end table and opens the drawer and takes out the pill bottles.* CARL *opens the window and throws out all the pill bottles.* MARILYN *calmly watches.*]

MARILYN: [*Cont'd.*] Close the window. All that hot air. He's a sick man. Have some pity.

[CARL *doesn't move.*]

MARILYN: [*Cont'd.*] Most of his childhood was spent in the infirmary of boarding schools. He showed me the pictures. Those infirmaries looked like my orphanage. He slept on musty mattresses. Ate bad food. His parents never came to visit him. Only the books came . . . Tolstoy . . . Dickens . . . Flaubert . . . Mann. He said he could grasp the head-bars of his sick bed and feel the presence of all the people who had ever slept in his bed before him . . . telling the short from the tall, the dark from the fair. He could perceive the murmuring of their hearts, the pulse from their weak wrist, the flutter of their breath struggling for air, the movement of listless legs. He could encounter the very character of all those who were sick before him. He could endure their moods: anger, joy, sadness. He knew their hesitancy, their deliberateness. He was experiencing the sensation of the

Western Indians who could smell camp fires that they were unable to see. That's how he got to sleep at night—putting his arms over his head and holding on to the metal bed-bars and feeling those invisible suffering souls before him. He could always tell who believed in God and who did not. He knew what part of the country they were from. There were as many cities and towns as philosophies. He knew what food they liked, what flowers they loved, whether they were fond of horses. He said holding on to those bars day after day made him understand human pain and human hope.

[*A beat.* CARL *slowly closes the window. Suddenly, the bulb over the bed begins to beep in red flashes.*]

MARILYN: Help me undress. Then you have to go . . . it's almost time. [*She gives him a short sweet kiss.* CARL *slowly begins to unbutton her dress. She is facing the audience. He helps her take off the dress as he stands in front of her so we can't see. He throws the dress to the side of the stage. She is standing naked. As* CARL *exits, she takes some pills she has hidden in a light fixture above the bed and she swallows all the pills from the bottle and lies down on the bed. After* CARL *exits, he stands by her closed door outside in the hall.* CARL *leans against the closed door and strums his guitar and talk-sings softly:*]

CARL: Marilyn,
  Marilyn,
  I'll never go so far
  from you
  that I won't see
  the same old stars
  and Venus, too
  as you.

  Marilyn,
  Marilyn,
  now my days are long,
  long,
  if I could sing with you
  I wouldn't need a song.

  Marilyn,

Marilyn,
I'll never go so far
from you
that I won't see
the same old sun
and moonbeams, too,
as you.

Marilyn,
Marilyn,
now my days are long,
long,
if I could sing with you
I wouldn't need a song.

[*A naval rope ladder falls down from above and clanks beside her window.* MARILYN *groans sluggishly her hand extended out toward the phone near her bed as the lights slowly fade.* CARL, *having finished his song, slowly exits from the hotel hallway.*]

END OF PLAY

John Ford Noonan

WHEN IT COMES EARLY

John Ford Noonan

WHEN IT COMES EARLY

JOHN FORD NOONAN

John Ford Noonan is a 1989 inductee into the French Society of Composers and Authors. He first came to prominence in 1969 with the highly acclaimed Lincoln Center production of The Year Boston Won the Pennant, starring Roy Scheider. It won Mr. Noonan an Obie, a Theatre World and a Pulitzer Prize nomination.

From 1972 to 1977 at Joe Papp's New York Shakespeare Festival, Noonan wrote *Older People* (a Drama Desk Award Winner), *Concerning the Effects of Trimethylchloride, Where Do We Go From Here?, All the Sad Protestants and Getting Through the Night*. In 1978 his play *The Club Champion's Widow*, with Maureen Stapleton, opened the premiere season of the Robert Lewis Acting Company.

In the 1980's he wrote *A Coupla White Chicks Sitting Around Talking*, which ran for more than 800 performances at the Astor Place Theatre, and *Some Men Need Help* (three months on Broadway). In 1987 Mr. Noonan's *Spanish Confusion, Mom Sells Twins For Two Beers, Green Mountain Fever* and *Recent Developments In Southern Connecticut* all ran simultaneously in Los Angeles (three of which won Drama-Logue Awards). In 1990, Mr. Noonan wrote his play *Talking Things Over With Chekhov* and also performed the male lead for six months at the Actor's Playhouse. In 1993, the WPA presented his play *Music From Down the Hill*. It was subsequently produced, under the direction of Dorothy Lyman, at the Odyssey Theater in Los Angeles.

Noonan has twice been nominated for an Emmy—in 1984 for an episode of *St. Elsewhere* called "The Women" (which he won) and in 1985 for the television adaptation of *Some Men Need Help*. On screen he has acted in such movies as *Brown Wolf; Next Stop, Greenwich Village; Heaven Help Us, Adventures in Babysitting*, and this past year he appeared in the hit movie *Flirting With Disaster*.

Mr. Noonan's proudest accomplishments to date are: 1) his children: Jesse Sage Noonan, Chris Noonan Howell, Olivia Noonan Howell, and Tracy Noonan Howell, and his secret and favorite fifth, Tom Noonan Nohilly; 2) his acclaim by *Rolling Stone* magazine as "the greatest white boogie dancer in the world"; 3) his being a founding member of the legendary punk band "Pinhead," as well as penning their anthem, *Kill Your Parents, Then We'll Talk*; 4) his being four consecutive times Junior Golf Champion at his home country club in Greenwich, Connecticut. He once shot a sixty-seven followed by an eighty-one; and 5) he loves sentences. His favorite utterance in his whole life was his mother's recent remark, "John, it's never too late to be normal."

CHARACTERS

J.C. WEBRING

MICKEY WEBRING

SETTING: *Bimney Park, Old Greenwich, Connecticut. A park bench USC. DSL a trash can. Neatly manicured grass and cement path winding through. On back of park bench and on front of trash can: PROPERTY OF THE TOWN OF GREENWICH, CONNECTICUT.*

TIME: *Early afternoon, the second week of May, just after 1 P.M.*

Lights up! MICKEY WEBRING *enters first. Early fifties, tall, blond, proud, she wears slacks, sport jacket, and blouse. She carries lunch basket. Puts down basket and crosses back to help husband* J.C. WEBRING. J.C. *is in his mid fifties, wearing large overcoat, gloves, and big floppy hat. He seems to have no hair. It has all been shaved off. He is tall and muscular and yet he moves tentatively and uncertainly.* MICKEY *offers a hand but* J.C. *pushes her away and "shushes" her over to the bench. She laughs and crosses back to the bench, sits, opens lunch basket, takes out red check table cloth and begins to lay out food: two hard-boiled eggs, two sandwiches in a wrapper, fruit in tinfoil and jug of orange-flavored ice tea. Next she takes out plastic forks, napkins, drinking cups, etc. Sets those out, looks up.* J.C. *has gotten half way to bench. She jumps up, her intention to help him but he waves her away again and "shushes" her back to her work.* J.C. *sits. She unfolds a napkin for* J.C. *only he grabs it and slaps it across his lap.* MICKEY *hands* J.C. *a hard-boiled egg. He begins to eat without cracking the shell.* MICKEY *grabs it back and peels it for him.* J.C. *eats egg.* MICKEY *peels own egg, begs us to eat, suddenly laughs.*

MICKEY: It's all changed so little. The pond's still there, so clean, pretty and pure. [*Pointing out over audience.*] The ducks, the swan, that weeping willow, and out there, the little boat house. In the winter they would enclose it, build a fire and all us girls'd help each other lace up. Boy could I skate!!

J.C.: You were a dandy.

MICKEY: What?

J.C.: Skating along. Flying by in your infamous outfit: white tights, short red skirt, red and white hand warmer, elf cap with the jingle bell on top.

MICKEY: Hold it! How do you—

J.C.: Oh, God! Look!!

MICKEY: Where?

J.C.: Freddy Di Stephano and Archie Manning are fighting over you again.

MICKEY: They were my first two. How do you—

J.C.: They're rolling in the snow. Cathy Nugent runs out onto the ice and grabs at you whizzing by. You scream to a stop. [*"Playing"* CATHY NUGENT.] "Mickey, they're fighting over you again. Do come stop them." [*"Playing"* MICKEY.] "Cathy, it's what I live for, my men killing each other over me."

MICKEY: That's exactly what I said. [*Quoting.*] "It's what I live for, my men killing each other over me."

J.C.: I know.

MICKEY: You weren't there.

J.C.: You told me.

MICKEY: When?

J.C.: The third night of our honeymoon. The Jug End Barn up in the Berkshires. January 8th, 1954. We were lying in bed. We heard shouting. We jumped up—looked out—skaters in the moonlight. It's when you told me. [*Laughing.*] Freddy Di Stephano and Archie Manning.

MICKEY: I don't remember telling you.

J.C.: I remember being told. [J.C. *takes* MICKEY'S *hand and kisses it, gently, fondly. Suddenly drops her hand and leaps to his feet.*] Oh God!

MICKEY: What's wrong now?

J.C.: There!

MICKEY: Where?

[*Pointing out over audience, counting something off in distance, whispering "One . . . Two . . . Three."*]

J.C.: The third bench past the big weeping willow?

MICKEY: Yes?

J.C.: That's where your father sat me down and read me the riot act.

MICKEY: J.C., this you're making up.

J.C.: You were away that weekend. Your college roommate Villette Kneeber.

MICKEY: She just got married again. Another dentist.

J.C.: Well, her brother Vincent had been killed on a motorcycle. I took you to the train. Villette lived in Scarsdale.

MICKEY: God, the things you remember!

J.C.: Your dad and I went for a walk. Through the village, up the hill by the railroad and then right over there.

MICKEY: Who spoke first?

J.C.: Who else.

MICKEY: Do his voice!

J.C.: [*"Imitating"* FATHER.] "Now listen here, pal. What are your plans for my gal?!!" [*"Playing"* SELF.] "I love her deeply. I love her totally. Sir, I'd like your permission to take Mickey's hand in marriage!" [*"Imitating"* FATHER.] "Son, does my Mickey ever scare you?"

MICKEY: He never said that!

J.C.: [*"Playing"* SELF.] "Sir, she scares the crap out of me."

MICKEY: You never said that!

J.C.: [*"Imitating"* FATHER.] "Me too!" [*"Playing"* SELF.] "Sometimes I get the feeling she'd kill to get what she wants." [*"Imitating"* FATHER] "Just like her Ma!"

MICKEY: I love it! I love it! More!! More!!!

J.C.: We laughed and laughed. He took my hand. God, what a grip! [*"Imitating"* FATHER.] "Son, what are your prospects?"

[*"Playing"* SELF.] "I'm going to make a million by the time I'm 35."

MICKEY: Which you did! You did, indeed!!

J.C.: "When I get into my 50s, I'm going to have a big, long black limousine with a full-time driver named Jocko. Your daughter and I are going to drive up here from our duplex on Park Avenue. We're going to get out of our big long black limousine and your gorgeous daughter and I, we're going to sit on one of these benches just like you and I are right now, Mr. McGriff."

MICKEY: And what did my father say?

J.C.: [*"Imitating"* FATHER.] "Son, I do believe you'll do it!"

MICKEY: Father was right. We're here. Our limo's right over there. Jocko's driving. We do anything we want. Go anywhere we want. There's nothing we're without. We lack very little. We're kind, open, warm and generous. Our children call regularly. We all get together for Christmas. Tom never did finish Yale and Callie's had an awful time with all those different husbands but we couldn't be prouder. We're looked up to. Respected. People are always asking us out. God-o-God, if only Freddy Di Stephano, Archie Manning and Cathy Nugent could see us now. [*Looks out over audience, sticks out tongue as though at old friends.*] Hey, you guys, look at who I ended up with!!! [*Puts arm around* J.C.] This man's a winner. This man's a champ. He's given me 26 years of sunshine and very few cloudy days. [*Waving to imaginary friends.*] Go ahead. Wave. Say "I'm J.C. I'm the great guy she ended up with!"

J.C.: There's no one there.

[MICKEY *takes* J.C.'S *hand and waves it for him. He pulls it away.*]

MICKEY: Boy, do I feel good. We're back. We're victorious. That's a big thing, to come back to Greenwich victorious. There's not much we've missed. We've missed very little.

J.C.: I miss getting here!

MICKEY: What?

J.C.: I look over at Jocko. [*Waving, yelling* O.S.] Hi, Jocko.

MICKEY: We won't be long, Jocko. [*Waving, yelling* O.S.] Isn't

Greenwich lovely? Say hello to the swan. Go as close as you like.

J.C.: And seeing Jocko I realize the last thing I remember is getting into the car back on Park Avenue. I don't remember the turnpike. The turn-off at Exit 5. Was I good along the way? Was I kind and caring?

MICKEY: Darling, you hugged me all the way. At exits you kissed me and screamed. [*"Imitating"* J.C.] "We're here, my lovey's hometown!!!!"

J.C.: Any swear words?

MICKEY: None.

J.C.: No four-letters?

MICKEY: Not a one.

J.C.: Oh God, that's good. I worry so much. I've been praying every night. [*Suddenly gets to knees, folds hands prayerfully.*] "Dear Lord God, no four-letter words and make these days easy on my gal."

MICKEY: J.C., back here, please.

J.C.: What?

MICKEY: You're on your knees.

[*He looks down. Startled to find himself on the ground. Reaches out, tests ground to make sure it's true.*]

J.C.: How did I get here?

MICKEY: Stand up.

J.C.: [*Standing up.*] I'm standing.

MICKEY: Sit down.

J.C.: [*Sitting.*] I'm sitting. [*Pause.* J.C. *seems to go away and come back.*] I'll bet you were dandy.

MICKEY: What?

J.C.: Skating along. Flying by in your infamous outfit: white tights, short red skirt, red and white handwarmer, elf cap with—

MICKEY: We already did my skating.

[*Pause.*]

J.C.: When do we eat?

MICKEY: Soon.

J.C.: I'm famished.

MICKEY: Here. [*She takes her sandwich out of the wrapper and hands it to* J.C.]

J.C.: I heard you make those calls last week.

MICKEY: I didn't make any calls last week. Every time I go near the phone, you scream and yell and foam all over.

J.C.: His name was Davis. Fucking Frank Davis. You made plans to take me up there a week from next Thursday. Fucking Frank Davis'll put me in with someone from Jersey who can't stop drooling. There'll be drool all over me. I'll never stop wiping. They'll run out of towels . . . but you, you won't run out of towels. Your new guy's a towel salesman. You'll be on your honeymoon cruise and you'll be on your honeymoon deck on your way to Bermuda, and this Martin guy, your new guy, your Martin Podlofsky from Wayne, New Jersey, well, he'll bend over to give you his honeymoon special . . . only the howl of me will come screaming across the water and it'll surround you. My scream'll say [J.C. *lets out this scream low, sad and very intense. It is the cry of a desperate baby.*] No words. Just a plea from behind my padded walls. You'll try to pretend it's the wind, Martin'll say [*"Imitating"* MARTIN.] "Isn't that the moon?" But no, no, no, that's J.C. Webring and his scream will never let you kiss. Yessir, if you can eat without me, there's no—

[MICKEY *suddenly stuffs half a sandwich into* J.C.'S *mouth. He eats it down—seems about to resume diatribe but instead laughs gaily, and flaps hands like a little boy.*]

J.C.: [*Cont'd.*] I love when you feed me.

[*He bites off half of the second half and won't take anymore.* MICKEY *tries to feed last bite but he resists.*]

J.C.: [*Cont'd.*] If you feed me the last bite nice, I'll kiss you real sweet twice.

[*She feeds him his last bite. He kisses her, one kiss on each cheek.*]

J.C.: [*Cont'd.*] Wipe me clean. I've got crumbs in my beard.

[*She pretends to wipe crumbs out of "imaginary" beard.*]

J.C.: [*Cont'd.*] Brush it out nice. Make it look full.

[*She pretends to brush it off, fluffing out "imaginary" beard so it'll look full. J.C. smiles, MICKEY, too. For a second he seems fine. As if out of nowhere, he begins loudly singing a song.*]

J.C.: [*Cont'd.*] When it comes early and you've still
        got most of your hair
        And your wife, she's dried up
        She's run out of care
        Who do you lean on?
        Where do you run?
        You're only 52
        But your life's all done.

[MICKEY *covers* J.C.'S *mouth with hand. Holds it angrily.*]

MICKEY: You going to be good? [J.C. *shakes head "yes."*] Promise?!

[J.C. *again shakes head "yes."* MICKEY *lets go of his mouth.* J.C. *is suddenly hungry again.*]

J.C.: So, when do we eat?

MICKEY: J.C., we just did that!!!

[*Pause—long silence.* J.C. *suddenly raises hands like he's catching the warmth of the sun.*]

J.C.: Warm.

MICKEY: What?

J.C.: The sun.

MICKEY: Very.

J.C.: It's smiling down.

MICKEY: Indeed.

J.C.: Can I have some?

MICKEY: Some what?

J.C.: Sun on my wound. [*Pause.*] Doctor Mischler said the more ultra-violet I get on it, the quicker it would heal.

MICKEY: What a lovely breeze. Feel.

J.C.: I want it all sealed tight. I don't want any more loss. That's what I keep thinking.

MICKEY: What a lovely swan. Look. What a lovely day. Smile.

J.C.: That after they finished in there, they didn't stitch it tight enough and that's why lots of little pieces and loose ends keep slipping out.

[MICKEY *cannot take it anymore. She starts to scream, only covers her mouth. As* J.C. *talks on, it becomes harder and harder not to scream.*]

J.C.: [*Cont'd.*] That's where my memories are sliding. Out the little slits that aren't closing up fast enough. If someone real soon doesn't—

[*The pressure of holding blows her hand away. She removes hat.* J.C.'S *head is shaved. A huge scar is on left side of his head back to front, each of 100 stitches clearly visible.*]

J.C.: How's it look?

MICKEY: Good.

J.C.: No oozing?

MICKEY: None.

J.C.: The double stitches in the front?

MICKEY: Beautiful.

J.C.: By my ear?

MICKEY: All dried up.

J.C.: Toward the back.

MICKEY: I just told you, everything's—

J.C.: No, no. Itch toward the back. I want something new, smooth, and different! Do me smooth! Do me slow!!

[MICKEY *begins to rub his wound. She is smooth and slow.*]

J.C.: [*Cont'd.*] Left!

[MICKEY *moves left, continues smooth and slow.* J.C. *moans.*]

J.C.: [*Cont'd.*] Back!!

[MICKEY *moves to back. Rubs.* J.C. *now moans much more loudly.*]

J.C.: [*Cont'd.*] Now toward the front. Yes! Yes!! Circular, like you're buffing...Oh, God!! Do double strokes and then blow little puffs of air in my ear.

[MICKEY *does double strokes and blows little puffs in* J.C.'S *ear. Moaning louder,* J.C. *suddenly grabs his groin—*MICKEY *slaps his hand away.*]

J.C.: [*Cont'd.*] Sorry.

[MICKEY *continues to blow and rub.* J.C. *is having a horrible time not grabbing his groin. He puts his hands every place but.*]

J.C.: [*Cont'd.*] Oh God! Oh God!! Rub and blow!! Rub and blow!!

[*Finally* J.C. *can't hold out. He grabs at his groin.* MICKEY *pulls hand away, resumes rubbing. Again* J.C. *grabs groin, again* MICKEY *pulls hands away.*]

MICKEY: If you're going to keep grabbing, I can't keep rubbing.

J.C.: It was your walk, you know. April 2, 1953. I was teeing off at Innis Arden. I have a yellow tee. I set my #3 Titleist down. Take a waggle, and see you walk. Your walk hooked me. Done there. Stop rubbing and scratch, scratch all the way up front.

[MICKEY *does as* J.C. *asks. She stops rubbing, and scratches in front of the wound.*]

J.C.: [*Cont'd.*] Harder, harder!!.

[*She rubs harder, he is aroused. Loud, screaming moan.*]

J.C.: [*Cont'd.*] I remember the first time I was in you. Boy, was I warm and safe. The only other time I ever felt as warm and safe was with a pitching wedge and I had 40 or 50 yards left to the green.

MICKEY: We never did it before the honeymoon.

J.C.: Three times.

MICKEY: Not once.

J.C.: The first time was in the car by the eleventh green at Tamarack up in back Greenwich!

MICKEY: I was pure. I earned my white organdie and silk.

J.C.: The second time—

MICKEY: Stop!

J.C.: Was after your dad took us out to dinner at Mamero's over on Steamboat Road, and he fell asleep watching a TV movie. Great. Real fingernails. Deep—deep—deep.

MICKEY: Will you stop talking if I dig deep? I love when you're quiet. When you're quiet, I can stay with what I'm doing. When you're quiet, I can play you like an instrument. I hate talk. I don't mind mild moaning, but the constant patter, and the wild screams, well, they just make me want to vomit. I wish we could've . . . wish we—

J.C.: Why'd you stop?

[*She kisses* J.C.'S *head.*]

J.C.: [*Cont'd.*] You're always stopping. I was so close. I need you! I fucking goddamn need you. I can never do it by myself. I fucking require your rubs, your blows, and your fucking deep, deep scratches. [*Lets out scream.*] Look, the more I rub, the itchier it gets. I'm not a good rubber. I'm not a qualified scratcher.

[*Stops scratching, She looks away, not taking gloves.*]

J.C.: [*Cont'd.*] If you don't finish me, I'll read you my list.

MICKEY: There's no list.

J.C.: It's of all the women I've messed with when you weren't looking.

MICKEY: Don't lie. I'm your only!!

J.C.: March 22, 1962—Marge McClure in the parking lot outside the club during the Spring Solstice Dance. [MICKEY *covers ears.*] Please do me! Please finish me off!

[*He grabs* MICKEY'S *hands to free her ears to listen, but she puts them back. He tries again, she puts them back again.*]

J.C.: [*Cont'd.*] April 3, 13, 21, 28 plus . . . May 8, 9 and 10, 1966. You were in the hospital for a D-and-C, right, well, I did it all those times with this waitress from up at Adams Corner.

MICKEY: No, no, no, I'm your only!!!

J.C.: October 7, 1971 with ... and then November 1974 ... no, 1975 with ... and, of course, for-three straight summers, 81 through 83 with ... Always cutting me off. Always leaving me short. Never there when I ache!! Always turning away when I bleed!!

[*He punches at his groin over and over like it was the most unreliable friend a man could possibly have.*]

Fuck! Piss! Shit! Bleed! Ache! Die!!
Fuck! Piss! Shit! Bleed! Ache! Die!!
Fuck! Piss! Shit! Bleed! Ache! Die!!

[*He stops. He goes through still another change. As dark as he was, he now is light and bright and full of smiles. He takes her hands away from her ears. Suddenly he grabs at the top of his head as though some minor miracle had transpired.*] The itching's gone and you did it. [*Picks up hat and puts it on. Poses proudly.*] I look normal. I look nice. I can pass another rich guy keeping it simple!

[MICKEY *tries to smile but she begins to cry. She sobs.* J.C. *smiles broadly.*]

J.C.: [*Cont'd.*] Finally I'm needed.

MICKEY: Are you?

J.C.: You're crying.

MICKEY: [*Touching eyes.*] Am I?

J.C.: Can I kiss them off?

MICKEY: Gently. One at a time.

[J.C. *reaches and begins kissing tears off* MICKEY'S *face. She's ecstatic. Suddenly* J.C. *does a slurping sound and licks, swallows and wipes away a wide bunch at once.*]

MICKEY: [*Cont'd.*] I wish you'd been gentler. I wish you'd studied the Europeans. They never rush. Never skip steps. Never get ahead!

[*Now* MICKEY *bursts into a river of tears. Sobs that come from a deep place. She suddenly stops sobbing and pushes* J.C. *away.*]

MICKEY: [*Cont'd.*] I'm crying. I need care. I need lips. What happened to your lips? Where's your care?!

J.C.: Look!

[J.C. *points off in direction behind bench.* MICKEY *looks around, finally sees where* J.C.'S *pointing.*]

MICKEY: Why's Jocko waving? Why does he keep pointing to his wrist?

J.C.: Eddy Joe Tammany's due any minute.

MICKEY: Tom's boyhood friend. The short little thing with a cowlick who always passed Tom the ball. Hold it! Why's he—

J.C.: He's doing the driving.

MICKEY: Where to?

J.C.: Here's your ticket.

[*From breast pocket* J.C. *removes AA plane ticket. He hands it to* MICKEY.]

MICKEY: Champagne First Class to San Francisco! God, we haven't been to Frisco—

J.C.: San Francisco!!

MICKEY: San Francisco since...since Tom was 17. He'd led the Southern Connecticut Catholic league in scoring and rebounding both.

J.C.: He was taller than everyone. What happened at Yale?

MICKEY: And Callie, she was just starting—[*Suddenly stops.*] Hold it! Where's your ticket?

[J.C. *pulls road map of U.S. out of pocket and spreads it out on bench. He is like a little kid.*]

J.C.: Red is our route. Blue are the places we stay over. Every night. I'll be calling you from a blue. Look—Wheeling, West Virginia—Springfield, Illinois—Lander, Wyoming. See, 13 days, 13 stops, 13 calls. "It's Wyoming, Mickey, but boy do I miss you!"

MICKEY: What about the three big green circles?

J.C.: Those are the two-day layovers to play golf. Oakmont,

Pittsburgh. Cherry Hills, Denver and last but not least, Pebble Beach. Thirteen days from now I'll be at Pebble Beach. I'll be standing on the sixth tee at Pebble looking down the fairway of this incredible 5-par that's surrounded by cliffs and ocean and back here you'll be at JFK boarding American flight #1 to come join me. I smash my drive, your 747 rockets into the air. We're both airborne. We're both looking forward to a reunion. A reunion? Why? 'Cause we've had the courage to take a break. A pause—a res ... res ...

MICKEY: Respite!

J.C.: You've always known more words. See, lately, we've been really—no, not we! Me!! I've been worse than ever—oh, God!

MICKEY: What?

J.C.: The sun's back on. [*Takes off hat. Again the "incredible scar."*] In the morning when I first look at you ... well ... I just want ... I mean, you look tired. Awful. Defeated. Beaten. I lock myself in the bathroom with my golf books, go practice my putting in my attic, take a walk down by the water. It doesn't matter what, and I cry. Cry, I mean it. I slump over and real tears flow. Why? I've made you old. I've robbed your beauty. But, Mickey, 13 days and you'll get a lot of it back. Now, I know how scary it is for you to—

MICKEY: What hotel?

J.C.: Come again?

MICKEY: In San Francisco.

J.C.: You mean you'll—

MICKEY: Which hotel, J.C., is it the Mark Hopkins?

J.C.: Jocko made the reservations. Check with him on the way home.

[MICKEY *gets up and starts to walk off. She is smiling hugely.*]

MICKEY: Good luck!

J.C.: Aren't you even going to—

MICKEY: See you in 13 days!

J.C.: But don't you want to—

[MICKEY *exits toward* JOCKO *and the waiting limousine.* J.C. *looks around nervously. Gets to feet—waves like a nervous diver about to attempt his last dive.*]

J.C.: [*Cont'd.*] Good-bye, Greenwich! Good luck, Connecticut!! [J.C. *starts toward pond a.k.a. the audience. Suddenly he is aware that his head is uncovered. He goes back to bench and puts on hat. He stands there several seconds. Addresses world around him.*] Good-bye, trees, bushes and birds and all other valued and living things.

[*He suddenly charges toward pond. Out of nowhere* MICKEY *comes on and tackles* J.C. *to the ground. He struggles to get away but* MICKEY *will not let go.* J.C. *screams and yells,* MICKEY *laughs.*]

MICKEY: You almost had me fooled. The hotel reservations gave you away.

J.C.: Let me go.

MICKEY: No, no, no.

J.C.: Let me jump in. Let me go under. Let me dive in and go directly to the bottom. I want to lie on my back. Count the ducks, open my mouth, and let the water all in. I want to—want to ... [*Pause.*] I can't anymore—I can't—I can't.

MICKEY: Can't what!!

J.C.: I can't get in the car on Park Avenue, and wake up here. I can't come to anymore, and see your eyes all scared and hurt. I can't—

[*He once more tries to break away and jump into the pond, but* MICKEY *holds him back.*]

J.C.: [*Cont'd.*] Every morning when I wake up, I tell myself, "J.C., don't go away today. Stay here, stay in the now!" But somehow, I keep slipping away, and ... and the harder I try not to, the more it comes.

MICKEY: J.C.?

J.C.: When I go away, am I still me? Do I talk the same? Do I kiss different? I can't stand the not-knowing!

MICKEY: Your not-knowing's all over!

[*She hands him present-wrapped package. He slowly opens it. It is a small cassette recorder. For a second he's baffled, but then he gets it. He claps his hands like a little boy.*]

J.C.: Every time I go away?

MICKEY: I'll press RECORD.

J.C.: And then when I come back?

MICKEY: I'll press STOP!

J.C.: Then you'll press REWIND.

MICKEY: And together we'll listen to where you've been. It'll all be different for me, hearing it not alone. I can't stand it alone. I hate things by myself.

J.C.: Why didn't I think of it first?

MICKEY: When things get bad, I see clear.

[*They laugh together.*]

J.C.: And, you're always ahead of me. You pretend like you're behind but, Mickey, thank God for the things you think of. Wow, the places you go—wow, I'm glad you're here! [*Suddenly* J.C. *freezes. A whole new mood comes over him.*] Please press RECORD.

[MICKEY *presses PLAY.* J.C. *looks around as if he just woke up. Takes* MICKEY'S *hand. She smiles. He smiles confusedly.*]

MICKEY: Are you O.K.?

J.C.: Who are you?

[*SLOW FADE*]

END OF PLAY

William Seebring

THE ORIGINAL LAST WISH BABY

WILLIAM SEEBRING

William Seebring grew up in rural Ohio. After leaving home for a well-paying factory job which did not suit him, Seebring drove a 1965 Pontiac LeSabre to Brooklyn where he taught himself the basics of structural and anatomical drawing. Adopting the pseudonym, Douglas Michael, Seebring published a series of underground comic books as well as an illustrated full-color travel guide to fictitious lands that were published, strangely enough, by a magazine catering to singles.

In 1986, Seebring returned to Ohio and bought a Honda Accord. Four years later, he moved to upstate New York with his wife and their dog where he began adapting his comics to stage plays while maintaining one of the finest cars ever assembled in North America. Under his assumed name, Seebring has dabbled in too many pursuits to mention including literary agent and country and western songwriter.

His only other completed plays to date are *The Geldings*, a western spoof about cowboys who have no genitals and *Das Wolfkin*, a darkly comic fairy tale written in an invented language.

CHARACTERS

There are as many as forty characters including thirty-seven speaking parts; however, the play can be performed with as few as five actors. A suggested breakdown of parts are divided as follows:

NARRATOR   male or female

ACTOR #1   male: Executive, Specialist #1, Customer #1, Crown-Features-Marketeer, Newsboy, Phoney-Last-Wish-Baby, Diner, Right-To-Extended-Lifer #2

ACTOR #2   female: Spokesmodel, Specialist #3, Welda Mae Forms, Network-Exec #3, Waitress, Guatemalan woman, Maitre d', Pundit #3, Right-To-Extended-Lifer #1, Pollster

ACTOR #3   male: Doctor, Man, Specialist #2, Network-Exec #2, Customer #2, Crown-Features-Pitchman, Lawyer, Daryl Wayne Trebleau, Pundit #2, Surgeon, Preacher, Politician #2

ACTOR #4   female: Nurse, Assistant, Ms. Kornfeld, Network Exec #1, Clara Collins, Crown-Features-Exec, Judge, Pundit #1, Politician #1

SETS: *Aside from a podium, the action of the play is best staged with pools of lighting and minor propping.*

Before rise, we hear tha-dump, tha-dump—the steady, rhythmic beat of a human heart. As this beat grows in base and intensity, a slide is projected. The slide is of a graphic of THE LAST WISH BABY. *As the beat slowly fades,* LIGHTS *come up on the narrator standing at a podium at far stage-right.*

NARRATOR: *The Original Last Wish Baby*, as researched, recorded and revised by William Seebring.

[*A* SLIDE *graphic of Cleveland, Ohio.*]

Cleveland, Ohio. Or, more specifically, the third-floor ma-

ternity room of the Holy Name Hospital on Cleveland's im-
poverished west-side where, at precisely seven-oh-one P.M.—

[SLIDE *graphic of an inner city hospital. We hear a crying baby.*]

A baby was born. Not just any baby, but the infamous, original, Last Wish Baby. The baby born without a heart.

[*Lights up on a* DOCTOR *and* NURSE *peering in on an infant's crib.*]

DOCTOR: No heart? Good Heavens, that's impossible.

NURSE: Check for yourself, Doctor.

[*The* DOCTOR *extends his stethoscope into the crib.*]

DOCTOR: Nothing, no pulse. Not a sound. And yet, this baby
clearly mimics life. A freak.

NURSE: [*Softly.*] No. A miracle.

DOCTOR: What's that?

NURSE: A miracle . . . the baby is a miracle.

DOCTOR: A miracle? This is Cleveland. It'll be a miracle if the
mother's insured.

[*Lights down on the maternity ward.*]

NARRATOR: Not only were the baby's parents uninsured, the identity of the baby's father was unknown. However, the birth
mother's name was given as Welda Mae Forms, a thirty-one-
year-old unemployed cosmetologist.

[SLIDE *graphic of* WELDA MAE FORMS.]

At the time, little else was known about Ms. Forms but
word of her remarkable progeny spread quickly from the maternity ward to the scrub rooms to the hospital's administrative
offices where a larger picture began to emerge.

[*Lights up on the Hospital's Administrative* EXECUTIVE *and his*
ASSISTANT.]

EXECUTIVE: A baby born without a heart? Sounds awful. Sounds
really awful.

ASSISTANT: Maybe not as bad as you think.

EXECUTIVE: C'mon Chet, how the hell do ya' window dress a missing heart? God knows we've had our share of high-risk deliveries here at Holy Name—little baby heads get smushed, tiny baby limbs get...it's messy, terrible, makes me shudder. But delivering a baby and not the heart—good God! [*Beat.*] What's our liability on something like that?

ASSISTANT: Well here's the thing, sir...the baby is alive.

EXECUTIVE: Alive? Without a heart? But that's, that's—

ASSISTANT: Impossible? Yes. Nevertheless, it's true.

EXECUTIVE: What—some kind of weird, auto-neuron tremors? Good God, is that what passes for life these days?

ASSISTANT: The baby is fully functioning, quite spirited and has a healthy appetite I might add.

EXECUTIVE: But for how long? An hour, maybe two?

ASSISTANT: Who can say? But, even if the baby were to, God forbid...Its short life could, with the right spin, be played out as the most incredible P.R. story of our time. What's more, the timing couldn't have been more...fortuitous...sir.

EXECUTIVE: What, the Sprag/Klockenheim takeover?

ASSISTANT: Precisely the kind of thing that could triple our name factor overnight. A miracle...and it happened here, in our hospital, under the care and guidance of our health care professionals. Think of it sir, *Holy Name, the get-well place where miracles happen.*

EXECUTIVE: *The get-well place where miracles happen*...Now there's a ball with some bounce to it! Call Delores Childs at Channel Five. If we can dazzle her, there's a good chance we could make the six o'clock news!

ASSISTANT: She's on her way, sir.

EXECUTIVE: Good boy. Oh, one other thing...the heart? Did anyone ever find the heart?

ASSISTANT: No. Actually, as far anyone knows, there never was a heart.

[*Lights down on the administrative offices.*]

NARRATOR: In point of fact, there was a heart. However, through one of those unfathomable anomalies which defy all logic, yet govern most things, the heart was delivered separately by a surprised New Jersey woman on her way home from the store.

[*Lights up on* MS. SYDNEY KORNFELD, *as she crosses the stage carrying a Nordstrom's bag. She is walking past a* MAN *when something like a beef-steak tomato falls from her skirt. The man regards it.* MS. KORNFELD *continues on, unmindful.*]

MAN: Yo, Miss...Ma'am! You dropped something.

[MS. KORNFELD *stops, turns and looks back.*]

MS. KORNFELD: Oh-my-god, what is it!

[*The sound of a thumping heart is heard as lights dim on* MS. KORNFELD *as she bends to retrieve the heart.*]

NARRATOR: That something would later be determined to be the baby's heart. However, at that particular moment, the New Jersey woman, later identified as Ms. Sydney Kornfeld, and who would soon become known as "The Baby Heart Mom," was not yet aware of the miracle baby story unfolding in Cleveland.

[SLIDE *of a graphic reading: THE FOLLOWING IS SPONSORED BY LIBBY'S AND THE TUPPERWARE CORPORATION. Lights up as a* DEMONSTRATOR *enters carrying a tupperware container, a beef-steak tomato, and a can of peaches.*]

NARRATOR: As for Ms. Kornfeld, she fortuitously retrieved the baby heart and returned immediately to her home in Paramus where, as the demonstrator shall faithfully recreate, she placed the pulsating vital organ into a clear, air-tight, number-seven tupperware container, which she then filled with a high-fructose, low sodium, heavy-syrup drained from a can of Libby's yellow-cling sliced peaches. After burping for a tight seal, Ms. Kornfeld placed the container in the crisper drawer of her refrigerator where, according to product designers, the heart could have been stored indefinitely and would remain every bit as fresh and vigorous as the moment she delivered it.

[*Lights down as the* DEMONSTRATOR *exits.*]

NARRATOR: [*Cont'd.*] Meanwhile, back in Cleveland, Ohio, ever more adept medical specialists were brought in to examine the so-called miracle baby.

[*Lights up on the maternity ward as three medical* SPECIALISTS *look into a crib and we hear a giggling baby.*]

SPECIALIST #1: Coo-chee-coo-chee-cooo.

SPECIALIST #2: No pulse. No pressure. This baby doesn't have a heart.

SPECIALIST #3: I'll be damned.

SPECIALIST #2: And yet... this baby is alive.

[*The Hospital's Executive* ASSISTANT *enters. He appears agitated.*]

ASSISTANT: Doctors, please, the press conference. They're waiting.

[*Lights down on the maternity ward. Lights up as the* THREE SPE-CIALISTS *and the* ASSISTANT *take their places at a table facing the audience. The table skirt advertises the Holy Name Hospital and its new slogan. The* NARRATOR *assumes the role of reporter.*]

ASSISTANT: [*Cont'd.*] Questions for the doctors?

NARRATOR: Yes. A living baby without a heart? How is this possible?

SPECIALIST #2: Technically, it's not.

SPECIALIST #1: The baby should be dead.

SPECIALIST #3: In fact, the baby could die any minute.

ASSISTANT: It's a miracle is what it is! And it happened right here in our—

NARRATOR: What about the baby's mom?

ASSISTANT: What about her?

NARRATOR: I'd like to hear her side of the story. I'd like to ask her a few questions.

ASSISTANT: [*Horrified.*] What, you mean talk with her?

NARRATOR: Why not?

ASSISTANT: No reason, uh, well, actually—that's impossible. I'm sorry, we're just, she's just—she's in recovery right now.

[*Lights down on the Press Conference.*]

NARRATOR: In fact, Welda Mae Forms was not in recovery. The so-called Baby Mom was not only alert and well-rested, she was, much to the dismay of hospital staffers, quite lucid and most out-spoken.

[*Lights up on* WELDA MAE FORMS, *in bed and under restraint. The* EXECUTIVE *and his* ASSISTANT *hover.*]

WELDA MAE FORMS: What's with the god-damned seat belts! And where's my kid! I come into this dump to pop off another slug, which is the last thing I need, and you-all got me tied down so I can't even see Oprah—big as she is!

EXECUTIVE: Ms. Forms, please, please calm down. There's something we have to tell you.

WELDA MAE FORMS: What, is my baby dead, or deformed, or some damn thing?

ASSISTANT: Uh, well, Miss Forms, actually, it's more than that.

WELDA MAE FORMS: Huh? Was that a hard question or are you really as stupid as you look? Listen here lap-dog, tell your fat ass boss that as far as I'm concerned I could care less if the little maggot's dead or mutated—hell, I never wanted one tuh begin with. Tried to have it flushed out in one of them clinics but them damn bible-thumpers chased me away and—

EXECUTIVE: [*Aghast.*] You were going to...! Cleveland's miracle baby...?

WELDA MAE FORMS: So, I figured I'd drown the slug in booze. Well, did it work or what?

EXECUTIVE: Ms. Forms, you've got to understand...you've made medical history here today.

WELDA MAE FORMS: Hee-doggie! Do tell, the little maggot's got three heads? Two weenies? Five titties? What? What?!

ASSISTANT: This is insane. We can't put that before the public. She'll ruin everything!

[*Lights down on* WELDA MAE'S *hospital room.*]

NARRATOR: Meanwhile, at that very moment, the afternoon press conference was being fed via satellite to network studios in New York.

[*Lights up on a roomful of* NETWORK EXECS *watching a monitor.*]

NETWORK EXEC #1: Can this be for real, a baby without a heart?!

NETWORK EXEC #2: The affiliate swears it's true.

NETWORK EXEC #3: Regardless, it's too late to break tonight.

NETWORK EXEC #1: Are you nuts! This stuff goes on immediately.

NETWORK EXEC #3: But, but we're airing a live feed from the White House!

NETWORK EXEC #2: Who cares? A baby without a heart! Now that's news!

[LIGHTS *down on the* NETWORK EXECS.]

NARRATOR: And news it was. Within the hour, satellite-beaming reporters from around the world had descended on Cleveland like the plague and every last one of them wanted one thing—a baby mom exclusive. Hospital officials acted with both haste and prudence.

[*Lights up on* WELDA MAE'S *hospital room.* WELDA *is still under restraint.* CLARA COLLINS, *a stylishly dressed woman, enters.*]

WELDA MAE FORMS: Who are you? What do ya' want?

CLARA COLLINS: Hello, Ms. Forms. My name is Clara Collins, I've been hired to be your image consultant.

WELDA MAE FORMS: Oh yeah? Well, does that mean you can reach up there and change the channel on the god-damned TV? Because that's all I've been trying to get from the lazy turds in white that run around here all day. And do they listen? Hell, no. Channel five—wrestling. You get me Bone-Crusher on the tube and lay a six-pack of Huedey Gold right here 'side my pillow and I'll be so happy I could pee green.

CLARA COLLINS: Well, I see I have my work cut out for me.

[*Lights down on* WELDA'S *room.*]

NARRATOR: Clara Collins proved she was worth every penny of her hefty fee. In short order, Ms. Welda Mae Forms was polished, enlightened and coiffured. At long last, cameras were admitted into her room and a nation known for its thirst of spectacle, tuned in.

[*Lights up on* WELDA'S *room. She is no longer restrained and her appearance has been transformed. Religious music is piped in and a* SLIDE *is projected of babies with angel wings and angel halos.*]

WELDA MAE FORMS: [*Her hands folded as if in prayer.*] With the Lord's help, my precious, precious baby will live. Of course, I can't begin to thank all you wonderful little people out there who have kept me and my baby in your thoughts and prayers. Bless you. Bless you all.

[*Lights down on* WELDA'S *room.*]

NARRATOR: With that one newsbit, the groundswell of public emotion became unquenchable. Overnight, Cleveland's miracle tot became America's most adored critical-list baby. There were news conferences every morning and afternoon and updates on the baby's condition flashed every hour on the hour, but it wasn't enough. Americans not only wanted to know more, they wanted to know what more they could do . . .

[*Lights up on a lunch-counter somewhere deep in rural America.*]

WAITRESS: And they say that baby could die any moment.

CUSTOMER #1: Hate to see that baby die and me not knowing if they was something I coulda' done.

CUSTOMER #2: By Gawd, I'd give my left nut for that sweet, little innocent lamb.

WAITRESS: Hell, Ross, baby don't need a go-nad. That baby needs a heart!

CUSTOMER #2: Can't give baby my heart. But I'd give that baby anything else. Anything a'tall.

CUSTOMER #1: Say, you know I hear baby likes to watch big time wrestling! What say we call the hospital and see if we could buy that baby a brand new color TV! Now wouldn't that make us all feel a whole sight better?

[*Lights down on the lunch counter.*]

NARRATOR: Calls from like-minded Americans jammed the hospital's switch-board. It was reported that in a single, twenty-four hour period more than twenty thousand color TV's were bought and delivered. Corporate America stood up and took note. Syndicate giant, GLAM ENTERTAINMENT, culled their best minds and put forward a most alluring concept.

[SLIDE *Graphic of Glam Entertainment logo. Lights up on an executive board meeting.*]

GLAM ENTERTAINMENT PITCHMAN: Every night we'll feature the baby mom, what's her name—

GLAM ENTERTAINMENT MARKETEER: Welda Mae Forms.

GLAM ENTERTAINMENT EXEC: Welda Mae? Where do you gotta' go to get a name like that?

GLAM ENTERTAINMENT MARKETEER: Welda, last stop before Zelda.

GLAM ENTERTAINMENT PITCHMAN: Whatever, we get her and we call it, "The Last Wish Baby Show." See, every night mom stands in front of the camera holding little baby no-heart in her arms like this and she's pouting 'cause the doc's are telling her how the baby's supposed to die any minute but, and here's the kicker, before baby goes, baby's made this one last wish . . . get it? Baby's last wish—Last Wish Baby!

[*Eyes widen with delight. Lights down on the meeting.*]

NARRATOR: A deal was proffered and quickly struck with Ms. Forms and her people. That very night, "The Last Wish Baby Show" blew out the ratings board with a whopping 75 share. Even more notable, the show's seamless tie-in with corporate sponsors set an industry standard.

[SLIDE *graphic of "The Last Wish Baby Show." Lights up on* WELDA'S *hospital room. A TV camera crew crowd* WELDA *as she clutches a cloth-wrapped bundle in her arms.*]

WELDA MAE FORMS: Poor, poor baby. Baby doesn't have a heart. Doctors say baby might have to leave us all for Heaven any minute now.

[*We hear the baby cry.*]

WELDA MAE FORMS: [*Cont'd.*] What's that Baby ... ? [*After leaning in to the baby,* WELDA *returns her gaze to the cameras.*] Awww. Baby wishes some nice person out there would buy us a uh ... a Sony XRK-35 Digital Game System.

NARRATOR: [*In an announcer's voice.*] That's right folks, the Sony game system could be Baby's Last Wish. Poor Baby. So open up that heart God so kindly gave you and call the 1-800 number you see now on your screen.

[SLIDE *of the 1-800 number. Lights down on "The Last Wish Baby Show." Lights up on* MS. KORNFELD'S *kitchen where a* GUATE-MALAN CLEANING WOMAN *removes a tupperware container and pops it open.*]

NARRATOR: [*Cont'd.*] Meanwhile, in a certain kitchen in Paramus, New Jersey, a certain Guatemalan cleaning woman was wiping down a certain refrigerator when she made an unusual discovery.

GUATEMALAN WOMAN: Eeeeee! Mios Dios! Eeeee!

[MS. KORNFELD *enters.*]

MS. KORNFELD: What? Que? Que esta? What the hell is it?

GUATEMALAN WOMAN: Esta la corazón de la nino con last wish!

MS. KORNFELD: What? What are you talking about?

GUATEMALAN WOMAN: Nino! Nino con last wish! Nino con last wish!

MS. KORNFELD: Baby? You mean that baby? That Last Wish Baby? The one on TV? Give me that! [*Studies the heart for a moment.*] Oh-my-God, it's alive! I have the baby heart! What should I do? What should I do?

GUATEMALAN WOMAN: Llama de medico! Pronto! Pronto!

MS. KORNFELD: Call a doctor?! Are you crazy? This is big, really big! I'm calling Howard Stern!

[MS. KORNFELD *reaches for the phone. Lights down.*]

NARRATOR: Ms. Kornfeld's call to the popular radio shock jock was quickly put through and she not only revealed that she possessed what she believed was the Last Wish Baby's Heart, listeners also learned her cup size and that she enjoyed lesbian sex while a sophomore at Harley Dickerson University.

[SLIDE *graphic of a woman's bra.* SLIDE *graphic of two campus co-eds.*]

Meanwhile, word of the whereabouts of the newly discovered baby heart spread fast and a race, of sorts, was on. EMS crews were first on the scene but no sooner had they readied the baby heart for shipment to Cleveland when ... the lawyers arrived.

[*Lights up on a* LAWYER *waving a writ.*]

LAWYER: Halt! Court order!

[*Lights down on the* LAWYER.]

NARRATOR: Motions were made. Injunctions issued. Larger questions loomed. The battle for custody of the Last Wish Baby had begun.

[*We hear the thumping heart.* SLIDE *graphic of the baby heart.*]

The hearing to determine the rightful custodial parents of The Last Wish Baby had barely opened when legal fees threatened to exceed even Ms. Welda Mae Forms' recently fatted purse-strings. However, with the baby show still posting record ratings, Ms. Forms saw fit to make full use of her forum.

[*Lights up on "The Last Wish Baby Show" set.* SLIDE *graphic of the show's logo.*]

WELDA MAE FORMS: [*Angelic.*] Poor, poor precious baby. Baby doesn't have a heart...know why? Hmmm? [*Bitter.*] 'Cause some East Coast floozy has got it and won't hand it over unless I give her half a' baby's royalties on the—

[*The baby cries.* WELDA *looks down.*]

WELDA MAE FORMS: [*Cont'd.*] Yeah, what is it? [*A beat to compose herself.*] Awww, but of course, baby. [WELDA *looks up again and composes herself.*] Baby wishes there was some nice, pro-bono law firm out there who would take Baby's rightful mother's custody case, and when that was all settled, and a certain individual from a certain so-called Garden-State was financially ruined, that same nice law firm might just be retained to negotiate with those shysters at Glum Entertainment for a more favorable contract...idn't that what baby wants? Yes, baby's so sweet. I just hope and pray this won't be baby's last wish.

[WELDA *smiles sweetly as lights darken on "The Last Wish Baby Show."*]

NARRATOR: But, no sooner had Welda Mae and her people retained new legal counsel than a shocking courtroom revelation hit the newsstands.

[*Lights up on a* NEWSBOY *hawking his papers.*]

NEWSBOY: Read all about it! "Last Wish Baby Show" Hoax! Read all about it!

[*Lights down on the* NEWSBOY.]

NARRATOR: Unsealed court documents alleged that the "Last Wish Baby Show" Baby was not the real Last Wish Baby, the baby born without a heart, but rather, a sixteen-year-old unemployed actor with a glandular condition. Americans shuddered. Did this mean the Original Last Wish Baby was dead? Or, Heaven forbid, was there even an original Last Wish Baby in the first place? Congressional spouses convened a hearing and demanded answers.

[SLIDE *graphic of congressional spouses. Lights up on a hearing room.* WELDA MAE, *the Hospital's Executive* ASSISTANT *and the* PHONY LAST WISH BABY *are seated together under a glaring light. The* NARRATOR *serves as inquisitor.*]

NARRATOR: [*Cont'd.*] Come forward. State your full name and occupation for the record, please.

PHONY LAST WISH BABY: Look pal, you can't nail this one on me! I'm not even Equity! The only reason I signed on to this sham was 'cause the Lady there got me tanked-up, then threatened to put my nuts in the grinder if I didn't—

WELDA MAE FORMS: Shut your trap you little—

PHONY LAST WISH BABY: Who are you calling little!? The only

thing little around here is your heart! You wanna' know why her kid's got no heart? I'll tell ya' why—

WELDA MAE FORMS: How dare you! And you said you loved me!

ASSISTANT: Stop it! Okay, look, it was all my fault. I agreed to pull the baby from the show and I was the one who okayed it when the Forms woman wanted to hire the little guy. But I only went along with it 'cause the doctors insisted on keeping the baby in intensive care. That's the God's-honest truth. There really is a Last Wish Baby, there really is a baby without a heart! I can prove it! I swear to God, I can prove it!

[*Lights down on the hearing room.*]

NARRATOR: Needless to say, Americans were skeptical and demanded that proof. Thus, the following night, "The Last Wish Baby Show" aired live from the Holy Name Hospital's pediatric intensive care unit. Viewers held their breath as the Baby Mom ushered the cameras toward the swinging doors which led to Baby's chamber.

[SLIDE *graphic of the "Last Wish Baby Show." Lights up on a hospital corridor.* WELDA MAE *and the* ASSISTANT *are wearing scrubs.* WELDA MAE *motions for the cameraman to follow her through a pair of doors.*]

WELDA MAE FORMS: Shhhh. Be quiet. This way, please.

[*A man* DARYL WAYNE TREBLEU *pushes by the* ASSISTANT *toward* WELDA.]

ASSISTANT: Watch it, he's got a gun!

[*Suddenly, the stage goes black. Four gunshots are heard and we see a series of quick* SLIDES *projecting images of chaos. The screen fills with the Emergency Broadcast test image and an accompanying high-pitched hum. This hum fades and the lights come up on the* NARRATOR.]

NARRATOR: Four shots, each one following its own fatal trajectory, were fired into the torso and cranial cavity of the woman most Americans knew only as the Last Wish Baby Mom.

[SLIDE *graphic of a "mug-shot" of* DARYL WAYNE TREBLEU.]

The assailant was identified as Daryl Wayne Trebleu, a slope-shouldered, itinerant floral designer from nearby Loraine, Ohio, and, purportedly, the man many believed to be the Last Wish Baby Dad.

[*Lights up on* DARYL WAYNE TREBLEU *standing solemnly.*]

Daryl Wayne Trebleu never uttered a single word in his own defense. Rather, he expressed himself through artfully-designed floral arrangements.

[SLIDE *graphic of* DARYL'S *bouquet.*]

Mr. Trebleu's "Not competent to stand trial bouquet" was a lovely and eloquent display of mums, gladiolus, and forty-four magnum shell casings set in a handsome earthenware bowl. Meanwhile, in another court in another state, the judge in the custody hearing for the Last Wish Baby had reached a verdict.

[*Lights down on* DARYL WAYNE TREBLEU. *Lights up on a* JUDGE *behind his bench.*]

JUDGE: As per the dictates of the honorable State of New Jersey, court of Domestic Relations, I, Judge Maliss T. Ward Nunn, have found as follows: Said infant, here-in-and-ever-after known as, "The Original Last Wish Baby," shall be granted ward status of this court, and thereby ordered to be joined immediately with heart. So be it, so help us God.

[*The* JUDGE *pounds his gavel. Lights fade on his courtroom.* SLIDE *graphics of close-in shots of medical procedures.*]

NARRATOR: With the "Last Wish Baby Show" having been abruptly pulled from the airwaves, no effort was made to appeal the Judge's decision. Thus, a medical team of the nation's leading cardio-vascular surgeons were assembled to carry out the court's wishes and, with God's blessing, prolong the baby's life. Meanwhile, high-minded pontificators from the academic, medical and legal communities pondered the implications of it all for the benefit of viewers at home.

[*Lights up on a televised round-table show.*]

PUNDIT #1: The baby phenomenon speaks directly to who we are as a nation.

PUNDIT #2: And who we, as a nation, are not.

PUNDIT #3: Yes, who we are, and who we are not.

PUNDIT #1: But more to who we are than who we are not.

PUNDIT #3: Then again, I think one could say this whole baby phe-
nomena says even more still to where we, as a nation, are going
than where we, as a nation, have been.

PUNDIT #2: Or not been.

PUNDIT #1: Or not, not been.

PUNDIT #2: Or not been, not been not.

PUNDIT #3: Yes, not been not. But not, been-been, not-not, been-
not-been.

[*This absurd chorus continues for a beat or two until:*]

NARRATOR: We interrupt this program to bring you a special Last
Wish Baby medical update. We take you now live, directly to
the Hoppscotch Medical Center in Tarmack, New Jersey.

[*Lights down on the pundits. Lights up on a bloody* SURGEON.]

SURGEON: The operation to implant the baby heart into the Last
Wish Baby was both...a success and...a failure. The heart
was successfully sutured and continues to pump vigorously.
Unfortunately, the baby, for reasons we do not fully understand, has ceased all other life sustaining functions and...ap-
pears to be in a rapid state of...decay.

[*Lights down on the surgeon. A series of* SLIDE *graphics showing the
Last Wish Baby in varying states of decay. All the while we hear the
thumping of the baby heart.*]

NARRATOR: There was no denying it. The Original Last Wish
Baby, the baby born without a heart, was now, and irretrievably,
a dead baby, but one with a very healthy heart. And that presented doctors and lawyers with an entirely new set of problems. For one, the baby could not be considered legally dead
unless the heart were either stopped or removed. However, if
the baby was not legally dead, then removing or stopping the
heart would be, in a word, murder. Therefore, despite all appearances to the contrary, the Last Wish Baby was, in the eyes

MOURNER: Bill was... he was a decent guy. A sensible guy. The kind of guy who let you know where he stood even when everything else around just got weirder and weirder—

[*Two* RIGHT TO EXTENDED LIFERS *enter and march around. They are wearing Last Wish Baby/Anti-Funeralists t-shirts.*]

RIGHT TO EXTENDED LIFER #1: Burial is murder! Burial is murder! Burial is murder!

RIGHT TO EXTENDED LIFER #2: Save the undead! Save the undead! Save the undead!

[*Lights down on the funeral.*]

NARRATOR: Despite their innocent-looking symbol, the movement stressed confrontation. Funeral homes were fire-bombed. Morticians and embalmers were forced to conceal their identities. Even limo drivers were suspect. Many believed reason would prevail and took comfort in the fact that the movement failed to win mainstream support. However, the ranks of the Anti-Funeralists continued to swell as old members never died off and new recruits were always just a few shovel-fulls away. Inevitably, highly-paid political pollsters were the first to see the writing on the wall.

[*Lights up on a Political Party staff meeting of* POLITICIANS *and their* POLLSTER.]

POLITICIAN #1: Speaking for my constituents, I say cut the heart out of that damned baby and you kill the movement, it's that simple!

POLLSTER: You're dead wrong. Give them what they want. Embrace these people now and they might remember you in the fall.

POLITICIAN #2: But that's insane. We'd be giving the right to vote to the dead!

POLLSTER: Dead, alive—c'mon, this is America—what's the difference?

[*Lights down on the political meeting.*]

NARRATOR: And so, in an historic Rose Garden ceremony,

of the law, very much alive. Further, this being a democratic ciety, it didn't take long for Americans to gaze upon their dearly departed loved ones and find similar cause to stretch definition of what constitutes life ... and death.

[*The thumping fades. Lights up in a restaurant where a* MAITRE *is calling out.*]

MAITRE D': Chatterwok, party of four, your table is r Chatterwok, party of four—

[*Suddenly, a* DINER *wheels in a corpse dressed in evening wear.* MAITRE D' *is appalled.*]

MAITRE D': Excusé-moi, monsieur! Excusé—Yo! What in name do you think you're doing?

DINER: Look here buddy ... my wife may look a little ripe t but she's still getting mail, and that, in my opinion, qualifi for your early bird special. Oh, and uh, non-smoking se please.

[*Lights down on the restaurant.*]

NARRATOR: Suddenly, Americans became embroiled in an e new moral debate—when did life end? The question was all as simple as it sounded. After all, who in this country with any real certainty when life begins?

[*Lights up on a* PREACHER'S *pulpit.*]

PREACHER: As the Bible so specifically tells us and I say ur brethren, Dust to dust!

ALL: Dust to dust.

[*Lights down on the* PREACHER.]

NARRATOR: With those words, the "Right to Extended Life ment was born. Also known as "Anti-Funeralists," th ment cannily usurped the image of The Last Wish F made it their own. Soon, that image was being bandi as a symbol of protest in nearly every cemetery and rium in the country.

[*Lights up on a funeral as* MOURNERS *stand over an open*

President Lance Ito signed the so-called, "Last Wish Baby Bill" into law. The bill not only granted the living-impaired the right to vote but also guaranteed entitlements and protections historically denied to members of this community, a community long regarded by many narrow-minded Americans as sloven, listless, and euphemistically-speaking, somewhat aromatic. [*Beat.*]

As the years passed and the American political spectrum calcified, living-impaired voters inevitably sought a candidate from among their own ranks. Republican strategists boldly exhumed a former California vote getter whose appeal cut across party lines and living tissue.

[SLIDE *graphic of a corpse-ish looking Ronald Reagan, still sporting a full head of hair.*]

During his first news conference as President, the newly re-elected Ronald Reagan announced his plan to fund and build a massive protective shield which he claimed would act as a deterrent to foreign aggression and help staunch the flow of illegal immigration.

[SLIDE *graphic of the North-American hemisphere as seen from space. Covering the entire continental United States is a huge Egyptian-style pyramid.*]

When completed, the shield did more than defend American shores, it stood as a symbol to all that here was a nation entombed, whose people sought no light to guide them and silenced any sound which might stir them. [*Beat.*] Except one...

[*We hear the growing sound of the thump-thump-thumping of the baby heart as the* SLIDE *of The Last Wish Baby is projected.*]

The never-ceasing, ever-pumping, always-thumping heart of the Original Last Wish Baby.

[*The thumping heart continues as lights slowly fade to black.*]

END OF PLAY

Paul Selig

THE MYSTERY SCHOOL

PAUL SELIG

Paul Selig has had work for the stage produced throughout the U.S. and the United Kingdom. *Three Visitations*, his trilogy of chamber operas with composer Kim D. Sherman, premieres this summer at The New Music-Theatre Ensemble in Minneapolis. His solo work *The Mystery School* will be produced in New York next season by En Gard Arts. Other plays include *Body Parts*, *Moon City*, *Terminal Bar* (published *Best Short Plays of 1988-89*, *Gay Plays 3*), *The Pompeii Traveling Show* (New York Drama League Award), and *Never Enough* (with Shapiro and Smith Dance Co.). He currently serves on the faculty of the NYU Tisch School of the Arts Dramatic Writing Program and Goddard College's M.F.A. in Writing Program. He is a graduate of the Yale School of Drama.

TONGUES

SETTING: *A woman in a church pew. Pantsuit, scarf, heavy makeup, cheap gold jewelry. The sound of a revival meeting in progress fades as she turns to face the audience.*

WOMAN: I am beginning to suspect that some people think that the gift of tongues is given out as freely as rejections to the Four Oaks Country Club. Eunice Blakey, she don't get tongues. She's fakin' it. Last week I was walkin' home from the motel an' I passed by her garage, an' there she was, waxin' her Pinto an' practicin' for Sunday. She's the first one struck down every service. First one passed out in the aisles with her dress up over her head an' her panties wavin' in the face of that cute new usher from Arkansas. First one to confess about pluggin' the milkman when her husband's away, first one to get redeemed every damn week, and don't you just know that it's to let old Arkansas know she's still available for another fall. Last week I got so fed up that as soon as her eyes started rollin' back in her head I jumped outa my pew an' started screamin,' "FAKER! FAKER! THE HOLY SPIRIT DON'T EVEN *KNOW* YOU!"

That shut her up.

She was waitin' for me, sure enough, in the parkin' lot after, like she meant some kinda trouble, an' she said "I do too get the gift of tongues." An' I said, "Yeah, every damn night over at the Motel 6 in every orifice you got. I get to clean up after your messes, case you didn't know, so you best watch your ass with me."

And she said, "Well, my Lord forgives me seventy times upon seventy."

An' I said, "Well, I been counting the condoms in your wastebasket for the past three years an' you done HIT that mark some time ago. Even Jesus got his limits. You best get your privates fireproofed, Eunice, 'cause where you're goin' you're gonna need another kinda protection."

An' she said, "My God is a God of forgiveness."

An' I said, "Not my Lord. Not my Lord."

How dare she pretend to know the Language of the End Times? And Mary Alice Johnson over there? Her son left the fold to be a tap dancer in Las Vegas. He'd send back pictures of his self with Lola Falana and Debbie Reynolds, and I will tell you which one looked like they had more paint on their faces. She buried him last year. Now she's over at the hospital every week spoonin' out her home baked goods to others like him. Who's just gonna be damned anyway. I don't know what she's thinkin. Might as well send 'em to hell on a full stomach. Burn with powdered sugar on their lips...

I was over there one day when my nephew got his hand caught in the disposal, an' I saw her comin' outa the Sin Ward with all her Tupperware.

An' I said, "Mary Alice, don't you come too close. Who do you think you're foolin'? You know why nobody never buys your damn fool pies at the bake sale? We know where your POTS have been. Don't you just think you're bein' NOBLE?"

An' you know what she had the nerve to tell me?

She said, "I thought I was bein' Christian..."

You'll burn in hell with the rest of them. See if I care. You can go bake for the pansies in the ninth circle of hell. Put your Betty Crocker over a flame down there an' see how fast your dough rises, Miss Mary Alice...

You know what's comin'. You know what's comin'. An' won't it be fine...

Let your cakes rise, Mary Alice, for I too will be rising...

Trudy Wilson what holds the Avon parties had us all in, an' I told her the first trumpet was gettin' ready to blow, an' I wanted to look my best for it, an' to give me the works...

An' she told me not to hold my breath because the trumpets and the breakin' of the seals was all symbolic. She'd seen it on "60 Minutes" where some China man was tellin' about the seven seals bein' the same as the seven centers in the body used for stickin' needles in acupuncture.

She said, "It ain't somethin' from the OUTSIDE that's comin, it's comin from the INSIDE."

An' I told her that if she was listenin' to some Bhuddist crap I would buy my face paint somewhere else. Dina Parks got a

Mary Kaye outlet outa her guest room, an' SHE'S been SAVED.

An' Trudy says "The scriptures say Our Father, not Our Father if you happen to agree with me."

An' I thought, you pitiful fool, you pitiful fool...

An' Sheila? She's callin' her Psychic Friend from work so many times they decided to dock her pay an' put a block on the 900 numbers.

I said, "What did your psychic friend tell you?" An' she said she got told it was gonna be a big year for her, an' I thought, yeah, well, burnin' in hell for an eternity ain't exactly a little event, an' that's where you're gonna go for listenin' to false prophets...

Every Friday at Bingo, each time somebody wins big, I think, take your money, take your money, you ain't gonna even have time to enjoy it.

All them people here. All them people who's goin' off smilin' an shakin' hands at the end of every service. Them people what's chaperoning the youth groups and sending money to the starvin' children every month and standin' in line like hucksters to ladle out soup for the homeless, who do they think they kiddin'? Who do they think is payin' attention to their works?

"It makes me feel so GOOD," they testify. "It makes me feel so GOOD to be of service."

An' I think, then, come over to MY house an' scrub MY floors, an' come over to the motel with ME an' YOU change the filth on the sheets an' YOU scrub out the toilets an' YOU peel the spunk off the walls that got shot there the night before by your husbands, your good neighbors and your children ...

You come and take this life that has been defiled and YOU fix it right. I'll take your money. I'll go over to the photo booth at the five and ten and send you pictures of ME smiling and write you all a letter every six months tellin' you what I REALLY think of you. It would be my damned pleasure...

You ain't saved. You will no more enter in my Father's house than I will be allowed entrance into your country club. You don't even know the language. And when it comes, you don't even understand...

The right way is narrow. Narrow is the path. I walk into this temple of Pharisees and I know that I am the only one that's leaving. I am the only one here that will not suffer the years of trepidation to come.

Politician's gonna get it. Take my money, give my jobs to wetbacks. Take the prayer outta the schools and teachin' them kids they was mutated outa fungus. I know who's image I am created in.

I tole my brother Larry, "You keep your guns out, Larry. You keep your rifles cleaned, because you ain't gonna be allowed where I'm a goin', an' you're gonna be left here when the locusts come and the Angels of Philadelphia and Smyrna break open their seals of pain upon this world. I will be long gone, but you keep your guns clean so you can shoot to kill. You watch who comes knockin' on your door on the dark night. You watch."

The darkness is real. Each time I kneel in prayer, I see my words moving into it. And it becomes stronger and stronger, and it is a force to be reckoned with. And each time I pray for the end, I see it getin' bigger an' stronger an' more an' more ready to come. More and more ready to topple the cities and smite the unfaithful and bring the glory of the kingdom through the wrath of my God.

Do they all think that He's sittin' up there on His cloud playin Parcheesi with His only begotten Son? Don't you think that the two of them got their maps spread out across the backs of the martyrs and they're stickin' their own black pins in an' plannin out what will be next? Don't you think that they have waited for this time and are GLAD?

Don't you think it's not comin'. It's comin' faster than a Cuban refugee can paddle. In the twinkling of an eye. Swifter than the rain and bigger than a nation and louder than a bomb blast.

For I KNOW the language of the end. It comes to ME. It speaks through ME [*Body tremor.*]. And the governments will tumble, for they are not in truth [*Body tremor.*] . . . And the mighty will perish, for they are not in truth [*Body tremor, almost speaking in tongues.*] . . .

It's a comin' it's a comin' it's a comin' it's a comin'.
It's a comin' it's a comin' it's a comin' it's a comin'.

And the years of waiting. All the years of prayin' without an answer will be because of this. When the fires come and the path is too narrow for any of you to follow, when I have been lifted out of my pew and through the roof of this temple, and when I am rising in the clouds and I am lookin' down upon the pitiable masses who have denied my Lord, who have given themselves over to the ways of sin, when my pantyhose is makin' runs in themselves because I am risin' so high and fine above you, and I look at your country clubs burn and I see your building's tumble, and your children, poor things, run screamin' on fire from the school house, while my hair turns into angel hair and my gold necklace melts and rises to become a halo around my head, I will be vindicated and my words will be finally understood . . .

[Her body begins to shake wildly as she breaks out into tongues. She rises in her pew, triumphantly, gloriously, for all her congregation to see and hear.]

AMELIA'S SECOND STEP

SETTING: AMELIA *sits smoking on a folding chair before a shade bearing the twelve steps of A.A. She is in her fifties, has a gray pageboy haircut, and wears a sweatshirt that reads "Serenity Sucks." Her hand is raised defiantly in the air as she glowers at the floor. She responds, as if called on.*

AMELIA: My name is Amelia and you *know* what I am.

First, I would like to make an amends to the group. It was I who put the dead cat in the collection basket during last Thursday's Promises Meeting.

It was an anniversary gift for my former partner, Ingrid, who, as you may know, has since resigned her post as treasurer of this group and has moved on in search of bigger livers to fry over at the Salvation Army Meeting on 14th Street.

Thank you for calling on me, Billy T. I was quite struck by your saying that maybe God gave us all two arms to reach for Him. It was almost as startling as Heidi M's triumph last week when she described herself as a little sober daisy cross pollinating the drunken fields of humanity.

Now, I know what step we're on today, which is why I have taken this opportunity to raise my little pink nailed hand for the first and LAST time in NINE DRY MONTHS to ask you all a question that has been burning itself into my detoxifying skull ever since I first got shanghaied into this rat cellar of Our Lady Of Perpetual Thirst Church.

HOW DO YOU DO IT?

HOW DO YOU MANAGE TO DO IT?

YOU PEOPLE ALL SPEAK OF COMING TO BELIEVE IN SOME HIGHER POWER AS IF IT WERE AS NATURAL AS A BODILY FUNCTION.

Ingrid FARTS and she calls it a spiritual awakening!

Ingrid! The love of my life and the bane of my existence, with whom I shared for fourteen years a room the size of a colostomy bag on Greenwich Avenue. And it was some kinda marriage and some kinda honeymoon. You coulda tied the beercans to our butts and sent us rattling down Seventh, if you could ever get us out the door.

"Did you take out the garbage?"

"Last week."

"Did you feed the cats?"

"Last week."

And so we lived in alcoholic bliss, surrounded by the multiple corpses of dead felines and enough trash to start a landfill in New Jersey.

And I honestly thought we were happy.

And then one day she shows up in the hole in the wall we called home and she has purchased a vacuum cleaner, with what should have been our beer money for the month. And she picks up the remains of Fluffy and Hiawatha and plops them into a Hefty Bag, and continues to ravage through the debris of our lives until she gets to me. And she gets to me, and she says, "Things are gonna change, Amelia. Things are gonna change, Amelia. Things are gonna change."

And, like a dutiful fool, I follow her here into folding chair hell, and we count our days in tandem, and we snigger at the personal revelations that are shared daily with the uniformity of a Geraldo broadcast. And I do the crosswords in the back, and Ingrid pretends to listen, and we keep each other away from the Schlitz and the barroom, and I thought we were still pretty tight, but something musta got by me.

Because one day old Ingrid comes home and announces that she's found God.

"I've GOT it," she says.

And I said, "Is it CONTAGIOUS?"

And Ingrid the Marxist, and one of the five most intelligent women I have ever known in my life, is standing there before me in her LEDERHOSEN telling me she has seen the proverbial Light.

"Where is it?" I said. "Underneath that stack of *Life* magazines in the hallway? Behind that fermenting catbox in the kitchen? Did the TOOTH FAIRY come and SLAM it under your dentures while you were sleeping?"

I would like to believe in fairies, Ingrid. I would LIKE to

believe in angels. I would LIKE to believe that Shirley McClaine did not accidentally high kick herself in the head during rehearsals for *Can Can* but is actually saying something of possible relevance."

And six months later, prayin' Ingrid's packing her rucksack to follow this light which, for some reason I cannot fathom, has told her to detach herself from toxic, co-dependent, farting old ME, who, unlike her, CANNOT SEEM TO KEEP HERSELF OFF THE SAUCE FOR MORE THAN THREE DAYS, NO MATTER HOW HARD SHE TRIES!!!

WHERE??? WHERE DO I LOOK, INGRID? AFTER YOU? YOUR FUTURE'S WRITTEN ON THE WALLS. SIX MONTHS FROM NOW YOU'RE GONNA BE STANDING IN FRONT OF THE SALVATION ARMY WITH YOUR LIPS WRAPPED AROUND A TUBA NOZZLE LIKE SOME REJECT FROM THE DAUGHTER'S OF BILITIS PRODUCTION OF GUYS AND DOLLS!!!

[*Bringing attention back into room, attempting to regain composure.*]

I heard you say while you were speaking that you didn't believe in coincidence anymore. That, perhaps, coincidence was your Higher Power's way of remaining anonymous. I found that very interesting. I will have to put that in my little sober thinking cap and let it ferment. But, I had a coincidence today. I ran into Ingrid.

Well, it was actually planned, as I had been up all night having a heated debate with an unopened bottle of scotch, which was making an irrefutable argument as to why I shouldn't just drink up, get it over with, and die. And in an absolute panic, I find myself tearing at the *Life* magazines, and lifting up the catbox, and running, running outa the apartment like a dry drunk outa hell.

And I am waiting, breathless, when Ingrid comes twelve stepping her way down the stairs of the morning meeting.

And I say, "Ingrid, I am not going to make it, and I don't understand..."

And she looks at me in all seriousness, and she starts talking about monkeys...

It seems there are these monkeys, see, on these little boney islands that polka dot the South Seas, and they are starving. And one day, these scientists go and dump all these sweet potatoes in the water, and they gather on the beach of this first island to receive the miracle of the yams.

Now, a YAM is not native cuisine to these creatures. In fact, they had never seen one before. But these little simians, out of sheer hunger and desperation, begin to go through the painful process of learning how to peel and eat a YAM. And first one does it, and then another. And when the hundreth monkey on this one little rock chip finally triumphs and heaves the thing into his gullet, all at once, all the other monkeys on all the neighboring islands, without having to GO through the abject PAIN and HUMILIATION of trial and error, without HAVING to slam their yams against their foreheads in frustration, without SCREECHING to the bloody SKIES that the FOOD which has FINALLY been offered them is inedible, suddenly and miraculously begin to eat them, too.

For, Ingrid is telling me, the new information had been picked up by the race mind. That the species had been permanently altered and filled, but that others had to go before them.

And that it didn't matter to her what I chose to believe in, so long as it was tough enough to keep me from killing myself one fucking day at a time.

And as she is walking away, Ingrid, the Diane Fossey of the A.A. Congo, turns and says: "For all you know, Amelia, you may be the hundredth monkey, and when you come to believe, what might happen then will be too beautiful for words..."

AM I TO TRUST THAT WHILE MY WHOLE LIFE IS TUMBLING THROUGH THE AIR LIKE A FLYING KARAMAZOV BROTHER, I HAVE ONLY TO REACH FOR THIS THING YOU SAY AND SOMEHOW TRUST THAT I WILL BE CAUGHT?

Because I fear things. I fear change, and I fear that there may indeed be some kind of peace to be found which eludes me. That I have encumbered myself with too many farting belief systems which preclude the simple state of willingness that you describe as the only prerequisite for faith. That I have maligned a truth in ignorance because I am constitutionally incapable of grasping the simplicity behind it. And that you people, who are kind to me no matter what I say and do, really have found some way.

Don't you think I would LIKE to believe in something? Don't you think I would LIKE to believe that the Red Sea did split in two like a dropped cheesecake? Or that a Bhuddha DID find enlightenment under a bodhi tree, or that some messiah did trod the earth two thousand years ago and still does in the hearts of those who've embraced him? Don't you think that even after crawling past the world's religions on my distended belly, I would still like to believe that this thing you've found can fill me, too?

And despite the fact that this action defies all rationality, despite the fact that it poses a terrific threat to all I have ever trusted and held dear, and despite the fact that it may be what is needed to save this cranky old life...

My arms, as if of their own volition...

They are reaching.

[*Lights dim on* AMELIA, *her expression is sad, yet hopeful.*]

DR. EDIE GIVES A COMMENCEMENT SPEECH

SETTING: DR. EDIE, *a happily disheveled woman in her fifties, takes her place at a podium festooned with flowers. She wears a ratty fur coat and a corsage. She looks out at her audience with what can only be described as love.*

DR. EDIE: I have been told that today is a special occasion, so I have worn my rat.

All occasions are special to Dr. Edie Kelvin, but I am especially honored because I have been told that I am here to address a room full of people who hear voices.

I have not felt moved to don the skins of a dead animal since the last time I took on a room, which was last Thursday, when I was escorted bodily from a meeting of the American Psychiatric Association, of which I am not a member, on the use of prescription drugs in medicating those suffering from auditory hallucinations.

There, I was heard to scream loudly, "JOAN OF ARC WOULDA BEEN ON PROZAK, MILTON WOULDA BEEN ON THORAZINE, AND *YOU* COCKSUCKERS WOULD HAVE TAKEN THE CANDLES AWAY FROM DICKENSON SO'S SHE COULDN'T BURN AT ALL."

I myself was born hearing voices. And I consider it to be quite a privilege to be invited to share my story with you, who not only hear them, but have the courage to follow what they say.

One winter, many years ago, when Dr. Edie was but a mite, her voices guided her to the bus stop outside the Yeshiva to lie in wait for her current beau, Morty Shine, the sexiest nine year old in Bensonhurst.

When Morty arrived, as the voices promised he would, little Edie was horrified. For Morty appeared before her for the very first time wearing glasses. Thick, ugly, bottle-busters with horned rims that lifted the pais from the sides of his head so's he looked like the Hassidic Pippi Longstocking.

Edie surveyed her ruined boyfriend, and a strange question

began to form in her mind. "Morty?" she said. "How did you know you NEEDED them?"

And Morty reported the following:

He hadn't known he needed them. It wasn't until the Festival of Lights, when he had reached to ignite the candles and instead sent his sister up in flames, that his parents wondered if there might not actually be something physically wrong. Because little Shula Shine, though spindly in frame, did not in the least bit resemble their menorah.

Morty Shine, it was revealed, was nearly blind. He had been his whole life. He had actually managed to survive for nine years on a planet firmly believing that there were nothing but shadows beyond him. And what shocked Edie even more was that up until that day, he had honestly thought that everyone else in the world saw that way, too.

To say that this bit of information confused little Edie would be an understatement. For she had never before conceived of the notion of a "subjective" reality. She had assumed, like Morty, that everyone else thought exactly as she did. And she began to mistrust herself, worrying that perhaps she, too, was wrong, and deceived by what she saw...and heard... around her.

And, as if enraged by her refusal to bear witness to her truth, the voices that had always accompanied her through her days began to turn...

And became cruel.

As Dr. Edie aged, they got louder. Harsh and horrible. They spoke of Dr. Edie's mistakes. Her failed marriage. Her unfinished dissertation. The child miscarried one night after an evening of ballroom dancing with a husband who was no longer hers. The voices told her that she was not enough, and Dr. Edie, frightened and alone, agreed.

In those days, Gawd spoke to her in different ways than he does now. He spoke to her in instances, unable to be heard through the clamor and din inside Dr. Edie's unprescribed head.

And the instances began to lead her, slowly, as she pulled herself through the thickness of days and the darkness of nights to a hotel room on West 72nd Street. Where the transients lived. Other women without settlements. Those who's voices had been silenced, by themselves, and by a world that no longer believes that simply being a human being is cause enough for respect.

For some people are born with less skin than others. Some people are born with almost none at all. They bleed through their clothing as they walk down the street, and their eyes shine brightly in the anticipation of being struck.

Gawd spoke to Dr. Edie in instances then. Through signs. Through symbols. Through the changing of a streetlight that might lead her down an alley, that might lead her to a stranger who might smile in passing, with a kindness in the eyes...

And then one day, when she was lookin' to get in outa the rain, she found herself standing in the doorway of Teachers College. And Gawd spoke to her directly, saying "Enter, Edie Kelvin, for I have made you for this love..."

"You made me for what?" I said. "Gawd, you made me for this love?" And I said to him "What is in it for me? Because being a cheerleader ain't my idea of success, and being kind ain't my idea of strength, and teaching the young five days a week ain't my idea of a high time, so's ya know."

Well, Gawd come back to me an' he said, "Edie, you have been created for this because you got the passion to prove me right. You got the knowledge of the night scares to make it better for them in the day, and they will recognize it. They will know it in your smile and see it in your eyes that the pain of being can be mellowed into compassion."

And I screamed, "Gawd, you got the wrong chickie here. You got the wrong bird."

And he said, "Who are you to tell me such things? You will do fine."

And so he sent me to Herbert Lehman High School in the Bronx, where the chairs in the faculty lounge ain't been upholstered since the WPA, and the water fountain sends up blisters for fluid.

He sent me to Herbert Lehman High School, where the students are black, and much to Dr. Edie's horror, all looked alike.

At first.

And then one day from her chalkboard she looked out across the sea of hope, and she began to notice how many shades of brown there were before her, and how much light was in the eyes of those she addressed, and how their potential radiated from them, like a flame threatening to devour her.

And she was humbled by this. She was humbled by their potential, and she was deeply ashamed at what she had done with her own. She had cried herself to sleep too many nights with what might have been, and there she was now, confronted with the possibilities of what could be, might be, with a little bit of encouragement.

And she began to teach to their potential as if it was the most holy thing ever created. Because in Dr. Edie's mind it was holy. And she saw in each of them the tree that might grow from the seed, and she never once let that vision slip from her mind. And every day her innocence was reborn. Every day, she saw the potential in them, the beauty that was created in them come forth, she was reminded of her own.

Because for all she had been through, and for all the wrinkles on her skin, she was not so different.

And suddenly, the flame that had lain dormant and hidden inside her own bosom began to burn, and the voices that had always been there, censoring her, demanding her silence, one by one, began to sing . . .

"WEND YOUR WAY, BABIES," I say now, and I watch them stumble forward into their lives, and they are so very brave. They have such expectation on their faces. They have such hope in their hearts.

And I SEE myself standing onna mountain screaming out, "WEND YOUR WAY, BABIES." And I wave, and I clap, and I applaud for 'em all, because they are righteous in their being, and they are noble in their efforts, and they are loved, LOVED by Dr. Edie Kelvin. Because they are making their way back into the forest and she knows what lays ahead. And, still they go. Still they go because they are young, and because they must. And perhaps when the nights are dark and cold, and the brambles on the path try to tear at their precious skins, they will remember old Edie, and what she said, and that someone once looked at them with the kindness in their eyes. And if they choose to, they have each other, and that is a fine and righteous thing.

SO WEND YOUR WAY, BABIES. WEND YOUR WAY. And you're gonna cry sometimes, but that's part of it. Because this is a Big School and you grade yourself, so you might as well be generous in your assessment. And if you don't do it, somebody else is gonna do it for you, and they might not be. Because in the long run, babies, what does it matter? What does it matter what they think and what they say? What does it matter what they do to ya? 'Cause you got yourself two feet made by Gawd, and you keep asking THEM to take you to the next fight place, and there you gonna be, babies. There you gonna be.

And if Dr. Edie could, she would walk before you. And she would bat away the terrors with the umbrella she carries with her always. She would beat away the monsters on the trail and she would make sweet beds of moss and leaves for her babies to lie in when they are tired.

But, then she would not be a good teacher. Then, she would not be wise and honor all the wisdom that she sees in her young.

So she prays at night for them. Loudly. And she celebrates them. Each and every mistake that is made along the way she applauds as loudly as the victories, because Dr. Edie KNOWS how learning occurs. And she says, "Lord, make their paths WIDE. No narrow paths for MY young. Make their paths WIDE, and let them know all there is to know. And let them suffer, and rejoice and grow wild in their own ways. But let them stay gentle. For gentleness is not weakness. It's an act of cowardice to be cruel, because you never gotta see the repercussions. People tend to cry in private, and by then you have turned away . . .

And those nights, when they come home from the jobs they said they'd never take, and they lay on their beds and think they are not enough, Dr. Edie will travel to them, travel through time and space with her rat flying and her umbrella beatin' at the wind, and say, "Oh, yes you are. Oh, yes you are."

And you practice your tuba on the subway. And you finish your novel in the attic room when the kids have gone to bed and the husband's had his fill. And you paint your pictures in grease on the skillet of the fast food if you have to, but then invite all the customers in to see.

And you tell your stories on the street corner, and at the tables in your twelve step meetings, and to the cop who gives you the ticket, and to the doctor who threatens to put you away. But you are never silent.

And you pray at night for the courage to continue expressing your truth, and know that Gawd always answers a prayer like that. And know that your truth may change, as Dr. Edie's has, before she remembered who she was. Because Dr. Edie divorced herself many years ago, and has paid alimony for it ever since. But she is NOT PAYING ANYMORE. And she will NOT BE SILENCED.

And she will continue shouting her truth, until the men in white come and carry her off screaming and hollering, and she will wear her rat proudly from this day forth. For hers is a Holy War, and she will always honor the voices that tell her where to turn...

And if you would accuse Dr. Edie Kelvin of being an idealist, just think for a moment, and know that you are the kind of person who believes that having an ideal is something to be accused of.

Because in the final analysis, babies, it's your own voices you gotta follow. Not old Dr. Edie's. She hears her own...

Let yours be kind ones.

CURTAIN

Mac Wellman

THE SANDALWOOD BOX

The Sandalwood Box was originally commissioned and produced by the McCarter Theater, Princeton, NJ.

MAC WELLMAN

Poet and playwright Mac Wellman was born in Cleveland and is a resident of New York City. Recent productions include: *Tallahassee* (Len Jenkin) at the Workhouse Theater; *Swoop* and *Dracula* at Soho Rep; *The Hyacinth Macaw* and *A Murder of Crows* (at Primary Stages and elsewhere); and *The Land of Fog and Whistles* (as part of the Whitney /Philip Morris "Performance on 42nd Street" series). He has received numerous honors, including both National Endowment for the Arts and John Simon Guggenheim Fellowships. In 1990, he received a *Village Voice* Obie (Best New American Play) for *Bad Penny*, *Terminal Hip* and *Crowbar*. In 1991, he received another Obie for *Sincerity Forever*. Two collections of his plays have recently been published: *The Bad Infinity* (PAJ/Johns Hopkins University Press) and *Two Plays* (Sun & Moon). Sun & Moon also published *A Shelf In Woop's Clothing*, his third collection of poetry, and two novels: *The Fortuneteller* (1991), and *Annie Salem* (1996).

The Maiden caught me in the Wild
Where I was dancing merrily
She put me into her cabinet
And locked me up with a golden key
from "The Crystal Cabinet"
    by William Blake

CHARACTERS

MARSHA GATES   A student and prop-girl at
    Great Wind Repertory Theater.

PROFESSOR CLAUDIA MITCHELL   A Professor of Cataclysm
    at Great Wind University.

BUS DRIVER

CHORUS OF VOICES including: DOCTOR GLADYS STONE; OS-
    VALDO (a sadistic monster); and others from the
    House of the Unseen.

*Note: The occasional appearance of an asterisk in the middles of a speech
    indicates that the next speech begins to overlap at that point. A
    double asterisk indicates that a later speech (not the one immedi-
    ately following) begins to overlap at that point. The overlapping
    speeches are all clearly marked in the text.*

SETTING: *In the rain forest of South Brooklyn.*

SCENE 1

We see MARSHA, *alone. Except for the table and the sandalwood box
itself, all scenic devising is done vocally. The actor speaking her*
VOICEOVER (VO) *appears in a pool of light down right; she bears a
strong resemblance to* DOCTOR CLAUDIA MITCHELL.

MARSHA (VO): My name is Marsha Gates. I lost my voice on the 9th of November, 1993, as a result of an act of the Unseen. If you think you cannot be so stricken, dream on.

CHORUS: I took the IRT every other day for speech therapy. In a remote part of Brooklyn. Avenue X. Where my therapist, an angelic person, resides. Her name is Gladys Stone.

SINGLE CHORUSTER: Doctor Gladys Stone.

[*The good* DOCTOR *appears.* MARSHA *tries to speak.*]

MARSHA: ... ?(!) ...

[DOCTOR STONE *tries to speak.*]

DOCTOR STONE: ... ! (?) ...

MARSHA (VO): Doctor Stone tried to cure me. Alas, she too was stricken.

[*Since neither can speak both give it up. Pause.*]

CHORUS: Dream on I did, but...

[*The good* DOCTOR *disappears.*]

MARSHA (VO): Parallel lines meet in Brooklyn. The East and West side IRT. This geometry is also of the Unseen. It is inhuman design, and therefore unnameable. Also, the knowledge of its mystery* is subject to error.

CHORUS: It is human to be so* stricken.

MARSHA GATES: I took the wrong train. We're on the wrong train.

MARSHA (VO): I took the wrong train and arrived at a strange place. A place I did not know. The air felt humid and tropical. The air felt not of the city I knew. A lush, golden vegetation soared up, up and all around the familiar landscape of the city, like a fantastic aviary. It was a fantastic aviary. A place full of exotic specimens. [*Pause.*] It occurred to me I might have lost my mind as well, although I did not think so because the idea gave me such strange pleasure, like the touch of a feather along the top of my hand. This place seemed a paradise. I laughed and fell asleep. I dreamed...

CHORUS: I am waiting at a bus stop, waiting to return to my home. Another person is standing there with me. We're at the bus-stop by the Aviary.

PROFESSOR CLAUDIA MITCHELL: Hiya.

MARSHA GATES: Hello.

PROFESSOR CLAUDIA MITCHELL: I'm Professor Claudia Mitchell.

MARSHA GATES: I'm Marsha Gates, a part-time student.

PROFESSOR CLAUDIA MITCHELL: I'm an archeologist, of sorts.

MARSHA GATES: I'm a student at City College. No declared major. I also work part-time in a theater. Great Wind Repertory. The plays are all shit. TV with dirty words.

PROFESSOR CLAUDIA MITCHELL: I see.

MARSHA GATES: I can't speak, either.

PROFESSOR CLAUDIA MITCHELL: So I understand.

MARSHA GATES: It's very aggravating.

PROFESSOR CLAUDIA MITCHELL: So it would seem. [Pause.] My specialty is human catastrophe.

MARSHA GATES: That's very nice, but you're making me nervous.

PROFESSOR CLAUDIA MITCHELL: So it would seem.

MARSHA GATES: Is this the Zoological Gardens? The beasts seem to be making a considerable noise. Perhaps the person who is sup-posed to . . . feed them—

CHORUS: Has been stricken,* like you, by an act of the Unseen.

MARSHA GATES: Like me. And Doctor Gladys Stone.

PROFESSOR CLAUDIA MITCHELL: I see. Perhaps so. Perhaps, how-ever, you mean an act of complete probabilistic caprice. A fly in the Unseen's ointment. An ontological whigmaleery. A whim of the die.

MARSHA GATES: I work in the theater. Philosophy makes me ner-vous.

PROFESSOR CLAUDIA MITCHELL: I see. What theater?

MARSHA GATES: I am a prop girl at Great Wind Rep. I told you.

[*The* PROFESSOR *throws back her head and laughs. Pause.*]

PROFESSOR CLAUDIA MITCHELL: An artist! Then surely you must appreciate the higher things in life. Knowledge. Ideas pertaining to a theory of the world Id. The power of the mind to crank out ideational constructs beyond mere calculation and desire . . . not to mention . . . mere mortality.

MARSHA GATES: This bus sure is taking a long time.

CHORUS: The bus arrives in a wild rotation of dust, hot fumes and the clangor of the unmuffled internal combustion engine. All are deafened. An instrument of noise close to the heart of disaster.

BUS DRIVER: Ever seen a bus before? This is a bus. Don't just stand there quaking. We in the bus business don't have all day. We live complex lives. We dream, gamble, seek, deserve a better fate than Time or Destiny, through the agency of the Unseen, allows. So, get aboard if you are going to. If you dare. There, there in the valley, someone is playing a saxophone among the peonies. His heart is broke. There's no poop in his pizzle and surely the will of the Unseen shall bear witness, and lift him up from the abyss of his . . . of his wretchedness, to the bright aire above where lizards, snakes and the mythic tortoise are . . . glub, glub . . . My basket of sandwiches flew off into the cheese that is the North end of the thing in the hot ladder. Groans and slavver. Spit and questions marked on the margin. A sale of snaps, larval coruscations. Sweet drug of oblivion. On a global scale. Flowers of unknown radiance, snarls of snails, all of a coral wonder. Just in time for the man who discovers himself stubbed, in an ashtray. Put out. All the work of the Unseen, like a wind in the sail of our hour, midnight, when we encounter the Adversary, anarchic and covered with hairs, in the form of our good neighbor's discarded sofa, left out for the garbage man to pick up. He would like to discover the truth about what can do no harm only if it is kept, safely under lock and key, in its cage, with no poop in its pizzle, aware of us but dimly, us lost in the crunching despair of our endless opening up before the doings of the Unseen, in all our sick, sad, pathetic innocence.

Innocence that is only the half-cracked euphemism for our woe, which possesses not even the required token for the train, or bus. Nor even the train to the plane. Not even the faith to enact that pizzle.

MARSHA GATES: I don't have a token.* Do you have a token?

PROFESSOR CLAUDIA MITCHELL: No, I don't have a token. Do you have a token?

[*They look at each other hopelessly. Pause.*]

BUS DRIVER: Then what are you wasting my time for?

PROFESSOR CLAUDIA MITCHELL: And he drove off, leaving us both in a brown study, abandoned. So I turned to my young companion, green with anxiety, and spoke in what I imagined were soothing tones... [*Long pause.*]

PROFESSOR CLAUDIA MITCHELL: [*Cont'd.*] I collect catastrophes. Vitrified catastrophes. Enchanted in a case of glass. Encased in glass,* that is.

MARSHA GATES: What a mess.* Farblonjet.

PROFESSOR CLAUDIA MITCHELL: You like messes?* Aha.

MARSHA GATES: What a* disaster.

PROFESSOR CLAUDIA MITCHELL: So you are fond of* disaster!

MARSHA GATES: What a catastrophe!

PROFESSOR CLAUDIA MITCHELL: Quelle Catastrophe! I collect them, you know.

MARSHA GATES: What did you say?

PROFESSOR CLAUDIA MITCHELL: I collect catastrophes.* Vitrified, of course.

MARSHA GATES: No, the other thing you said.

PROFESSOR CLAUDIA MITCHELL: Vitrified. Encased in glass. They are very beautiful. Would you like to see my collection? My estate is very close, just beyond the lianas.

MARSHA GATES: No, no. The other thing* you said.

PROFESSOR CLAUDIA MITCHELL: Never mind. Never mind. That was in the French language. The language of love.

[*They exchange long, hard looks.*]

CHORUS: So I went to her house. In the deep Forest, near Avenue X. I went with her, although I knew there was something about it not quite right. [*Pause.*] Something, in fact, quite wicked.

MARSHA (VO): I suspected that my hostess, Doctor Claudia Mitchell, harbored heretical views on the topic of the Unseen.

CHORUS: Heh-heh ... [*Pause.*] ... heh-heh ...

[*She looks hard at the* PROFESSOR.]

MARSHA (VO): I could not bring myself to ask. Her draperies were of the finest brocade, purple and stiff, annihilating the out of doors with its pedestrian bird-cries, bus fumes, the horror of the city's ... hullabaloo ...

CHORUS: Tick-tock ... tick-tock ... [*Repeat, etc.*]

PROFESSOR CLAUDIA MITCHELL: I poured a large glass of sherry for the young girl, and myself, and led her into my studio.

MARSHA (VO): There, upon a long, dark-grained, baroque table of immense, carved teak, supported by four, grotesque, dragon-faced whorls of some other, strange wood, lay ... tada!

PROFESSOR CLAUDIA MITCHELL: My sandalwood box. Within it, my dear Marsha, is nestled my collection.

MARSHA (VO): The deep plush of the box's dark interior ... took my breath away.

[*The* CHORUS *joins* MARSHA *and the* PROFESSOR *around the sandalwood box.*]

PROFESSOR CLAUDIA MITCHELL: This is ... [*She holds up a small, bright object.*] Seoul, Korea. December 25th, 1971. The worst hotel fire in history. An eight-hour blaze at the 222 room Taeyokale Hotel. A total of 163 persons are incinerated or succumb to the horrors of noxious inhalation. Two workmen are later sent to prison for terms of three to five years, convicted of carelessness in the handling of gasoline. [*Pause. She replaces it in its place and holds up another.*] This is Clontarf, Ireland in the

year 1014 A.D. Danish raiders under chieftain Sweyn the First
(Forkbeard) are repelled by the forces of King Brian Boru. The
Danes are mauled, with a loss of 6,000, and driven back to their
stumpy ships. Both Boru and his son are killed. Forkbeard is
slain later that year. And another. Saint Gotthard Pass, Italian
Alps. 1478. During the private war between the Duke of Milan
and another feudal lord, an array of 60 stout Zurichers, allies of
the Milanese are flattened by an avalanche in the early afternoon, with the solar furnace blazing away so innocently above.*
And another. Kossovo, in former Yugoslavia. 1389. Prince
Lazar's Serbian army of 25,000 meets the Spahis and Janazaries
of Sultan Murad in the morning mists of the 28th of June. In
accordance with a prophecy of the Unseen, the entire Serbian
force is annihilated, thus clearing the way for Turkish mastery
of the region for over half a millennium. And another. The
Johnstown Flood. May 31, 1889. A wall of water 30 to 40 feet
high bursts down upon the town as the entire damn collapses.
Over two thousand people are drowned, or dragged to their
deaths over tree branches, barbed wires and overturned houses.
Victims continue to be unearthed, some far upstream, for the
next seventeen years. Yet another. The retreat of the French
Army from Moscow, begun on October 19th, 1812. Hounded
cruelly by marauding Russian guerrillas, the Grande Armee is
soon mangled, and beaten—reduced to a desperate, starving
horde. Snows begin to fall on November 4. Ten days later
Napoleon is left with only 25,000 able-bodied fighters. At the
River Berezina 10,000 stragglers are abandoned in the crossing
on the 29th. French losses are the worst in history: 400,000
men, 175,000 horses, 1000 cannon. [*Pause.*] This wonderful
collection constitutes only a merest part of the world's catastrophe, which in toto comprises the dark side of the Unseen's id.

MARSHA (VO): But I hardly heard the words she spoke because of a
curious feeling that stole into my mind, and I began to wonder,
out-loud—

MARSHA GATES: Why is the night better than the day? Why do the
young become old, and not the other way around? Why is the
world made mostly of clay? Why can't a person always tell what

is wrong from what is right? Why does the full weight of the Unseen fall most heavily upon the visible, like brass? Why can't we see what it is that compels both cause and effect to be so interfixed? Why can't I find a number beyond which nothing can be enumerated? Why can't I know what will come of what I do, think, and say? Why can't I know truth from lies the way I do "up" from "down." Why is one person's disaster not catastrophe for all? And who knows why these things are called unaccounted. Unaccountable. Uncountable. And why, oh why, don't we know who does know the answers to these things? [*Pause.*] ... because isn't it so that if we possess, and are possessed by a question, the answer must, too, be hidden somewhere, somewhere in the heart of someone, someone real, and not a phantom of the Unseen?

CHORUS: Dream on, they did. Dream on ...

MARSHA (VO): When, however, I perceived at last the true sickness of her id ... her sick, squat, demented id ... I stepped quietly behind her while she was focused on her precious set of vitrified catastrophes ... and picked up a large, blunt object to bludgeon her with, but ...

[*Picks up a chair, freezes. The* PROFESSOR *turns to her, freezes. Pause. They look at each other a long time.*]

MARSHA (VO): When I saw she wanted me to do it ... she wanted me to do it ... out of a curious ... covetous ... vexatious ... perversity ... [*Slowly* MARSHA *lowers the chair.*]

PROFESSOR CLAUDIA MITCHELL: I am a recovering alcoholic, and a fraud.

MARSHA GATES: And I knew she was neither ... so—

CHORUS: Out of a curious, covetous, vexatious perversity ...

MARSHA (VO): [*Very softly.*] I refuse, I refuse, I refuse* to do it ...

CHORUS: I REFUSE TO BLUDGEON* HER.

MARSHA GATES: Simply put: I refused to do* it.

CHORUS: She refused.

[*She laughs. The* PROFESSOR *roars out a command.*]

PROFESSOR CLAUDIA MITCHELL: Osvaldo! Osvaldo! Throbow hobero obobout.

[The CHORUS *beats her up, and throws her out. As this is being done we hear the following, sung by the* PROFESSOR *and* MARSHA (VO).]

PROFESSOR CLAUDIA MITCHELL AND MARSHA GATES (VO):
In the name of Id
And all the Id's work
Show me what dark works
Are done in the dark.
In the name of disaster.
In the name of catastrophe.

[Pause. She lies outside the door of the PROFESSOR'S *house, dazed. We hear birds cry.]*

MARSHA (VO): Her man, an ape named "Osvaldo," beat me, and threw me out, but... *[Pause. She opens her hand revealing one small, glimmering object.]*

CHORUS: As I lay, bloody and beaten, on the Forest floor amongst dead leaves and whatnot, nearly poisoned by lethal inhalation of spoors, and accidental ingestion of strange moss and fennel...

PROFESSOR CLAUDIA MITCHELL: Wicked id's fennel...

MARSHA (VO): I opened my hand, and my voice returned. I had stolen one small, nearly perfect catastrophe.

[A slow blackout begins.]

MARSHA GATES: April 4, 1933. The United States dirigible Akron goes down in heavy seas, in a remote spot in the middle of the Atlantic Ocean with a loss of 73 nearly perfect lives.

[Pause.]

MARSHA (VO): It was the most perfect jewel of that Sandalwood box.

END OF PLAY

THE
BEST
AMERICAN
SHORT
PLAYS
1996–1997

To Howard and Marianne Stein

INTRODUCTION

"Mr. Albee," one of Edward Albee's early admirers once accosted him after a performance of *Sandbox*, "I love your work so much. I simply cannot wait until you write a full-length play." "Madam," Mr. Albee responded, "there's no need for you to wait any longer. You'll find that all my plays are full-length."

Albee's reply might be the motto of this series. The short play is not short on anything. It's as full as the longest play by Lope de Vega. The short play isn't missing anything either — it wouldn't know where to put a second act. Short plays need more length the way sonnets need a fifteenth line. A short play may be briefer than a "full-length" play, but is no less complete.

Sandbox debuted in print in the 1960 edition of this annual, under the editorship of Margaret Mayorga. Since Ms. Mayorga's remarkable tenure other editors — including Stanley Richards, Ramon Delgado, Howard Stein, and myself — have endeavored to keep her standard flying equally high. In this volume, then, as in the sixty preceding volumes of the series, a dozen "full-length" plays await your fullest attention.

The following is a short, cordial introduction to each of this year's dazzling dozen:

The student in Neena Beber's *Misreadings* balks at the syllabus and thumbs her nose at the final exam, but both student and professor earn a grade of woefully incomplete by play's end. Each is called to account by the other in a way that invokes — yet leans ironically on — Aristotle's maxim of "the unexamined life."

In *The Rehearsal, A Fantasy* J. Rufus Caleb strums up vibrant, echoing shadows of Jimi Hendrix and Little Richard in a marathon dual jam session of Oedipal proportions. As they play back the tape of their previous night's concert, both rockers also rewind through the drama of their lives together. Young Jimi, no longer content simply to support his mentor's music, looks longingly for an exit to the beginning of his own sound. The pain and ambivalence of their onrushing split turns the volume and tone up louder and shriller, producing a verbal music both mournful and electric.

The machines have the orgasms in Edward de Grazia's "opera," *The Vacuum Cleaner*, while human beings sputter and peter out — pun intended. The spring in de Grazia's characters' steps is not related to love in the air. The lyrics they sing are robotic platitudes, decrepit vestiges of a long lost language of a nearly extinct race. Lifetime warranties, it turns out, only apply to mechanical psyches nowadays.

Information and data petulantly refuse to be tamed into knowledge and wisdom in Christopher Durang's *Mrs. Sorken*. The title character, in her best Ladies' Club style, wishes to share with us her intelligent observations about The Theatre. (She enthuses somewhat in the style of Chekhov's lecturer in *The Harmfulness of Tobacco*.) What issues forth, however, is a tangled torrent of dreamlike malapropisms, the underlying subject of which is our current pathetic degeneration from the heights of true classical theatre tradition.

Gus Edwards' subject, in his play *Four Walls*, is the easy fraudulence of life. Fakes of all brands and species are a lot easier to come by than the genuine article. But, with time, what's false may prove as dangerously seductive as the real thing. The cheap facsimile of life that Edwards' characters assemble becomes a shrine to which they not only offer worship but are sacrificed.

In Herb Gardner's *I'm With Ya, Duke*, Sam may be in utter misery at being ignored by history, but he takes surprising pleasure in his lament. His complaints about his son, "Dopey," and his larcenous business partner, Shimkin, are rich comic arias of blissful discontent. Sam may even forfeit his last chance for a life-saving operation because he's too busy taking a swipe at every suspect enemy. It takes a WASP doctor to set Sam straight about who's responsible for his fate. In facing the answer to the doctor's challenge, Sam finally faces his most challenging enemy, himself.

The patter of familiar domesticity in Susan Hansell's *My Medea* exudes a force much deeper than any from our own experience. Hansell's play, with its hip choral voiceover that makes it rap, is not merely a 90's L.A. cosmetic makeover of the Medea myth. Hansell also exercises her plot with originality and vigor. Nor is her gilded, hyperbolic invocation of O.J. Simpson & Co. throughout the play merely the rhetoric of clever political parody. Hansell's MEDEA cries out for blood with the authority and judgment of hard-core tragedy.

An emotionally challenged brother (a.k.a. the typical macho sports-car-driving yuppie) meets his physically challenged younger sibling in Rich Orloff's *I Didn't Know You Could Cook*. They finally network a dinner together amidst Mark's planes and other upwardly mobile appointments. Jerome is a stripped down version of his older brother: paraplegic, a teacher in an urban public school, gay; he has a specially adapted basic Ford in the garage. But Jerome isn't serving any empty calories tonight. He's dishing up a stiff brew of reality to wake his brother up to the relationship they've been miss-scheduling for a lifetime.

"I'm keeping very busy with external activities so I don't have to experience any inner feelings," explains Gary in *The Tunnel of Love*. In Jacquelyn Reingold's universe, professional inspectors (shrinks, physicians, analysts, and other experts) have effectively closed down not only Gary's but everyone's most basic instincts of creativity and introspection. The high-priced Peeping Toms with diplomas in *The Tunnel of Love* even replace our congenital reflexes with their committees on feelings. Reingold's tunnel might at first seem a one-way express lane for female metaphor, but the traffic backed up in this underground passage includes us all.

A contemporary master of the short play, Murray Schisgal can sock more power and complexity into a few pages than the earnest long-fellows can sandwich into a triptych of evenings. The audacious whimsy of Schisgal's writing teases then sweeps us into a gyration of collapsing time and place. His characters are ever eloquent, yet their brief conversation across the page rivals a haiku for economy. His *Fifty Years Ago* is no exception. What begins ostensibly as a first wedding anniversary tête-à-tête eventually invokes, involves, and invites the greatest celebrities of the Second World War. And while the couple's anniversary also celebrates the breaking out of peace on VJ Day, we are not permitted to forget that peace on all fronts, domestic and otherwise, is a temporary "occasion" performed in front of a backdrop of violence and war.

Lance in Lanford Wilson's *Your Everyday Ghost Story* tiptoes around the periphery of life, negotiating past unpleasantness with his famous charm and wit. He deflects dangerous realities as skillfully as he avoids a dying friend on the street. As his gay friends suffer and evanesce physically, however, Lance himself becomes increasingly insubstantial spiritually. The ghosts in Wilson's story are not the deceased but those survivors who keep themselves a dimension removed, forever superficial and forever without the solidity of real compassion.

Past the paparazzi, past the police blockades, a real estate agent escorts her prospect into the house that is the notorious scene of a recent crime in *Wildwood Park*. Seller and buyer traverse Doug Wright's ominous blank stage and, of course, we the audience follow them, urging the grand tour on to scenes of ever more grisly horror. "I'm a monster!" chirps the well-heeled agent. As we are drawn deeper into the dark web of speculation, we catch a glimpse and a whiff of the victims and the perpetrators, but we never learn any hard and fast details of the crime. And Wright never actually tells us what happened. Our final speculation must be that the crime is in the heart of the beholder and that the property offered for sale can only be purchased — however dearly — by the imagination.

— GLENN YOUNG
December, 1997

Neena Beber

MISREADINGS

Neena Beber

MISREADINGS

Neena Beber

Neena Beber's plays include *A Common Vision, Tomorrowland, The Brief but Exemplary Life of the Living Goddess, Failure to Thrive,* and *The Course of It.* Theatres that have produced her work include The Magic Theatre, New Georges, Watermark, circus minimus, Workhouse Theatre, Padua Hills Playwrights Festival, and En Garde Arts. Her plays have been workshopped and developed at The Playwrights Center's Midwest Playlabs, Audrey Skirball-Kenis Theatre, New York Theatre Workshop, The Public Theatre's New Works Project, Circle Rep Lab, South Coast Rep, MCC, GeVa Theatre, and Lincoln Center's Directors' Lab, among other places. Her short film, *Bad Dates,* was based on her one-act *Food.* Beber has received commissions from Amblin Entertainment/Playwrights Horizons and Sundance Children's Theatre, and a MacDowell Colony Fellowship. She has contributed articles to *American Theatre, Theatre,* and, *Performing Arts Journal.* Her writing for children's television has garnered Emmy and Ace Award nominations. She graduated *magna cum laude* from Harvard, specializing in Latin American Literature, and received her M.F.A. from N.Y.U.'s Dramatic Writing Program, where she was a Paulette Goddard Fellow. Beber grew up in Miami, Florida.

Misreadings was commissioned by Actors Theatre of Louisville and included in the 21st annual Humana Festival of New American Plays.

CHARACTERS

SIMONE   a student

RUTH   a teacher

A college professor's office, minimally represented: a desk with a very tall stack of blue exam composition books on it.

[*Lights up on* SIMONE.]

SIMONE: It's important to dress right. I want to look slick. To look sleek. To look like a fresh thing. I've got a message. I'm the message. Study me, baby, because in ten minutes, I'll be outta here.

[SIMONE *lights a cigarette. Lights up on* RUTH.]

RUTH: What are the issues for which you would kill?

      I like to ask my students this on their first day of class. I assign novels where the hero or heroine kills, or is killed. I try to bring it home.

      They tell me they would kill to defend their family. They'd kill to defend their friends. I ask them if they would kill for their country... for their freedom... what would it take?

SIMONE: I'd kill for a pair of Prada velvet platforms in deep plum. Those are to die for.

RUTH: Simone. I didn't know what she was doing in my class. Neither did she, apparently.

      [*To* SIMONE.] Nice segue, Simone; would we be willing to die for the same things we'd kill for?

      [*Out.*] She usually sat in the back, rarely spoke, wore too much lipstick and some costume straight out of, what, Vogue. When she did speak, it was always — disruptive.

SIMONE: I'd die for love except there ain't no Romeos, not that I've seen; I'd take a bullet for my daddy but he's already dead; I'd die of boredom if it were lethal, but I guess it isn't.

RUTH: If I couldn't inspire her, I wanted her gone. I'd asked her to come to my office hours. I asked her several times. She was failing, obviously. I would have let her drop the class, but it was too

RUTH: [*Cont'd.*] late for that. She never bothered to come see me. Not until the day before the final exam. She wanted me to give her a passing grade.

[RUTH *turns to* SIMONE.]

RUTH: How can I do that, Simone? You haven't even read the material. Have you read any of the material?

SIMONE: I don't find it relevant.

RUTH: If you haven't read it, how do you know?

SIMONE: I read the back covers.

RUTH: You may find yourself surprised...*Anna Karenina* is wonderful.

SIMONE: It's long.

RUTH: Why not give it a shot?

SIMONE: The books you assign are depressing...I don't want to be depressed. Why read stuff that brings you down? Kafka, Jesus Christ — I started it, okay? The guy was fucked up.

RUTH: So you were moved at least.

SIMONE: Moved to shut the book and find something more interesting to do.

RUTH: That's too bad; you might have found one of these books getting under your skin, if you stuck with it. Haven't you ever read something that's really moved you?

SIMONE: Nothing moves me, Dr. Ruth.

RUTH: I'm going to have to ask you to put out that cigarette.

SIMONE: Okay, ask. [*But she puts it out.*] See art or be art. I choose the latter.

RUTH: Somebody must be paying for this education of yours. I imagine they expect a certain return for their money.

SIMONE: How do you know I'm not the one paying for it?

RUTH: I don't believe someone who was spending their own money would waste it so flagrantly.

SIMONE: Okay, Dad chips in.

RUTH: Would that be the same father you said was dead?

SIMONE: That was a joke or a lie, take your pick.

RUTH: You're frustrating the hell out of me, Simone.

SIMONE: I don't consider it a waste, you know. I like the socialization part.

RUTH: If you fail out of this school, you won't be doing any more "socialization."

SIMONE: You assume that I'm failing the others.

RUTH: So it's just this class, then? That you have a problem with?

SIMONE: [*Referring to her grammar.*] Dangling. [*Beat.*] Do you enjoy being a teacher?

RUTH: Yes, I do.

SIMONE: So I'm paying for your enjoyment.

RUTH: It's not a sin to enjoy one's work, Simone.

SIMONE: I just don't think you should charge me, if it's more for your pleasure than for mine.

RUTH: I didn't say that.

SIMONE: Did you ever want to teach at a real school, not some second-rate institution like this?

RUTH: I like my job. You're not going to convince me otherwise.

SIMONE: Four-thousand two-hundred and ninety-eight.

RUTH: That is—?

SIMONE: Dollars. That's a lot of money. Do you think you're worth it? Do you think this class is worth it? Because I figured it out: this is a four credit class, I broke it down. Four-thousand two-hundred and ninety-eight. Big ones. Well, do you think that what you have to teach me is worth that? Come on, start talking and we'll amortize for each word.

RUTH: You're clearly a bright girl. You can't expect an education to be broken down into monetary terms.

SIMONE: You just did. That's a lot of money, right? It's, like, food for a starving family in a fifth-world country for a year at least. It's

SIMONE: [*Cont'd.*] a car. Well, a used one, anyway. Minus the insurance. Suddenly this number doesn't sound so huge. It's a couple of Armani suits at most. I don't even like Armani. So hey, come on, can't you even say "Yes, Simone, I am worth two Armani suits. I have that to offer you . . ."

RUTH: I can't say that, no.

SIMONE: No useful skills to be had here.

RUTH: The money doesn't go into my pocket, by the way.

SIMONE: I think it should. It would be more direct that way; you'd feel more of a responsibility. To me. Personally. Don't you think, Dr. Ruth?

RUTH: I'd prefer that you not call me that.

SIMONE: Wrong kind of doctor, man. All you're interested in is a bunch of books written a hundred years ago, and the books written about those books; you're probably writing a book about a book written about a book right now, am I right?

RUTH: If you don't see the connection between books and life, you aren't reading very well. I want you to try. Can you do that? Books might even show you a way to live.

SIMONE: I'm already living, Dr. Ruth. Are you? Because it looks like you haven't changed your hair style in twenty-five years.

RUTH: Well, you weren't even born then, Simone.

SIMONE: Stuck in your best year? Because I see you in a close-cropped, spiky thing.

RUTH: That's enough.

SIMONE: P.S.: You might want to do something about the way you dress.

RUTH: Have you been in therapy?

SIMONE: Don't think that's an original suggestion.

RUTH: I'm not suggesting anything. I simply want to point out that this is not therapy. I am a teacher, not your therapist. You can't just waltz into my office and say whatever hateful thing you please.

SIMONE: I don't know how to waltz.

RUTH: I'm giving up here, Simone. You don't like my class, you don't like me, you want to fail out, I can't stop you.

[RUTH *goes back to her work.* SIMONE *doesn't budge.*]

RUTH: What?

SIMONE: Drew Barrymore would move me.

RUTH: Who?

SIMONE: I think Drew would do it. Getting to meet Drew.

RUTH: Who's Drew Barrymore?

SIMONE: Damn, you really should know these things. She's extremely famous. She's been famous since she was, like, born. I saw her on TV yesterday and she was so real. She connected. You know? You really might relate to your students better if you got a little more up to date.

RUTH: You might be right. But you might not be so behind in class if you spent a little less time watching television.

SIMONE: Drew is a film star, she's in films.

RUTH: You said you saw her on television. Don't you even go to the movies? Probably only the ones that are totally L-Seven. And I know you don't know what that means. [*She forms a square by making an "L" and a "7" with her hands.*]

SIMONE: Square? Anyway, Drew was on TV because she was being interviewed. They have these daytime talk shows nowadays?

RUTH: I've heard of them.

SIMONE: And this chick was in the audience and she started to cry. Because she couldn't believe she was there in the same room with Drew, who's been famous forever, right? She was just, like, sitting there sobbing. And this chick, she had her bleached blond hair pasted down real flat, and she was wearing a rhinestone barrette just like Drew used to, but that whole look is so old Drew, so ten-minutes-ago Drew. The new Drew is sleek and sophisticated and coiffed and this girl, this girl who wanted to be Drew so bad, she wasn't even current.

RUTH: I don't think we're getting anywhere.

SIMONE: And that is so sad. Because the thing about Drew is, she is always changing. It's a constant thing with her, the change.

And that is, like, what you've got to do . . . keep moving or you die. Drew knows that. How to invent yourself again and again so you can keep being someone that you like, the someone that you want to be. And once you're it, you've got to move on. Now where was it you were hoping we'd get to?

RUTH: The exam is tomorrow morning at 9 A.M. If you read the material, any of the material, I might actually be able to give you a passing grade. But right now I don't think we need to waste any more of each other's time.

SIMONE: [*Starts to go.*] You might have said that I go to the movies the way you read books. I would have pointed that out, Dr. Ruth.

RUTH: Well I suspect we don't think very much alike.

[SIMONE *goes, turns back.*]

SIMONE: A wall between our souls?

[RUTH *looks at her, about to say something, about to reach out.*]

SIMONE: [*Cont'd.*] I'm sorry if I've been rude. I'm sure a lot of people like your class. Maybe I wasn't raised well. I'm sure somebody's to blame. [SIMONE *goes.*]

RUTH: The next day she showed up at nine on the dot. I felt a certain pride that I had somehow managed to reach her, that she was finally going to make a real effort, but she handed in her blue book after a matter of minutes. I was rather disgusted and let it sit there, until a pile formed on top of it, a pile of blue books filled with the scrawling, down-to-the-last-second pages of my other more eager, or at least more dutiful, students. Later I began to read them straight through from the top, in the order they were stacked in. I wasn't looking forward to Simone's.

In answering my essay question about how the novel Anna Karenina moves inevitably toward Anna's final tragic act, my students were, for the most part, thorough and precise. They cited all of the events that led to Anna's throwing herself in

RUTH: [*Cont'd.*] front of the train, touching on the many parallel plots and the broader social context. I was satisfied. I felt I had taught well this last semester. My students had learned.

In the blue book she had written "All happy people resemble one another, but each unhappy person is unhappy in their own way." So I guess she had read Anna K.; the opening sentence, at least. My first instinct was to correct the grammar of her little variation. There was nothing else on the page. I flipped through the book; she'd written one more line on the last page: "Any world that I'm welcome to is better than the one that I come from." I'm told it's a rock lyric. Something from the seventies. Anna was written in the seventies, too, funnily enough, a century earlier.

I would have given Simone an F, but I noticed she had already marked down the failing grade herself, on the back of the book. Or maybe the grade was for me.

By the time I came to it, days had passed. I didn't leap to conclusions. Come to think of it, Anna's suicide always takes me by surprise as well, though I've read the novel many times and can map its inexorable progression.

[SIMONE, *just as before* . . .]

SIMONE: That's a lot of money. Do you think you're worth it? Do you think this class is worth it?

[RUTH *turns to her.*]

RUTH: I live in worlds made by words. Worlds where the dead can speak, and conversations can be replayed, altered past the moment of regret, held over and over until they are bent into new possibilities.

[RUTH *tries to reach toward* SIMONE . . .]

SIMONE: Do you think I'm worth it? Am I? Am I? Am I?

RUTH: I live there, where death is as impermanent as an anesthesia, and the moment of obliteration is only . . . a black-out.

[SIMONE *lights a cigarette as lights black out.*]

SIMONE: Ten minutes, time's up — told you I'd be gone by now, baby.

[*The flame illuminates her for a moment, darkness again.*]

J. Rufus Caleb

THE REHEARSAL
A Fantasy

"I know *now* Hendrix was on the set with Little Richard."
  —Walter Norcross
   owner, Mustang Lounge
   Greenville, South Carolina

J. Rufus Caleb

In 1973, J. Rufus Caleb joined the faculty of Dickinson College where he taught writing and African-American literature, until 1975, when he moved to the Community College of Philadelphia, where he is an Associate Professor of English, and Director of the Annual Spring Writers Workshop. He has received grants from the Pennsylvania Council on the Arts, the Pennsylvania Humanities Council, and the National Endowment for the Arts.

In 1981, Caleb's play *Benny's Place* received the Eugene O'Neill National Playwrights Conference Theatre Award for "Best Conference Play," as well as other award nominations. It was soon produced for ABC Television, featuring Louis Gossett, Jr. and Cecily Tyson. In 1986, People's Light and Theatre produced *City Lights — An Urban Sprawl*, directed by Murphy Guyer, featuring Ray Aranha and Darryl Edwards. Two years later the Germantown Theatre Guild of Philadelphia commissioned and produced Caleb's *Prologue to Freedom*.

Caleb returned to television in 1989, when WHYY-TV, PBS, Philadelphia produced his play *Jehovah's Witness*. The following year, the New Orleans Center for the Performing Arts staged *Jean Toomer's Cane* (an adaptation of *Cane* by Jean Toomer). *The Devil and Uncle Asa*, commissioned by WNYC Radio Stage, was aired in 1991. *The Devil and Uncle Asa* received the 1993 "Special Achievement Award" from the National Association of Community Broadcasters. In 1992, Caleb was commissioned by New American Radio and Performing Arts to write, direct and produce *The Ballad of Mistuh Jack*. In 1993, Caleb received an NEA grant to write, direct and produce for radio *Moods For Jazz*, an adaptation of *Ask Your Mama: Twelve Moods for Jazz* by Langston Hughes.

Caleb has published fiction and poetry in a number of magazines, including Hoo Doo, Black Series, Journal of Black Poetry, Obsidian, PoetryNOW, Salomé, Shenandoah, Maryland Review and the William and Mary Review.

The Rehearsal: A Fantasy was commissioned for The Radio Stage, a co-production of WNYC, New York Public Radio and the Radio Stage Consortium and broadcast in 1996, by WNYC, produced by Sarah Montague and directed by John Pietrowski. The subsequent stage version of *The Rehearsal* was developed with the assistance of The Playwrights Theatre of New Jersey in 1996.

CHARACTERS

JIMI, nineteen years old

RICHARD, late thirties

SETTING: *A small, cramped juke-joint, in Macon, Georgia. A late, rainy, summer night, 1963.*

A light rises on RICHARD, *stage right, in limbo. He is in profile, facing a pay phone. He is dressed to go on stage. He reaches out towards the phone, stops, drops his hand and shakes his shoulders to settle his jacket on his frame. He pivots to the audience, one hand slicing into his buttoned jacket; the other hand giving a hip gesture. With small movements of his free hand, he could be either counting telephone rings or beats. When he speaks, he jumps into his monologue, addressing hand, initially, and then moves his monologue out to some, indefinite point beyond the audience.*

RICHARD: Art Rupe? This the Art Rupe from Specialty Records? [*Pause.*] Yeah, Art, it's me. Same wonderful Richard. Like a bottle of champagne been laying on its side for a hundred years—but I'm even better, 'cause Richard don't give no hiccups. I ain' going too fast for you, now? I wake you up? Don't tell me you been waitin' up for me to call. [*Coyly.*] How you even know I come back on the scene? Yeah? What he say? Bet he give you a blow-by-blow of the whole show. Excited, was he? Hmmm. 'Bout lovely me? I know you mean he was excited 'bout my playing. I ain' that slow. Of course, I got new material. Bring in a few tunes each stop of the tour. O, no, we playing Macon at the moment. But we ain' but a car ride from Atlanta. Got us booked in a sweet spot. Macon's my hometown, you remember. Go' be jam packed the whole week we there. You understand, Art Rupe, all my friends go' fall by on some one of them nights. Don't want Specialty Records to miss out, being how good together we been in the past. But you know, when Richard go on tour, he can't keep it secret forever. [*Pause.*] I know I disappeared? Dead—who told you that lie? Richard just needed some time off the highlife, after that last world tour. You ain' heard where I been? Well, I started me a little church, way back

RICHARD: [*Cont'd.*] behind Nowhere, Georgia. Had my barber cut down my pretty pompadour. Trimmed my fingernails. And I devoted my life to the ministry: studied, and got ordained. Richard built a fine little church in a little grove of trees. And folks come in droves to hear me preach. Uh-huh, near the whole six years I been off the scene. [*Pause.*] Now, you ain't heard me say I give up music, just the scene. I even took my choir into a studio. Made us a nice little rockin' version of "Walk in the Sunshine." Art Rupe, it ain' yo' fault you missed it. My little gospel record wouldn' a showed on the charts you look at in New York. [*Quickly.*] No, I ain't on a gospel tour. This ain't a gospel tour. Wouldn't be talking to you, Art, was this a gospel tour. [*Pause.*] I put together a band of unknowns. Young boys. Now, don't talk no trash: yeah, they look good, but these boys can play. I spent six months, looking all over the country till I found the right mix. [*Pause.*] O, yes, six years is a long time to be away from the scene. But now I'm back, we go' get together in Macon? Y'know, Art, there ain't been much news outa Specialty since 1957, when I was the news. [*Pause.*] Then who you go' send? O, yeah? But is he coming with his briefcase? O, you definitely excited. Ou-we, my, my, my.

[RICHARD *immediately settles his clothing, shakes down his watch to his wrist, reads the dial, pivots back to the payphone, and begins to dial.*]

[*The light drops.*]

[*A light rises on* JIMI, *downstage center, sitting on a bar stool. A guitar amplifier is nearby. Nothing else is seen.*]

[JIMI *does not have a guitar; and later* RICHARD *will not play the piano. Using their bodies and small gestures, the actors will suggest the instruments, and the music coming from them. The music will be played by two musicians seen in hazy silhouette, from behind a scrim upstage.*]

[JIMI *is preparing to begin a song. The tilt of his torso and the design his fingers make abstractly establish a guitar in his lap. He is focused on his hands in his lap. He nods, his hands having found the place to begin. He launches himself into "Going Home, Tomorrow." He knows the tune perfectly, but he is also exploring, so that as he 'plays' and sings,* JIMI *makes discoveries, nods as he finds ideas he can keep. On occasion, he drops the lyrics and listens to the guitar's notes. But for the flashy print shirt he wears, his persona is the solitary bluesman, anchoring the beat with the heels of both feet, coaxing the music from his instrument. Within this moment,* JIMI *is playing within himself, and playing for himself. Only his voice is heard.*]

JIMI: Going home, tomorrow,

Can't stand your evil ways

Baby, I'm going home, tomorrow

Sick and tired of yo' evil ways.

I'll be better off without you—

I'm in misery all my days.

[JIMI *stops and looks off, left, then fiddles with knobs of his amp. When he begins anew, the wall will light up, and the guitarist will be seen and the guitar heard.*]

JIMI: I'll be better off without you—

I'm in misery all my days.

[*At the bridge,* JIMI's *guitar cries for a few brief moments. He closes the guitar down with the beat of his heel, and launches into the next verse.*]

JIMI: Don't ever try to find me

Don't even call me on the telephone

Hear me, babe, don't ever try to find me,

No need to call me on yo' telephone.

I'm better off without you,

Why don't you leave poor me alone.

[JIMI *repeats the bridge, note for note. However, he stops his heels, while playing. At the last note, his guitar takes off into the realm of pure sound, looking for a way to make the guitar squeal like a saxophone.*]

[*The set lights come up.* RICHARD *is standing, dripping with rain, within a few yards from* JIMI. *He wears a raincoat and a hat.*]

[*When* JIMI *senses, then sees* RICHARD, *he clamps down on his guitar neck.*]

[*For the first time, the steady, summer rain is heard falling on the club's tin roof.*]

[*The lights reveal the cramped OASIS CLUB in Macon, Georgia. However, only the bandstand is emphasized. It is a small platform, with an abused upright piano, electric guitar case, a few music stands, stools. A fullsize tapedeck sits on one stool. Center of the platform is an all purpose amplifier, from which two cables run: one to a wah-wah pedal, and the other off the bandstand, to* JIMI's 'guitar.']

RICHARD: [*taking off hat and coat*] O, don't stop, Jimi. Go on. Ain't nobody said the only thing can be done with a guitar is to play music. Keep on stomping them boats under your ankles. Must still be at least one-two snakes you ain't drove from beneath the floor. I run into a whole slew of 'em snaking out, whilst I'm 'bout to come in the door. Them snakes had they hats and coats on, and mad—disappointed, Jimi. Was talking: man, it's Friday night, my one night off from doing evil in the world, and all I wanna do is slide under the Oasis Club, curl in the dust for a while, but here come some fool banging dirt down on my head. You can tell when a snake mad—don' wiggle, he slide straight, and the smoke just coming outen his ears. I'm curious, so I follow this line o' steamin' snakes, and see 'em duck in under the rinky-dink Midway Bar, which ain't never had no business even being in business. I look down where they going in, 'n' one aft' t'other, they pay they little snake cover charge, go on in. Snake owner put the money in his snake pocket. They order from the kitchen, snake owner put little more money in his snake pocket. You buy a drink, snake money in his pocket. And ever' time he drop money in his pocket, he say 'Thank you, Jimi; thank you, Jimi; thank you, Jimi.'

JIMI: What you talking 'bout, Mistuh Richard?

RICHARD: Maybe you trying not to understand me, Jimi. I'm talking 'bout snakes. Snakes do' like wet. Out in the country—

[JIMI *has turned away; playing a few idle notes.*]

RICHARD: Guess you musta thought I was done talking.

[JIMI *turns immediately back.*]

RICHARD: [*Cont'd.*] Out in the country, when a snake know it go' be a heavy rain, you see 'em sliding up the winda pane.

JIMI: [*Pauses.*] Mistuh Richard. We got snakes in Seattle.

RICHARD: I been to Seattle, Jimi.

JIMI: Snakes don't talk; snakes don't drink in a bar; and they don't smoke out their ears.

RICHARD: Then I must be dumb, huh?

JIMI: Yeah, you think I'm dumb. So you can just tell me a dumb story. It's a dumb story, Mistuh Richard.

RICHARD: What's on your mind, Jimi.

JIMI: [*Deliberate sigh.*] Mister Richard, its four o'clock in the morning.

RICHARD: Tell me something 'bout yourself I don't already know.

JIMI: I been waiting here on this barstool. Just like you told me.

RICHARD: I didn't tell you to rev up that amp.

JIMI: I couldn't just sit here. So I just wanted to hear a little bit of what I was thinking about.

RICHARD: And confused yo'self.

JIMI: I knew where I was going, Mistuh Richard.

RICHARD: But ever'body else was sliding in the opposite direction. How long you had that amp on?

JIMI: I didn't mean to disturb anybody. [*Pauses.*] I didn't even know really if there was anybody else here. I didn't hear nobody.

RICHARD: [*Pauses.*] What would you know—last two hours you been listening to that marble rolling 'round in yo' head. [*Immediately.*] You ain't using the strings I told you to buy. If you throw'd 'way that money, it come right outen—

JIMI: They're in my case. [*Pause.*] You want to see 'em?

RICHARD: I want to hear 'em on your guitar.

JIMI: [*Pause.*] I'll put 'em on, Mistuh Richard. [*Pause.*] Now?

RICHARD: All right, for now, Jimi. All right, for now.

JIMI: [*Pause.*] Mistuh Richard. Where you been?

RICHARD: Now, Jimi, that's not a proper question to ask your employer.

JIMI: [*Nods a few times; then.*] Mistuh Richard, where's my money? C'mon.

RICHARD: That's the question you been waiting to ask, Jimi. Only reason you here, four o'clock in the morning. Otherwise, you'd be out running the streets all night.

JIMI: C'mon, Mistuh Richard, where's my money.

RICHARD: [*Pauses.*] That's what I been doing in that office. Getting some advance money, so's I can put it in your hand.

JIMI: [*Slight whine.*] C'mon, Mister Richard. You paid the whole band right after the show.

RICHARD: 'Cause I stretched my pocket. When I come to your hand, I was down to counting copper Abe Lincolns and a handful of buffaloes. And I know'd you needed bigger money than that. [*Pause.*] So I had to go in an' sweet talk the owner for a while. [*Smiles.*] Walked him right to his car—so he'd understand: even big a star as Richard is, he don't mind getting wet for a club owner what invite Richard in for a week's engagement. Tucked him right in the seat, just like they do in New York.

JIMI: But you got my money, right, Mister Richard?

RICHARD: O, he 'vanced me soon's I asked.

JIMI: [*Pause.*] But I don't see my money, Mister Richard.

RICHARD: I can't just walk in, say money-honey and walk out. He wanted to hear stories.

JIMI: You two could talk tomorrow. At least let me know you're gonna be three hours.

RICHARD: Can't leave the stage, Jimi, till the audience release you. Couldn't do nothing but keep talking. 'N' he lapped up every word. Just like you did. O, gimme more, Mister Richard.

JIMI: I never said that, Mister Richard.

RICHARD: Tell me what it's like to be a star. Back in Seattle? Like my little lap dog, Jimi.

JIMI: All right, Mister Richard. I know all your stories.

RICHARD: Like my little lap dog, Jimi. You remember.

JIMI: Y'know what my favorite of all was? About that teen angel chick. Stripped naked in the back seat of your cadillac. Cruising Norfolk, Virginia for soldiers on leave.

RICHARD: Sailors on leave, Jimi. Git it right.

JIMI: Broke off the daggone rearview mirror trying to get a look.

RICHARD: Was a funny story when I told it.

JIMI: I never thought so.

RICHARD: I should never'a told you that story, Jimi.

JIMI: How the owner like that story?

RICHARD: You don't tell folks down here that motel room stuff. That man 'member when my daddy was 'live. This is my home-town. What's wrong with you?

JIMI: I need to have my money. And you not acting like you gonna give me my money.

RICHARD: And if I propose not to pay you right this minute, what you gon' do—cut my tour again?

JIMI: Uh-huh, I see, Mister Richard. So you not gonna pay me.

RICHARD: And would that not leave you a Seattle Negro in Macon, Georgia. With no money—and no cause to be this deep in Klan country—'cept to play Richard's music. Well, I ain't go' fire you, and I ain't go' not pay you. But I for sure am not gonna pay you till we get done one thing. [Crosses to piano and plays a flurry of notes.]

JIMI: [Pause.] What you talking about, Mistuh Richard?

RICHARD: Boy, you and me gonna have a rehearsal, right here and right now.

JIMI: For what?

RICHARD: Cause I don't like the way you been playing, of course. [*Pause, then bursts.*] This is Richard's tour. You just 'long for music decoration. Any other sideman cut the fool like you, I'd'a fired his butt first time. Wasn't for my pledge to your daddy.

JIMI: Now, Mister Richard, you ain't made no pledge to my daddy.

RICHARD: Was you there when we set eye-on-eye?

JIMI: I'd have known if you'd been talking to him. Well, where you talk to my daddy? He wasn't in Seattle when you came through. I'm the one you talked to. [*Pause.*] 'Bout the big venues you had lined up.

RICHARD: Don't play with me, boy.

JIMI: [*pause*] Yessir, Mister Richard. Yessir. [*Pause.*] Can I have my money now, Mister Richard? And you won't have to worry 'bout me acting up again.

RICHARD: I'm serious. We gonna have a wee-hours in the morning rehearsal. Then you get yo' money.

JIMI: C'mon, Mister Richard, what's going on? I need my money. Places I need to be. I sat on this stool, 'n' you said you'd be right back.

RICHARD: Boy, you want to get paid? Well? Does you or doesn't you?

JIMI: [*Sighs.*] What you want to rehearse?

RICHARD: You don't think I know?

JIMI: I know you know, Mister Richard.

RICHARD: Then wait 'till I tell you. Right now, you get back on the bandstand. You rewind tonight's show tape, like I told you? [*Pause.*] I don't s'pose you listened to it? [*Moves to bandstand.*]

JIMI: Same two chord changes every night.

RICHARD: You ain't even wired the deck. [*Runs tape deck cable into guitar amplifier.*] And it ain't been the same every night. You

RICHARD: [*Cont'd.*] been playing a whole lot more notes than I told you, and you making the rest of us sound raggedy.

JIMI: [*Small jump onto bandstand.*] Hey, Mister Richard, say anything you want, but don't put down my playing. When I lay the sound of my ax on the chicks, the chicks can't dance 'cause they starting to juicy-up.

RICHARD: Don't even talk that trash. You think these "chicks" come to see some no-name Seattle nig-grow play guitar 'tween his legs? Boy, turn on that tape 'fore I forget you got a daddy.

JIMI: [*Turns on deck; quietly.*] I should be getting some credit, too.

RICHARD: Naw, baby, I'm the one had a string o' six hits. You ain' done shit.

[*The show tape kicks in with the band warming up the audience; screaming fans in a small space; guitar out front.*]

RICHARD: [*Cont'd.*] That's me they calling for.

ANNOUNCER [Show tape.]: And now, ladies and gentlemen, live on our stage, himself, the father of rock 'n rhythm, rhythm 'n' soul. Put your hands together for—

RICHARD: [*Screams.*] Me-e-e. Now, I come on stage. And listen to how they love me. O, I love you, too. [*Mimics show tape.*] Thank you, thank you. We-e-e, it's sure good to be back home, in Macon, G-A. All right, now. We gonna ask the band to slow it down a teeny little bit. Here come something from the heart for all my special guests out there.

[*On cue, the show tape band's tempo changes, and it segues into their introduction of "Good-night, Irene." The guitar picks out, and breaks down, the vocal part. The crowd responds. The piano adds a few occasional notes, in punctuation.*]

RICHARD: Right there—lemme jump in, Jimi.

SHOW TAPE RICHARD: All right, let's give that young Seattle boy on guitar a big Macon welcome.

[RICHARD *stops tape.*]

RICHARD: I ain't supposed to be waiting on you to let me play, Jimi.

JIMI: Sometimes you can't help but feel a groove, Mister Richard. Gotta jump on those times. [*Plays a quick burst of notes.*]

RICHARD: Uh-huh. [*Starts tape.*]

[*The show tape guitar continues to break down "Irene," but never loses the melody.*]

SHOW TAPE RICHARD: I don't know what you doing back there, Jimi, but you tearing it up. [*Pause.*] Now c'mon, Jimi, Bring it back home.

[*The show tape guitar loses "Irene" completely, and sounds as if it is saying 'What'? The show tape guitar calls out, hoots, pants.*]

RICHARD: What you doing behind my back, boy?

JIMI: Aw, Mister Richard, you should'a turned around.

RICHARD: And be part of yo' audience? I be damned.

[*The show tape guitar illustrates* JIMI's *monologue. Periodically,* JIMI's *rehearsal guitar adds a new layer of notes.*]

JIMI: I wasn't tryin' to be the show. This girl in the corner of the floor was the show. I tried to get you to look. 'Mistuh Richard, Mistuh Richard, look'a that girl out there.' I lost some notes trying to get your attention. I couldn't keep my eyes off her from the time she walked in the door. She was just moving, moving, squeezing hands, kissing cheeks and moving to the stage. Then she's dropping a little purse in his hand, and he must be her old man. She's in the corner. I aim my ax right at her, but I know: Aw, girl, you don' need me. You don't even need the drummer to groove. Don' lie to me. You playing with me, girl, you playing with me. All right. There's where I jumped in and played all over her: O, look'a her out there with that cherry red dress on. O, don't she know, don't she know, how to shake her thang. [*Pause.*] She's just grooving now, Mister Richard, climbing up my notes, her big coconuts shaking in her dress. Then she kinda cups 'em up, and just throws 'em out her dress. And quick as a dream, she tucks those mountains back. Now here she come slinking, slinking, slinking to the neck o' my ax. Aw, come on girl, throw your head back, let your eyes roll back in delight. Look'a that girl, shining cherry red. O, my.

JIMI: [*Cont'd.*] O, my, girl. And there. I'm lowering down my guitar. Gonna pick you right up, wrapped in the hot sides of your thighs. O, chile, lemme take you, and I take her, and I take her. And I take her.

RICHARD: [*Stops tape.*] Boy, I don't know where in the white wilderness of Seattle you learned that. But tonight, you will unlearn it. [*Starts the tape.*]

[*The space left by the guitar is taken by the piano, which picks out the crisp opening notes of "Irene." The rest of the band, with guitar, follows and settles into the even rhythm. The Introduction does begin to drive, but the arrangement is mechanical.* RICHARD *listens intently to the tape;* JIMI's *mind is wandering.*]

RICHARD: [*Continues; humming.*] Finally, you sounding like you can count.

JIMI: Aw, Mister Richard, I just wanna make my music.

RICHARD: [*Humming.*] Have to be able to read music to write music.

JIMI: Why you want to start that again.

RICHARD: Well, can you can, or can you can't read music? Don't know why your daddy ain't teach you to read. Wonder, he figure you too dumb—there. Listen. You making mistakes. And your A-string's gone flat. But you just playing on.

[*The show tape continues with* RICHARD's *vocals rendering the verses.* RICHARD *is listening to everything, mimicking various instruments, passing judgment with his body or guttural sounds. "Irene" ends in applause.* RICHARD *turns off tape, angrily.*]

RICHARD: 'Nough of you playing the fool. Aw-right, we gonna take it from the top—or what s'posed to been the top.

JIMI: We going through the whole show?

RICHARD: Yessir. From 'good evening' to 'good night.' Just like I wrote the show.

JIMI: [*Flash of anger.*] That show's two hours. You must be crazy.

RICHARD: Naw, I'm the boss. [*Explodes.*] Nigga, I got deals riding on

RICHARD: [*Cont'd.*] this comeback tour. So don't mess with me. You think we playing for some hussy in a red dress. So you can lay in the crack of some girl you can buy for a fried fish sandwich? This tour's for them two slack-eye white boys was here for the show. An' before we went on, I 'specially looked at you Jimi, and tol' yo' simple self: what go into these white boy ears tonight is important. They from New York. And the only white folks come this deep south is important white folks. 'N' Jimi, you even nodded and grinned like you understood me. So what happen when the show's over? I jump off the bandstand, and they gone. Just gone. [*Pause.*] So, if yo' guitar is plugged in, despite yo' brain, pick up the beat and stay with me. We go' watch the sun rise from the woodshed. One-two-three. One-two-three.

[RICHARD and JIMI *play the introduction to "Irene."*]

RICHARD: [*Cont'd.*] All right, now. You settling into the groove. [*Pause.*] I want you to leave off playing under the verses; come in on the chorus.

[JIMI *stops.* RICHARD *stops.*]

JIMI: Well, Mister Richard, what's the point of me playing at all, if I'm just gonna strum like a banjo?

RICHARD: 'Cause I prefer to go for a different sound.

JIMI: Just your piano.

RICHARD: O, no, my piano ain't go' be holding y'all together on this one. Richard just go' sing on "Irene." What I'm looking for is for everybody to just rock 'long: da—da—da; da—da—da. Build off that. Then I jump in with the drum, conga, and bass.

JIMI: Why I have to drop out?

RICHARD: You back in on the chorus.

JIMI: [*Edge.*] Well why we not practicing with the others?

RICHARD: They don't need to rehearse. They parts don't change. I'll keep you company for now. You ready?

JIMI: [Pause.] And you gonna pay me when we get done, right, Mister Richard?

RICHARD: That's the onliest deal you go' get, Jimi.

JIMI: But we don't have to do the whole show, right Mister Richard? I do have someplace I'm supposed to be.

RICHARD: Well, Jimi, I need you to play better.

JIMI: All right, Mister Richard.

[RICHARD *cues* JIMI *with notes. Both play the exact Introduction.*]

RICHARD: [*Exact delivery as on show tape.*] Thank you, thank you. Aw right, now, here come something from the heart. [*Pause.*] Saturday night we got married/ Me and my wife settled down/ Now me and my wife we're parking/ Gonna take another stroll downtown. [*Beat.*] Irene, good night/ Irene, good night—well, sing, Jimi.

RICHARD/JIMI: Irene, good night/ Good night, Irene/ I'll see you in my dreams.

[RICHARD *and* JIMI *play the bridge.*]

RICHARD: [*Pause.*] To the bridge. Shom—da—da—boom.

Both stop on the note.

RICHARD: [*Continues.*] Well? What you think?

JIMI: [*Playing a B. B. King riff.*] I guess it's different.

RICHARD: Not the note, boy. I mean can you see the feeling I'm after. The colors.

JIMI: [*Another riff.*] Mister Richard, I just can't get into this hillbilly waltz music.

RICHARD: Jimi, yo' job is to get into it.

JIMI: [pause] I hear you tonight, I'm thinking you could go higher than Robert Johnson. You got the voice for some blues, Mistuh Richard.

RICHARD: What you know 'bout blues? You ain't even got a sense of humor.

JIMI: Then what was I doing in Seattle? I know my blues, Mister Richard.

RICHARD: Say who?

JIMI: Albert King, that's who.

RICHARD: Where you play with some Albert King?

JIMI: [*Pause.*] In St. Louis.

RICHARD: When your butt ever sit in St Louis.

JIMI: [*Pause.*] You don't know everywhere I've been, Mr. Richard.

RICHARD: I may not've been there when your mama dropped you off in the world, but since then I know you been in Seattle and on my band bus.

JIMI: So you wanna think.

RICHARD: Them two weeks? O, you wanna claim you was in St. Louis.

JIMI: Mostly. I went to some other places on the way.

RICHARD: You lying. You was shacked up with that goofy country girl what followed you 'round in Greenville.

JIMI: [*Slyly.*] I just told the fellas that.

RICHARD: Why you lie? What—you think I was go' come running after you?

JIMI: I couldn't tell *what* you were going to do.

RICHARD: [*Pauses fully; slowly.*] Then you should'a checked yo' ID. Now is probably when you lying. You shack up with whoever you want.

JIMI: I swear, Mistuh Richard; I saw Albert King—sitting in Arch Recording.

RICHARD: Arch Recording!?

JIMI: [*Pause; smiles.*] In the lobby. Mister Albert was just sitting there, plugged into this nice little amp, driving his ax like a freight train. [*Guitar burst, similar to one at open, on "Going Home."*]

[JIMI *moves into the limbo area, as the light there rises on a low stool. He cradles his guitar upright.*]

[JIMI *approaches the stool, reverentially.*]

JIMI: I got as close to him as I could. I was trying to see his finger-work, while he was leaning over his ax, checking out my shoes.

[JIMI *bends towards* ALBERT's *left hand. Then he pivots in* RICHARD's *direction and personifies* ALBERT, *playing soundlessly, and checking out* JIMI's *shoes.*]

RICHARD: He like them shoes?

[ALBERT *"approves" of the shoes.*]

JIMI: Then Mistuh Albert looked up, real perplexed, surprised. [*Sits on stool, tilts his head up to*] You colored. Don't think I ever seen a colored boy wear shoes like them. I just nodded. Then he said: Son, you make a better door than a window. I'm just standing there, staring at his hand after he stopped playing. So he just pushed me a little to the side and said: I got to keep an eye out for the man. I asked 'What man'? And he asked me: What's in there, Sonnyboy—meaning my guitar case. I'm still so knocked out that it's Albert King, I say, 'My guitar.' He cracked up, and I felt real stupid. But he told me: Sit on down. He meant what kind of guitar do I play. I'm opening up my case, and he goes: You must be in love, Sonnyboy, 'cause that's some kin'a shirt you got on. Go' git me one, next time I'm pass-ing through Puerto Rico, France. I knew what he was gonna ask next: Can you play. [*Over to Richard.*] And he didn't mean can I play the guitar.

RICHARD: Can you play it.

JIMI: [*Doing a mock tuning.*] I could tell he liked me, but he wasn't going to loan me his guitar cord. "A strong man may not need a zipper to get ready, but a bluesman—

JIMI & RICHARD: —better have his long black snake. Sonnyboy, plug into that empty socket, and light up.

JIMI: I surprised him, and went way back to his first album. I wasn't gonna put one note in Mistuh Albert's ear but what I learned from his album.

[JIMI *plays and the music heard* is *the blues, but with a nod to the polished surface of rhythm and blues. The music is cousin to B B King: ironic, sly, with mocking pauses. Who the mockingbird be is*

*clear—but who is the mock-ee? The music is distant cousin to B. B.
King: full, broad notes, ornate, even riddled with random riffs: gut,
guttural, all down in the gutter.* JIMI *plays on a delicate blues.* JIMI
is winding down the music.]

JIMI: Yeah, put the baby to bed, Sonnyboy. Turn off the light. And
tip-toe. Out the. Room. [JIMI *releases the strings, clamps down on
the neck.*] Then he said: O, you didn't have to be that nice to my
stuff, Sonnyboy. And for a while, that's *all* he said. Then he just
started showing me all kinds of stuff with his ax. How to anchor
the guitar with my elbow, so I can pick different strings with
both hands. To re-tune on the fly, and when to do it so that that
stretching string folds right into the music. [*Reveling.*] You
know, Mistuh Albert's got these big hands, like me, and he can
wrap 'em 'round the neck, and make 'em go like pistons. He
don't even use a pick.

RICHARD: Who don't know 'bout Albert crusty thumbnail?

JIMI: And he plays upside-down and left-handed, too.

RICHARD: And I know that. [*Pause.*] Albert ask after me? [*Pause.*] O,
you ain't tell Albert you worked for me?

JIMI: [*Pause.*] After a while.

RICHARD: [Quickly.] What chu tell him?

JIMI: He asked what you had in the set. [*Pause; smiles.*] He said,
"Good-night, Irene" was too country for him.

RICHARD: Albert ain't call *me* country. Albert from too deep in
Mississippi to call *me* country.

JIMI: [*Edge of condescension.*] We weren't talking about you. We just
agreed that for 1963, "Irene" just too country.

RICHARD: You can't tell a whole note from a fly on the wall, but you
will arrange my set.

JIMI: We were talking about Leadbelly.

RICHARD: What *you* have to say 'bout Leadbelly?

JIMI: I'd heard about him, Mister Richard.

RICHARD: Well then, I wanna hear.

JIMI: He was real big, real country and a real bad man.

RICHARD: All right, you know some Leadbelly.

JIMI: [*Warming.*] Near the whole of his adult life, the state of Louisiana would run him in and out of jail for shooting folks.

RICHARD: [*Amused.*] You talking Albert King now.

JIMI: Uh-huh. Mister Albert says Leadbelly had him a pistol called a left-handed Wheeler. Made from magnet metal. And he would stick that left-hand Wheeler right 'gainst his Leadbelly, 'stead of a holster. And when he died, the undertaker pulled enough bullets out of Leadbelly's gut to line his coffin. [*Shrugs.*] Hard to believe *that's* the man that wrote "Goodnight, Irene."

RICHARD: You don't know Albert jiving you with them tall tales?

JIMI: Mr. Albert was showing me something. How Leadbelly started out with something special, only he lost it. [*Pause.*] Mister Albert says I got something special, too. And I told him, don't worry 'bout me: I'm going to keep my special thing.

RICHARD: Leadbelly and Jimi occupying the same sentence?

JIMI: I won't ever write some slow-drag "Goodnight, Irene."

RICHARD: [*Pause.*] Lemme tell you one more story 'bout "slow-drag Leadbelly." One of them times he was in Angola Prison, the gov'nor of the state of Louisiana, Huey P. Long—ever hear o' the kingfisher? Thought not. Well Kingfisher sent word in to Leadbelly: Write me a song, and I will set you free. But the warden say: Wait a minute, Gov'nor, Leadbelly in for life this time. We gotta cure this colored man of killing taxpayers. So Kingfisher sent another word in to Leadbelly: I better like that song; otherwise, you don't walk. Leadbelly got to thinking, got to working. Wrote out "Irene," the first night, and put that pretty tune here in his back pocket. Then he wrote six more tunes he know'd was dogs. Sent 'em up the gov'nor's mansion, one-at-a-time. And each time Kingfisher throw'd a dog in the trash, that warden show'd Leadbelly his red neck. [*Pause.*] You understand what I mean by "showing his red neck," don't chu? Even a Seattle Negro must'a heard what that mean.

JIMI: [*Thoughtfully.*] Yessir, Mister Richard.

RICHARD: All right, you listening. Well, when Leadbelly was ready, he sent out "Irene." And damn if he ain't walk a free man soon's the Kingfisher could tap out the notes to the words. Call Leadbelly country, and more bad news than a nightmare—but he was slick, too.

JIMI: I bet he was sweating scared.

RICHARD: He know'd what he was doing.

RICHARD: You can know what you're doing and still be scared.

RICHARD: What you doing to be scared 'bout?

JIMI: I'm not talking 'bout me. What if that Kingfisher had thrown "Irene" in the trash, too?

RICHARD: Like you would'a, huh?

JIMI: Well, Mister Richard? You get your stuff right and send it out there and you got your whole life depending on it.

RICHARD: [Pause.] You better have more'n your 'special stuff' to depend on. You better know what you doing.

JIMI: I know what I'm doing.

RICHARD: No, you don't, Jimi. Did you know, you wouldn't'a run from me to a few sessions with Albert. Lucky I took you back.

JIMI: I knew you would. 'Cause you know what you doing, what you got.

RICHARD: Albert planning to give you more work? [Pause.] How much he paying you for a session?

JIMI: I didn't say I got a job with Mister Albert.

RICHARD: O, I see. I'm still the onliest one to offer you some real work. So, what kind o' stuff Mister Laundromat Blues doing at Arch?

JIMI: We didn't talk about that.

RICHARD: His stuff so secret, he ain't let you listen from the booth? [Pause.] Well then, what Albert say 'bout his deal?

JIMI: Nothing.

RICHARD: Laundromat? And didn't go on and on 'bout his deal?

JIMI: Don't always have to be 'bout business, Mister Richard.

RICHARD: What else but?

JIMI: [*Pause.*] Mister Albert understands what it's about.

RICHARD: Since when?

JIMI: [*With some poignancy.*] The blues is about playing what you done lived, so everybody what hear yo' blues, got to live it, too. How you wake up so lonely in the morning, you make a deal with the devil, just to talk to somebody on the phone. The blues is sadness, pain and sorrow so deep down in a black man's soul...

RICHARD: Aw, Jimi, that's the stuff Albert s'posed to say when they put you on the TV not what he said when they put him on the TV that one time. Lord'a'mercy. [*Pause.*] I bet you wore that same Honolulu shirt you tried to wear tonight. Ha. And them stingy-crotch blue jeans you think you look so good in.

JIMI: What you driving at, Mister Richard. [*Meekly.*] What?

RICHARD: [*Begins laughing.*] I know Albert take one look at you and saw a Seattle nig-row, who ain't know'd but 'bout six colored people growing up, and what learned all the little he know about colored music from the half-dozen 'blues' records some white deejay choose to let him hear.

JIMI: You don't know what Mister Albert was thinking.

RICHARD: I know he talk to you like you was a white boy.

JIMI: I don't have to grow up eating hominy grits on some plantation to play the blues, Mister Richard.

RICHARD: Who told you that?

JIMI: Well then, to play my blues. I'm telling you the truth, Mister Albert says I got something special in my hands. I just gotta find a way to get it out.

RICHARD: [*Shakes head.*] So you can be like Albert—sitting in that lobby throwing out every new note he got, sweating the varnish off his guitar. Hoping some doped-up or drunked-up slack-eye white man give him a contract. But he ain't giving out no contracts to colored to sing the blues. He waiting for some more

RICHARD: [*Cont'd.*] white boys to learn to play it. Look what been done with Elvis. Ain't give Elvis a contract to sing hillbilly. Elvis just happen to be the first singing cracker to come 'long when Sam Phillips put out the word that could he find him a good-looking white boy could sound like a 'nigger' he could make a million dollars. Shoot, let's go on to the second verse, 'fore I forget you got a daddy out there somewhere. Pick up the bridge.

[*Piano and guitar hit the bridge exactly.*]

RICHARD: [*Continues; hums few bars of verse.*] Wait for me. I'm trying something. [*Hums entire verse, exactly as on tape.*] All right now. [*Pause.*] Sometimes I run to the country, babe/ Sometimes I roam downtown/ Sometimes I take a great notion/ To jump in the river and drown. [Pause.] Everybody, go—

RICHARD & JIMI: Irene good night/ Irene good night/ Good night Irene/ Good night Irene/ I'll see you in my dreams.

[JIMI*'s angry guitar solo overtakes the bridge, and begins to drive.*]

RICHARD: Don't drift, boy.

[JIMI *stops.*]

JIMI: Elvis got his contract because kids don't want to hear Pat Boone no more. Man, Elvis scares them middle-class old folk.

RICHARD: That what they tell you back in Seattle? Elvis come on the scene when slack-eye couldn't put over Pat Boone doing covers of Little Richard songs. Missed on Pat, went on and hired Elvis, to cover Big Mama Thornton's "Hounddog."

JIMI: Aw, Mister Richard, you know Elvis can sing.

RICHARD: He don't need a colored boy to broadcast that. You know what Elvis say: "All nigras can do for me is shine my shoes and buy my records." [*Pause.*] Well, is it is, or is it ain't?

JIMI: Mister Richard, that don't sound like Elvis.

RICHARD: I know it don't to you.

JIMI: He talks all the time about listening to Negro music growing up. Just because he's from the south don't mean he's prejudiced. It's 'cause you're from the south you think like that.

RICHARD: You right, there.

JIMI: You just jealous, 'cause Elvis' stuff is a hit.

RICHARD: And I ain't had the hits? And back on the scene for some more.

JIMI: [Pause.] Elvis got the stuff everybody want to see.

RICHARD: O, I see. [Picks out notes.] Like the little stuff you got, huh?

JIMI: [Eager.] You wrong, Mister Richard, my stuff's big and plentiful.

RICHARD: Mmmm, goodness, this boy think he got a package.

JIMI: I know I can play better'n Elvis. And shoot, when I get my shot, I'm'a make Elvis' hips look as tame as Pat Boone's shoes. [Plays a fast, hard riff.]

RICHARD: So you think feeling up a guitar go' get it? Like you claim it does for these little colored girls.

JIMI: Damn right it does. And I'm gonna fire up the white chicks with the same stuff.

RICHARD: Boy, they ain't go' let you do yo' raunchy stuff 'fore little white girls.

JIMI: I was already doing my stuff back in Seattle. And all there was were white chicks.

RICHARD: Now, Jimi, you wasn't doing all that dirty stuff in Seattle. You even got the chance to unbutton your shirt 'cause them little girl daddys wasn't watching.

JIMI: Shoot, Mister Richard, nobody was worried 'bout that stuff. You been dealing with these crazy Georgia rednecks too long. This place ain't even America, really.

RICHARD: [Pause.] I'm just trying to teach you some things, Jimi, that your daddy neglected.

JIMI: [Fast, hard riff, directed at RICHARD.] I believe the truth is, you don't got nothing to teach me. I could take you places.

RICHARD: Now I know yo' daddy, and I know he taught you more respect than you showing.

JIMI: What's he gonna teach me in a three minute phone call from on the road? I've been putting my stuff together all by myself.

RICHARD: Jimi, Jimi, Jimi. Slack-eye ain' go' be able to do nothing with your stuff.

JIMI: He won't have a choice. Mister Richard, you know I'm good.

RICHARD: O, you got some talent. But it take more'n that to make a package.

JIMI: I'm gonna get my contract, Mister Richard. Then I'm gonna blow everybody's mind with my record. You saw my stuff back in Seattle, and you dug it like everybody else. Then you hired me on the spot.

RICHARD: 'Cause you could play guitar, and on the rare occasion when I needed something a little special, I could teach you to deliver. Jimi, the onliest thing different slack-eye go' let out there is a package like Elvis on the one side and me on the other side. Nothing else go' squeeze through the door—least not for the big time contract that's gleaming in your eye. I wasn't brought up to dress in those costumes I wear on stage. My people don't even want me to sing the very songs I wrote. I'm nothing but the devil on stage. I know that. And I'll tell you something, boy: Had I my will and my way, I'd be singing the Lord's music on this tour. But I'm the first king of rock 'n' rhythm. When I got the urge six years ago to sing what I ought to [*Gentle, gospel phrasing.*] I had to jump my own world tour to do it. Back then every color of people was crazy 'bout my rock 'n' rhythm. Nineteen-hundred-and-fifty-seven, headlining a world tour. We had played Japan. And had filled a giant airplane hangar in Manila.

[JIMI's *guitar, with spare, resonant notes, joins* RICHARD's *phrasing.*]

'Bout to wrap up Sydney, Australia. But that evil Russian man put up his sputnik in the air, and like to scare the life out the world. And that very night was the only time my daddy come to me in a dream. Stood the foot of my bed and tell me, I was making music for evil. Was all he said. Son—

[*Both arrive at the same note.*]

RICHARD: [*Cont'd.*] — you making music for evil. Here I'm the father of rhythm 'n' rock. String of hits, and the very next morning I get on a cross country bus out'a Sydney, going north. I didn't care where, I don't know why. Once we leave the city behind, that bus started to pass all manner of brown people 'long the way. They would smile right up to Richard in that bus, and wave; Richard smile right back out the window, and shake a little wave down on 'em. Bus drove me through a scrubbrush desert, up an endless mountain, till it rolled down into the smell of the dank sea. And the Lord, he stopped that bus and took me off—just like the Lord, he had put me on a bus in the first place. Here, Richard, dwell amongst these little brown people. Dead of night, weren't nobody 'round. But Richard walked, down a dirt road, that could have been any country road in any country—with just 'nough moonlight to see ahead. [*Pause.*] I begin hearing this sound. A kind'a "wang-wang." A sound like could be made on a Jews-harp. Or like that thing you can do with the pedal.

[RICHARD *creates the sound of a didgeridoo. He shakes his hands, and he makes a steady drone.*]

[JIMI *processes a note through the wah-wah pedal.* JIMI *creates the sound of the didgeridoo. He captures the gentle sameness of its sound, and at the same time lets us know that* RICHARD *is walking closer to the source of that energy.*]

[RICHARD *adds his hands clapping.*]

RICHARD: I was sure it was God setting the night a-buzz. [*Pause.*] I come a little closer and hear the beating of sticks-on-sticks. And there they all was, in a clearing, lit by torchfires. Hundreds of brown people and I'm watching. Watching a dance I could not comprehend. Men in pointed caps, who writhed on the ground like snakes. Women with exposed breasts, who acted like men. Men who were women. Men with feathers covering they bodies. And all throughout, the air smelled of blood, sweat and the dank sea.

[JIMI *stops playing.*]

[RICHARD *creates the* didgeridoo, *and takes us out of that night.*

Again JIMI *comes in under him, and relieves him of the music. Jimi adds various touches to the sound, that reflect the next part of* RICHARD's *monologue.*]

[JIMI's *guitar carries* RICHARD *back to the piano; he sits.*]

RICHARD: [*Chuckling.*] Come morning, they talking to me, but I don't understand a word they was saying. When they realize I couldn't, they kind'a drew back from me. So, Richard give 'em his signature, to pull 'em right back. [*Shakes out his hands.*] Lord, don't they give Richard his signal right back. Then they looked at each other, and shrugged. They didn't know who Richard was. Even the ones what spoke English didn't know me. Had not one of my records. I come to find out, all night, they was thinking I'm somebody son or brother what done come back home for this special ceremony.

[RICHARD *lays down a series of happy gospel notes.* JIMI *bends his sound to echo* RICHARD's *notes. But with the shift in* RICHARD's *monologue,* JIMI's *guitar becomes bluer and bluer.*]

RICHARD: Seem like for a month, I'm singing my church songs to them; they singing they religious chants to me. O, we was having a joyous time. [*Pause; stops playing.*] But slack-eye found me, as far in that outback as I was. Pull up in a big French car, covered with wanted posters: "Have you seen this man." "The king of rock 'n' rhythm done run 'way." O, slack-eye pulled on me, and he pulled on me. You letting everybody down. Gonna miss the high-life, and the big paychecks. Called me madman, gonna call the FBI and put me in jail. Made it so Richard had to go back. But soon's that tour was done, got on another bus, back to Macon, back to the little church what give me my first life. [*Pauses.*] Only the money is so good. And the whole time I was off the scene, my fans was sending me they love through the mail. [*Pauses.*]

[JIMI *fills the space with a pure blues. Clear, clean notes, without irony, without lyrics to shape our response, to filter the pain.* JIMI *is drifting, and with a note placed here and there,* RICHARD *"flags" the places* JIMI *discovers.*]

RICHARD: [*Cont'd.*] I'll tell you one thing, Jimi: many a night I've

RICHARD: [*Cont'd.*] lied awake on this tour, my soul torn in two, hoping my daddy'd come and show his face again. [*Pauses.*] You ever hear, that when you gone, supposed to cross your shadow on the foot of the bed of somebody you close to? [*Pause.*] Daddy never throw'd his shadow 'cross my mama's bed. The dead s'posed to do that, ever'body say so. [*Pauses.*] Long gone, these twenty-five years, he never throw'd his shadow 'cross the foot of mama's bed. [*In rhythm.*] Not nair', one sign, good-bye. Left her 'lone, crying on the deep-down ache in her head. [*Pauses.*]

[JIMI *continues, deeply lost in his blues phrasing.* JIMI *is only a conduit for the notes.*]

RICHARD: [*Continues.*] Nice, Jimi.

[RICHARD *hums a few bars, then scats along, feelingly and leading the guitar's phrasing.*]

[*Voice and guitar come together as if rehearsed.* RICHARD *is intent on the intense* JIMI, *hunched over his guitar.*]

RICHARD: [*Drifting into his private world, then in rhythm.*]

Ever hold a man

so close

smell the gin

cigarette

the blood

bubbling from his throat

cause he has been shot down

by his best friend

ove' a twenty-cent glass

of gin.

When you coming home, daddy

When you coming back, tonight

Will you give me some sugar

in the morning

RICHARD: [*Cont'd.*] Is you ever go' do right.

Was a low-roof juke-joint place

Way back in the devil's woods.

[*Stops abruptly.*]

[JIMI's *guitar repeats the lines, then continues through the verse's resolution. He fills the space with a flurry of notes, extends the phrasing.*]

RICHARD: Jimi? [*Grasps* JIMI's *knee.*] Jimi? [*Slowly.*] Was my daddy what died that way, Jimi. I saw that nickel-plate coming out. Knew what it was, 'cause I'd seen it so many times before. Then I saw it go 'pop.' My daddy come stumbling over to me. Need to get over to me. Pulled me down to the floor. Like we could'a been wrastling. Died with my eyes on his face. Here I am, a lad of ten, tagging 'long 'hind his daddy. Lord'a mercy, my long gone daddy. [*Recovering composure.*]

[JIMI's *guitar 'repeats'* RICHARD's *last sentence, syllable-for-syllable.* JIMI's *guitar repeats the first phrase of its phrasing of* RICHARD's *sentence, with embellishment. The guitar plays a set of spare random notes. The guitar is stuck.*]

JIMI: C'mon, Mister Richard. Gimme something to work on. [JIMI *is excited, scared and desperate.*] We got something going. Where we going, Mistuh Richard. C'mon, Mistuh Richard, take it. [*Trails off playing.*] Mister Richard? [*Realizes* RICHARD's *hand on his knee, and springs off his stool.*] Keep your hands off me.

RICHARD: My daddy usta grab my leg like that, when I done something that tickled him. Strongest thing I remember—

JIMI: [*Intense.*] I told you before, I ain't no faggot.

RICHARD: I just wanted to touch somebody. [*Open and vulnerable.*] Wasn't you listening to me? Wasn't touching you that way.

JIMI: I was playing. Trying to find something. And I almost got it.

RICHARD: I heard you, Jimi. You was there right with me. I just... [*Shrugs.*]

JIMI: You ruined it.

RICHARD: We can get it back, Jimi.

JIMI: We? I was doing it. Staying out the way. Letting it come.

RICHARD: Here's what you was doing. [*Poised to play; cannot remember.*]

JIMI: [*Pauses.*] I'll get it back.

[JIMI *retrieves guitar case, and opens it on floor. He unplugs his guitar, and as a ritual, kisses its neck quickly and nestles it into the case.*]

RICHARD: [*A little shaken.*] What you doing, Jimi? Now, now, we ain't done. Whole lot more o' this tape to do.

[JIMI *unplugs his small amp from the larger band amp, begins to coil the two cables and tape the loops. When he is done, he will have a small pile of possessions.*]

JIMI: I'm done, Mister Richard. I want the money I earned for two weeks work.

RICHARD: [*Placating.*] I tol' you, I got your money, Jimi. [*Pause.*] Won't be no more loans coming.

JIMI: I won't need none.

RICHARD: Go on 'n' spend it on whatever hussy you got waiting.

JIMI: I'm not going to no girl. Why you keep saying that. I almost never bother with those girls hanging 'round. Mister Richard, when I'm not in one of these bars playing, I'm back in whatever cheap room you got me in—creating my music. I hear you all talking about me in the morning. If you don't hear me, it's cause I don't need to plug in my amp to hear what I'm playing. [*Finishes piling.*]

RICHARD: [*Tentatively.*] Where you going, Jimi.

JIMI: [*Pause.*] To the bus station.

RICHARD: [Weary.] Jimi, don't play with me.

JIMI: I'm going to New York City, Mister Richard.

RICHARD: Boy, you going' where?

JIMI: [Pauses.] Mister Richard, I'm going to be on the Ed Sullivan

JIMI: [*Cont'd.*] Show. He don't know it yet. He don't even know my name yet, but you watch. I'm gonna do exactly what Mister Albert did: be patient. Plug in and fire up right in the lobby.

RICHARD: You can't do that country stuff in New York City. I been there. Country only works in the country.

JIMI: Just because you can't, doesn't mean I can't. I'm gonna get a crowd of 'em 'round me, and show 'em all my tricks. And when I do get my shot, I'm gonna play all over the place. Play some blues like they ain't never heard before.

RICHARD: Shoot, you be back to my tour. The little money I got for you barely carry you past the subway.

JIMI: I'm not coming back this time, Mister Richard.

RICHARD: [Pause.] Jimi, I can't get 'long 'out a guitar.

JIMI: What about when I was in St. Louis?

RICHARD: I didn't bring you clear 'cross the country, cause I could not find a guitar player.

JIMI: So you know. [*Pause.*] Mister Richard, you owe me something. For what I can do; for what I did for you on this tour. [*Shrugs.*] But I'm always the one who's got to pay. [*Pause.*] You said you have my money. I got someplace to be, Mistuh Richard.

RICHARD: [*Suspicious.*] What them slack-eyes from New York promise you, Jimi?

JIMI: I don't know what you talking about, Mister Richard.

RICHARD: [*Bit nervous.*] You lying to me, boy. They ain't come all this way, and just disappear the same night. I been huntin' they damn asses all over Macon—Naw, if they wanted your stuff, they'd give'd you bus fare. [*Pause.*] All right, Jimi. All right.

[RICHARD *pulls out money clip; counts out one-hundred-twenty dollars, which he hands to* JIMI. RICHARD *pivots back to face piano.* JIMI *pockets the money, loads up his stuff, surveys for anything overlooked.*]

JIMI: Mister Richard. This is more than I need for bus fare.

RICHARD: That's yours, Jimi. And you will need every penny, and a hundred times more. I just missed with you, Jimi.

[JIMI *nods.* RICHARD *shakes a wave.* JIMI *exits, closing the door softly.*]

RICHARD: Well, well, well. Well, well. Ev'body long gone. [*Tickles the keyboard; begins to pick out "Goodnight, Irene," in a bluesy/gospel tone, toying with the verse; sings.*] Stop gambling and rambling all over town/Stop staying out late every night/Come home to your wife and your family/And dine by the fireside bright. [*Continues through chorus.*] Sometimes I live in the country, babe/Sometimes I live downtown/Sometimes I take a great notion/To jump in the river and drown. [*Trailing off.*] Irene, good night/Irene, good night/Good night, Irene/Good night, Irene/ I'll see you in my dreams.

THE END

Edward de Grazia

THE VACUUM CLEANER

An Opera in One Act

Edward de Grazia

Edward de Grazia took his law degree to Washington, D.C., where he practiced at the F.C.C. bar, did what little was in his power to combat McCarthyism, wrote book reviews for the *New York Times* and *Washington Post*, and alerted the press of the country to the operation of federal literary censors when he went to court to save a rare-edition copy of Aristophanes' *Lysistrata* from being destroyed as obscene by the U.S. Post Office Department. This marked the beginning of the end of the censorship of literature and art by Post Office officials, a practice de Grazia described and documented in the *Journal of Law & Contemporary Problems*. After that he went to Paris where he worked at UNESCO for the improvement of cultural relations and progress in human rights, and studied the emerging Absurd theatre. Returning to the States after Joe McCarthy but not "McCarthyism" was finished, he began to write absurdist plays of his own.

The Swings had its premiere at Gene Frankel's Weekend Repertory Theatre in New York, was also performed at the Arena Stage in Washington, and published in *Evergreen Review*. *Borgeois Gentleman* and *Hoo Fasa* had staged readings at the Washington Theatre Club. *Myrtilus* (with music by Dina Kosten) and *The Americans* were performed at Ellen Stewart's La Mama Experimental Theatre in New York.

After de Grazia met Barney Rosset, the legendary founder of Grove Press, the two worked together to free from censorship the Grove editions of William Burrough's *Naked Lunch*, the Swedish film *I Am Curious — Yellow*, and Henry Miller's *Tropic of Cancer* (in the U.S. Supreme Court). During the Vietnam War he was associated with the Institute for Policy Studies, served as a lawyer for the Mobilization to End the War in Vietnam and was an organizer of Volunteer Lawyers to Defend the Demonstrators at the Pentagon.

De Grazia is a member of the founding faculty of the Cardozo Law School (Yeshiva University) in Greenwich Village where he continues to teach and write about, among other subjects, the freedom and censorship of literature, art, and film in America. He is the author of a history of the struggle for artistic freedom in the United States called *Girls Lean Back Everywhere: The Law of Obscenity and the Assault on Genius* (Random House and Vintage).

CHARACTERS

WIFE

CHILDREN, A DAUGHTER AND SON

HUSBAND

THE NEIGHBOR'S WIFE

THE APPLIANCES

SCENE: *The living-dining area of a cheap two-bedroom brick bunga-*
low in a development forty minutes from a metropolis. There is a
great "picture-window" which looks out upon a row of identical
cheap two-bedroom brick bungalows with identical great "picture-
windows" looking out upon identical . . . etc., etc. Within the win-
dows may be seen pantomime scenes identical to that which takes
place on the stage. The furnishings are American "Colonial"; they
clash with the modern dress of the husband and his wife. On the
wall, a crocheted portrait of the American flag, and other oddities.
The place is in dreadful taste, but the couple raising their family
there are trying.

    There is a giant-size TV screen in constant operation, its im-
age visible, even oppressive, to the audience. The volume is at max-
imum, probably in an effort to overcome the terrible, ear-splitting
and brain-deadening sounds coming from THE AIR CONDITIONER,
THE AUTOMATIC DISHWASHER, THE AUTOMATIC WASHER-
DRYER COMBINATION, THE AUTOMATIC DISPOSAL, THE RE-
FRIGERATOR-FREEZER, *and* THE TANK-TYPE VACUUM
CLEANER, *which interminably grind, humm, swish, tumble, buzz,*
bang, shift gears, roar, gurgle and groan—obscuring the human
sounds that the characters seek, from time to time, to make. In fact,
their sweet docility is best accounted for by their final submission to
the aural vitality of these mechanical helpmate devices.

    As the scene opens, the TV image is delivering a late-afternoon
"soap-opera," the heroine of which is an aging, once-beautiful
mother whose marriage is going on the rocks, whose teenage son has
just been arrested for smoking marijuana in high school, whose
beloved father is dying of cancer, and who has suddenly grown aware
that she is fast becoming, if not already there, an alcoholic, etc. The
sound from the TV, when it surfaces above the raging ocean of

sounds coming from the other appliances, is apparently out of sync. Worse yet, as gradually becomes evident, the dialogue is from another "soap-opera" — D.H. Lawrence's Lady Chatterley's Lover.

When the CHILDREN *enter, the TV image will deliver animated cartoons, with a soundtrack composed of readings from the book* Auschwitz *or* Letters From Vietnam, *or another.*

When the HUSBAND *enters, the TV image will deliver the news and weather of the day with soundtrack running smart personal commercials for ladies, à la* Vogue, Glamour, *etc. He will be very tall and thin, with a mustache; neatly dressed in a gray flannel suit, etc. The* WIFE *will enter with a rush, from the Kitchen* [O.S.]. *She will wear ballet slippers, tapered slacks, a frilly tea-apron, a ladies-model man's shirt, no make-up, and hair-curlers under a kerchief. A cigarette will dangle from her lip. She will wear her* ANXIETY *mask, as from an impossible number of household chores to be done by an impending deadline. The living-dining room, however, appears immaculate.*

The WIFE *enters, and all the* APPLIANCE *sounds come on. She moves to* THE VACUUM CLEANER, *takes its neck or handle, in her hand, doesn't switch on the power, stands and looks at the TV screen. Her body, rigid at first, relaxes slowly. She goes rigid once more, then relaxes, still watching the TV. As the reading from Lady Chatterley's Lover becomes recognizable, she turns on the power but does not push the machine.* THE VACUUM CLEANER'S *sound grows and subsides, huskily, having a life of its own. As the* READING *becomes a bit tense, the* WIFE's *body also grows tense, and* THE VACUUM CLEANER *has an orgasm in the* WIFE's *hand. The* WIFE's *body sort of sags.* THE VACUUM CLEANER'S *sound subsides. The other mechanical sounds grow remote and smooth out.*

The CHILDREN *enter the house. They are twins, boy and girl, aged 5. They carry schoolbooks underarm. When they enter, they stand impassively at the threshold.*

The WIFE *springs to life, cuts off* THE VACUUM CLEANER, *darts to and around the* CHILDREN, *and all around the room. Her mask of* ANXIETY *flickers with lights of* JOY. *She returns to her original position, facing them at the door, lays her hand upon* THE VACUUM CLEANER *handle or neck, and speaks.*

WIFE: [*Singing.*] Watch what you are doing!

Don't make a mess of things!

Where have you been all day?

Go to your room and play!

[*The* CHILDREN *remain immobile. The boy, however, makes a faint move with his hand or mouth, as though he wishes to speak; this propels her once more into agitated motion, around the room, around them, and back again as before.*]

WIFE: [*Singing.*] Do you want something to eat?

[*The* CHILDREN *lick their lips and she springs OS into the kitchen.*]

WIFE: [*OS*] [*Singing.*] All right! I'm coming! All right!

All right! All right! All right!

I'm coming! All right!

[*Enters with cookie jar.*] All right!

[WIFE *stuffs cookie after cookie into their mouths, boy, girl, boy, girl, etc. They swallow as fast as they can. She gets an extra cookie into the boy when the girl's swallowing falls behind . . .*]

WIFE: [*Singing.*] All right! All right! I'm coming! All right!

[*pause*] All . . . right . . .

[WIFE *watches them swallow the last cookies and, as their faces suffuse with dumb contentment, her mask changes from* ANXIETY *to* JOY.]

[*The* CHILDREN *shake the crumbs from their hands and continue to smile contentedly. The* WIFE *leaps and dances around them and the room, joyfully, returning to her first position.*]

WIFE: [*Singing.*] All right!

Then watch! But I have so many things to do.

Please stay out of my way!

Here!

[*She takes them up by their coat collars, as a cat her kittens, and deposits each on a hook of a coat rack standing in a corner of the room.*

They dangle there, their smiles of contentment marred a bit by the helplessness of their situations.]

[WIFE *returns to her* VACUUM CLEANER, *switches it back on; it and the other household sounds mount once more to a raging ocean of sound.*]

WIFE: [*Sings.*] Busy day!

Busy day!

Every one is such a busy day!

Busy day!

Busy day!

Every one is just a busy day...

[WIFE *slows ("runs") down to immobility, looking at the TV screen.* THE VACUUM CLEANER'S *sounds subsides too; but all the other sounds of the* APPLIANCES *grow in power and variety and run rampant through the room. A LONG TIME passes.*]

[*The light outside the "picture-window" fades.*]

[*The door opens again.*]

[*The* HUSBAND *enters carrying a briefcase and a mask of FATIGUE.* WIFE *springs to life. The other mechanical sounds subside to buzzes and a hum.* THE VACUUM CLEANER *returns to life with a welcoming roar and a new surge of power, which drown out the words* HUSBAND *has to say upon entering.*]

[WIFE *darts to him, pecks his cheek, closes the door, darts around the room, back to him, pecks his other cheek, takes his briefcase,* EXITS *with it into bedroom, enters without it, darts to bar, makes* GIANT MARTINI, *darts with it to him, takes his nose in her fingertips, opens his mouth, pours* GIANT MARTINI *into him, watches him swallow and go glassy-eyed. She looks at him lovingly.*]

WIFE: [*Sings.*] Darling, you can use a drink.

When you come home from work.

You can always use a drink.

[WIFE *returns to bar, makes another* GIANT MARTINI, *returns*

*to him, feeds him it in the same manner as before, watches lovingly
as he turns even more glassy-eyed than before.*]

WIFE: [*Sings.*] There! There!

> There!
>
> That's better, dear?
>
> Isn't it? Better, dear?
>
> There! There?
>
> There!

[WIFE *studies him, remembers something, moves up to him, loosens
his tie, unbuttons his shirt collar, removes his hat, smooths down his
hair, caresses his shoulder, singing:*]

> There . . . ?
>
> There . . . ?
>
> There . . . ?

[WIFE *rubs against him.*]

HUSBAND: [*Responding.*] Unng!

WIFE: There . . . ? [*Pause.*] Stop! [*She looks around the room.*]

> Not before the children . . . Don't forget our chil-
> dren! Think about . . . the children [*Looking
> around, unable to locate the children.*]

HUSBAND: UNGHHhhh . . .

WIFE: Besides! Wouldn't you like another . . . ?

[*She goes swiftly to bar, pours another* GIANT MARTINI, *returns, feeds it to him in the same manner as before.*]

> There!

HUSBAND: [*Wobbling, caving, straightening, caving.*] Enhhhh......

WIFE: [*Helping him to sofa.*]

> Hard day. You've had a hard day.
>
> All work and no play means
>
> Dad-dy's had another hard day.

WIFE: [*Cont'd.*] [*She sits him down on the sofa, he caves, she sits him up, he caves, she props him up with pillows.*]

>It's all right! All right! It's all right!

>There!

[WIFE *looks around, spies the* CHILDREN *who are staring at them, dashes to them.*]

>[*Singing.*] All right? Is everything all right?

[*She darts out and returns with more cookies.*]

>[*Singing.*] If you'd rather not go and play in your room

>You may stay and watch......

[WIFE *stuffs more cookies into their mouths.*]

>But please don't spoil your appetite!

[WIFE *goes to the* HUSBAND, *takes* GIANT MARTINI *glass from him, smiles.*]

>You mustn't spoil your appetite either!

[WIFE *exits with glass, returns to* VACUUM CLEANER, *begins to sweep.* THE VACUUM CLEANER *and all the other* APPLIANCES *roar back to life.*]

WIFE: [*Singing madly above the turbulent ocean of sound.*]

>Happy day! Happy day!

>Every one is such a happy day!

>Happy day!

>Happy day!

>Every one is just...a happy...day...

[*The* WIFE *slows ("runs") down, into immobility.* THE VACUUM CLEANER *subsides. The other* APPLIANCES *rock and roll victoriously about the room.*]

[*The* NEIGHBOR'S WIFE *enters.*]

[*The* WIFE *snaps back to life, darts to her, then around the room, leaving* THE VACUUM CLEANER *standing, dusting all the furniture, the walls, doors, etc. then returning to original position.*]

WIFE: Won't you come in!?

Come in!

How very nice to see you.

You're almost like a stranger.

Come in! Won't you come in!

It's been so very long. Let's see...

N.W.: [*Drily.*] Before lunch. I dropped in before lunch.

WIFE: Let me see...

N.W.: To borrow some sugar. We talked 'til...

WIFE: Let me see...

N.W.: ... o'clock. Three or four. O'clock.

WIFE: How could it have been three... or four o'clock. You're mixing up today with yesterday... o'clock. O'clock.

N.W.: [*Drily.*] Yesterday, I dropped in after breakfast.

To try out your electric blender.

We talked 'til five or six... [*Looking around.*]

That was yesterday.

WIFE: [*Flitting around room, dusting, etc.*] Ha! ha!

Oh dear! Ha! ha! Well...

N.W.: Whenever I drop in

We talk 'til three or four.

Or five

Or six... [*Looking around.*] o'clock... o'clock.

WIFE: What?

N.W.: O'clock. What would my husband say?

WIFE: What?

N.W.: Yes. What would your husband say? O'clock.

WIFE: I wonder.

N.W.: I wonder, too.

WIFE: I wonder.

N.W.: I wonder . . . too.

too . . . O'clock.

Too . . . [*She stares at the* HUSBAND, *glassy-eyed on the couch.*] *o'clock!*

WIFE: [*Following her eyes.*]

What in the world did you drop in at this time for, Nicole? It's

so

very . . . late . . .

N.W.: [*Staring at* HUSBAND.]

I know.

WIFE: You know how much I love to stop

And hear you talk.

You shouldn't stay too long, . . . Nicole?

N.W.: [*Staring at* HUSBAND.]

I know.

WIFE: This time. O'clock.

N.W.: [*As before.*] I know.

WIFE: Please don't misunderstand my meaning . . .

N.W.: [*Turning to go, seeing the children, pop-eyed on the coat-rack.*]

No. O'clock.

WIFE: They're so dear to me. I want to be prepared.

N.W.: [*Staring at the children.*] The children . . . the children . . .

WIFE: And don't forget my husband. He'll be home too, soon. He'll . . . be home . . . soon, too. O'clock. I have to be prepared. [*She starts* THE VACUUM CLEANER *and the other* APPLIANCES *begin also to come on.*]

WIFE: [*Cont'd.*] The children come first

But my husband comes, too.

You see?

Don't you see?

I want to be prepared.

[*Stopping abruptly.*] [*Leaving the* APPLIANCES *on.*]

I wonder where they can be?!

They're home so late from school.

Maybe they're outside playing.

Should I go out and see...? [*Putting on a scarf.*]

Excuse me? Excuse me! [*Exiting.*] But I'd better

go out and see...

N.W.: [*Staring at the closed door, looking around the room. listening to the appliances, noticing* THE VACUUM CLEANER.]

[*To audience.*] She must be crazy! [*Moving to sofa.*] O'clock.

[*Sitting down beside* HUSBAND *who, as before, smiles glassy-eyed at all and nothing.*]

HELLO.

I think your wife must be crazy. O'clock. O'clock.

Running out on you this way. O'clock.

I think your wife must be crazy...

Hello... [*He doesn't change countenance: she seizes his shoulders and kisses his lips, passionately.*]

I know how long you've been waiting to do that, to me

How long. Too long. I saw how you were watching me... so long.

Through my window. For so long. [*Pause.*]

N.W.: [*Cont'd.*] She can't satisfy you, can she? [*Seizing and kissing him again, more passionately.*]

You're not like all the other men, here, around here.

N.W.: [*Cont'd.*] All the other men around here . . . aren't men at all.

They all look exactly the same, no matter what's their name.

Horn-rimmed glasses and a gray-flannel suit.

Smiley-mouth and glassy-eyed, too.

You're . . . different! [*She kisses him again and removes his coat and shirt.*] [THE VACUUM CLEANER *revs up and the D.H. Lawrence reading begins to repeat.*]

What's different about you is . . . brains . . . [*Kisses him.*]

I like a man who can . . . think and see . . . [*She unbuckles his belt and starts to remove his trousers.*] [THE VACUUM CLEANER *is running amuck.*]

I like a man . . . who's a MAN . . . [*She pulls down his trousers so that he sits wearing only underwear and shoes and gartered socks.*]

[*The* CHILDREN'*s eyes pop out unbelievingly*]

With a big DICK . . . for me . . . oh! [*She has found his tiny dick.*]

[THE VACUUM CLEANER *subsides with an uncharacteristic whistle, but the other* APPLIANCES *run and grind and whirl and tumble and gyrate and scream raucously, as the* WIFE *enters.*]

WIFE: Dear, oh dear! Dear, oh dear!

Where in the world can the children be?!

[*Spotting children.*] Oh!

[*Rushing to them, kissing their faces.*]

There you both are! I almost forgot!

N.W.: [*Swiftly re-making her face: new lipstick, powder, eyebrow pencil, mascara.*] Excuse me . . . Excuse me . . . I didn't look . . .

I didn't . . . see.

WIFE: How you were!

What love was all about!

[*She hugs them lovingly and the* CHILDREN *start to scream, hideously, piteously, as if all the horror which they have seen was only now felt. Their screams encourage even more heroic efforts from the* APPLIANCES, *and* THE VACUUM CLEANER *starts to huff and puff.*]

[*The* NEIGHBOR'S WIFE *rises from the sofa, straightens her clothes, straightens up the* HUSBAND *on the sofa, kicking his outer clothes underneath and starts to leave.*]

N.W.: So nice to see you!

Too bad. Too bad.

Maybe they are hungry!

I think he could use some sleep. [*Exits.*]

Too bad. I'll drop in again soon. Too bad.

I'll be seeing you . . . soon . . .

WIFE: [*Taking the* CHILDREN *down from their hooks, carrying them OS into a bedroom.*]

Don't cry, my darlings!

Brave children don't cry

Please don't cry my darlings

Tomorrow brings a brighter day. . . .

[*The* APPLIANCES *quiet down. The* HUSBAND *remains as before, seated in his underwear, glassy-eyed, his face now smeared with red. There is a long silence. Then the* WIFE *enters, very slowly, stops, looks at her* HUSBAND.]

WIFE: Hello.

I almost didn't see . . . you.

Hello.

[*The* HUSBAND *topples over onto the floor.*]

WIFE: You've been drinking again, haven't you.

Oh Tom, you've been drinking so much again,

Haven't you!

WIFE: [Cont'd.] Trying to unwind.

We know you're only trying to unwind ... but ...

[*She takes him by the feet and draws him gently OS from the room.*]

WIFE: Silly day.

Silly day

Every day is just a silly day.

Silly day.

Silly ... day ...

Christopher Durang

MRS. SORKEN

Christopher Durang

Christopher Durang has had plays on and off-Broadway including *The Nature and Purpose of the Universe*, *Titanic*, *A History of the American Film*, *Baby with the Bathwater*, *Beyond Therapy*, *Laughing Wild*, and *Sex and Longing*.

His play *Sister Mary Ignatius Explains it All for You* won Obie Awards for him and actress Elizabeth Franz when it originated at Ensemble Studio Theatre. A subsequent production by Playwrights Horizons on a double bill with his *The Actor's Nightmare* transferred to Off-Broadway, where it ran for two years. *Sister Mary* has had productions around the country and the world.

His play *The Marriage of Bette and Boo* also won him an Obie Award, as well as the Dramatists Guild's prestigious Hull Warriner Award, when it premiered at the New York Shakespeare Festival. Durang also played the part of Matt in that production, sharing with the other nine actors an Ensemble Acting Obie Award. The play's director, Jerry Zaks, and designer, Loren Sherman, also won Obie Awards for their work on that play.

Among his most recent work was *Durang Durang*, an evening of six one-acts directed by Walter Bobbie at Manhattan Theatre Club. Included in this evening were *Mrs. Sorken*, *For Whom the Southern Belle Tolls* and *A Stye of the Eye*.

Mr. Durang has also acted in movies, such as *Housesitter*, *The Butcher's Wife*, and *Mr. North*. He sang in the Sondheim revue *Putting it Together*, which starred Julie Andrews at the Manhattan Theatre Club. He also performed with Sigourney Weaver in their co-authored cabaret, *Das Lusitania Songspiel*; and with John Augustine and Sherry Anderson in the *Chris Durang and Dawne* cabaret.

Durang is a graduate of Yale School of Drama; a member of the Dramatists Guild Council; and with Marsha Norman is the co-chair of the playwriting program at the Juilliard School Drama Division.

CHARACTERS

MRS. SORKEN

Enter Mrs. Sorken to address the audience. She is a charming woman, well-dressed and gracious, though a little scattered. She is happy to be there.

MRS. SORKEN: Dear theatregoers, welcome, and how lovely to see you. I've come here to talk to you about theatre, and why we all leave our homes to come see it, assuming we have. But you have left your homes, and you're here. So, welcome!

Now I have written down some comments about theatre for you, if I can just find them.

[Searches through her purse.] Isn't it refreshing to see someone with a purse?

[Looks some more through the purse.] Well, I can't find my notes, so I'll have to make my comments from memory.

[From here on, she is genuinely winging it — some of it may be thoughts she prepared, much of it is thoughts that pop into her head as she is speaking. She is not nervous, though. She loves talking to the audience.]

Drama. Let's begin with etymology, shall we? ... etymology, which is the history of the word.

The word "drama" comes from the Greek word "dran," which means to do, and which connects with the English word "drain," meaning to exhaust one totally, and with the modern pharmaceutical sedating tablet, Dramamine, which is the tradename of a drug used to relieve airsickness and seasickness and a general sense of nausea, or *nausée* as Jean-Paul Sartre might say, perhaps over a cup of espresso at a Paris bistro. How I love Paris in the spring, or would, if I had ever been there; but Mr. Sorken and I haven't done much traveling. Maybe after he dies I'll go somewhere.

We go to the drama seeking the metaphorical Dramamine that will cure us of our nausea of life.

Of course, sometimes we become nauseated by the drama itself, and then we are sorry we went, especially if it uses the F-word and lasts over four hours. I don't mind a leisurely play, but by 10:30 I want to leave the theatre and go to sleep.

Frequently, I prefer Dramamine to drama, and only wish someone would renew my prescription for Seconal.

Secondly...we have the word "theatre," which is derived from the Greek word "theasthai," which means to view.

And nowadays we have the word, "reastat," a device by which we can dim the lights in one's house slowly, rather than just snapping them off with a simple switch.

And thirdly, we have the Greek god "Dionysus," the last syllable of which is spelled "s-u-s" in English, but "s-o-s" in Greek, the letters which in Morse code spell "help" — "Dionysos" is the god of wine and revelry, but also the father of modern drama as we know it.

The Greeks went to the theatre in the open air, just like the late and wonderful Joseph Papp used to make us see Shakespeare. Shakespeare's language is terribly difficult to understand for us of the modern age, but how much easier when there's a cool breeze and it's for free. If it's hot and I have to pay, well, then I don't much like Shakespeare. I'm sorry, I shouldn't say that. He's a brilliant writer, and I look forward to seeing all 750 of his plays. Although perhaps not in this lifetime.

But back to the Greeks. They went to the open-air theatre expecting the drama they saw to evoke terror and pity.

Nowadays we have enough terror and pity in our own lives, and so rather than going to the theatre looking for terror, we go looking for slight irritation. And rather than looking for the theatre to evoke pity, we look merely for a generalized sense of identification as in "Evita was a woman, I am a woman." Or "Sweeney Todd was a barber, I go to the hairdresser." Or "Fosca in *Passion* should have her moles removed, I know a good dermatologist." That sort of thing.

But did the Greeks really experience terror and pity? And if so, what was it in all that matricide-patricide that so affected them?

I know that seeing Greek drama nowadays, even with Diana Rigg in it, really rather baffles me, it is so very different from my own life. My life with Mr. Sorken is not something that Diana Rigg would wish to star in, even on PBS. My life, I'm sorry to say, is not all that interesting.

Indeed, addressing you at this very moment, I'm sorry to say, is the high point of my life to date.

Could I have lived my life differently? Women of my generation were encouraged to marry and to play the piano, and I have done both those things. Is there a piano here? I don't see one. I might have played a sonata for you, or a polonaise.

But back to my theme — Drama, from the Greek word "dran."

When we leave the drama, we return to our homes feeling "drained." And if it's been a good night in the theatre, we leave feeling slightly irritated; and feeling identification with Evita or Fosca or that poor Mormon woman in *Angels in America*.

And so, drained, we get into our nightgowns, we adjust our reastats from light to darkness, we climb into bed next to Mr. Sorken, we fall into a deep REM sleep, dreaming God knows what mysterious messages from our teeming unconscious; and then in the morning we open our eyes to the light of the new day, of the burgeoning possibilities.

Light from the Greek word "leukos," meaning white, and the Latin word "lumen" meaning illumination. In German, *der Licht*; in French, *la lumière*. All art leads to light.

Light. Plants need light to grow. Might people need art to grow? It's possible. Are people less important than plants? Some of them are certainly less interesting.

But there is some connection between theatre and light, and people and plants, that I am striving to articulate. It's about photosynthesis, I think, which is the ingestion of light that plants go through in order to achieve growth.

And you see, it's "light" again — "photo" comes from the Greek word, "phos," which means light and which relates to phosphoresence, or the "light given off." And synthesis comes from the Greek prefix, "syn-" meaning together, and the Greek word "tithenai," meaning to place, to put.

Photosynthesis — to put it together with light.

We go to the theatre, desperate for help in photosynthesis.

The text of the play is the light, the actors help put it together, and we are the plants in the audience.

Plants, lights, theatre, art. I feel this sense of sudden interconnection with everything that's making me feel dizzy. Dramamine, of course, is good for dizziness.

Now to wrap up.

Dear theatregoers. I hope you enjoy your evening this evening. I'm not quite sure what you're seeing, but whatever it is, I'm sure it will be splendid.

And, by the way, if you are ever in Connecticut, I hope you will drop in and say hello to me and Mr. Sorken. He prefers that you call first, but I love to be surprised. So just ring the bell, and we'll have cocktails.

And I hope you have enjoyed my humbly offered comments on the drama. I have definitely enjoyed speaking with you, and have a sneaking suspicion that in the future, it is going to be harder and harder to shut me up.

[*Either end with that, or possibly add and end with: "And so, the high point of my life to date being over, I leave you with the play."*]

Gus Edwards

FOUR WALLS

Gus Edwards

Gus Edwards was born in the Caribbean, but studied theatre in the U.S., where he worked as an actor. Mr. Edwards is the author of thirteen full length plays produced by the Negro Ensemble Company (NEC) and other places. Titles include *The Offering, Weep Not for Me, Lifetimes on the Streets,* and most recently, the single-character play *Confessional.* He has also written for PBS-TV.

Edwards, who has received grants from the Rockefeller Foundation, National Endowment and the Arizona Commission for the Arts, currently teaches Theatre and Film Studies at Arizona State University, where he also runs the Multi Ethnic Theatre Program.

Publications by Gus Edwards include *Old Phantoms* and *The Offering* (Dramatists Play Service), *Three Fallen Angels,* (Centerstage Anthology), *100 Monologues* (Mentor Books), *Classic Plays from the NEC* (University of Pittsburgh Press) and Monologues on Black Life (Heinemann Books).

Four Walls was originally presented by the Writers Circle and the Actors Theatre of Phoenix at the Herberger Theatre (Stage West) on August 1, 1996 with the following cast: Ellen Benton as Rose, Ken Love as Ralph and Lillie Richardson as Judy. It was directed by Glorianne Engel.

This play is dedicated to Glorianne Engel and the Writers Circle.

CHARACTERS

RALPH   A man in his twenties.

ROSE   His wife — late forties

JUDY   An attractive but tough looking girl between 18 and 23.

SETTING: *Despite the title, a room without walls. Sort of a lighted area surrounded by a void of darkness. Furniture should be kept at a minimum. A sofa, two chairs, and something that represents a replica of an old statue. It doesn't have to be very elaborate — just suggestive.*

TIME: *The present.*

SCENE 1

Night. Late. ROSE *is sitting alone in the room doing needlepoint. Music from a radio can be heard softly in the background. The feeling is lonely, even bleak.* ROSE *remains in her chair for a while quietly doing her work. Outside the room a dim light illuminates* JUDY *and* RALPH.

RALPH: Take just about a minute. Don't move.

JUDY: You sure?

RALPH: Told you, I'll handle it.

JUDY: Ralph —

RALPH: Baby —

JUDY: Okay man. It's your scene. [*He kisses her.*]

RALPH: Be right back.
    [*He moves into the room as the lights fade on* JUDY.]

ROSE: Ralph?

RALPH: Hey Rose, I didn't think you'd still be up.

ROSE: I was just going in.

RALPH: Oh, yeah . . . Kinda late for you ain't it?

ROSE: I was doing, some stuff . . . You hungry?

RALPH: No . . . No thanks. Er —

ROSE: I have food all prepared. Sure you don't want something?

RALPH: No. I ate already. Downtown you know.

ROSE: Oh.

RALPH: Yeah, it was getting late, I was getting hungry so —

ROSE: Alright.

RALPH: But, thanks anyway.

ROSE: Sure.

RALPH: Listen — er — Rose.

ROSE: Yes?

RALPH: I got a favor to ask you.

ROSE: Uh-huh?

RALPH: And if it ain't okay, you tell me.

ROSE: Sure. What is it?

RALPH: Well, you see, I ain't exactly alone.

ROSE: Oh.

RALPH: I have a friend with me. Somebody I met — well — tonight.

ROSE: A woman?

RALPH: No not a woman. A child. Couldn't be no more than — Oh I don't know. A child anyhow. I met her wandering around the streets. No place to go. Talking about sleeping in the subway, on a night like this. So — I told her she could stay the night. Here on the sofa. That's if it is okay with you.

ROSE: Yes. It's all right.

RALPH: Look — you don't have to say so if it ain't.

ROSE: I know.

RALPH: I mean this is your place too. We — both live here.

ROSE: I know.

RALPH: So if it ain't okay—

ROSE: But it is, Ralph.

RALPH: You sure?

ROSE: I told you before, yes.

RALPH: Alright.

ROSE: Where is she?

RALPH: Outside. One minute. I'll get her.
[*He exits.* ROSE, *almost as a reflex, begins straightening up things in the room. After she's finished, she pauses for a moment staring off into space. Her appearance and manner give the impression of great weariness. Moments later* RALPH *returns with* JUDY.]

RALPH: [*Cont'd.*] Honey, this is Judy—the person I was telling you about. Judy, this is my wife Rose.

JUDY: Hi.

ROSE: How do you do?

JUDY: Oh—I'm fine. How are you?

ROSE: I'm fine too. Thank you.

RALPH: Hey, hey, everybody's fine. Well that's nice. Real nice.

ROSE: Yes.

JUDY: Uh-huh.

ROSE: Have a seat, won't you.

RALPH: Yeah, sit down. Rest your bones. I was just telling Rose how I met you.

JUDY: Oh. Yeah—I was hanging out, with no place to go, then I met Ralph.

ROSE: Are you new to the city?

JUDY: Nooo. Well—kinda new, I guess. Came in from Detroit. I been living with this guy couple a months now. And, well, we had this fight. Dumb stuff. Everything will probably be okay tomorrow when I see him. But tonight I'm kinda stuck. No money—and no place to go.

ROSE: Don't you have any family or friends?

JUDY: Oh I know a couple of people, but I'm kind of embarrassed to go knocking on their door at this hour. I'd rather sleep in the subway.

RALPH: But you don't have to. At least not tonight anyway.

JUDY: Yeah. Thanks. You're really kind.

ROSE: Thank Ralph. He's the kind one.

RALPH: You're in it too, honey.

ROSE: Yes. I guess.

JUDY: Well, thanks to both of you.

RALPH: Hey, the least we can do is give somebody a helping hand from time to time. Ain't that so baby?

ROSE: Yes.

RALPH: I mean if we don't look out for each other, who gon do it. Right?

ROSE: Right

RALPH: Black folks got to stick together and that's a fact.

JUDY: Right.

RALPH: Absolutely.

> [*There's a pause in the conversation as everybody tries to think of something to say.* JUDY, *looking around the room, begins to take interest in the statue.*]

JUDY: That thing is nice. Real nice. Where'd you get it?

RALPH: Rose made it. Down in the cellar. She makes all kinds of things. That's how she makes her living.

JUDY: Yeah?

ROSE: Uh-huh.

RALPH: When somebody wants a copy of some famous statue or sculpture all they have to do is order it and Rose goes to work.

ROSE: My father was a sculptor, so I took up his profession. Only,

ROSE: [*Cont'd.*] he could make beautiful, original things. Me, I just have a talent for reproduction.

JUDY: Well, I don't know what to say except I think they're really, really good.

ROSE: Thank you . . . that's nice to hear. [*She rises.*] It's getting late. I guess we better prepare some place for you to sleep.

JUDY: Look, I don't want to put you to any trouble.

ROSE: No trouble. No trouble at all. I'll get some pillows. [*She goes off.*]

JUDY: Ralph —

RALPH: It's okay.
        [ROSE *returns.*]

ROSE: Here you are. The bathroom's over there. I'll get you some clean towels.

JUDY: I wish you wouldn't go to —

ROSE: Don't worry about it.
        [ROSE *gives her the towels.*]

JUDY: Thank you.

ROSE: I forgot to ask. Have you eaten?

JUDY: Yes, that's how I spent the last money I had.

ROSE: Can I get you anything?

JUDY: No, thanks.

RALPH: We got beer in the box. You want a beer?

JUDY: Well, if somebody else is having one.

RALPH: Rose?

ROSE: No, I don't think so.

RALPH: Come on honey, break down.

ROSE: No. Not tonight. I'm tired.

RALPH: Suit yourself. Well, it's just you and me, Judy. Two beers, coming right up. [*He goes to get them.*]

ROSE: You're an attractive young woman.

JUDY: Thank you.

ROSE: But you should take better care of yourself. You look a little — tired.

JUDY: I been up a long time.

ROSE: It shows.
[RALPH *returns.*]

RALPH: Here you go. [*He gives* JUDY *a beer.*] Sure you don't want one, Rose?

ROSE: No. It's late. I'm turning in.

RALPH: Oh, alright. Let me just finish this. I'll be right behind.

ROSE: Take your time. Goodnight, Miss —

JUDY: Judy.

ROSE: Judy.

JUDY: Goodnight Rose. Thank you.

ROSE: Thank Ralph. [*To* RALPH.] Goodnight.

RALPH: See you in a while, baby.
[ROSE *exits.* JUDY *and* RALPH *stand there looking at each other.*]

JUDY: Ralph I —

RALPH: Shhhh — [*Indicating* ROSE *in the bedroom.*]
He goes over to the radio and turns it up a bit, but not too loud. Then returns to Judy who's staring out of the window.

RALPH: It's a quiet night out there. And cold.

JUDY: [*Sensing him but not looking back.*] Ralph, I don't know.

RALPH: But in here it's cozy.

JUDY: Ralph —

RALPH: Don't talk. Turn around. Look at me.
[*He kisses her lightly, then draws her more firmly to him, kissing her more strongly.*]

JUDY: Ralph, I don't know.

RALPH: Baby, why you have to talk? There's only you and me, baby. Just you and me. And the long night ahead of us.

[*They kiss again. Somewhere in back we see* ROSE *not looking at them, but present almost as a witness to their coupling. She makes the sign of the cross and begins to pray.*

Lights fade to black.]

SCENE TWO

Morning.

RALPH *enters partially dressed carrying a leather jacket.*

RALPH: Rose. . . Rose?

ROSE (OS): Yes.

RALPH: Listen baby. I need some money.

[*While he's waiting,* RALPH *puts on the jacket and inspects it in the mirror.* ROSE *enters.*]

RALPH: [*Cont'd.*] What do you think, baby? Real leather. Bought it off a guy on the street. Sixty bucks.

ROSE: It looks nice.

RALPH: I'm talking about the fit. In back.

ROSE: It fits fine. Looks good on you.

RALPH: Smells good too. Here, take a whiff. English leather. You can't beat the price.

ROSE: Was it hot?

RALPH: Of course. That's the only time you get a bargain in this city. But, you got to know what to buy. There's a lot of junk out there. But this was a good deal. A real good deal. [*Admires himself some more in the mirror.*] You know, that's what you ought to do. Get yourself some new clothes and things.

ROSE: Why?

RALPH: Make you feel good.

ROSE: But I feel good already.

RALPH: I mean happy — inside.

ROSE: I feel happy.

RALPH: You sure? Because sometimes I look at you and you look like the loneliest woman in town.

ROSE: I'm not lonely.

RALPH: You sure?

ROSE: Yes. I have you, don't I?

RALPH: Course, you do. And don't you ever doubt it. [*He holds her close to him.*]

ROSE: I won't. . . . Ralph.

RALPH: Hmmmm?

ROSE: That girl, did she leave?

RALPH: Yes.

ROSE: Is she coming back?

RALPH: No. She asked me to say good-bye. And to thank you.

ROSE: I'm not the one she should thank.

RALPH: Well, she thank you anyway.

ROSE: That was nice of her.

RALPH: You didn't mind her spending the night, did you?

ROSE: No.

RALPH: You're really great. You understand me so.

ROSE: I love you, Ralph.

RALPH: I know. And I love you too baby.

ROSE: Yes . . . How much do you need.

RALPH: Ohh—I think about twenty'll do.

ROSE: Here.

RALPH: Thanks. [ROSE *gets her shawl.*] You going out?

ROSE: I'm going to church.

RALPH: Yeah? You been doing that more and more.

ROSE: It makes me feel good. Inside.

RALPH: Well, that's where it counts, I suppose.

ROSE: Yes.

RALPH: Look, I probably won't be here when you get back. I'll see you later tonight.

ROSE: Alright. I'll cook something for you to eat.

RALPH: You don't have to.

ROSE: I know.

RALPH: I'll see you later then, baby. Have a good day.
[*She leaves.* RALPH *goes back to the mirror and finishes dressing as the lights fade.*]

SCENE THREE

Night. Late. The same as in Scene One.
    ROSE *rises, puts away her stuff, turns off the radio and the lights, then goes in. Moments pass. Suddenly there's a desperate pushing on the buzzer, followed by a frantic knocking on the door.*

RALPH (OS): Rose! Rose! Wake up, baby! Hurry! Wake up, please. Hurry!

ROSE: [*Returning.*] Ralph?

RALPH (OS): Rose! Rose, open up.
[*She rushes off stage to him.*]

ROSE (OS): Oh my God! My God! Ralph — what happened?

RALPH: [*Stumbling in.*] Help me honey . . . Help me! [*He's clutching his stomach, his shirt is quite bloody.*]

ROSE: [*Hand over her mouth.*] Ralph —

RALPH: I'm hurting baby. Hurting bad . . . I got cut. Some guys up the street jumped me. They wanted my money . . . I gave it to them, but they cut me anyway.

ROSE: Oh Jesus, Ralph . . . Jesus. [*She begins to cry.*]

RALPH: Don't cry baby . . . Don't cry. I'm hurt and bleeding. Bleeding real bad . . . You got to help me.

ROSE: Yes. Yes, of course.

RALPH: You got to go get me to a doctor . . . Call emergency or something.

ROSE: Yes . . . I will, I will. But — first we got to get you warm. And comfortable. You're shivering. You look cold.

RALPH: I am cold . . . Rose!
   [*She goes for a blanket.*]

ROSE: [*Returning.*] I'm here. Not going anywhere. I'm right here. [*She puts the blanket around him.*] Now doesn't that feel better?

RALPH: Yes . . . yes it does. But you got to move baby. You got to call a doctor . . . Or an ambulance. This thing is bad. I can feel it.

ROSE: Yes darling, yes. I will. I will . . . Now put your head on this pillow. Rest softly.

RALPH: Honey, I mean it. I'm bleeding to death . . . I — I ain't joking . . . this is for real. I'm bleeding and my guts is falling out.

ROSE: I know.

RALPH: Then for God's sake Rose, do something! Call somebody, hurry.

ROSE: Okay. Just rest and relax. All will be fine.

RALPH: Honey . . . Honey, you saying that, but you ain't moving.

ROSE: Just lie still. It'll be easier if you don't move so much.

RALPH: Easier? What are you talking about? Call the man. I'm about to pass out.

ROSE: Rest easy, baby. Lie still.

RALPH: Honey —

ROSE: Relax —

RALPH: But Babe —

ROSE: Please Ralph. Don't move.

RALPH: Don't —? [*He tries to rise.*] Why?

ROSE: It's alright, honey. I'm here. Here to make it easy for you.

RALPH: What you talking about? Make what easy? Baby, you okay?

[*He rises,* makes two steps toward the phone, then falls.] Rose, please help me. Call somebody.

ROSE: Can't. The phone's been broke for a week.

RALPH: [*Shouting with his last strength.*] Well gooddamnit then. Do something! Go outside, get a cab . . . [*A plea.*] Do something.

ROSE: I can't leave you alone like this. Not now. Not when you need me.

RALPH: Baby, baby — you ain't understanding. I'm hurt and bleeding. I'm dying and I can feel it. My life is just —

ROSE: I love you Ralph. Love you very much.

RALPH: Honey, please —

ROSE: From the first time we met I loved you. And, as time went on, I loved you more.

RALPH: Oh God — Jesus — somebody, Help me!

ROSE: They said you were too young for me. And that I could never hold you — but I did, didn't I? You may have strayed but you never left.

RALPH: [*A cry of pain.*] Rose!

ROSE: Hold unto me, baby. Just hold unto me. I'm right here.

RALPH: Honey — baby . . . I'm cold.

ROSE: [*Rocking him.*] Sleep . . . Sleep baby . . . sleep.

RALPH: [*Pulling away from her.*] You . . . you want me to die. [*A sudden realization.*] That's what it is. You ain't doing nothing because . . . because — you want me to die. You glad this is happening to me. You happy! You — you — Oh my God — you hate me!

ROSE: I love you, Ralph.

RALPH: You — been hating me — all this time.

ROSE: I been loving you — loving you all this time.

RALPH: Well, if you do, help me. Call the police.

ROSE: No.

RALPH: I — don't understand you. I — ain't following —

ROSE: Because this is the end, Ralph. The end — here with me.

RALPH: No — no it can't be. [*Shouting.*] SOMEBODY PLEASE, HELP ME!

ROSE: [*Calmly.*] You've had a good life. A rich life. Roof over your head, clothes, money, love . . . and all the women you could get. You've had a lot, Ralph. A whole lot. And now it's all over. This is the end — here with me.

RALPH: Oh Jesus — Jesus. You gone nutty baby. Talking this strange . . . weird talk . . . Oh God . . . you gone crazy . . . burying things in the yard, being by yourself all the time . . . It messed you up . . . it's this place . . . This goddamn place. Staring at these four walls. It done something to you . . . and all that church going. You been praying on me — praying for something bad — Oh God . . . Jesus — I don't want to die. I don't want to —

ROSE: Ralph . . . Ralph, don't worry. Everything will be the same. I love you baby. I love you, and always will. There'll never be anybody else. Ever. You hear. Every year on your birthday I'll put flowers in your room. I'll light candles in church and say prayers. You'll have a nice funeral. Flowers, organ music, everything. I'll shine your shoes myself. And you'll wear your new suit and gold cuff links . . . There'll be a Cadillac, a long shiny black one to drive you on your way . . . And there'll be more, lots more . . . Nothing's too good for the man I love.

[*She rises, goes to the phone and dials.*]

ROSE: [*Cont'd.*] Yes I want to report an emergency . . . My husband has just died in my arms. Yes . . . yes, I'll be right here waiting. Thank you. [*She returns to the sofa where* RALPH *is still lying.*] There now it's all taken care of. Everything is going to be just fine.

[ROSE *then sits with his head on her lap. After a while she begins to rock him and hum as the lights fade.*]

THE END

Herb Gardner

I'M WITH YA, DUKE

Herb Gardner

Herb Gardner is the author of *A Thousand Clowns*, *The Goodbye People*, *Thieves*, *I'm Not Rappaport* (which won the 1986 Tony Award for Best Play, the Outer Critics Circle Award for Outstanding Play, and the John Gassner Playwriting Award), and *Conversations With My Father*. His one-act plays include *How I Crossed the Street for the First Time All by Myself*, *The Forever Game*, and *I'm With Ya, Duke*. For his film adaptation of *A Thousand Clowns*, Gardner won the Best Screenplay Award from the Screenwriters Guild as well as Academy Award nominations for Best Screenplay and Best Picture of the Year. He also wrote the screenplays for *Thieves*, *The Goodbye People* (which he also directed), and *Who Is Harry Kellerman and Why Is He Saying Those Terrible Things About Me?* — this last being an adaptation of one of his several short stories, which appeared in *The Best American Short Stories of 1968*. In addition, Mr. Gardner is the author of a novel, *A Piece of the Action*. He is currently adapting his award-winning play *I'm Not Rappaport* for the screen.

CHARACTERS

SAMUEL MARGOLIS

DR. ALBERT MACINTYRE

NURSE'S VOICE

RED BARBER'S VOICE

SCENE: *A semi-private room in a brand new wing of St. Mary's Hospital in Brooklyn; 1975. A hanging rod and curtain separate the two beds. One is unoccupied, the mattress folded, and can be seen through the pulled-back curtains.*

In the other bed, asleep, is SAMUEL MARGOLIS; *late seventies, several days' growth of beard, wearing a baseball cap with "Dodgers '55" printed on it. He is attached to a heart-monitoring machine by two slim tubes to his chest, a travelling line on the screen indicates heart and pulse beats, which are regular. An I.V. tube is attached to his left arm: to the Right of the bed is an intercom button and speaker, a table with a phone and a manuscript. This is* SAM's *will. A television set is mounted high and at the Center of the wall opposite the bed, to the Right, a simple wooden cross. On the right wall a somber but tasteful painting of the crucifixion.*

AT RISE: *It is 8:30 at night and the darkened Brooklyn skyline is seen through the large window at Left.* SAM *is asleep. We hear the regular hum and blip of the heart-monitor machine.*

SAM: [*Murmuring.*] Yessir. Yessir. All fresh today. Strawberries. Beauties. Do yourself a favor. The bananas, forget it. I don't personally recommend...

[*He opens his eyes, squinting.*] What the hell is this? What's going on here?

[*He looks about, sees crucifix.*] Oh boy... oh boy... Terrific.

[*Sees the I.V. on his arm and the two tubes for the heart-monitor.*] One thing sure... I'm not visiting here.

[*He sits upright.*] Okay. What's up? What's cookin' here? What's doin'?

[*Punches intercom button.*] Hello somebody! This is Margolis! Speak to me!

NURSE'S VOICE: [*On intercom.*] Yes, Mr. Margolis.

SAM: Who I got here?

NURSE'S VOICE: This is Nurse Carswell.

SAM: O.K. What am I doin' here? Where am I?

NURSE'S VOICE: Mr. Margolis, every night at this time you ask me the same —

SAM: I'm not looking for hot news. Answer me again, I wouldn't be bored.

NURSE'S VOICE: Mr. Margolis, you are on the eighth floor of St. Mary's Hospital in Crown Heights. It is Tuesday night, eight p.m....

SAM: Perfect...

NURSE'S VOICE: You have suffered a coronary occlusion...

SAM: Expensive...

NURSE'S VOICE: You were brought here under emergency circumstances...

SAM: Five, six hundred dollars...

NURSE'S VOICE: and have been here exactly one week.

SAM: Fifteen hundred dollars, easy. I gotta get outta here, one more week they'll name a pavilion after me. A week? A week I'm here.

[*To intercom.*] Yes, I knew it was a week. Of course, a week. I knew that.

[*To himself.*] A week. Wow... who's watching the fruit store? Shimkin, the thief. A whole week now. There won't be an orange left.

[*To intercom.*] Who brought me here?

NURSE'S VOICE: Your son.

SAM: Which one? I got one in Europe, finding himself. One in Los Angeles, a lawyer puts you to sleep on the telephone, and the Dopey. The Dopey put me here, right? Jack. Jack the Dopey. Look where he put me. Of course, only Jack.

[*His hand to his heart.*] I remember now... I was in the store... Bingo...

SAM: [*Cont'd.*] [*Into intercom.*] You're the Night Nurse, *Cars*well ... I remember now ...

NURSE'S VOICE: Yes, sir.

SAM: [*Leaning toward intercom.*] Listen, it wouldn't hurt you could lose a couple pounds. [*He looks at the empty bed.*] Ortega. Where's Ortega? I was just talking to Ortega ...

NURSE'S VOICE: Oh, I thought you knew ... Mr. Ortega ... Mr. Ortega expired early this afternoon.

SAM: Expired? What was he, a driver's license? [*Quietly.*] Dead. Ortega. He died. Well, that'll teach me, you can't make friends in a place like this. Talked to me all night. Told me his whole life. That's what people do, Carswell. Something tells them they're dying and they hand it over, the inventory ...

NURSE'S VOICE: Mr. Margolis. Your surgeon, Dr. MacIntyre, will be visting you shortly to discuss the operation tomorrow —

SAM: Save him a trip. I'm not doing it. I lost interest. That's enough living. That's it. [*Turns off intercom. Dialing phone, singing very softly.*] "Who stole my heart away ... who ..." [*Into phone.*] Hello, Dopey. Let me tell you about my will; you're not in it. How come you put me here? ... I don't care emergency; look where I am! How could this be a hospital? It don't have the word "Sinai" in it. Listen, Dopey. No operation. The release form. I'm not signing. No signing. No operating. I'm seventy-eight-and-a-half. It's enough. Love to the children. [*Hangs up.*]. [DR. ALBERT MACINTYRE *is standing in the doorway. Late 30's, a tasteful suit with a vest and a near smile that has carried him through many rooms and many conversations like these.*]

DR. MACINTYRE: Mr. Margolis ...

SAM: What?

DR. MACINTYRE: Hello, I'm Dr. Albert MacIntyre ...

SAM: [*Correcting him.*] No, you're his son, you're Dr. MacIntyre's son! What is it, a child surgeon? How old are you?

MACINTYRE: I'm thirty-seven.

SAM: Come back when you're fifty-two; we'll talk business.

MACINTYRE: I've been asked by your internist to look in on you ...
[*Sits on chair next to bed.*] Dr. Cramer and I both feel that I
should describe to you the purpose and necessity of tomorrow
morning's surgery ... The purpose is, of course, to prolong life.
In your case, I would safely say, by several years. Life in relative
physical comfort, with a minimum chance of future attack. We
have located an obstruction in the anterior descending branch
of the coronary system. That part of the heart, which this artery
supplies, is being deprived of blood and oxygen. Now, what
we'll be doing tomorrow, Mr. Margolis, is inserting a bypass, a
small new channel for the blood to get through, a supplemen-
tary vessel that will be—

SAM: Speaking of boats, Al, I came to this country on a boat, the
Princess Mara, me and Benny Kalsheim; April the Seventeenth,
Nineteen Seventeen, three and a half years older than the century. A lot of people aren't informed but half the boats went to
New Orleans which is where I was. Came to New York later, up
the river like Jazz from the South. We went, me and Benny,
first to Tompkins Corners in South Carolina. They made me
the sheriff there. Could you believe it? Sheriff Margolis! The
only English I knew was "Hello" and "What's goin' on here?"
In my wallet there, a picture of me, the Sheriff. I had a uniform
and a star and dreams you wouldn't believe. A fruit store was
not on the horizon. Benny is still there, he stayed and I came to
New York City. Why am I telling you this? You should know
me. You should know whose heart you're talking. [*A small moment of fear.*] Or maybe I'm just doing what Ortega did with me
yesterday ...

MACINTYRE: Of course. Well then ... [*Takes out a Xeroxed drawing of
a heart and a pencil from vest pocket.*] Mr. Margolis, let me sketch
for you, roughly, what we'll be doing tomorrow morning ...
[*Sketching briskly on the heart-drawing.*] Now, the operation is
designed to improve the circulation of blood through this area
of the heart muscle ... [*Pencil slips from his hand and falls to the
floor.*] Oh, I ...

SAM: [*Cups his hands around his mouth, shouting to the room in general.*]
Cancelled! Operation cancelled! Forget it! Unavailable! Not

SAM: [*Cont'd.*] even considering at this time! [*Punches intercom button.*] Nurse! Nurse! There's a kid in here plays with knives! He'll hurt somebody. Get him outta here!

MACINTYRE: That's amusing, the pencil...

SAM: Listen, there's a call for you. I hear them calling you...in the hall...

MACINTYRE: Mr. Margolis, we—

SAM: [*Quietly, genuinely.*] Listen, Al...The fact is I'm putting you on altogether... I got no intentions for this operation. I'm not doing it anyway. I just been stringing you along; you're a busy fella, goodnight.

MACINTYRE: Is there something about the operation that...

SAM: No, it's a cute operation. I'm saving the picture.

MACINTYRE: What is it that you object to?

SAM: Living. It's time to go. I'm not interested no more.

MACINTYRE: Is there some particular reason that you—

SAM: Look out the window. I'll show you.

MACINTYRE: Mr. Margolis—

SAM: Al, go look...

[*MacIntyre goes to the window.*]

SAM: [*Cont'd.*] That's it. You see what they're doin'? Whatever they're doin', I don't want to be party to it no more. The times, these times, ain't my time. They took too much away without a snappy notion what to put instead. When I was sheriff there was still dreams for things. They don't do that no more; cash and carry and what's for supper. I personally knew this a long time, and last week my heart found out. You see the cap? Brooklyn Dodgers of Fifty-five. I do them honor.
      [*Sitting at edge of bed.*] Nobody came to take their place... They took Ebbets Field away. You take the pyramids away from Egypt all you got is sand and rotten weather. Walter O'Malley, he sells them like shoes without even discussing. What's left? Banks! You don't got *teams* now, MacDonald, you got Marine

SAM: [*Cont'd.*] Midland plays Chase Manhattan! The heart went with them and Brooklyn started to die. What's to root for? Without what's to root the voice goes away. Duke Snider! He went away! A lifetime in the afternoon hollering "I'm with ya, Duke, I'm with ya," never dreaming for a moment that he wasn't with me. Edwin Donald Snider, six feet tall, a hundred and eighty pounds, bats left, throws right, lifetime average Two Ninety-Five — a person you *knew*, went to Los Angeles, which doesn't even exist. They threw the lions to the Christians. They all went. The names, just say the names, you could sing them: Amoros, Gilliam, Campanella, Furillo, Hodges, Padres, gone, even the sound is gone... What's left? A cap. I got a cap. Dodgers Fifty-five, and sometimes I hear in the summer, on the wind, Red Barber's voice... [*Leans toward the Doctor; quietly.*] It's a sign of the whole thing. Time got my heart, the Dopey's got my name, and Shimkin the Thief got my fruit store by now. What was, isn't. What could be, didn't happen. Altogether: check-out time for Margolis!

MACINTYRE: Mr. Margolis —

SAM: Forget it —

MACINTYRE: If you would —

SAM: Listen, they had an expression for this in the old country: [*Shouting.*] "Get outta here!"

MACINTYRE: Certainly, Mr. Margolis. I am not particularly attracted to your abuse. And any further time spent listening to your farewell address does not interest me. [*He rises.*] You will not enjoy dying, Mr. Margolis. Without this operation another coronary occlusion will be fatal, and this attack could occur at any hour, perhaps tomorrow, the next day; next week. But make no mistake; you are killing yourself. It won't be the world, or Walter O'Malley, and certainly not me. I've been listening to you; I thought you were at least angry enough to live. [*Silence for a moment.*] Am I mistaken? Answer me, Mr. Margolis.

SAM: [*Silent for a moment, then he points to the Crucifixion painting.*] It's a hospital; they couldn't put somebody in better shape on the wall?

MACINTYRE: Good evening, Mr. Margolis. [*Goes to door.*] I can't say that it's been a pleasure.

[*He exits.* SAM *sits, frustrated, pulls his cap down sharply, brooding for a moment.*]

SAM: [*Suddenly shouting.*] Hey you! Macintosh! Hey, Al!

[MACINTYRE *has been standing just outside the doorway. He steps back in.*]

MACINTYRE: Yes . . .

SAM: O.K. I'll give you a break.

MACINTYRE: You changed your mind. Why?

[*No response.*]

MACINTYRE: [*Cont'd.*] Why?

SAM: [*After a moment.*] Curiosity !

MACINTYRE: You'll have to sign the release paper.

SAM: Yeah. O.K. [*He writes something on the paper, then signs it, looks up.*] You're a drinker? You drink a little?

MACINTYRE: Only while I'm operating. [*Looks at release paper.*] You wrote something here . . .

SAM: I added a clause to the contract.

MACINTYRE: "C.O.D"?

SAM: Yeah, you deliver me back in the shape I gave you: that is, living; and then you get paid. On delivery.

[MACINTYRE *smiles.*]

SAM: [*Cont'd.*] Look, I could die from this operation, right?

MACINTYRE: There is that possibility. Not a strong one, but a possibility.

SAM: O. K. I'll see you tomorrow.

MACINTYRE: Fine.

SAM: No parties . . .

MACINTYRE: O.K. [*Going out the door.*] Good night.

SAM: [*Shouting.*] Hey, Butterfingers!

MACINTYRE: Yes . . .

SAM: [*Quietly; a genuine threat.*] You kill me and I'll make your life miserable . . . I'll haunt you, Sweetheart; you understand? I'll haunt your closet and your suits'll make you crazy.

MACINTYRE: Good night . . .

SAM: [*As* MACINTYRE *goes out the door.*] Good night! Go home and go to sleep!

   [SAM *alone in the empty room. A moment of fear, of weakness, of exhaustion. He quickly picks up phone, dials. Speaks into phone: brightening, his energy returning . . .*] Hello, Dopey? Here's the latest on the will; you're still not in it. They say I could be dead tomorrow so here's last wishes. Instruct my lawyer, Klein, all money goes to Benny Kalsheim, Tompkins Corners, South Carolina. Tell him it's from the Sheriff. Call Shimkin, tell him whatever he's doing he'll never get away with it. Tell your daughter Jennifer, start the guitar lessons again; music is a good thing. Tell your mother the Doctor says absolutely her cooking did it. Meanwhile, if I don't see you again, goodbye and good luck.

[*He hangs up; enormously satisfied by this burst of energy. He closes his eyes. We begin to hear the sound of* RED BARBER'S VOICE, *barely audible at first and then building very gradually as it fills the room. The sound of cheering fans builds with the excitement of his familiar voice.*]

BARBER'S VOICE: . . . the pitch to Lavagetto, swung on and missed. Fast ball, it was in there, strike one. Gionfriddo walks off Second, Miksis off First, they're both ready to go at anything; two men out, last of the Ninth. The pitch — swung on, there's a drive out toward the Right Field corner, Henrick is going back, he can't get it, it's off the wall for a base hit . . . here comes the tying run . . . and here comes . . . the winning run . . .

[*Barber's voice is lost in the sound of the cheering crowd as*

THE CURTAIN FALLS.]

Susan Hansell

MY MEDEA

Susan Hansell

Susan Hansell is a native of California. She graduated from Berkeley with high honors in 1981. Plays of hers which were produced on the west coast in the 1980s include *Pink Rope*, *A Day In*, and *14 Ladies in Hats*. A commissioned work, *American Rose: Our Gals on the Homefront, 1941-1945* premiered in 1997 at the Ohio Theatre in New York City. Her new plays are *Rollover Othello* (nominated for a Pushcart Prize as published in *Oasis* Jul-Sep 1996), *Queen of Sheeba*, *Romance with Jana*, and *Quicksilver, Quicksand*. *My Medea* was first published in *Oasis* Oct-Dec 1996. Ms. Hansell has had poems, essays and dramatic texts published in magazines and anthologies, including Heinemann Press's 1996 *More Monologues by Women for Women*. She resides in Brooklyn, New York, where she is employed as an adjunct lecturer in the CUNY system.

CHARACTERS

HOUSE BOY
CHAUFFEUR
M.J. MEDEA
CHORUS OF LOS ANGELES MEN
TWO POLICEMEN
MRS. MEDEA
BEST FRIEND OF M.J.
THREE ATTORNEYS
THE MEDIA
A STREET PREACHER

Also, in non-speaking roles:
MRS. MEDEA'S MOTORCYCLE ENTOURAGE

SETTING: *A wealthy Los Angeles subdivision, in front of the Medea mansion, as represented by scaffolding or like structures which allow view of the interior.*

HOUSE BOY: [*Entering from the house.*]

God I wish man never launched jets across the skies,

    Flying through blue, or cut stadiums or cities

    From the earth's blood. If only men weren't men at all,

    And black and white weren't colors; then My Man wouldn't

    Be hot like some thermo-nuclear thing, with his

    Head in a melt-down, just thinking about this wife.

We worship M.J. Medea in this country.

    What reason is there for a wife to leave The Man.

    Now there's hatred in every suburb, and love looks

    Like trash. She refuses him, and he calls on the

    Public to witness her vacancy sign. In the

    Motel of stars, NO is no answer for M.J.

HOUSE BOY: [*Cont'd.*] When night falls, he feeds his global ap
   petites.

   With white lines and love from the ladies. Left alone,

   He throws his head back and shouts out for his mother,

   And for the family he left when he married such

   A chick. My Man, wanted mucho by the whole world,

   Has discovered the suffering of any lame guy.

M.J. Medea won't tolerate such treatment.

   Why should he? Celebrities have toxic tempers;

   Plus, the stuff of my dumb life is too low to

   Be touching him. The situation is tense, man.

   If he unnerves, he could quake us all down. Check it out.

   I'm too young and good-looking to grieve. Got that?

CHAUFFEUR: [*Entering.*] Why are you standing outside talking to
   yourself?

   Mr. M.J. wants you inside, to watch the house.

HOUSE BOY: Listen, old man, if you were truly good help you'd

   Feel for the boss when his luck ran out. Have a heart.

   I've worked myself into a full-on anxiety attack.

   I had to come outside and tell my troubles

   To the green, green lawn here, and to the spacious air.

CHAUFFEUR: The man's mood is still poisonous, day and night.

HOUSE BOY: Still. Are you kidding? It's the BEGINNING of it.

CHAUFFEUR: Oh well — not that it matters what I know or do

   But we oughta be worried about what's coming—

HOUSE BOY: What are you saying? Do you know something? Spill
   it.

CHAUFFEUR: Nothing. Forget it. Nothing to be done.

HOUSE BOY: Hey, we work together. You can't keep things from
        me.

Fair is fair. [*Pause.*] Do you think I'm a gossip or what?

CHAUFFEUR: Alright, alright. I heard some people, who will go
        Unnamed, talking the other day, in the garage
        Where I get the Rolls serviced. According to those
        In the know, Mrs. Medea plans to stick it
        To M.J. permanently. The Missus. is fed
        Up with the fans he lets see him, suck him, and shake
        His hand. He ain't easy to talk to, neither, she
        Says; says he leaves her alone, nine nights out of ten.
        So she won't take him back; he's like any Common
        Joe. She's got a regular lawyer, and she split
        With his kids. A come-down for us all, eh? No good. [*Pause.*]
        That's what I heard anyway. But what do I know.

HOUSE BOY: No good. Are you crazy? This is the worst possible
        Thing. How could Our Man deprive his public of...
        What's she thinking? She can't think one woman'd be
        Enough for him. Impossible. Insulting. [*Pause.*] Can the
        Missus. take the children from him? I don't believe it.

CHAUFFEUR: Out with the old and in with the new. [*Pause.*] Yet
        I doubt Mrs. M. knows just what's going on around here.

HOUSE BOY: I'm starting to hate her. It's her fault these clouds
        Above us are so hard. It looks like sixty nights worth.

CHAUFFEUR: Well you didn't hear it from me. And keep your flap
        Shut. He's mad enough without hearing news from us.

HOUSE BOY: Can you believe their mess. I wish she were dead.
        No I don't. Understand. She's a nice lady —

CHAUFFEUR: Are you that young? People seem nice, but love can

CHAUFFEUR: [*Cont'd.*] Hurt like hell. No one knows what goes on
    behind closed

    Doors. Besides, we only love ourselves when pushed.

HOUSE BOY: Maybe I have a lot to learn. It's weird, but like,

    I don't wanna be in that house with him. He cuts

    His eyes at anyone who happens by. One minute

    He's hot; the next, he's cold. Somehow his cold is

    Worse than his hot—

CHAUFFEUR: —Earthquake weather, my mother said.

    Mrs. M. oughta know better'n to piss him

    Off. I know I sure won't be anywhere around.

       [*CHAUFFEUR exits, muttering.*]

M.J. MEDEA: [*As seen within the house, pacing etc.*]

    I won't take this. No. NO. I WON'T.

    This won't happen. Not to me. NOOOOOO —

    I was created. To have my

    Way. MY WAY. I. Am. MEDEA.

HOUSE BOY: Oh no. What did I tell you. Is that bad or what.

M.J.: No. No. No. NO WOMAN tells me

    How it's gonna be. People love

    Me. ME. I'm The Man here, goddamnit.

    That's the way it is. Shit. No

    Woman leaves me. Never. NEVER.

    It can't happen here. It won't. NO.

    Who does the bitch think she is. Shit.

    She'll burn before I fall. MOTHER.

    NO NO NO NO NO NO NO NO.

HOUSE BOY: It's true. Our heroes aren't admired for their

    Moderation. No, humble mediocrity

HOUSE BOY: [*Cont'd.*] Never inspired a goddamned thing. The flip side

Is, everyone's afraid to contradict him.

And here's how the man-made-gods get by with their murders,

While the rest of us chickens sweat it out. Watch.

CHORUS OF LOS ANGELES MEN: [*Entering, the* CHORUS *members speak their sentences/sentence groups/ sentence fragments as both individuals and as groups or choral sub-groups, which may correspond to a specific choreographed pattern.*]

I heard the voice, I heard the yells

Of Our Wretched Idol, M.J.

Our father in heaven, he raves;

Across the valley, on the shore,

From the freeways that divide our

Homes; I heard his shouts, I heard

His moans. I'm sorry for The Man;

We're all outraged for this . . . loss. No

Woman can get away with chip,

Chipping away at his Holy

Marble. [*Pause.*] Hey, you there, house boy. What's

The latest word on Medea?

HOUSE BOY: Americans bury the bodies of mortals.

You cheer for the good guys with the horses-n-guns.

What can winning at such games mean to the Medea.

Which peons will be torched in his bitter grip.

CHORUS: What? Talk English, man. And speak up!

M.J.: [*From within.*] Death is better than this defeat.

I'll wipe-out the whole town for this

HUMILIATION. I want rain,

M.J.: [*Cont'd.*] Mud-slides, fires and riots. AAAAARRRRRRHHH.

She'll pay for this. THE WHORE. Somehow.

CHORUS: Jesus Christ. Did you hear that shit.

We can't let her bring him down. And

We can't let him start wishing

For death-n-destruction. He could

Make it happen. This is M.J.

We're talking about. Yeah. The Man

Can do whatever he wants. Yeah.

Let bygones be bygones is the refuge

Of chumps. Everyone deserves

What they get in the end. Listen.

M.J.: She will NOT cripple me. NO SLUT

Will show me up. [*Laughs.*] Your Barbarian!

I was the outcast who soared

To the top. I'm The Man of all

Men. Now I call the shots. No woman's

All that. I'll teach her a damned

Lesson she'll be sorry about.

For the city to see, for men

To hear: She'll find out what's up.

HOUSE BOY: Do you hear how he's talking, and the threats he makes.

On our Lady of Guadalupe, virgin of

Faith and necessities, I'll pray for roses. But

Only a crown of thorns will satisfy his thirst.

CHORUS: [*Chiming in.*] It's our time to aid and comfort

M.J. The Man needs his fans. Yeah.

He's my friend, and I'm willing to

CHORUS: [*Cont'd.*] Help, no matter what. We're on his
   Side. Yeah. What other side is there?
   Shit, man, no one can touch HIM. That's
   The way it is. Yeah. [*To HOUSE BOY.*] Why don't you
   Go in and tell him we're outside. [*Pause.*]
   Hurry up, boy. Now he needs us.
   His wrath isn't chump change. Move it.

HOUSE BOY: OK, OK. But I doubt if it'll do squat.
   Whenever I approach . . . well, if looks could kill
   You'd have to find someone else to order around . . .
   [*Pause.*] Did you ever think about how stupid
   Your pop music is? Your favorite songs yak all day
   About love and how great it is. Why don't you have
   Songs about betrayal and disappointment. [*Pause.*] I'm going.
   But I think the radio should play songs that help
   People deal with how things really are.
   Either that, or songs shouldn't have words at all. Sounds
   Alone can't fool, or be taken away to dust.
         [*HOUSE BOY exits into the house.*]

CHORUS: I hear M.J.'s cries against the
   Woman who wronged him. Betrayal
   Of love is an abyss
   Unlimited as the sea.
   M.J., over us, does not merit this hit.
         [*M.J. enters from the house.*]

M.J.: Men of Los Angeles. I have come outside to
   Show you a thing or two. Our situation is
   About to improve. I know. Life isn't easy

M.J.: [*Cont'd.*] For the average man. Don't think I've forgotten
   My roots. I haven't. A guy has to make money
   Just to get a woman, and if you marry her,
   She wants more. Yet it's worse to be without one.
   There's no escape. And you never know if you'll take
   A good or a bad one. So once married, a dude
   Has to be a mind reader to understand the
   Creature in his bed. If she's a saint, then life's great.
   If she's a whore, then your whole world's better off dead.
   She takes your money and goes shopping. She's happy.
   A man goes out every day into the desert
   Of the streets. He's a refugee; he's a warrior.
   He sees the worst that life offers. The only thing that
   Keeps him going is knowing his woman is at
   Home, behind him, no matter what, always. You know
   What I mean. In the end, a guy needs his heroes;
   Men need to be fans of a MAN BEYOND their own
   Meagerness: To give glory to an image of
   MAN UNBOUND by work-a-day worlds. After
   The oil change, after monogamy and the
   Orthodontist, you're owed your sweet fantasies. My
   Medea will live on for you, conquering the women
   You can't touch, as master of cities you'll never
   Visit. For your dreams, it's my duty to strike out
   Any mortal who seeks to destroy your source.
   I ask only this from you, that my way of pay-back,
   My plan of vengeance, will be honored among us.
CHORUS: Yes, I promise. And I swear.

CHORUS: [*Cont'd.*] You're right. It's fitting to

> Maintain the order. Common
>
> Men are crippled enough. True.
>
> But our Medea... NO. Yeah,
>
> It's a stinking landfill of
>
> A town we live in. No, none
>
> Of us should put up with it.
>
> Look how she treated him. Yeah.
>
> Pictures in the *National*
>
> *Enquirer.* Shaking her
>
> Stuff up and down Rodeo Drive.
>
> Shit. She had everything she
>
> Could want. And still she wasn't
>
> Satisfied. Typical broad.
>
> Yeah. Of course we're angry. Of course
>
> HE'S angry. Of course you're angry!

M.J.: In all ways, a man must be like steel, strong and

> Uncomplaining. But when his beliefs are wronged, a man
>
> Must hold thoughts of blood. Come, hear my mighty-fine
> plan.

CHORUS: Wait up. Two of L.A.'s finest.

> What do they want? What's up with this?

TWO POLICEMEN: [*Entering, they alternate lines, with one cop domi-
nating and speaking most of the longer lines, while the second cop
punctuates the first's, speaking most of the short lines/words.*]

> Mr. M.J. Medea? Of course, we know who
>
> You are. Right. We hate to bring you bad news. Our job
>
> Is never easy. Try to understand. We have
>
> To follow orders. That's the way it is, you see.

M.J.: I hope nothing's wrong, officers. What could be, uh?

POLICEMEN: It's none of our business. Of course not. The facts can't

Be right. They're exaggerated. No doubt. But still . . . .

M.J.: Spit it out guys. I can take it. What's the problem?

POLICEMEN: Right. This isn't easy. Sure, I know how women

Can be. But it seems that your ex has filed a

Complaint against you. Right. She says you entered her

House, broke a few things and slapped her around a bit.

A misunderstanding, huh? Right. She mentions some

Prior incidents. Marriage is no picnic, that's

For sure. Looks like she's taking legal action to

Keep you away from her and your kids. That's too bad.

See this complaint form? It comes with a warrant. We

Should take you downtown with us. Right. Just to talk . . .

M.J.: Guys, guys, is that really necessary? Come on.

Now whatever's going on with the woman, this

Here's between the men. You know how they can change things

Around. Before you know it, they've got it all fixed

Against ya. If she's having a bad-hair-day, look

Out. Don't mention it if you ran into one of her

Friends at the Beverly Center. You'll be fast

Accused of spousal abuse, or worse. A guy can't win.

This complaint, and the warrant? Impossible, uh?

Female imagination gone crazy. I say,

The crime is my children are hers, and my wife's out

With her Hollywood crowd, in the vehicles I

Bought with my bucks. I have to go downtown with you?

POLICEMEN: Of course we sympathize with you. I'm on your side,
     Mr. Medea. We all know how wives can be.
     But it looks like yours is serious here. You've got
     To prepare yourself for a fight. Allegations
     Like these won't die of their own accord. If your ex
     Persists, she can drag you in front of the judge, and
     Then there won't be a thing we boys-in-blue can do
     For you. Right. That's the way it is. If she wants
     To make trouble, well, I hope for your sake she don't.

M.J.: So what happens now, with today's little problem?

POLICEMEN: Tell us about the events she cites. Are they true?

M.J.: It hurts me to know you would consider them so.

POLICEMEN: I have to ask, sir; it's my job. I don't like it.

M.J.: Of course, of course. How insensitive of me, boys.

POLICEMEN: If we'd found you not at home . . . It's possible . . .

M.J.: M.J.? He's out in Malibu now. No problema.

POLICEMEN: I guess we can keep this visit between us men.

M.J.: What visit? [*Laughter.*] Do you want a drink before you go?

POLICEMEN: How about an autograph, Mr. Medea?

M.J.: Sure, sure. And call me M.J., boys. Anything else?

POLICEMEN: I think you better steer clear of your ex-wife, sir.

M.J.: What do you mean? I haven't seen the bitch in weeks.

POLICEMEN: Right, right. Then this complaint is really not true.
     Wow.

M.J.: I told you, the bitch lies. I don't want to see her.

POLICEMEN: It's for your own good; for the court, and custody.

M.J.: Of course, of course. I'm just kidding you. Is that it?

POLICEMEN: Right. We'll be going. But don't forget, we weren't
     here.

[*All laugh.*]

M.J.: And since I wasn't either, I won't say good-bye.

[M.J. *salutes sarcastically;* POLICEMEN *salute back, then exit.*]

CHORUS OF L.A. MEN: What a bitch. What a travesty.

'S up with those cops, man. Without their

Blue suits they'd have no huevos to

Ask the time. And forget about

Telling M.J. what to do. Like

They're doin' him a favor. I

Don't think so. Nope. Nothin' but

A homeboy when push comes to shove.

M.J.: Down, boys. Don't worry about it. I don't need your

Sympathy. Everything's under my command. I've

Got the plan. It's normal for the boys-in-blue to

Take a swing at the big block. Don't sweat it; I'm up

To the challenge. Inside, I'm still the kid from your

No-where-lands. You all know my pavement-to-the-

Paradise-of-Los Angeles story. You know how.

The Beautiful People love a kid who fights for

Their gold. Don't think I've gotten FAT. Look at me, uh?

I remember Oak-town. I remember myself;

The kid who out-ran, out-spit, and out-thought all of

God's children. And I was Enough to know what to

Do with it. I became your sportsworld gladiator,

Your dollarbill hero, your global-trade-magnet, and

Your biggest hero of intercourse idol-making ever, uh?

Now, this bitty pestilent female trouble,

A test of my manhood and brains? HA.

I know precisely what to do. She's dead meat.

CHORUS: Right. For sure. He's in control.
　　He's making sense. Go M.J.
　　Ride, man. Dude, we're with ya.
　　Yeah. You know it. No high-horse
　　Answers to the judge of the
　　Foot-men. We have no choice.
　　But M.J.? He's too high to die.
M.J.: I am your Medea, and I
　　Will never disappoint Our
　　Expectations of Fame and its
　　Omnipotent Fist. [*Pause.*] How the day goes.
　　I will execute the vengeance
　　Due, and its fall-out will rain
　　Acidly on any woman who
　　Dares take out our way of life.
　　　　[M.J. *exits into the house.*]
CHORUS: Fly, fly, sails and planes. Flow back
　　To the source; restore the status.
　　Women are deceitful, their vows
　　Are loose. Men must be paid their dues.
Stop the love-songs, stop the singing,
　　Or I'll answer the opposite sex:
　　It's not a happy ending; it's
　　Either boredom or betrayal.
From the bombed-out inner-city,
　　He radiated for all men;
　　His strengths jumped exponentially
　　With every task and contest won.

CHORUS: [*Cont'd.*] He left a mother and a first

> Wife, with his glittering torso,
>
> For her. The woman doesn't know
>
> The meaning of sacrifices.
>
> In America, a sense of
>
> Shame should blot out the sun, and make
>
> Every unfaithful bed cold, cold,
>
> Cold. Vows are vows, and lies are lies.
>
> > [*Pause; the* CHORUS *indulges in self-congratulatory asides.*]

MRS. MEDEA: [*Entering on motorcycle, accompanied by an entourage of attractive motorcycle-riding L.A.-types. The revving of this group's engines may punctuate the ensuing dialogue between* M.J. *and the* MRS., *or, the* MRS. *might flash a signal which results in their silence.*]

> This isn't the first time I've heard men yabba
>
> Yabba yabba-ing about things they make up in
>
> Their heads. Shut up. Get a life. You know nothing here
>
> About nothing here. There's two sides to a story.
>
> And what does your pledge mean? 'Til death do us part? Ha.
>
> More like another woman's panties on the floor.
>
> Sacrifice? Don't make me laugh. [*She laughs.*] Are you kidding?
>
> I know a thing or two about "great" men, and the fibs behind
>
> Them. Men lie and it's called second nature.
>
> Cute. To be expected. Women lie and they're dirt.
>
> My children will NOT be raised to believe this, or
>
> To perpetuate the sickness in your heads. Go!
>
> Get Medea for me. I want him to hear this.

CHORUS: [*Pause; shifting uncomfortably, then loftily.*] It's a strange form of anger, difficult to cure,
When those with fortune turn hatred upon themselves.

MRS.: Oh I know how men like you think. Understand?

Don't bother changing your tune for me.

Ok? I'm not buyin' it. Save it for your wives.

And don't you dare talk down to me. Go fuck yourselves.

[M.J. *enters from the house without being called.*]

M.J.: I thought I heard the unmistakable tone of

White trash. Whatever you want, take it elsewhere, tramp.

MRS.: [*A bit cowed initially by his presence, but bouncing back fast.*]
You know what I'm here for, your two spoiled brats; but

First things first. My sources tell me you want to give

Me a hard time over my right to divorce. Now

Listen; it makes no sense. You don't want me. Right?

We should both let each other go. And for the sake of

The kids, we should act like adults, and try to get

Along. Ok? I'm sick, sore and tired of this,

And that's putting it mildly. Ok? What are

We fighting for, anyway? It's ridiculous.

Let's stop the insanity, and do the right thing,

I'll take my half and leave you in peace. Whatever.

M.J.: Be careful woman; I'll tell you the way it is.

You're mine and you always will be. It doesn't matter

If I don't want you or if I do. You have no rights.

Period. End of story. I'll take care of that.

And your beef with my behavior? It's not

Your place to complain. It's enough to have touched me.

Every American adores ME not you, uh?

And they have their inalienable right to revere

ME, without your petty interferences. Babe,

You coulda learned a few new tricks from their acts.

MRS.: I don't quite see things like that. To hear it from you,
   I've never given you my worship; how untrue.
   You know, the charisma of a zeus can turn a girl's head.
   I wanted you. You were like, a king, surrounded
   By awe; you got the best seats, the best smiles, the
   Best sensational press. I wanted to be part
   Of you too. But I found out that wasn't your game.
   Yeah, you married me, but never made me a queen.
   No. You were the gold, and I was the brass. Well now, as
   You see, I've got my own devotees, and they do
   Whatever I ask. Not your kind of crowd, yet no
   One's really what they appear to be, right, M.J.?

M.J.: There oughta be a brand on women to tell the
   True from the false. You're at least a two-headed one.
   You'll never be anything more than the trashy
   Waitress you were when I met you. You shoulda been
   Grateful for every night you got your claws around
   Me. Your tickets for steak started here, along with
   Meals at my table for all your hangers-on.
   You're a disease. You think you can take me down, with
   Your tabloid tits and your low-life cohorts. Think again.

MRS.: I coulda had my pick of men; you weren't exactly
   Hurt by the young beautiful blonde on your arm.

M.J.: It's bleached.

MRS.: So what?

M.J.: You're a witch.

MRS.: Can I talk?

M.J.: Know your place, woman. You weren't meant to talk back.

MRS.: I have a mind, if you hadn't noticed, it's mine.

M.J.: NO. I gave you all the life you were entitled to.
    If you were meant to get any more bliss from life's
    Bank, it woulda come from me, when I gave the word.

MRS.: Jealousy from you is hypocritical,
    Dontcha think?
    Change your ideas, cantcha?
    Obedience and your
    Possessiveness are out of style.
    Get with it. Realize: women
    Aren't dogs; neither are wives
    Cows with rings through their fingers.

M.J.: I come into a room, you
    Should be turning to see me.
    I step out, you should be waiting.
    I'd like to hear the sound
    Of my voice: Play it back for me.

MRS.: Better. Here's a mirror for you.
    Knock yourself out. Go for it.

M.J.: To love, honor and obey.

MRS.: You mocked those words first, not me.

M.J.: The only proof is your lies.

MRS.: My lies? The one you cherish
    Is you, and always will be. [*Pause.*]
    They're all watching for your fall,
    Ya know. The only thing they'll
    Feel is relief not to have been
    Stars themselves, and bound to explode.

[*Pause; they turn their backs on one another.*]

CHORUS: Although the things she says sound sort

    Of reasonable . . . Still I think,

    Though you might not agree, she has

    Wronged Medea and acted badly.

    Anyway, we don't care about the

    Woman or what she says. We want

    To find out what happens to our

    Hero. It's his story that makes

    Us shudder, that makes us moan, or

    Groan. Maybe we do want to project

    Ourselves into his fate and

    Live vicariously. So what?

M.J.: DON'T YOU EVER TURN YOUR BACK ON ME DO
    YOU HEAR. [*Pause.*]

MRS.: Look. Let's make a deal. Of course I still want you.

    That is, more like, I want to be in your party;

    I want my own bliss; I want to be on a throne;

    I want the same special treatment. Please. Let me

    Finish. Sure, I went after you; what girl wouldn't?

    You were a god to like, the whole world. But now I know

    You're all too human. Ok? You're a man like

    Any other, and you can't control me; you don't own

    Me. Wait. This is it. Make me a goddess, equal

    To your level, and I promise I'll worship you

    Like everyone else; erotically, neurotically,

    Whatever you want. Only, no more screwing

    Around; no more reminding me of my dependent

    Place. Can't you see, we need each other, M.J.

MRS.: [*Cont'd.*] And I wanna be just as important as you.

M.J.: You're a fool. You're crazy. No one cares about you.

You're off the deep end if you think you can try to

Manipulate ME. I've got the power to prove

You'll be sorry, bitch. I'll see this world dead before

I cave to your, to any woman's demands. You're nuts.

You're here to take orders, not give them. Get it.

MRS.: What's the point. This is useless.

M.J.: You got that right, and how. I

Read you like a see-through book.

MRS.: You're stubborn and arrogant.

M.J.: AND THAT'S WHY YOU FELL FOR ME.

MRS.: I was young then, and stupid.

M.J.: ENOUGH. Go on. GET OUT. I've been

More than patient, listening to you.

Another thing you're too selfish

To see. Your time's up. Get lost. NOW.

What are you waiting for, uh? GO!

MRS.: Fine. I don't need this abuse.

But send out the children. They're

Coming with me. I won't see them growing up to—

M.J.: NO. You WILL SEE. You will see what the future holds.

Soon enough, woman. You're temporary. And MY

Children? They're staying with ME. I know you. You'll get

Sick of 'em and ship 'em back in NO TIME at all.

MRS.: That's not true! They're half mine too! Everything is, well,

Just like the money should be. Why can't you share with—

M.J.: [*Laughing loudly.*]

    HALF? HA. What's mine will RUIN you. What's mine will

    STARVE YOU. Poison bitch. What's mine. Is mine. THAT
       matters.

MRS.: I don't know why you have to get so angry. I did

    Some important things for you. I got you into

    Places. The best places. Circles for only the

    Beautiful and you know what I mean. When we first

    Met you were just another jock. But with me you —

M.J.: With YOU. With WHO? Where do you get the gas to
      pump

    This shit? Somethin's gettin' you higher than your height.

MRS.: You never appreciated me. You never

    Valued what I gave to you. Not even the kids —

M.J.: THE CHILDREN ARE MINE. All children belong to
    men.

MRS.: What are you saying? I have no rights, period?

M.J.: She walks. She talks. Maybe she has a brain in there.

    How many blondes does it take to change a light bulb?

MRS.: That does it. You and your friends think your egos

    Are above even the laws of this land? Well, I'll

    Prove that's a hoax too, just like you. Inferior?

    Subordinate? Stupid? You just wait. Hahaha.

M.J.: I WOULDN'T LAUGH IF I WERE YOU. IF YOU
      WERE A

    FORTUNE-TELLER YOU'D BE SCARED ABOUT
      NOW GODDAMN

    YOU. NO. YOU WAIT. YOU ARE WAITING. YEAH.
      FOR NOTHIN'.

MRS.: No one. Not TV, not the trades, not the children

　　Will think you The Man when I'm through exposing you.

　　You're not the god you think you are. Whoring around

　　For advertisers. Selling some faded image

　　To prop-up your castle. This system's about to

　　Go down. Get ready for the crash M.J. But first,

　　Send out the kids. I'm their mother. And I want them.

　　With me. They won't be reared with your idiocy.

M.J.: YOU DON'T GET IT DO YOU. MY CHILDREN? I'D
　　　SEE THEM

　　DEAD BEFORE I'D LET YOU HAVE 'EM. THAT'S
　　　RIGHT. I'D KILL

　　THEM MYSELF TO STOP YOU. HALF? HALF. YOU
　　　WANT HALF? HA.

　　YOU'RE NOTHING. NOTHING. I'M WHAT MAT
　　　TERS. ME. ME. MY

　　GOLDEN VOICE. Shall I sing you THE BALLAD OF
　　　HOLLIS

　　BROWN, baby? Or the one about the dude in

　　Long Island who blew his whole family away?

　　Nah. I don't wanna spoil the show. I hate it

　　When somebody gives away the plot. NOW GET LOST.

　　BE GONE. THERE'S PRECIOUS FEW BREATHS TO
　　　WASTE TIL THE END.

MRS.: What are you saying? It doesn't have to be this

　　Way. God why couldn't I have had a normal life.

M.J.: [*Laughs.*] OH IT'S WAY TOO LATE FOR THAT. GO
　　　WHILE YOU STILL CAN.

　　BUT YOU BETTER GO REAL FAR. WAY FAR FROM
　　　HERE. AND

M.J.: [*Cont'd.*] IF YOU DON'T, IF YOU THINK YOU CAN
    BRING MY LIFE TO

    YOUR FEET, THEN YOU BEST KISS THE THINGS —
    AND WE ALL KNOW

    THEY'RE THINGS YOU LOVE GOODBYE. SAY BYE-
    BYE BLOOD SUCKER.

MRS.: I don't know what you're talking about. We could've

    Been so good together. If only you would see—

M.J.: OH I SEE. I SEE THE PAST. I SEE THE FUTURE.

    AND I AM THOSE. I KNOW WHAT YOU WANTED
    ME FOR.

MRS.: You're becoming a real loser M.J. I never

    Thought I'd hear you feeling sorry for yourself.

    I'm above that. And people'll worship me

    For myself. I don't need you. Or your money.

    And eventually the law'll side with me too.

M.J.: WE'LL SEE WHO'S WEAK. YOU WANNA FIGHT.
    YOU GOT IT GIRL.

    THESE HANDS KNOW. KNOW WHO AND HOW IT'S
    GONNA FALL OUT.

MRS.: We'll see.

M.J.: OH YEAH.

MRS.: Fine.

M.J.: Right. GET OUT. I'M SICK OF YOU.

    [*Exit* MRS. MEDEA *with her entourage.* M.J. *paces. Long pause.
    The* CHORUS *shifts uncomfortably, then regroups.*]

CHORUS: In matters of love, and in

    Matters of money, learn this:

    Desire in excess is AIDS like

    Nothing else. If love can heal,

CHORUS: [*Cont'd.*] The opposite is true. Hatred
   Can shatter and greed can kill.
   The best marriage is a boring
   And dispassionate one; it makes
   For a peaceful home. Ah! let my
   Emotions be harnessed just so!
   But realistically, we
   Are men, and what we want at
   Home, we seldom want in bed!
      [*General laughter amongst the chorus.*]
   It's true. But with every seduction,
   A later rejection is implied.
   And as far as this story goes,
   The public is always hungry
   To eat a tasty Donald Trump. Yeah.
   And why not? If a god has clay
   Feet, then a man needs friends.
   To be a celebrity
   Is a nice fantasy, but
   To be a regular guy means
   Never to sink from fame. If
   A man never knows the crests and peaks
   Of grace, he'll be saved a
   Drowning in anonymity.
M.J.: [*Pacing and muttering.*]
   Women. MEN! Do you see how she believes she can
   Exploit me. ME!? I AM NOT IN DECLINE. WHAT.
      WHAT?!
   NO-O-O-O-O-O-O-O-O-O-O-O-O.

M.J.: [*Cont'd.*] MEN. You heard her threats and half-baked plans.
Now I say,

Whatever happens she brings on herself. SHE LOVES IT.

Medea. MEDEA. The worship of CONTROL.

A man's children are HIS; his blood, his line, his

PRESERVE. In my image. In my mind. What I am.

SHOWS. NO. WEAKNESS. For in his domain is he defined:

OURS. THE MAN who stopped not raising himself up.

FOR OUR WORLD MEN. The Man will now DEFEND
us.

It's a sacrifice I take on with THE FORCE OF

THE U.S. MARINES. THE EMPEROR STRIKES BACK.
Yes.

He will call on the four winds. He will summon the

Powers dark and the powers light, and the henchmen,

The real men, of our man's world, will not hesitate

To play their rightfully righteous positions

For our man's game. For you, men. THE MAN. Who is HE?

MEE-EE-EE-EE-EEE-EE-EE-EE-EE-EE-EEEEEEEEEE.

> [*The* CHORUS *shifts awkwardly; long pause.* M.J. *dances. Enter the* BEST FRIEND.]

BEST FRIEND: Hey, I saw your ugly mug all over the covers
Of the scandal-sheets, man. What's up with that shit?

M.J.: My brother. Where ya been, sport? I need my back-up.

FRIEND: I guess so, man. The press is gonna eat you
Alive. And so is the public, man. Kiss the
Endorsements goodbye. Not to mention that high cloud
You sit on. If you drop, how far down, man. How far.

M.J.: I'm gonna put a stop to her way before that.

FRIEND: How far can she rock you, man? It's probably nothin'.

M.J.: I'll see to that. Don't fret. This'll be some good shit now.

FRIEND: The women these days. Always tryin' to make the
World shift out from under our feet. I like them when
They're young and stupid, man. Know what I mean. Pussy.
[*Pause.*] Life's no cakewalk for me, neither. But I'm listening.

M.J.: You've got troubles, it's true. But I've gotcha covered.

FRIEND: I've got alimony, too. I've gotta think
Of myself. I need a pay-off, with no jail time.

M.J.: Not to worry, Jack. *Mi casa es su casa.*

FRIEND: So what's your plan, man? I know the bitch's schedule.

M.J.: HOW'S THAT?

FRIEND: The dame's been makin' the rounds, M.J. That's it.

M.J.: [*After a pause.*] Don't' sweat it. I'll tell you everything impor-
tant when
You need to know. A man is judged by his actions.
If you help, I'll protect you. If not, you're free; go.

FRIEND: How can you question my loyalty. I'M HERE.

M.J.: You swear to do anything I ask, regardless?

FRIEND: Relax, M.J. I'm your back-up. [*Pause.*] I swear, alright?

M.J.: What happens to guys who back down on their pledges?

FRIEND: We all know they're nothin' but women, God help 'em.

M.J.: Enough. I won't forget it. Or you. Now wait for
Me in the trophy room, and prepare yourself well.

[*The BEST FRIEND exits into the house; M.J. paces slowly.*]

CHORUS: Each fissure in the old world
Requires a new boot. Sure,
Nostalgia is natural; too is
Defending our way of life.

CHORUS: [*Cont'd.*] M.J. protects us; he acts

> Through us, for us on our behalf.
>
> If he's tarnished so aren't we.
>
> No. Whatever he chooses,
>
> We must uphold him. Failure
>
> Is not an option. How can we change?

M.J.: MEN. Revenge will hit the freeways; San Pedro is

> My harbor; I'm about to launch my plot. Now for
>
> The whole idea; wait, don't speak. I've thought this through
>
> Completely. NOW ALL OUT with its wrath. To swing it
>
> Straight from this height, like the guillotine, the pitchfork
>
> The scythe. Medea, Medea, Medea MINE.
>
> She'll nourish. Feeding my eyes with her velvet blood.
>
> A gushing murder of the constellations.
>
> After all, we can't get away from violence in
>
> America. [*He laughs.*] I'll play the grieving Hollywood
>
> Legend. It is sad, for things to come to this.
>
> BUT I WILL NOT BE BROUGHT DOWN TO HER.
>   And ALL children
>
> WILL grow to adore me. Our ways ascendant, uh?
>
> Not bad. And the sympathy won't hurt my stock. Nope.
>
> I'm forever loved; this is just a small growth spurt.
>
> Painful, perhaps, but I've already decided.
>
> That's that. I know you're with me. So tallyho, boys.
>
> It's not enough to stew and brood on our fury;
>
> It's time for the future that I make. I TAKE.
>
> She must die! Or else she betrays me, and all men!

> [M.J. *prepares to exit;* CHORUS *pipes up quickly.*]

CHORUS: But the mother of your children? Think
      Of the kiddies' deprivation, shouldn't you?
M.J.: They'll forget. They'll have me.
CHORUS: Hmm... Perhaps civilization has
      Some advantages. You could control
      Yourself. It might be better.
M.J.: That's easy for you to say.
      You live on the ground. I'm cut way
      Above. YOU EXPECT ME TO GANGWAY?
CHORUS: Of course not. Still, now that you've shared
      Your plans with us, why not reconsider?
M.J.: She's a vessel, that's all; she doesn't matter.
      Who cares about her. One more aging female, the
      Scourge of our Earth. I'm doing a public service.
CHORUS: It's murder. Can it be forgotten
      At the drop of night? More likely,
      You'll relive it when you look at
      Their little faces. You'll see yourself
      A murderer. And come on, you'll
      Remember their mother's blood.
M.J.: NO. It's my blood that counts, you wimps. Aren't you men?
      NO. You're whipped. And that's the difference between us,
      uh?

      [M.J. *exits into the house.*]
CHORUS: [*After clearing their throats.*]
      Once upon a time, yeah, men came
      From across the globe to harness
      The bounties of this continent;
      They carved cities, roads, towns and farms

CHORUS: [*Cont'd.*] Like nothin' ever seen before.

    History flew ten times fast, faster

    Still; men drew up sweet-sounding

    Documents for liberty, justice;

    Laws created to improve

    Society. The lady with

    The scales is beautiful, man,

    Because she's a picture of civilized

    Equality. In reality,

    Things didn't always factor out

    So fair, but the ideal

    Lives on, and needs our protection.

    M.J., if you willfully kill,

    How will you live within this country?

    Murder is against all principles

    Of freedom and independence.

    It's wrong; it'll change you, it'll

    Change your life. But you'll have to

    See for yourself it seems. Like all

    Men, we only realize afterwards

    What's right. The desire for

    Dominance is a strong one, no doubt.

    But we must be more than this, right?

    Stop yourself. Don't do it, M.J.

      [M.J. *enters from the house.*]

M.J.: Who's ruling here, girls? You sound like so many tamed

    Animals. WhatRya? Gettin' laid and gettin' used to it;

    Lettin' yourselves be led around by the heads. Which ones?

M.J.: [*Cont'd.*] I'm not surprised. But with the way they want to make

You into robots and machines, can't you see, they

Deserve what they get; they're askin' for it, in fact.

When they yak their twisted ballyhoo at us, well,

They're damned lucky not to get slapped or screamed at.

Yeah, they're wrapped up in their way, but you don't hafta

Agree. Get a spine. No woman's gonna fuck me or make

Me think like her. If you spoil them like that, they'll

Just wanna go higher. My ex is evidence

Of female ambition. What a hoot. A dime a dozen.

The ordinariness of bimbos after

A few years can't be hidden by dark glasses

Or all sorts of lotion; one face is as good or

As bad as another. Should you do what they say

So THEY'LL be satisfied with YOU? I DON'T THINK SO.

That's not what I'm here for, or you. NOW WATCH as I

Show you the stuff of the myths. There's more I could say,

But I'm tired of this. Just look what they're doing.

To you, but NEVER ME. I've got the iron hand. Look-n-learn

From THE MASTER. This ain't no bullshit magazine.

[M.J. *snaps his fingers. The* BEST FRIEND *enters from the house. The two men exit the stage together,* M.J. *leads.*]

CHORUS: [*After a pause.*]

A man wants a diamond, and thinks about nothing

Else. The color, cut, size, weight and cost of the stone

Takes up all of his considerations. He strives

And saves and plots and cheats and competes for the rock.

CHORUS: [*Cont'd.*] He knows, he believes, when he finally holds
the
   Gem in his hand, he will be happy, and want for
   Nought. One day, the diamond is his. He mounts it, on
   A ring, on an arm-charm. It sparkles, it glitters;
   He glows from inside. He shines it, he cleans it, he
   Tucks it into its velvet box. He's happy.
   Then one day the worries begin. What if it's lost.
   What if he's mugged for it. What if, while crossing a
   Street, his rock slides away, and into the gutter,
   Falling through the sewers and into the sea. What
   If, even when locked within its red-velvet pouch,
   He returns home to find it violated. What
   Will he do without it? What will he do without
   The trappings of himself, without the things of his
   Self that he believes make up him?

   [*Pause. Night falls. The sound of one lonely dog barking. Pause.
   A limousine slowly enters. It appears to be driving itself. It stops in
   front of the house. Pause. Lights fade up slowly to the loud sounds of
   birds and/or an urban cacophony, which ceases abruptly when three
   lawyers dart from the automobile. The* LAWYERS *are dressed in expensive suits. A group of* MEDIA *rush on stage and surround the ve-
   hicle/lawyers.* THE MEDIA *shouts ad-libbed questions until the
   lawyers respond.*]

MEDIA: Where's M.J.? Where's M.J.? Where is he?
   Do you know where he is? Can you tell us anything?

THE THREE LAWYERS: Mr. Medea has no comment, no comment,
   No comment, please. Ladies and gentlemen, please.

MEDIA: We aren't leaving. The public has
   A right to know. M.J.! Where is
   He? What does he have to say now?

MEDIA: [*Cont'd.*] Will he come out and speak to us?

M.J., M.J.? Where is he? Where?

LAWYERS: Please, please. Mr. Medea plans to cooperate

Fully with the authorities. He will be —

[M.J. *appears, climbing the house-walls/scaffolding. He is drenched in blood. Everyone is momentarily stunned. The* LAWYERS *go into a huddle and many cameras flash.*]

MEDIA: M.J.! M.J.! How does it feel?

Tell us M.J.! We still love you!

We want your point of view! M.J.!

Over here! M.J.! Talk to us!

LAWYERS: Mr. Medea will not be making a statement

At this time. Please. Allow us to consult with—

[M.J. *continues to climb; blood drips.*]

M.J.: I AM MEDEA. I AM MEDEA. The woman

Is mine, MINE. So now she knows; now you all know.

Who the fuck cares. No one laughs at me. I showed her,

You, all men, me, I AM DEBASED. NO! Can't slip. Can't.

THE ROCK, I will NOT fail. Am not falling WILL NOT.

MEDIA: This'll sell the commercial spots.

Wow. Get it all. M.J.! M.J.!

Over here M.J.! M.J.! M.J.!

The cops say her throat was slit

Like a pig's. Any comment on this?

M.J.! M.J.! Talk to us! Tell —

M.J.: Who says she's dead? SHE'S NOT dead until I SAY!

Take a good look at me. [*Pause.*] SHE DIED OF YOUR
    OWN DISEASE!

Thou art on thy deathbed. Down Strumpet! It's too late!

MEDIA: Can you answer some questions for

Us, M.J.? M.J.? Medea!

If you give us an exclusive,

Well, we'll see, we'll talk. Who knows how

High the brass'll pay for this dish.

Whaddaya say M.J.? M.J.?

LAWYERS: As your lawyers, we advise:

Say no more, or they'll kill you M.J.

M.J.: A MAN'S SKIN CAN BE BURNED AWAY BY THE
  FIRES

OF HELL BUT THE COURAGE TO AVENGE HIM-
  SELF MAKES

A MAN IMMORTAL LIKE THE GODS. I AM FLYING.

MEDIA: Did you get that? Did you catch it?

No matter what, we'll get our story.

And what a story, holy cow.

Play the race card; play the battery.

It's pure Americana.

M.J.: OH SHE WAS SURPRISED. Never thought. I'd spring.
  Knew she

Had NOT the weapon to make me a beggar. NO!

The long white neck. The most beautiful eyes. Murder.

Her eyes, widening, Then OUT out out out. My wife.

I HAVE NO WIFE. NEED NONE. Nothing. BRING ME
  THE CHECK!

Only I have money to burn! Only I have.

LAWYERS: It'll be two mistrials and a

Plea bargain. Time served. No jury

Will slap the fate of conviction

On any rich celebrity.

M.J.: [*Climbing higher, hounded by the press.*]

>Women don't have souls. That was proven by
>St. Augustine a helluva long time ago. She knew.
>She knew that too. Everyone loved me. After all.
>Maybe I didn't kill her. And if I say I
>Didn't, then I didn't. I'll believe it myself.
>I decide, I decide what to DO SAY THINK BE.
>AND NO ONE CAN TOUCH ME. No one can touch me
>now.

MEDIA: Are you getting this? Get it ALL.

>M.J., over here. M.J.! M.J.!
>Hey, Medea! What's the matter?
>Didn't she give good head?

>[*General loud laughter amongst the members of* THE MEDIA.]

M.J.: Oh, She was foul! Whose breath these hands have newly stopped!

>Horrible. But no. I'll become richer now. MORE!
>[*Hysterical laughter.*]
>These Americans. This sky. My fans. HE IS WHAT.

LAWYERS: We're outta here. See ya in court.

>We'll do lunch. Or catch us on
>*Entertainment Tonight*. It's his, his
>Story, but it's our dough. Right.
>We'll soak him. We'll get our fees.
>First'll be the book, and then all
>Our royalties. What's next? The best
>Parties in high society!

>[LAWYERS *move to exit;* M.J. *climbs; the scaffolding bursts into flames. The* LAWYERS *do not exit; they, and all the cast, watch. The flames rise.*]

M.J.: No. I had to. Or fall. Killing her, I fell. No. This

Falling isn't. Is it. I am not. He is what.

It's still all me. All about me. All. I am not.

All. My verge of. Nothing. I am not. He is what.

DON'T SHOOT UNTIL YOU SEE THE WHITES OF
THEIR whatnot.

I can't look back. Won't. Plunge. No. KILL THE MESSEN-
GER.

[M.J. *burns.* THE MEDIA *films/photographs. All cast-members
who previously exited now enter.* M.J. *burns, climbs higher, then out
of sight.*]

[*Enter the* STREET PREACHER.]

STREET PREACHER: Repent I say! No man is guilty! Jesus saves!

[*As the fire burns out,* THE MEDIA *can be seen interviewing* THE
HOUSE BOY, THE CHAUFFEUR, THE LAWYERS *and* THE BEST
FRIEND. THE POLICEMEN *pick haphazardly through the wreckage.*
THE PREACHER *hands out pamphlets, etc. The following dialogue
may be played separately or layered simultaneously.*]

MEDIA: Get the Chauffeur! Get 'im before

He leaves! Lighting! Sound! Over here!

Mr. Chauffeur! Mr. Chauffeur!

Tell us your side of the story!

CHAUFFEUR: I saw nothin'. Get your cotton-

Pickin' hands offa me. What the . . .

Wait. Whatsit to ya? Huh? How much?

How much am I gonna git for it?

MEDIA: House Boy, House Boy. Come on kid, give.

HOUSE BOY: Well, Mr. Medea was

Never easy to work for, that's for

Sure. But that's because he was like

One of those Aztecs, man. Fire

HOUSE BOY: [*Cont'd.*] And Ice. Oh yeah, I was close to

The Man, sure. I loved working for

A Star. Ya never know, working

For them, what's gonna happen to

You. It could be like the Lotto.

Sure, I dream a little dream. Why

The hell not? Why else work for such

Snots. No. We were very close. I

Loved the Boss. He always told me

All of his secrets. What? I can't

Tell you that! They're priceless, the

Stories I have on our Medea.

MEDIA: 50 grand! 80! A mil!

What can I authorize for this?

Get me a hookup with Murdoch! Now!

[THE LAWYERS *and* THE BEST FRIEND *attempt to exit; they are swamped by cameras, etc.*]

LAWYERS: No comment. No comment now. No.

Read the book. It'll be out soon.

[THE LAWYERS *exit.* THE BEST FRIEND *pushes past all without talking.* THE STREET PREACHER *attempts to leaflet them before they exit.* THE MEDIA *changes its focus to* THE POLICEMEN, *who have been picking clumsily through the chaos.* THE MEDIA *ad-libs questions to* THE POLICE. THE POLICEMAN *who did most of the speaking earlier steps forward. He holds up his hands dramatically to quiet the press.*]

POLICEMAN: [*Deliberately.*] I'm speakin'... under the

Condition... of a-non-y-mi-ty.

[*General, loud laughter from all present.*]
[*Continue ad-lib dialogues between* THE MEDIA *and their*

*interview subjects. Also ad-lib intra-police and intra-media confer-
encing. A widespread hubbub as the* CHORUS *begins its final passage.*]

CHORUS: Is heaven the overseer of all our doings?

What we think, and what we expect, are not confirmed.

Once upon a time, a big black bear was poor and

Despised, yet he grew up to be our hero.

We, who needed an idol, both feared and cherished

Him; and we built him to the skies. In fact, his

Violence dwelled also within us, and, in terms of

His authority to tyrannize us, well, we sorta

Lived through him. It's true. But if no animal is

An island, then similarly, no creature is

Beyond reproach. Thus we, who placed Medea in

Repose, are as much to blame for this mess. Uh-huh.

It's difficult to say just why we've done this. Yeah.

Money changes everything. But when anybody's

Excesses are tolerated to the point of

Destruction, then we create our own Monsters;

Our Medeas. And so it is in this story.

Rich Orloff

I DIDN'T KNOW
YOU COULD COOK

Rich Orloff

Rich Orloff's plays have been seen at such regional theaters as American Stage Company in New Jersey, Arizona Theatre Company, Florida Studio Theatre, the Bathhouse Theatre in Seattle, Philadelphia Festival Theatre for New Plays, and the Key West Theatre Festival. His full-length plays include the comedies *Veronica's Position* (winner, 1995 New Plays in America Festival), *Damaged Goods* (winner, 1995 Festival of Firsts), *Someone's Knocking*, *Water Boy*, and the drama *Days of Possibilities*, based on true stories of college life during the Vietnam era.

His many one-acts include *The Whole Shebang*, which was published in *The Best American Short Plays 1994-5*, and which has since received over thirty productions in theaters and schools throughout the country. His short play *August Afternoon* was recently published as part of *Ten-Minute Plays from Actors Theatre of Louisville, Volume Four*.

I Didn't Know You Could Cook began as a ten-minute play for the National Theatre Workshop of the Handicapped. Expanded and revised, the play was produced by the Carousel Theatre Company in New York along with two more of Rich's one-act comedies, *Oedi* and *Mars Needs Women But Not as Much as Arnold Schecter*, under the umbrella title *Sexy People*. That production of *Cook* was directed by Vicki Meisner and featured William-Kevin Young and Christopher Kirk Allen. The play was also produced in the spring of 1977 by the Sackett Group, directed by Valerie Harris, and featured Kelly AuCoin and Dan Haft.

The author would like to give special thanks to Rick Curry, artistic director of the National Theatre Workshop of the Handicapped, and to the actors in that company, whose experiences and talent inspired this play.

CHARACTERS

JEROME   mid-20s, paraplegic, uses a wheelchair

MARK   near 30, his older brother

SETTING: *The kitchen of a modest urban apartment.*

TIME: *Dinner time.*

NOTE: *In a kitchen used by someone confined to a wheelchair, the higher shelves would be empty, and all appliances would be in easy reach.*

As the play begins, JEROME *and* MARK *are at the kitchen table finishing dinner.* JEROME *has gone to some effort to make the meal setting look classy.*

MARK: Anyway, so he pulls up to the stoplight, and he begins revving up his little Corvette engine, and I think, give me a break.

JEROME: Uh-huh.

MARK: I didn't get my Porsche to be macho or anything. I just like how it feels.

JEROME: Uh-huh.

MARK: But he keeps revving his engine, rhhm, rhhm, rhhmmmm, so, so right before the light changes, I roll down my window—

JEROME: Yeah.

MARK: And I say, "I think you've done a wonderful job of compensating for a small penis."

JEROME: You didn't.

MARK: Light changed; I took off; left him in the dust.

JEROME: Wow, it's so cool they gave you a Porsche as a bonus.

MARK: Hey, if you ever want to get into sales...

JEROME: I think I'll stick with teaching.

MARK: Well, if you ever want me to help. After all, what's a brother for?

JEROME: Thanks. Not that I could drive one, anyway.

MARK: I'm sure they could adjust it.

JEROME: Bucket seats? Low to the ground? I think I'll stick with my Ford.

MARK: I'm sure they could adjust anything, if you pay them enough.

JEROME: I'll stick with my Ford. We've developed a very intimate and trusting relationship.

MARK: You know, in a just world, they'd give teachers cars as bonuses.

JEROME: That'll be the day.

MARK: Well, you work hard enough for it.

JEROME: I'm just glad they finally put all the ramps up.

MARK: I thought they had to do that years ago.

JEROME: They did.

MARK: Then why didn't they?

JEROME: They hadn't run out of excuses yet.

MARK: [*Finishing eating.*] This was delicious, Jerome. Absolutely delicious.

JEROME: I'm glad you liked it.

MARK: I'm really impressed. I didn't know you could cook.

JEROME: Millions of people can cook, Mark. Maybe billions.

MARK: Not me. I tried making pasta once; a couple of pieces are still stuck to my wall.

JEROME: Would you like some dessert?

MARK: Oh, no, I'm stuffed.

JEROME: It's chocolate mousse pie. Made it from scratch.

MARK: Sorry. No room.

JEROME: You don't need room for chocolate mousse pie. It just fills the crevices around the food you've already eaten.

MARK: Can't do it. I've already met my caloric maximum for the day.

JEROME: I forgot how disciplined you are.

MARK: Even a small paunch can negatively impact a woman's first response to you.

JEROME: I'll remember that.

MARK: Besides, I, I probably should be heading back to the hotel.

JEROME: It's early.

MARK: I know, but I have another meeting first thing in the —

JEROME: [*Overlapping with the above.*] But we've hardly —

MARK: [*Overlapping with the above.*] They didn't fly me this far so I could —

JEROME: [*Overlapping with the above.*] I just hoped we could —

MARK: [*Overlapping with the above.*] Next time I'm in town —

JEROME: Right. Sure.

MARK: Hey.

JEROME: You know — you know how long it's been since we've spent any real time together?

MARK: Six months?

JEROME: Five years.

MARK: What do you mean? I saw you at Mom's birthday thing, and Uncle Ted and Aunt Lisa's fiftieth anniversary, and at Daniel's wedding.

JEROME: Those are family things. Nobody really talks at them.

MARK: Sure, they do.

JEROME: Mark, the reason they're called family *functions* is because that's about all you can do at them.

MARK: Well, we've talked the last hour, haven't we?

JEROME: Yeah. I guess. [JEROME *starts taking the dishes to the kitchen sink.*]

MARK: Can I help with the —

JEROME: I got it.

MARK: I'd be glad to —

JEROME: I got it... Would you like some coffee?

MARK: Caffeine after seven? Never.

JEROME: I have decaf.

MARK: I really can't stay —

JEROME: Right.

MARK: Hey, Mom sent me that article about you in the paper.

JEROME: About the disabled schoolteacher all the third graders adore?

MARK: It was a good article.

JEROME: It was your generic "Let's admire the handicapped" piece. They just filled in the blanks with my name.

MARK: Nobody writes about me.

JEROME: Look, it was a fine article; I, I just don't like being

JEROME: [*Cont'd.*] written up because I can do what people *assume* I can't do. If they were honest, the piece would have been titled, "Local Crip Transcends Expectations."

MARK: Well, *I* liked the piece.

JEROME: I'm glad.

MARK: And even if this isn't . . . correct, I'm really impressed by how well you've learned to manage on your own.

JEROME: And I'm impressed by how well you've learned to manage on your own, too, Mark.

MARK: All I mean is, well, I never thought you'd move out and live on your own. I mean, I knew you could. I knew you could do anything you put your mind to.

JEROME: I think professional ski jumping is out.

MARK: Well, anything practical.

JEROME: The jumping I could finesse; it's the lifts that frighten me.

MARK: I'm still proud of what you've done. I'm sorry if that bugs you, but it's true.

JEROME: I haven't done anything special.

MARK: I'm not sure I could have done what you've done.

JEROME: You just haven't been tested.

MARK: Still, to live alone when you're, well, you know — I think it's quite an accomplishment.

JEROME: Well, it's not like I'm completely alone.

MARK: Why? Is someone hiding in the bedroom or something?

JEROME: No, no, it's just, well, to quote Ringo, or was it George, anyway, to quote one of them, I get by with a little help from my friends.

MARK: Oh, does some social agency help —

JEROME: No, I mean friends. You know, *friends*.

MARK: I know, *friends*. The people you put in your Rolodex who aren't business connections.

JEROME: I also, um, well, I, there's, there's also one special friend.

MARK: No, really?

JEROME: Really.

MARK: Who?

JEROME: Oh, just . . . just someone special.

MARK: Who?

JEROME: Well —

MARK: What's her name?

JEROME: Louie.

MARK: Louie?

JEROME: Louie.

MARK: Well, if there can be an actress named Glenn Close, I guess there can be a woman named Louie.

JEROME: Louie's a man.

MARK: Oh, so he's just a friend.

JEROME: We're more than friends.

MARK: He's a good friend.

JEROME: We're more than good friends.

MARK: He's a good, good friend.

JEROME: We're lovers.

MARK: He's a *very* good friend.

JEROME: Mark, I'm gay.

MARK: You can't be gay.

JEROME: Why not?

MARK: Because our father isn't henpecked and our mother isn't castrating.

JEROME: I'm still gay.

MARK: What makes you think you're gay?

JEROME: Well, for one thing, I'm extremely enamored with the male form.

MARK: So you have a heightened sense of aesthetics.

JEROME: I also have a lover named Louie.

MARK: Are you sure you're not just doing this to be trendy?

JEROME: Mark, I'm a homosexual.

MARK: Well, I'm stunned. I'm really stunned.

JEROME: I —

MARK: I never even knew you were sexual.

JEROME: Of course, I'm sexual.

MARK: Well, I thought, since the accident...

JEROME: Only my legs went limp; nothing in between...I'm one of the lucky ones.

MARK: You mean, you really can, uh—

JEROME: Uh-huh.

MARK: Really?

JEROME: Yes.

MARK: Really?

JEROME: Well, it does take me longer to climax, but I've never gotten any complaints about that.

MARK: Well...what do you know.

JEROME: To be honest, after the accident, I wasn't sure what I'd be able to do. At the rehab center, they didn't deal with our sexuality at all. At all. Then about six months later, I—I was

JEROME: [Cont'd.] watching this Mel Gibson movie, and he started getting real sweaty, and inside I started getting real excited, and outside I got real excited, too.

MARK: Mel Gibson?

JEROME: I know you're shocked that I'm turned on by Mel Gibson. [*Lightly.*] But then, I'm shocked when I meet someone who isn't.

MARK: You're just doing this to be different, aren't you?

JEROME: No.

MARK: Isn't it enough that —

JEROME: Stop it! Look, I, I . . . I know you have trouble accepting things sometimes.

MARK: Like what?

JEROME: Like after the accident, when you visited from college and you offered me a hundred bucks if I took five steps.

MARK: I thought you needed encouragement.

JEROME: My spinal cord had been severed, Mark.

MARK: I know.

JEROME: It was physically impossible.

MARK: Miracles do happen, Jerome!

JEROME: That's exactly what I thought during the Mel Gibson movie.

MARK: Look, I just thought you needed a little push to get better.

JEROME: I was getting better.

MARK: Well, you know, the way the whole family was coddling you;

Mom and Grandma were so glad you were alive, they weren't going to ask anything of you.

JEROME: Well, you know, c'mon, they were devastated.

MARK: I didn't want you to get too ... comfortable.

JEROME: That wasn't likely.

MARK: I didn't see anybody pushing you to get better.

JEROME: You almost made me think —

MARK: Everyone always coddled you.

JEROME: Dad never coddled me.

MARK: Dad never knew either of us existed.

[*This stops the conversation for a moment.*]

JEROME: You're right.

MARK: Look, about this, this deciding to be gay thing, I ... well, I just can't say I approve.

JEROME: Well then, I guess I'll just have to stop. Next time my pecker rises during a Mel Gibson movie, I'll have to say, "Stop that. Wait till Sharon Stone comes on the screen."

MARK: This doesn't sit right with me, that's all. It just doesn't.

JEROME: Do you want to pretend I never said it?

MARK: This doesn't sit right, that's all. Maybe by your friends it does, but, but not by me.

JEROME: Oh.

MARK: You always get these ideas in your head and, and everyone coddles you...

JEROME: Look...

MARK: It's not healthy.

JEROME: Mark —

MARK: So I'm giving you a choice.

JEROME: What?!

MARK: I'm giving you a choice.

JEROME: What?

MARK: You can be gay or disabled, but not both.

JEROME: But I *am* both!

MARK: Why can't you be satisfied just being disabled?

JEROME: I don't know. Maybe I'm just selfish.

MARK: Have you considered seeing a shrink about this?

JEROME: I've seen a shrink.

MARK: And what did he say?

JEROME: He said I should accept myself for who I am and stop worrying about whether or not I can please my older brother.

MARK: That sounds like something a shrink would say. Does the school know about this?

JEROME: I'm sure some people suspect, but no.

MARK: 'Cause I'm sure a lot of parents would get pretty upset.

JEROME: I know. Some of them are already nervous about me. I think they're afraid that with me as a role model, some of their kids will want to grow up to be disabled.

MARK: You never used to have this edge.

JEROME: I never used to live in the real world.

MARK: Look, Jerome, about this uh — you sure this isn't just another phase you're going through, you know, like when you were eight and you were positive you wanted to become an astronaut?

JEROME: I don't think —

MARK: You were very serious about it. You had pictures of constellations up on your walls and everything.

JEROME: It's not the same.

MARK: Maybe you think women won't be attracted to you because... you know.

JEROME: Mark, I've been with women. I wasn't attracted to them the way I am with men.

MARK: What do you mean, "been with"?

JEROME: I mean everything you think I could mean.

MARK: Even, uh...

JEROME: Uh-huh.

MARK: Were these women . . . you know?

JEROME: Hookers?

MARK: No! . . . You know.

JEROME: Virgins?

MARK: No.

JEROME: Disabled?

MARK: Yeah.

JEROME: Some were, and some weren't.

MARK: Where'd you meet 'em?

JEROME: Oh, I don't know. School, bars, the post office.

MARK: You picked up girls at the post office?

JEROME: Oh, sure. [*To an imaginary woman.*]"Here, let me hold your package in my lap . . . No, it's no effort at all." [JEROME *gives the imaginary woman a big smile.*]

MARK: So then women find you attractive.

JEROME: Well, not an uncontrollable number . . .

MARK: And you've had sex with them.

JEROME: Some of them.

MARK: Well, that proves it. You're attracted to women.

JEROME: No! I, uh, the women were, oh, I don't know. I guess, I guess they were an experiment. I mean, I thought I might be gay even before the accident; actually, I was pretty sure of it. Still, I kept thinking, "Maybe if I meet the right woman..." Hell, most of the time the only way I could get it up with them was if I fantasized I was with —

MARK: I know. Mel Gibson.

JEROME: Or Tom Cruise.

MARK: You know, both of those men are straight.

JEROME: I don't hold it against them.

MARK: Why do you have this obsession about seducing straight men?

JEROME: I don't have an obsession about seducing straight men. Louie does, but I don't.

MARK: Then he must think you're straight.

JEROME: He doesn't think I'm —

MARK: Well, you said —

JEROME: I just meant —

MARK: If you're not sure —

JEROME: I'm sure —

MARK: You don't sound sure.

JEROME: Mark!

MARK: Why can't you just be disabled?!

JEROME: Look, damn it, I'm disabled and I'm gay, and that's the way it is, whether you like it or not or I like it or not or anybody in the world likes it or not. I didn't ask to be either. I always figured I'd get married someday and I'd walk down the aisle, and surprise, I'm not going to do either. I know I should be proud that I'm gay, and accepting that I'm disabled, and I suppose I am, but damn it, I've sure had to give up a lot of fantasies, a whole truckload of fantasies.

MARK: Look, if you've decided to be gay, that's your decision. I —

JEROME: Oh, yes. That's what it was, a decision. One morning I woke up and thought, "I wonder what I'll do today. See a movie? Go shopping? Turn homo? That sounds interesting."

MARK: Look, I'm sorry, I know this must be hard for you, but I just can't approve.

JEROME: I'm not asking you to approve; I'm asking you to, to accept.

MARK: Well, I'm not sure I can.

JEROME: Why, because I can't be who you want me to be?

MARK: What?

JEROME: It's like when you offered me that money to walk again. I think about that a lot. Was that for me or for you?

MARK: What do you mean?

JEROME: If I could walk again, then you wouldn't have to face the fact that I couldn't.

MARK: I was just trying to help.

JEROME: You or me?

MARK: Damn it, it wasn't my fault you hurt yourself. Just because I had a motorcycle, you didn't have to borrow the neighbors'.

JEROME: That's not why I —

MARK: I didn't do anything wrong.

JEROME: I'm not saying you did.

MARK: I was trying to help.

JEROME: [*a surrender, not an agreement*] I know.

MARK: Look, Jerome, it's, you know, I'm sure you don't approve of everything I do —

JEROME: I don't want your approval, Mark.

MARK: I mean, I'm sure all your friends think this is perfectly —

JEROME: I don't need your approval.

MARK: Then why did you tell me?!

JEROME: Because you're, you're my brother.

MARK: I know, but —

JEROME: Because you let me tag along with you when you went to get ice cream. Because you explained long division to me

JEROME: [*Cont'd*] better than my teacher. Because you taught me how to play catch.

MARK: You threw like a girl.

JEROME: I don't think it was a sign.

MARK: You know, you could've given me a little hint along the way or something.

JEROME: Like what?

MARK: I don't know. You could've had copies of *Playgirl* lying around.

JEROME: I prefer *Gentleman's Quarterly*. I enjoy mentally disrobing them.

MARK: [*Uncomfortable.*] Really?

JEROME: What?

MARK: Well, I pick up *GQ* at the newsstand sometimes, and it never occurred to me that people might think —

JEROME: Don't worry, Mark. I'm sure lots of heterosexuals read *GQ*. Hundreds maybe.

MARK: You don't act very gay.

JEROME: I'm sorry. Would you like me to wax eloquent about Barbra Streisand?

MARK: I love Streisand.

JEROME: Uh-oh, be careful. First *GQ*, now this.

MARK: I'm not worried about me.

JEROME: Do you ever refer to another guy as "that bitch"?

MARK: It's just, it's a scary time.

JEROME: I'm careful. We're careful.

MARK: Still —

JEROME: You sure you wouldn't like one piece of — [*One of* JEROME's *legs starts to spasm. It's not significant, but it's noticeable, and it lasts ten to fifteen seconds.*] Uhp, there goes Old Faithful.

MARK: I thought you were taking medication —

JEROME: I stopped years ago. I'm used to them; they don't bother me.

MARK: [*Overlapping a bit.*] Do you ever get spasms at school?

JEROME: Oh, sure. Not often.

MARK: How did the kids react?

JEROME: Oh, the first time, they were freaked out. Then I told them that whoever got the highest mark on the division quiz would get to ride me next time it happened. They got used to it after that.

MARK: You have a lot of guts, Jerome.

JEROME: I just do what I have to do, that's all.

MARK: So why do you think you turned out gay?

JEROME: I don't know. Why do you think you turned out straight?

MARK: I don't know. Jay Wertheimer, remember him?

JEROME: Yeah.

MARK: Jay and I used to sneak looks at his dad's *Playboys* when we were in junior high. Maybe if you had had some experiences like that...

JEROME: Will you stop being so damn superficial?!

MARK: Hey, if I have to accept you're gay, you're going to have to accept I'm superficial. I don't examine things like you do.

JEROME Do you know what Socrates said about the unexamined life?

MARK: It's easier on the nerves?

JEROME: Mark....

MARK: Look, Jerome, the only magazine I read regularly is *People*, and that's only because I fly a lot. My main source of news is the car radio, and half the time I'll switch stations. I work hard, and I don't bother anyone. I may not be a great role model, but nobody's asked me to be.

JEROME: Well, I'm sorry if I'm bothering you with my news.

MARK: You don't have any more surprises for me tonight, do you? You haven't joined a religious cult or anything. You're not a gay disabled Moonie, are you?

JEROME: And if I were?!

MARK: I don't know!

JEROME: Look, I, I... I know this must be hard on you...

MARK: Well, you know, it's like one moment you think the universe is one way; the next moment, it's another way.

JEROME: No, the universe is always the same. The only thing that changes is what you know about it.

MARK: This Louie guy, is he, you know ...

JEROME: An Episcopalian?

MARK: No. Is he, you know ...

JEROME: Handicapped? Crippled? Physically challenged? Lame? Euphemism of the month?

MARK: I don't know why you're so angry.

JEROME: It's because I'm afraid that if I ever turn into one of those "nice" cripples, I'll end up on a Jerry Lewis telethon.

MARK: Hey.

JEROME: No, Louie's not disabled.

MARK: How'd you meet?

JEROME: At a gay bake sale. He bought one of my cookies, and then he came back and bought another, and then he came back and bought five more. You know, what they say about the quickest way to man's heart is absolutely true.

MARK: Is that why you took up cooking?

JEROME: No. I took it up because I like to eat.

MARK: Look, I, I'm sorry, I really gotta go.

JEROME: Right.

MARK: If you want, we can discuss it again —

JEROME: Yeah.

MARK: Look, you're going to do whatever you want anyway. You always did.

JEROME: I'm not your little brother anymore, Mark. There's nothing you have to protect me from.

MARK: From what I've read —

JEROME: Let's just drop it, okay?

[MARK *gets ready to go.*]

MARK: Look, dinner was delicious. I won't tell Mom; she'll feel threatened.

JEROME: Goodbye.

MARK: You know, this is a real burden you're laying on me. A real burden.

[JEROME *just looks at* MARK.]

MARK: [Cont'd.] You're asking me for more than I can give. You've always done that. You want me to make everything okay.

JEROME: I don't —

MARK: You wanted the bribe to work. You wanted me to be right. When you were laying in that bed, and everyone else was crying and going nuts, you looked at me, and maybe you don't

MARK: [*Cont'd*] remember, but God, you really wanted someone to believe you could walk. I didn't think you could either, but if you wanted me to think you could, I was willing to play that role.

JEROME: You didn't think —

MARK: Hell, no.

JEROME: I didn't know.

MARK: Older brothers don't give out all their secrets.

JEROME: Any other secrets you kept from me?

MARK: Yeah. I hated it when you tagged along with me to get ice cream.

JEROME: I'm sorry.

MARK: It's okay. It's just that you always insisted on getting a double cone, and halfway through the first scoop there'd be this lava flow coming down your arm.

JEROME: Thanks for cleaning it up.

MARK: Hey, what are older brothers for?

JEROME: Good question.

MARK: Does anyone else in the family know you're —

JEROME: No, I thought I'd try it out on you first.

MARK: So how'd I do?

JEROME: You were —... [Starts to cry.] I ... Shit.

MARK: Jerome ...

JEROME: I'm sorry, I ...

MARK: Hey, you don't have to —

JEROME: I wanted to look so together tonight.

MARK: Hey —

JEROME: I just wanted — shit, shit.

MARK: Calm down.

JEROME: I . . . I lied.

MARK: You're not gay?

JEROME: No, I mean, yes, I'm gay. I lied about . . . Yes, damn it, I, I want your approval, and I want your acceptance, and your love, and maybe I'm stupid, maybe I'm stupid for wanting so much from you . . . Consider it a disability.

MARK: Look, Jerome . . .

JEROME: I'm just so sick of pretending. I'm so tired of Aunt Debbie always asking me when I'm going to meet that special person. Damn it, I've met that special person.

MARK: Well, you know, Aunt Debbie —

JEROME: I mean, I have a pretty good life, and I know it. But sometimes, I . . . Sometimes I don't know where to put my sorrow.

MARK: I . . . I don't know what to say. I don't know what you want me to say.

JEROME: Say you'll stay five minutes and have a piece of my damn pie!

[MARK *looks at* JEROME *a moment.*]

MARK: Okay if I stay five minutes and have a piece of your damn pie?

JEROME: Well, since you asked.

[JEROME *brings the pie to the table. It's beautiful.*]

MARK: You really made that from scratch, huh?

JEROME: That's right.

MARK: Look, you know, I, I'm not sure when I'll be in town next...

JEROME: That's okay. You don't have to —

MARK: It's just that, I don't know, it's —

JEROME: I understand.

MARK: I just want to see what we've got here.

JEROME: Mark —

MARK: So you've really had sex with women...

JEROME: Yes.

MARK: You've had sex with disabled women...

JEROME: Uh-huh.

MARK: And with non-disabled women...

JEROME: Uh-huh.

MARK: And with disabled men...

JEROME: That's right.

MARK: And non-disabled men.

JEROME: Yep.

MARK: So the bottom line is ... you've probably had more sex than I have.

JEROME: It wasn't intentional.

MARK: Well, I just don't think it's right. I'm your older brother, damn it!

JEROME: I'm sorry if I broke the rules.

[MARK *eats a bite of* JEROME'*s pie.*]

MARK: Mmm, this is delicious.

JEROME: I'm a damn good cook, Mark ... You'll just have to accept that.

[MARK *and* JEROME *look at each other.*]

THE END

Jacquelyn Reingold

TUNNEL OF LOVE

Jacquelyn Reingold

Jacquelyn Reingold's play, *Girl Gone*, was produced off-Broadway by the MCC Theatre, and then in 1996 at the City Garage in Los Angeles. It received the Kennedy Center's Fund for New American Plays Roger Stevens Award, and is published in *Women Playwrights: The Best Plays of 1994*. Her one-act, *Dear Kenneth Blake*, was produced in Ensemble Studio Theatre's Marathon '94, and by Theatre Geo in Los Angeles in 1997, where it won a Dramalogue Award in Playwriting. It is published in *The Best American Short Plays 1994-5*.

Jacquelyn's other plays, which include *Freeze Tag, Lost and Found, A.M.I., Joe and Stew*, and *Creative Development*, have been seen in New York at Ensemble Studio Theatre, Naked Angels, MCC, Primary Stages, the Working Theatre, the Circle Rep Lab, as well as at theatres across the country and in London. Her work has been published by Dramatists Play Service, Samuel French, Smith and Kraus, and in *The Quarterly*. She has written and directed plays for inner city kids at the 52nd Street Project, and is a member playwright of New Dramatists and Ensemble Studio Theatre.

Tunnel of Love was first workshopped at Naked Angels, directed by Ethan Silverman, and acted by Kimberly Flynn, Susan Greenhill, Merrill Holtzman, Karen Kandel, Martha Plimpton, and Tisha Roth. It was first produced in Ensemble Studio Theatre's Marathon '93, directed by Ethan Silverman, and acted by Amelia Campbell, Bill Cwikowski, David Eigenberg, Christine Farrell, Karen Kandel, and Angela Pietropinto. It was produced in 1996 at Theatre of NOTE in Los Angeles where it received a Dramalogue Award in Playwriting, and in 1997 at the Shadowbox Theatre in Columbus, Ohio.

CHARACTERS

SUSIE — Quirky, confused, trying to cope as the world spins around her. Wears an oversized "Laura Ashley"-type dress. In her early 20s.

GARY — A guy guy. Trying hard to do his best. In his 20s.

DOCTOR CHECKUP

DOCTOR MUFFIN

DOCTOR BEAVER

DOCTOR SNATCH

DOCTOR TOO-LIPS

JO

FIFI

THERESA

WOMAN 1

WOMAN 2

WOMAN 3

WOMAN 4

TIME: Now.

NOTE: An ensemble of three women and one man play all roles except SUSIE and GARY. Also, there are no blackouts between scenes.

SCENE 1

Doctor's office. SUSIE *sits in a tiny child sized chair.* DOCTOR CHECKUP *sits in a large chair. He looks very big. On his chest is a name-tag that reads, "Dr. Anton Checkup." He has a Russian accent.*

DOCTOR CHECKUP: So. I'm Dr. Anton Checkup. And you're — [*He looks at a paper.*] Susie. So. Any aches and pains?

SUSIE: No.

DOCTOR CHECKUP: Ongoing childhood diseases?

SUSIE: No.

DOCTOR CHECKUP: Shortness of breath?

SUSIE: No.

DOCTOR CHECKUP: Runny nose?

SUSIE: No.

DOCTOR CHECKUP: Post-feminist depression?

SUSIE: No.

DOCTOR CHECKUP: Tummy ache?

SUSIE: No.

DOCTOR CHECKUP: Heartache?

SUSIE: Um, well, no.

DOCTOR CHECKUP: Problems with peeing or pooping?

SUSIE: No.

DOCTOR CHECKUP: Exercise?

SUSIE: Stairmaster.

DOCTOR CHECKUP: Ulcer due to backlash anger?

SUSIE: No.

DOCTOR CHECKUP: Eyes? [SUSIE *points to her eyes.*] Ears? [*She points to ears.*] Nose? [*She points to nose.*]

DOCTOR CHECKUP: Married?

SUSIE: No.

DOCTOR CHECKUP: In a relationship?

SUSIE: Uh, no. I was, but he um, just left me.

DOCTOR CHECKUP: [*He looks at her.*] Anorgasmic or orgasmic?

SUSIE: Excuse me?

DOCTOR CHECKUP: Have you had one or haven't you?

SUSIE: Umm.

DOCTOR CHECKUP: Hmm. And no trouble peeing or pooping.

SUSIE: No.

DOCTOR CHECKUP: My wife's a social worker, I recommend counseling. Otherwise, you're healthy. Come back next year. Find a man. Pay 600 dollar bill at desk.

SUSIE: Wait.

DOCTOR CHECKUP: Yes?

SUSIE: I do have a problem.

DOCTOR CHECKUP: Yes.

SUSIE: With.

DOCTOR CHECKUP: Yes?

SUSIE: My.

DOCTOR CHECKUP: Yes? [*She crosses to him and stands on tiptoe to whisper in his ear.*] Oh. Go on. [*She whispers.*] Interesting. I'd like to have a look at that.

SCENE 2

Phone call. GARY *in his apartment, fixing something with his tools.* SUSIE *at home.*

SUSIE: Gary?

GARY: Yeah?

SUSIE: Hi, it's Susie.

GARY: Oh, hi. Hang on. [*He uses his screwdriver.*]

SUSIE: What are you doing?

GARY: Fixing objects so that I can feel like I have infinite power over my world.

SUSIE: Nice.

GARY: Sorry things didn't work out with us. I just couldn't handle it. I mean, I still can't. I mean, let's cut to the chase here. Why are you calling?

SUSIE: I just wanted to say that— [*He drops something.*] What are you doing?

GARY: Breaking things so that I can fix them so that I can feel like I have infinite power over my world.

SUSIE: Oh. Well, I went to the doctor.

GARY: Good. It's good to take action.

SUSIE: You were right.

GARY: It's good to be right. Tough break for you, though.

SUSIE: Well, the doctor said there was hope.

GARY: Oh? You mean like a repair job?

SUSIE: And I was wondering, if they can, you know—

GARY: I see—would I want to be a couple—movies, dinner, nesting, that sort of thing.

SUSIE: The doctor recommended it.

GARY: Look, uh, my, my phone is ringing.

SUSIE: It is?

GARY: I mean, the door is ringing.

SUSIE: I have an appointment with a specialist.

GARY: Hey, well, like, I don't know, I mean, yours seemed like a problem even I couldn't fix. So, let me know what happens, if you get it worked out or worked in or whatever, Susie. You're a sweetheart. Gotta go. [*He exits.*]

SCENE 3

Another Doctor's office. SUSIE *sits on her little chair, or on a table with wheels.* DOCTOR MUFFIN *appears.*

DOCTOR MUFFIN: I'm Dr. Muffin.

SUSIE: Hi, Dr. Checkup gave me your name. I was—

DOCTOR MUFFIN: Oh, yes. Mind if I take a look?

[SUSIE *spreads her legs.* DOCTOR BEAVER *appears.*]

DOCTOR BEAVER: I'm Dr. Beaver.

DOCTOR MUFFIN: Interesting.

SUSIE: Hi, Dr. Muffin gave me your name. I was wondering—

DOCTOR BEAVER: Interesting. Mind if I take a look?

[DOCTOR SNATCH *appears.*]

DOCTOR SNATCH: I'm Dr. Snatch.

SUSIE: Dr. um, Beaver gave me your name. I was wondering if—

DOCTOR MUFFIN: So, you growing potatoes in there?

SUSIE: What?

DOCTOR BEAVER: Are you married?

SUSIE: No.

DOCTOR SNATCH: Oh, yes, Mind if I —

SUSIE: — take a look?

DOCTOR BEAVER: In a relationship?

DOCTOR MUFFIN: Post-feminist depression?

SUSIE: Ooh.

DOCTOR SNATCH: Interesting.

DOCTOR BEAVER: Are you seeing a psychiatrist?

SUSIE: Ow.

DOCTOR MUFFIN: Do you mind it when men sit with their legs spread apart?

DOCTOR BEAVER: My cousin's an analyst.

DOCTOR SNATCH: I'd like to take a look.

DOCTOR MUFFIN: I like to look.

SUSIE: Doctor, do you think—?

DOCTOR MUFFIN: Let me call in my partners.

[DOCTOR TOO-LIPS *apppears.*]

DOCTOR TOO-LIPS: I'm Dr. Too-Lips.

DOCTOR BEAVER: Get the camera.

SUSIE: Hey.

[SUSIE *is spun around and/or pulled around the stage. Or perhaps it's just the* DOCTORS *that are moving. At some point strange, large, examining instruments appear.*]

DOCTOR MUFFIN: I think there's someone else I'd like you to see.

DOCTOR TOO-LIPS: Do you have a boyfriend?

DOCTOR BEAVER: I think I'd like to see.

DOCTOR TOO-LIPS: Do you have a friend?

DOCTOR SNATCH: I'd like you to come back.

DOCTOR BEAVER: We think it can be fixed.

DOCTOR TOO-LIPS: Do you know any men?

SUSIE: Hey!!

DOCTOR MUFFIN: Interesting.

DOCTOR SNATCH: I can't see.

DOCTOR BEAVER: Let me look.

DOCTOR TOO-LIPS: I'd like to see.

[DOCTORS *in a circle around* SUSIE, *passing the instruments to each other. Fast:*]

DOCTOR MUFFIN, DOCTOR BEAVER, DOCTOR SNATCH, & DOCTOR TOO-LIPS: I can't see ... Let me look... Interesting ... Do you have a ... Interesting ... I'd like to see ... I can't see .. boyfriend? ... Do ... I can't see ... Let me look ... Interesting ... you have a Interesting ... I'd like to see ... I can't see ... friend? ... Do you ... I can't see ... Let me look ... Interesting ... have a boy-Interesting ... I'd like to see ... I can't see ... friend? ... Do you?

DOCTORS: I'd like to take a look. [*They aim the instruments at her.*]

SCENE 4

Support Group. WOMEN *drink from styrofoam coffee cups. The scene should start realistically, in chairs, then move into a heightened, presentational staging, and then back to chairs.*

JO: Hi, my name is Jo.

GROUP: Hi, Jo. [*Applause.*]

FIFI: Hi, my name is Fifi.

GROUP: Hi, Fifi. [*Applause.*]

THERESA: I'm Theresa.

GROUP: Hi, Theresa. [*Applause.*]

THERESA: I didn't know 'til I was married.

JO: I thought my life was ruined.

FIFI: My life was over.

THERESA: I'd never really looked.

JO: It looked normal from the outside.

THERESA: My husband was surprised.

FIFI: I read about it in Cosmo. [*Holds up* Cosmopolitan *magazine.*]

JO: They wrote about it in Cosmo. [*Holds up* Cosmopolitan *magazine.*]

THERESA: We read about it in Cosmo. [*Holds up* Cosmopolitan *magazine.*]

GROUP: [*Reading from* Cosmo.] Sometimes nature slips up.

JO: Cleft palate—

THERESA: —harelip—

FIFI: —clubfoot—

JO: —but there is one abnormality few of us have heard of.

GROUP: Yet today, there are twenty to thirty thousand women, like us, in the U.S. alone who were born with: CAV.

THERESA: [*Not from* Cosmo.] I found out on my wedding night. We were in Bermuda. I was still a virgin.

FIFI: [*Not from* Cosmo.] I found out as a teen ager. You know, on my own.

JO: [*Not from* Cosmo.] I found out at the doctor.

THERESA: My husband was unable to penetrate. Much to our displeasure.

FIFI: I knew right away something was wrong.

THERESA: For months I was still a virgin.

JO: I was having an examination. He called in his partners.

GROUP: We were diagnosed with C.A.V.

THERESA: Congenital—

FIFI: — absence —

JO: — of —

THERESA: — the —

GROUP: [*Loud whisper to* SUSIE.] — vagina.

THERESA: I became hysterical.

FIFI: I felt like I wasn't a woman.

JO: I was a freak.

THERESA: I had surgery as fast as possible.

[*Overlapping section:*]

FIFI: [*Reads from* Cosmo.] Skin from the buttocks is wrapped around a mold, held in place by suturing. Fourteen days later the mold is removed.

JO: [*Reads.*] Nature, unfortunately, recognizing the opening as foreign, wants to close it down.

THERESA: [*Reads.*] A patient must keep it open with frequent coitus or by using dilators regularly.

[*Overlapping ends.*]

GROUP: [*Reads.*] One day a doctor heard of a woman who created hers through coitus, and it didn't close down.

JO: He thought it would be possible—

FIFI: —to create a neo vagina without surgery—

THERESA: —and he began experimenting.

JO: He had a—

FIFI: —patient sit on—

THERESA: —a stool with—

JO: —a lucite—

FIFI: —dilator for—

THERESA: —15 to—

JO: —30 minutes—

FIFI: —a day.

JO: It—

THERESA: —involved—

FIFI: —time—

JO: —patience—

THERESA: —and—

FIFI: —motivation—

GROUP: —but it worked.

GROUP & SUSIE: Once CAV was a devastating diagnosis for any young girl. But today, women, like us, can lead satisfying, sexually active lives.

THERESA: I had the surgery. You have to keep it in use. My husband loves it.

FIFI: I used the stool.

JO: I had the surgery, then it closed, then I used the stool.

THERESA: I'm a changed woman.

JO: I stare at skyscrapers.

FIFI: My husband really loves me now.

THERESA: I like to keep objects inside of mine.

JO: I was afraid after my first one closed down.

THERESA: Spare change, my keys, date book. Things I don't want to misplace.

JO: My boyfriend was very supportive. He loves it.

FIFI: They love it.

GROUP: Your boyfriend will love it.

SCENE 5

Phone call. GARY *with money, a computer, calculator; wearing athletic/career clothes. Loud sounds of TV sports.*

SUSIE: Gary, it's Susie.

GARY: Oh hi. [*He catches a football.*]

SUSIE: What are you doing?

GARY: [*He counts money.*] I'm keeping very busy with external activities so I don't have to experience any inner feelings.

SUSIE: Oh.

GARY: [*He works on a computer.*] You know sports, cars, sex, money, career advancement. I'm very busy, not much time to talk.

SUSIE: I see.

GARY: [*He watches a game on TV, yells at the set.*] Pass! Run! Jump! GO!

SUSIE: Well I just wanted to let you know I'm getting one.

GARY: Oh? [*He pulls out the tv remote. Silence*]

SUSIE: It should be ready in a while. I think you'll love it. I'll be a virgin, Gary.

GARY: [*With reverence, he puts on a baseball cap. A baseball bat appears, he takes it.*] Give me the chance, I'll hit a home run.

SUSIE: Yeah?

GARY: Let me know when it's opening day. [*He swings the bat.*]

SCENE 6

Doctor's waiting room. Sexy looking women sit.

WOMAN 1: I'm having my breasts enlarged.

WOMAN 2: I'm having mine reduced.

WOMAN 4: I'm having my lips inflated.

WOMAN 3: I'm having my hips deflated.

WOMAN 4: Collagen injection.

WOMAN 2: Silicone rejection.

WOMAN 3: Nipple lift.

WOMAN 4: This is my fifth.

WOMAN 1: Chemical peel.

WOMAN 3: Cheeks revealed.

WOMAN 1: Liposuction.

WOMAN 2: Bulge reduction.

WOMAN 4: Ribs removed.

WOMAN 3: Jaw—

WOMAN 2: —reimproved.

   [ALL *look at* SUSIE.]

SUSIE: [*Whispers.*] Vagina. [*Full voice.*] I'm getting a [*Whispers.*] vagina.

WOMAN 2: Really?

WOMAN 3: Wow.

WOMAN 4: A new one?

WOMAN 1: I never thought of that.

SCENE 7

   Phone call. GARY *is drumming.*

SUSIE: Hi, it's Susie. What are you doing?

GARY: Drumming. I'm reading that revolutionary "pumping iron in the john" book. [*He drums.*] My name is Gary, son of Barry.

SUSIE: I wanted to give you an update.

GARY: [*Stops drumming.*] I'm finding my manhood. If you're gonna talk about—about, I mean, women's parts and—eew—you know—eew.

SUSIE: Well, I'm in the middle of a session. I've been sitting here. Expanding. And, Gary, do you want to know what I think about?

GARY: What?

SUSIE: Sometimes I think about you. [*He turns to her.*] And, Gary. It's beginning to work.

GARY: It is?

[*He drums with enthusiasm.*]

SCENE 8

Support group.

SUSIE: It's beginning to work.

GROUP: How do you feel?

SUSIE: Different.

JO, **THERESA**, and **FIFI**: Yes? ... I knew it ... I told you.

SUSIE: I have — I have this yearning feeling.

JO, **THERESA**, and **FIFI**: Oh yes, oh yes ... Oh really? ... Tell us.

SUSIE: Like I need to nurture someone.

JO: Try volunteering.

SUSIE: And an interest in children.

FIFI: I bought a puppy.

SUSIE: And a need to relate to other relationships.

THERESA: Try the afternoon talk shows.

SUSIE: And at the same time I feel angry. I see, I see injustice and sexism and it makes me angry. It's confusing. Things are getting very confused.

FIFI: Oh, that.

JO: Being a woman.

THERESA: Try therapy.

JO: Oh, yes.

FIFI: Being a woman.

THERESA: Counseling.

JO: Oh, that.

FIFI: That.

GROUP: Oh, *that*.

SCENE 9

SUSIE *alone. Almost like a nursery rhyme.*

SUSIE: The Freudian said penis envy. A Jungian, animus fear. Psychiatrist said chemical imbalance. Psychopharmacologist thought Prozac needed here. The psychic said the answer is the future; psychologist, the future's in the past, don't fear. Internist called a gynecologist, support group says—

[SUPPORT GROUP *appears.*]

GROUP: Just keep stretching it, Dear! [GROUP *exits.*]

SCENE 10

[SUSIE, *alone.*]

SUSIE: Oh my God. I have, I have, this empty feeling. I feel so, so, empty. I want to find fulfillment. I want to fill this empty feeling. I want to be pretty. I have to help others. I want to wear silk teddies and push-up bras. I want men to open the door for me and then I want to say "Do I look like I have no arms?" I want to go dancing in high heels and let men lead, and then I get mad when they don't know the steps and I'm not supposed to show them. I want men to notice me and then I want to punch them when they stare. I want to feed children in the third world and scream at the white male cold war politicians who sent the guns there and screwed it up in the first place. I want to shoot guns at truck drivers and bomb operation rescue. I want men to give me a seat on the subway and I want to tell

SUSIE: [*Cont'd.*] the one next to me to stop taking up so much room, why don't you close your legs, what have you got between them, an aircraft carrier?! I want to lash back at the backlash. I have a hole inside me now. All of this because of a hole?

SCENE 11

GARY *dials the phone. He takes a deflated blow up doll out of a box.* SUSIE *picks up.*

GARY: Susie.

SUSIE: Hi.

GARY: Listen, I'm — I'm, uh, practicing for the big day, you know, exercises, technique, defining goals to make sure we achieve them, you know, win the gold medal, blue ribbon, first place, one for the gipper.

SUSIE: Gary, you make me really angry.

GARY: Oh. [*He drops the doll.*]

SUSIE: I — I want to hurt you.

GARY: Well, then, I — I want to get away from you.

SUSIE: I wouldn't nurture you if you were the last human on earth.

GARY: I wouldn't get near you with a ten foot pole.

SUSIE: Well your testicles are hairy!

GARY: And your vagina is — missing!

SUSIE: [*She talks directly to him.*] Not anymore.

GARY: [*He talks directly to her.*] It isn't?

SUSIE: No.

GARY: Can I come over?

SUSIE: I'm wearing crotchless panties.

GARY: I'll be right there. [*He exits.*]

SCENE 12

[SUSIE *unbuttons her two top buttons and puts on lipstick.* GARY *enters wearing a test pilot outfit.*]

SUSIE: Hi.

GARY: Hi, Sexy. You ready?

SUSIE: What are you wearing?

GARY: Test pilot, ready for take off.

SUSIE: Gary, before we go any further, I just have to tell you—

GARY: Go where no man has gone before.

SUSIE: That I think you're a jerk.

GARY: Can I touch it now?

SUSIE: And a pig.

GARY: Oink oink. Now can I?

SUSIE: The way you dumped me then and the way you want me now.

GARY: Come on, baby, let's go exploring.

SUSIE: All because of a hole.

GARY: I want to be your Christopher Columbus.

SUSIE: Gary.

GARY: Cortez, Ponce De Leon. Neil Armstrong. Stormin' Norman. [*He puts on the goggles.*]

SUSIE: That does it. I changed my mind.

GARY: What?

SUSIE: I'm not interested, I'm just not interested. It's my vagina. It is. I made it, it's mine — V-A-G-I-N-A. I don't have to share. I can have a satisfying life without sharing it with you. So, no. It's my hole. And if I want to spend my life crawled up inside of it without you or anyone, then I will. And if you don't like it, you can go. If that's all you're here for, leave. Find yourself another hole.

GARY: [*Stunned. Looks at her, confused.*] Well. What about your mouth?

SUSIE: Well, what about the inside of one of your drums? Or why don't you hollow out your baseball bat? I know, just unzip your pants and head for the Holland tunnel. Even better, Gary, use your own hole, the one between your ears, just put your dick in you head and fuck what little you have of your own brains out!

GARY: [*Beat.*] Nice. I'm really glad you've found yourself.

SUSIE: Me too. [*Pause. They stand there.*] So, what are you waiting for? Leave. I'm not the only hole in the universe.

GARY: [*Pause.*] I don't want to leave.

SUSIE: Why not?

GARY: I don't know.

SUSIE: Why did you ever even talk to me in the first place?

GARY: Mmm. Your face. I think. Something about your face. Made me want to say hi. And then, something about what you said.

SUSIE: What did I say?

GARY: "Hi." But it was the way you said it. "Hi." And when I asked if I could see you sometime and you said, "That would be nice," that was nice. I guess I liked you. And, well, I guess I kinda like you feisty even better.

SUSIE: Oh.

GARY: Why did you talk to me?

SUSIE: You had nice buns.

GARY: Yeah?

SUSIE: [*She shrugs.*] I looked at you and I knew I wanted—to wrestle.

GARY: [*Beat.*] Susie. I know I can be a jerk. I couldn't—I didn't know how to—I—Sorry. Look, what if we—what if we just, you know, tried to be, like, close.

SUSIE: What do you mean?

GARY: You know, like, lie down and do the close thing.

SUSIE: What?

GARY: You know, that talking and feeling thing. How would that be?

SUSIE: I don't know.

GARY: Yeah. Forget it.

SUSIE: [*Beat.*] It might be ok.

GARY: Yeah?

SUSIE: Yeah.

GARY: We could try.

SUSIE: We could. Take off the helmet.

> [*He does. Music plays. They take off their shoes as the* ENSEMBLE *enters with sheet and pillows to create a vertical bed. They 'get in bed,' on opposite ends. They, very gingerly and slowly, get close. They sigh. They smile.*]

GARY: So, how is it?

SUSIE: It's — nice. How is it for you?

GARY: Nice.

SUSIE: Gary?

GARY: Yeah?

SUSIE: Do you sit on the subway with your legs spread?

GARY: Yeah.

SUSIE: Why?

GARY: Just born that way, I guess.

SUSIE: Oh.

GARY: I think I'm gonna fall asleep now. Good night.

SUSIE: 'Night.

> [*He snores, then pushes her all the way to the edge of the bed.*]

SUSIE: Gary?

GARY: [*Asleep.*] Huh?

SUSIE: [*With clarity.*] Move over.

[*He rolls over to his edge. They are apart.* SUSIE *reaches out her hand across the bed,* GARY *reaches out his hand. They touch.*]

[*BLACKOUT.*]

THE END

Murray Schisgal

FIFTY YEARS AGO

Murray Schisgal

Murray Schisgal has had six plays produced on Broadway, a good many Off-Broadway, Off-off-Broadway, and in regional and foreign theaters. He was nominated for a Tony for his play *LUV*, an Oscar for co-writing the film *Tootsie* (it won the New York Film Critics, Los Angeles Film Critics, National Society of Film Critics, Writers Guild of America, and Hollywood Foreign Press Association Awards). His original TV screenplay, *The Love Song of Barney Kempinski* won an Emmy Award. His other credits include *The Typists* and *The Tiger*, which received the Outer Circle and Vernon Rice Awards. Twelve of his one-act plays have appeared in various anthologies. *Slouching Towards the Millennium*, three one-act plays, was produced in 1997 at the 42nd Street Workshop.

CHARACTERS

DONALD

PATRICIA

SETTING: *The Lumleys' living-room in a brownstone on West 88th Street, Manhattan.*

TIME: *August 14, 1995. Day.*

AT RISE: *Folding chairs have been added to the armchairs and sofa, set in a semi-circle, to accommodate the guests who are coming to a party. Canapés and appetizers are on a silver plate; nuts and potato chips in carnival-glass bowls; bottles of champagne, wine and mineral water on coasters or in ice buckets; etc. Several crepe-paper streamers crisscross overhead. Fresh-cut flowers also decorate the room.*

A door to the bedroom is on the right; a door to the ping-pong room is on the left; the entrance door is upstage, left.
PATRICIA is dressing in the bedroom, DONALD in the ping-pong room. The doors to both rooms are open, but we can't see the occupants.
PATRICIA and DONALD are in their seventies.

DONALD (*Offstage.*): Patty m'girl? [*No response; louder.*] Patty? [*No response; a folding chair is thrown against the wall in the ping-pong room, clattering to the floor.*]

PATRICIA (*Offstage.*): [*In a panic.*] What is it? What was that? Are you all right, Donald? Did you hurt yourself? Did you fall or have an accident? Did you break anything? Talk to me! Talk to me!

DONALD (OS): [*Cool as a cucumber.*] I am perfectly fine.

PATRICIA (OS): Then what was that horrible noise? What in God's name happened?

DONALD (OS): It seems the only way I can get your attention when I speak to you is by making you think I've had an accident or I suffered a debilitating stroke!

PATRICIA (OS): [*Heavily emphatic.*] That is not true. That is blatantly not true!

DONALD (OS): It is! It is absolutely true! I've learned something being married to you for one full year!

PATRICIA (OS): What, may I ask, is it that you've learned?

DONALD: [*Only his head is visible in doorway; he is wearing shower-cap; shouts.*] You're hard of hearing! [*Head retreats back into room.*]

PATRICIA (OS): I am not hard of hearing! I'm preoccupied. I have to get dressed. My focus is on getting dressed, not on being convivial!

DONALD (OS): I don't mean to offend you. And I certainly don't mean to quarrel with you on this very special occasion. But I do recall during my first marriage . . .

PATRICIA: [*Only her head is visible in doorway; her hair is dyed with a reddish hue and is rolled in purple, plastic curlers.*] Don't do this to me, Donald. Please, Please, do not do this to me.

DONALD (OS): [*Heedlessly.*] If I coughed, if I sneezed, if I cracked my knuckles, Bertha was at my side, immediately, with a handkerchief or a band-aid or a glass of alka seltzer!

PATRICIA: [*Rigidly.*] I take it you're talking about the first . . . [*Pinched voice.*] . . . Mrs. Lumley, Mr. Lumley.

DONALD (OS): I am. I cannot, after all those years of living with another woman, disregard my experiences with her. I would merely whisper her name in the bedroom — and she would instantaneously rush in from the garden, an unplanted rhododendron bush still in her hands!

PATRICIA (OS): [*Retreats into bedroom.*] I forbid myself, and I have forbidden myself in the past, to utter a single derogatory word against the first Mrs. Lumley. Is that not so, Mr. Lumley?

DONALD (OS): It is. As is befitting and proper in view of the fact that Bertha is gone from this earthly vale of tears.

PATRICIA: [*Head appears in doorway; no curlers.*] To me, Donald, your first wife, whatever her name might be, is still with us. Literally speaking, she will always be with us.

DONALD: [*Head appears in ping-pong room doorway; shaving cream on his face; no shower-cap.*] That is an oxymoron!

PATRICIA: That is not an oxymoron!

DONALD: How can you explain to me the following: "Literally speaking, she will always be with us."

PATRICIA: Because, my dear husband...May I call you my dear husband?

DONALD: Legally, I cannot prevent it.

PATRICIA: Because, my dear husband, she is constantly about us, in the air we breathe, in the water we drink, in the food we eat. Like a pollutant.

DONALD: Be forewarned. Beee forewarned! You are talking of the mother of my three, *priceless* daughters! [*Retreats from sight.*]

PATRICIA: [*Nodding mournfully.*] How well I know it. Full well do I...[*Suddenly in a panic; shouts.*] Donald, I love you!

DONALD: [*Head in doorway at once; no shaving cream on face.*] And I, you! I, you, my sweet, my treasure, my heart!

PATRICIA: Oh, I float on air. I'm in a land of dreams.

DONALD: Do you remember the vow I took one year this evening in our marital chamber?

PATRICIA: Vividly. Lucidly. As well as I remember the day we first met.

DONALD: Fifty years ago.

PATRICIA: In Manila.

DONALD: In the far reaches of the Pacific.

PATRICIA: On VJ Day.

DONALD: Fifty years ago.

PATRICIA: A twin celebration, my darling. Our first anniversary and the anniversary of the unconditional surrender of the Japanese.

DONALD: Happy days. Happy days. [*Stretches his hand out.*] If only I could touch you.

PATRICIA: [*Stretches her hand out.*] My fingers ache for your fingers.

DONALD: What vow was it, my sweet, that I took in our marital chamber one year this evening? [*They withdraw their hands.*]

PATRICIA: That death itself would not separate us.

DONALD: So shall it be. I vow it again, two-fold, ten-fold, a hundred-fold! And now ... Are you ready, Patty m'girl? Are you dressed? Are you made up? Can we begin our party?

PATRICIA: Yes, yes, but ... You come out first.

DONALD: I need another minute. You come out first. Please, I beseech you, I beg you. Let's not make an issue of this.

PATRICIA: I'll be magnanimous.

DONALD: As you are inevitably!

PATRICIA: I'll come out first, but you are not to laugh, smirk, smile, grin, or make a single snide or critical remark!

DONALD: I wouldn't. Never. Am I not in the same boat as you are? Am I not susceptible to the same calumnies as you are?

PATRICIA: Keep that firmly in mind. Lastly, you are not to look at me either directly or surreptitiously until I call your name. Agreed?

DONALD: Agreed!

PATRICIA: Return to the ping-pong room, please.

DONALD (OS): [*Retreats.*] I'll finish dressing. Don't take too long. Our guests will be arriving momentarily!

[PATRICIA *looks about, wanting to make certain that there's absolutely no one watching her. Tentatively, timidly, she steps out of the bedroom. She's wearing a WW2 nurse's uniform. It's too small on her, as are the white shoes and cap. She feels miserable.*]

DONALD (OS): [*Cont'd.*] Patty m'girl? [*No response; louder.*] Patty? [*No response; a folding chair is thrown against the wall, clattering to the floor.*]

PATRICIA: [*Almost in tears.*] If you must come out and gape at me, come out and gape at me. I think your idea of how to celebrate our anniversaries is positively ridiculous and infantile and unworthy of a man of your intelligence. I cannot, for the life of me ...

[*She stops in mid-speech at the sight of* DONALD *entering. He's wearing his pitifully too small WW2 navy uniform; a wide belt or suspenders hold up his trousers and a white cap is perched at the rear of his head. Two rows of campaign ribbons are on his chest and his left arm has a Radioman 3rd Class insignia. He beams like a poppycock. He feels, and believes he looks, terrific.* PATRICIA, *wide-eyed, raises her finger to point at him; her cheeks blow up and a hawking, throaty laugh erupts from her, building to a howling crescendo.*]

DONALD: [*Perplexed.*] What's funny? [*Is she laughing at him?*] What, may I ask, is so funny?

PATRICIA: [*Interrupted laughter.*] That . . . That . . . That . . . [*Screwing her face in to a somber expression.*] I think you look very attractive in your uniform. [*She has to turn away from him; lips glued together.*]

DONALD: [*Pulls down on blouse.*] All things considered, I'd say we both look very attractive. We put on a few pounds, but it's only natural. It's nothing to be ashamed of. [*Pointing at her.*] You see, Patricia, that's the difference between us. I speak what has to be spoken, objectively, not emotionally. I acknowledge the circumstance, I deal with it, correct it, and go beyond it. That's something you've never learned to do.

PATRICIA: [*Thinks; magnanimously.*] You're right. You're one of the most perceptive and brilliant men I know. My first husband . . .

DONALD: I prefer we do not discuss your first husband.

PATRICIA: Donny-o, I also do not want us to quarrel on this auspicious occasion. Having said that, however, I will say that I reserve unto myself the inalienable right to talk about my first husband, my inestimable son, and the life I lived prior to our matrimony!

DONALD: [*Glances at wristwatch.*] Talk, talk if you must! But talk fast. Our guests are practically knocking on the door. [*He sits on sofa; picks up a handful of nuts.*]

PATRICIA: [*Sits on chair; pours mineral water.*] Must we go on with this charade? Why can't we just have a nice little celebration, an intimate *petit dejeuner deux*? We can dance, we can drink champagne, we can enjoy the fruits . . .

DONALD: Patty m'girl, you have given me your word, your solemn, sworn word that you'd go along with what I deem to be the most momentous anniversaries of our mortal existence. Are you, and I ask you this calmly and unperturbably, are you reneging on your solemnly sworn word?

PATRICIA: [*Thinks; magnanimously.*] No. I am not. I thought I might convince you of an alternative means of celebration. But since I cannot, I will greet our ... guests and I will act in an appropriate manner. I do, however, continue to reserve unto myself the inalienable right to talk to our guests as an unfettered, individual entity who also served her country in a time of national crisis. And for the record, let me add, I volunteered of my own free will and volition. I was not drafted as some others I can mention.

DONALD: [*Grievously offended.*] I knew I should never have told you everything about my private life before we were married. I knew it in the deepest recesses of my being. But I said to myself, I'm in love with this woman, there should be no secrets between us; besides, she would never be soooo insensitive, soooo vindictive as to throw it all back in my face in a fit of postmenopausal distemper!

PATRICIA: Be that as it is, may I continue to tell you what I was going to tell you about my first husband?

DONALD: Legally, I do not have the power to stop you.

PATRICIA: Then as I was saying, you, you are one of the most perceptive and brilliant men I know. My first husband, Herman ...

[DONALD *cringes at the mention of his name.*]

... being by profession an actuarial statistician was also a perceptive and brilliant man ... And I am compelled by maternal instinct to add another name to that honor roll: my son, Jonathan.

DONALD: [*Dubiously.*] Your son, Jonathan, a perceptive and brilliant man.

PATRICIA: Yes.

DONALD: The same Jonathan who has not been employed for the last five years.

PATRICIA: Yes.

DONALD: The same Jonathan who is still without wife at the age of forty-six.

PATRICIA: He's a genius.

DONALD: Jonathan.

PATRICIA: Yes. He's writing an encyclopedia.

DONALD: For whom? For baboons? For... [*Anguished.*] Ohhh, what am I saying. What's wrong with me? [*In a panic; on his knee beside her.*] Patricia, my precious, my sweetheart, my darling, my wife, my reason to get up in the morning, my reason for going to bed at night. I love you, I love you, I do love you!

PATRICIA: And I, you! you! you! Oh, dear, dear Donny-o, where would I be without you! What life would I have? What day or week or month would I have if not for the warmth of you next to me?

DONALD: Let's not ever, ever, ever quarrel again!

PATRICIA: Why do we? What is this insanity? I... like your three daughters.

DONALD: Do you?

PATRICIA: They're... lovely girls.

DONALD: Say their names, sweetheart.

PATRICIA: Maria, Pinta and Nina.

DONALD: Thank you. Thank you. Did you say they were lovely?

PATRICIA: Yes, I did. Lovely and so polite and prolific.

DONALD: They gave me six grandchildren.

PATRICIA: [*Peeved.*] I know full well how many grandchildren they gave you! You don't have to remind me because I don't give a horse's ass how many grandchildren they gave you!

DONALD: [*Rises; warningly.*] Patricia, we can't...

PATRICIA: Sorry, sorry. Sorry, sorry, sorry, sorry. It's not easy for a

PATRICIA: [*Cont'd.*] woman of my age to recognize she'll never be a ... biological grandmother ... with her own little grandchildren to put talcum on their tushies, to slip them into their little doggy pajamies, and to watch telly with them on Saturday night while eating french fries with ketchup! [*And she starts bawling.*]

DONALD: [*Embraces her.*] There, there, don't, honey. You'll be a grandmother one day. Jonathan ...

PATRICIA: Jonathan is a bimbo! He still wears buttons on his fly!

DONALD: [*Laughing.*] That's what I've been trying to tell you. He ...

PATRICIA: [*Suddenly flares.*] Are you laughing at my son? Is that what you're doing?

DONALD: Sorry, sorry. Sorry, sorry, sorry, sorry.

PATRICIA: And I'm sorry, sweetheart. Lately, I have great difficulty restraining myself. It seems the older I get the more I have to give vent to my emotions.

DONALD: I understand. I have the same problem.
      [*They sit down again.*]

PATRICIA: In an odd way, I feel so much less inhibited, less fearful of what other people will think since I'm a senior citizen.

DONALD: Amazing. It's the same for me. I'm not afraid of any human being living on this planet anymore!

PATRICIA: You're not. I know you're not. You're incredible.

DONALD: I used to be such a fraidy-cat, all through elementary school, high school, college, my twenties, my thirties, all those years. But now? Did you see how I walked up to those four hoodlums who were sitting on our stoop last Sunday?

PATRICIA: Fearless. You were positively fearless.

DONALD: "Hey! Hey! You! Yeah, it's you I'm talking to. The four of you! Get off that stoop this minute or face the consequences! [*A beat.*] Yeah, yeah, I'm the consequences!"

PATRICIA: My heart stopped beating. I couldn't believe what I was hearing.

DONALD: Did they get off the stoop as I ordered?

PATRICIA: Each and every one of them. I can't imagine what you were thinking.

DONALD: I'll tell you what. I was thinking the worst thing that could happen is that they kill me. [*A beat.*] And then I was thinking, if they killed me, the worst thing that could happen is that I'd be laying in my coffin a few months earlier than I expected.

PATRICIA: Thank God they didn't hurt you.

DONALD: [*With insouciance.*] Who cares? Who cares? We have to go sometime. That's the deal we made when we started collecting our social security checks. We have to go so there'll be checks for the people who don't have to go until after we go!

PATRICIA: I am the luckiest woman in the world to be married to you.

DONALD: I know. [*A beat.*] Now I have to say, in all honesty, I do like Jonathan. He has a wonderful sense of humor.

PATRICIA: Doesn't he? Isn't he amusing?

DONALD: I can't find the words to describe how amusing he is.

PATRICIA: Now it's my turn to be honest with you. Your first wife...

DONALD: Bertha.

PATRICIA: Yes. Bertha. You lived with her for over forty years and yet, after her demise, you were able to remarry another woman.

DONALD: You.

PATRICIA: Yes. Me. That you didn't loathe women after living with Bertha for over forty years... It's extraordinary.

DONALD: And a tribute to my first marriage to Bertha.

PATRICIA: Yes, that's what I wanted to say. But couldn't.

DONALD: I'm glad that you at last acknowledge... [*Turns.*] Did I hear the doorbell ring?

PATRICIA: I didn't...

DONALD: [*On his feet.*] I heard it. They're here! They're coming. Answer it, Pat. I'll open up a couple of bottles of mineral water. Who do you think it is? Who do you think is the first one?

PATRICIA: [*This is silly; not at all easy for her.*] I have no idea. Donald, do we have to go through with this? It's ...

DONALD: You promised! You gave me your solemn word: I don't want to hear anymore of that! Now will you or won't you answer the door? Our guests are arriving!

PATRICIA: [*Resolved to do her best; moves to door, taking off cap.*] Yes, yes, I'm going, I am. I'll see who it is. [*At door.*] Are you ready?

DONALD: [*Removes cap; brushes off uniform.*] Ready.

PATRICIA: The party begins. [*She throws open door.*]

DONALD: [*Hushed voice.*] Who? Who is it?

PATRICIA: [*Hasn't the faintest.*] It's ... It's ... It's ...

DONALD: Who! Who!

PATRICIA: [*Desperately.*] Harry James!

[DONALD *gasps loudly; beyond his wildest dreams.* PATRICIA *beams. Thank God she came up with a winner.*]

PATRICIA: [*Cont'd.*] Come in, come in, Mr. James. We are so, so happy you were able to come to our party this afternoon.

[*Her eyes follow an imaginary* HARRY JAMES *as he enters; she closes the door.*]

May I introduce you to my husband, Mr. James? [*A beat.*] Harry? You prefer I call you Harry? [*A beat.*] Yes, of course. We are like old friends. My husband has been a fan of yours for... eons. He loves your music. [*Clears throat; formally.*] Harry, I have the distinct pleasure of introducing you to my husband, Mr. Donald Lumley, an amply decorated veteran of the 1941–1945 conflagration.

DONALD: Mr. James... Harry. [*Swallows.*] Harry, this is an event,

DONALD: [*cont'd.*] the likes of which I have not experienced since I saw Frank Sinatra at the Paramount Theater on October 12th, 1944. [*Hand on heart.*] I'm choked. I'm literally choked up and can't stop my voice from trembling.

PATRICIA: Donald probably has the largest collection of your records in the Tri-state area.

DONALD: [*Emotionally.*] My favorites are "You Made Me Love You," "I Cried for You," "I Don't Want to Walk Without You," "I Had the Craziest Dream," "I've Heard That Song Before," and so many, many more, including your trumpet virtuosity with Benny Goodman in "Sing, Sing, Sing," and... I could go on and on... but it hurts too much, Harry, for me to remember those days of yesteryore.

PATRICIA: [*At record collection.*] These are all your recordings, Harry. They're on 78s and V discs that Donald collected in the service and here are tapes and CDs... [*She plays a record or CD. We hear James's "I Walk Alone," or another of his tunes.*]

[*Holding out hand.*] Donald.

[DONALD *puffs out his chest and takes her extended hand. They dance, lovers on a cloud. After a moment or two,* DONALD *stops the dance.*]

DONALD: We should return to our guest, sweetheart. Thank you for the dance. [*He kisses her on cheek; moves to* HARRY.] We dance to your music all the time, Harry. There's nothing around like it. Do sit down. Make yourself comfortable. My home is yours.

[DONALD *sits on last folding chair, right;* HARRY *on the next;* PATRICIA *on the third.*]

PATRICIA: May I get you a drink, Harry? A bourbon? A scotch? A banana daiquiri?

DONALD: I didn't know you could make a banana daiquiri, dear.

PATRICIA: Oh, yes, I learned years ago. From a native of Patagonia.

DONALD: [*A thoughtful beat; whispers to* HARRY.] Don't take everything my wife says literally. She tends to exaggerate a bit. [*Then.*] Honey, why don't we wait until the others arrive before

DONALD: [*Cont'd.*] we serve drinks? I would like to start with champagne, to toast the occasion.

PATRICIA: Shall we wait for the others, Harry?

DONALD: [*Leans towards him.*] I'm sorry. I didn't hear you. What did you say? [*Bursts out in laughter; to* PATRICIA.] He said he already drank half a bottle of bourbon this morning. He prefers to wait.

PATRICIA: As you like, Harry. I don't know if you're aware of it, but besides celebrating VJ Day we're also celebrating our first anniversary.

DONALD: Does that surprise you, Harry?

PATRICIA: It surprised everyone. Our children were vehemently against our getting married.

DONALD: They thought we were too old to go a second time around.

PATRICIA: They were embarrassingly wrong. We've never been as happy as we've been this past year.

DONALD: You know the expression "made for each other?"

PATRICIA: We were unequivocally made for each other. And, mind you, we both had excellent first marriages.

DONALD: No doubt about it. Excellent first marriages.

PATRICIA: I was sincerely in love with my first husband.

DONALD: And I my first wife. She was a sweetheart, an absolute sweetheart.

PATRICIA: And yet...

DONALD: Patty and I...

PATRICIA: We were made for each other.

DONALD: Unequivocally.

PATRICIA: The fact is we do everything together.

DONALD: Everything. Golf, stretching exercises, a two mile walk in the park every morning...

PATRICIA: Trips to the museum, Atlantic City, an East Side restaurant at least once a week, the cinema... We love the cinema.

DONALD: And I'll tell you a secret, Harry, we have an incredibly active sex life.

[PATRICIA *grins widely, rolls her eyes upwards in gratitude.*]

PATRICIA: My husband is a regular hound dog. It's exhausting.

DONALD: Fortunately, we exercise and eat a lot of fish!

PATRICIA: What you don't know, Harry, is that we met on VJ Day, fifty years ago.

DONALD: In Manila. We were on active duty.

[*They nibble on finger foods, offering the same to* HARRY.]

PATRICIA: I was stationed aboard a hospital ship while Donald was temporarily stationed at Subic Bay, waiting reassignment.

DONALD: By pure happenstance, we were both on leave in Manila.

PATRICIA: I remember I was having drinks with some friends in an unspeakably dark and dirty bar called The Piggly Wiggly.

DONALD: I just walked into The Piggly Wiggly when someone ran in and shouted the war was over! The Japanese had surrendered!

PATRICIA: And everyone was shouting in the street, "The war is over! The war is over!"

DONALD: For a minute or two minutes or three minutes there was total silence, not a peep out of anybody.

PATRICIA: But then... [*Jumps to her feet.*] ... everybody in the bar started screaming and yelling...

DONALD: [*Jumps to his feet.*] It was absolute pandemonium!

PATRICIA: Chaos! It was sheer chaos!

DONALD: I don't know how it happened...

PATRICIA: But the next thing I know...

DONALD: We were holding hands!

PATRICIA: Jumping up and down!

DONALD: Yelling to beat the band!

PATRICIA: Singing, too!

PATRICIA/DONALD: [*Singing.*] "Happy days are here, are here again [*Or some such tune.*]

DONALD: We hit it off!

PATRICIA: Right from the start! From the very beginning!

DONALD: It was like we were drunk, drunk on the exhiliration of being together!

PATRICIA: We couldn't stop ... touching one another.

DONALD: And we danced. For hours and hours. To the jukebox.

[*They dance, barely moving.*]

"I'll Be With You In Apple Blossom Time."

PATRICIA: "Be Careful It's My Heart."

DONALD: "There Will Never Be Another You."

PATRICIA: "People Will Say We're In Love."

[*Eyes only for each other; stop dancing; whisper.*]

DONALD: We hit it off.

PATRICIA: Unequivocally.

DONALD: What did we do? What did we talk about? How did the day go so fast?

PATRICIA: And the night. Where did it go?

DONALD: I remember I got back to the base late and the C.O. bawled me out, but I didn't hear anything or see anything. My head was filled with you.

PATRICIA: And mine with you, only you. [*Breaks out of it; moves to sit beside* HARRY.] You see, Harry, so much was going on during those weeks, there was such an incredible fever, excitement ...

DONALD: [*Sits on his chair.*] Before we knew it, we were being shipped back to the States.

PATRICIA: We were going home, to live with our parents, to be with our friends.

DONALD: There were major decisions to be made.

PATRICIA: I didn't want to pursue a nursing career I couldn't, not after . . .

DONALD: She had nightmares. She still has them. Of the soldiers brought on the hospital ship . . . to die there.

PATRICIA: I often wonder, do they know the direction the world has taken since . . . then? Are they grieved by the turn of events? Do they think now that they died in vain, for no earthly purpose . . . or reason? Do they know that we've forgotten all about them?

DONALD: That's not true, Patricia. Not everyone! Not some of us! [*Softer tone.*] Besides, this is not the time to go into it. We're here to memorialize the very men you're speaking of. [*To* HARRY.] I was always interested in the law so . . .

PATRICIA: Donald went to law school. I went to City College to become a guidance counselor at a junior high school in the Bronx.

DONALD: I eventually specialized in real estate law and did quite well for myself.

PATRICIA: As for Donald and me . . .

DONALD: We wrote to one another, regularly . . .

PATRICIA: We spoke on the phone, frequently . . .

DONALD: And we dated . . . at the beginning . . .

PATRICIA: You see, Harry, the Bronx and Brooklyn are at opposite ends of the world.

DONALD: It took me over an hour, by subway, to get to her place from mine. And that's not counting the long walk to and from the subways.

PATRICIA: Even when we were going to school we had part-time jobs.

DONALD: I used to work six days and Sunday mornings, too. It wasn't that easy getting together. [*A beat.*] She started going out with other men.

PATRICIA: And?

DONALD: I started going out with other women. I was very sought-after as a young man.

PATRICIA: I didn't go out with other men. I went out with Herman, my first husband.

DONALD: The next thing I know she calls me and tells me she's getting married and moving to Chicago.

PATRICIA: Herman worked for Metropolitan Life. They offered him a substantial raise and promotion.

DONALD: I didn't waste any time. Within three months I was married myself, to Bertha Hoffmueller, a wonderful gregarious and attractive woman who worked as a buyer for S. Klein's on Union Square.

PATRICIA: Herman was six feet two inches tall, a very handsome and dynamic man. He loved to travel and we visited, during the course of our marriage, London, Paris, Rome, Budapest, Casablanca...

DONALD: [*Interrupts.*] Harry may I speak to you a moment, privately? [*To* PATRICIA.] Excuse us. [*He leads* HARRY *to the side, right, looks back to* PATRICIA, *thinks she might be able to overhear him, leads* HARRY *further downstage; whispers.*]

You won't get the truth out of her when it comes to her late husband. Take my word for it, he was not a nice man. And he was taller than six foot two. Whenever he was in a room his head would be up there in the chandelier. He'd be talking to the lightbulbs. A very unsociable man. They used to come to New York from Chicago a couple of times a year, to go to the theater, restaurants... Pat would phone and our families would get together for a few hours. It was painful. Bertha and Pat didn't get along, Herman and I had nothing in common, the kids didn't hit it off, and every time I saw Pat it'd break my heart. I ...I still had very strong feelings about her and...We stopped seeing one another. That was the end of it until...Bertha passed away several years ago and I phoned Pat, out of the blue, out of loneliness, out of despair, without knowing that Herman had passed away ten years before Bertha did.

PATRICIA: Donald?

DONALD: Yes, dear?

PATRICIA: I feel abandoned.

DONALD: I'm sorry, sweetheart. Forgive me.
[*Moving to her,* HARRY *in tow.*] I was just telling Harry how we finally got back together again.

PATRICIA: You may think it's silly of me, Harry, but, in my opinion, what happened between Donald and me qualifies as divine intervention.

DONALD: [*Listening a beat.*] What was that?

PATRICIA: What was what?

DONALD: Didn't you hear the doorbell ring?

PATRICIA: I didn't hear anything.

DONALD: Did you hear it, Harry? [*Tilts head towards him.*] Harry heard it, too. You should see a doctor about your hearing, dear.

PATRICIA: Do you want me to ... ?

DONALD: [*Moving to door.*] No, I'll get it. You entertain Harry. [*Throws open door; gasps.*]

PATRICIA: Who? Who is it?

DONALD: [*Turns to her in awe.*] What does the name Betty Grable mean to you?

PATRICIA: Noooo.

DONALD: [*Nodding fervently.*] Yes! Yes! [*Turns to door.*] Miss Grable, won't you ... ?

PATRICIA: Wait! Wait! [*Waves for him to join her.*]

DONALD: [*To imaginary* BETTY.] Excuse me, Miss Grable. A moment. I'll be right back. [*Rushes to* PATRICIA; *whispers impatiently.*] What? What is it?

PATRICIA: [*Whispers.*] They're divorced!

DONALD: Who's divorced?

PATRICIA: Harry James and Betty Grable.

DONALD: [*Horrified.*] What a *faux pas* we made inviting her!

PATRICIA: We didn't invite her! You invited her!

DONALD: She was at the door! I didn't... What should we do?

PATRICIA: Put her in the ping-pong room!

DONALD: The ping-pong room?

PATRICIA: We'll keep them apart. They'll never meet. We'll avoid a major social embarrassment!

DONALD: Good idea. Excellent idea. Leave it to me. [*He rushes back to door; expansively.*] Come in, Miss Grable. Do come in. Let me introduce you to my lovely wife, Patricia.

PATRICIA: I am delighted, overwhelmingly delighted to meet you, Miss Grable—I loved your acting in "Down Argentine Way" and "I Wake Up Screaming." You were superb. Now if you'll follow me... [*Leads* BETTY *to the ping-pong room.*] You'll have privacy in here and you won't be annoyed by any of the other guests. We'll drop in now and then to converse with you. Help yourself to anything in the refrigerator. [*She closes door.*] She'll be happy. It must be so annoying for a star to... [*Listening a beat.*] Ah, the doorbell! I'll get it, dear. [*She moves to door which has remained open; sees guests; turns to* DONALD; *glowing.*] You are going to be very pleased with those who have taken the time off from their pressing duties to be with us here today. [*Turns to door; announces.*]

   General Douglas MacArthur!

   [*She salutes.* DONALD *snaps stiffly to attention, clicks his heels and salutes smartly.*]

PATRICIA: [*Cont'd.*] General Dwight D. Eisenhower! Admiral Chester Nimitz! [*She salutes, twice.* DONALD *salutes and clicks his heels together, twice.*]

DONALD: Sirs, this is indeed a great, great honor, one that I thought would never occur during my lifetime. [*Gestures.*] Please, take a seat next to Harry James, the world-renowned trumpet player. If any of you would like to converse with Betty Grable, the pin-up girl to millions of servicemen, she's in the ping-pong room. [*Turns.*] Patty...

PATRICIA: [*Now enjoying it all.*] One second, dear. There are more guests coming. I see... [*Hand to heart.*] I don't believe it!

DONALD: Who? Who's coming?

PATRICIA: [*To entering guest.*] I am so thrilled by your presence at our party, Mrs. Roosevelt. I can't describe . . . [*Listening a beat.*] Of course. Eleanor. [*A proud look to* DONALD.] Eleanor, I must tell you, both my husband and I worshipped your late husband. It was a terrible shock to us when we learned the reason why we never saw him standing up. But do come in and make yourself comfortable.

DONALD: Having you in my home is beyond my wildest dreams . . . Eleanor. [*Listening a beat.*] Donald. Radioman 3rd Class Donald Lumley. Incidentally, I visited your home in Hyde Park last summer. Lovely place. Excellent landscaping. And the antique oriental rug in your living-room . . . It must have cost you a bloody fortune! [*Moving towards the empty chairs with her.*]

We have some guests here I'm sure you know. Some military men who served under your husband. [*He improvises introductions, sotto voce; chats, laughs, offers food, etc.*]

PATRICIA: [*To entering guests.*] I'm speechless! I don't know what to say to you, Mr. Einstein. Thank you. Thank you so very much for taking the time from your scientific work to be with us today. [*Gestures.*] My husband, who is chatting over there with Mrs. Roosevelt and Admiral Nimitz will introduce you to our guests. [*Turns back to doorway.*]

Is that . . . Is that really you, Joe Louis? Ahh, how kind . . . But who's that with you? Lou Gehrig, the Yankee slugger? Come in, come in, gentlemen, please. My first husband talked about you two incessantly. [*Gestures.*] Do introduce yourselves to my second husband, Donald. Oh, yes, I was married twice. It does have its advantages.

[*Laughs frivolously; turns to doorway; in amazement.*] Noooo . . . It's not true. You came . . . You . . . You travelled three thousand miles to be here with me on this . . . on this the most important day of my life.

DONALD: [*Moving to her.*] Patricia . . .

PATRICIA: [*Ignores him.*] How can I ever repay you, Mr. Gable, except . . .

DONALD: Patricia...

PATRICIA: [*Parodies Judy Garland.*]...to let you know...that my heart is beating like a hammer...whenever I see you in a picture show...

DONALD: Patricia, I'm talking to you!

PATRICIA: Excuse me, Mr. Gable.
    [*Shouts at* DONALD.] What is it? I am talking to Clark Gable!

DONALD: [*Through clenched teeth.*] We have other guests, Patricia! They are hungry. They are thirsty. I cannot do everything myself. I am, whether you and Clark Gable want to recognize it or not...[*Shouts.*]...a senior citizen!

PATRICIA: [*Heartfelt.*] And I am such a fool!

DONALD: No, no, you're not! I am! I am!

PATRICIA: You're everything to me.

DONALD: I would long ago have been a bag of bones if not for you.

PATRICIA: I love you, Donny-o.

DONALD: And I, you, Patty m'girl.

PATRICIA: [*Brightly.*] I'll introduce Mr. Gable to our guests and pass the canapés and hors d'oeuvres. Mr. Gable...if you'll follow me...[*She moves towards empty chairs; improvises introductions, sotto voce; chats, laughs, offers food, etc.*]

DONALD: Ah, the doorbell! I have it, sweetheart! [*Moves to doorway; looks out.*] Why, it's...Rita Hayworth! [*Turns.*] Rita Hayworth is here, Pat! She looks absolutely stunning.

PATRICIA: What is she wearing?

DONALD: A white, satin nightgown and a black, lacy brassiere! [*Turns to* RITA.] Come in, come in, Rita. No, no, you're not late. Who's that with you? Ava Gardner? Come in, yes, you, don't be shy. You brought...Lana Turner? Wonderful! And do I see Eva Marie Saint and Rhonda Fleming out there? Who else? Dinah Shore and Dina Merrill? With Dana Andrews? Wonderful! Wonderful! Do come in, all of you! [*Laughing.*]

DONALD: [*Cont'd.*] Oh, this is wonderful, terrific, the cream on the cake! [*He closes door; crosses with his guests.*] Pat, I want to introduce you to Rita, Ava, Lana, Eva, Rhonda, Dinah, Dina and Dana.

PATRICIA: I'm delighted to meet each and every one of you. And may I introduce you to Harry, Douglas, Dwight, Chester, Eleanor, Albert, Joe, Lou and Clark.

DONALD: [*Opens bottle of champagne.*] And if any of you would like to speak to Betty Grable, she's in the ping-pong room. [*The cork pops out of the bottle.*]

PATRICIA: [*Applauding.*] Bravo! Bravo! Don't spill any, dear.
      [DONALD *pours only a drop in several glasses on table—for the guests; he fills two glasses for* PATRICIA *and himself.*]

PATRICIA: [*Cont'd.*] Everyone, everyone, may I have your attention, please? [*A beat.*] First of all, let me say, my husband and I can't thank you enough for coming today.

DONALD: Speaking for myself, I am genuinely appreciative of your taking the time off from your incredibly busy schedules to be at our party.

PATRICIA: [*Taking champagne from* DONALD.] Please, help yourselves to the champagne. I'd like to make a toast.

DONALD: [*Applauding.*] Speech! Speech!

PATRICIA: [*To guests.*] My dear ... heroes, for that is what you are to me ... my heroes. Many of you sacrificed yourselves, unequivocally, to help bring about peace in the world ... whatever peace we have in the world. Like the peace we had in Korea, and the peace we had in Vietnam, and the peace we had in Belfast and in Jerusalem and in Afghanistan and in Bosnia and so on and so forth ... as we listened over the years to the well-tailored politicians intoning "this is the war to end all wars, for a better world of love and brotherhood, never again will we slaughter the innocent children for the sake of flag or boundary, for the sake of religious, ethnic, cultural differences, or for this, that and the other thing, never again until we go to war ... the next time."

DONALD: [*Peeved.*] Patricia, you are being rude to our guests! They came here to join us in a celebration of victory, not to listen to a diatribe of your dissatisfaction with politicians!

PATRICIA: [*Firmly.*] I'll be done in a minute. Please, be patient.

[*To guests.*] I often wonder, do they, those who died fifty years ago, do they know the direction the world has taken since then? Are they grieved by the turn of events? Do they think now that they died in vain, for no earthly purpose or reason? Do they know that we've forgotten all about them?

DONALD: [*Almost a whisper.*] Patricia, I asked you . . .

PATRICIA: [*Won't be silent.*] I often wonder, if they came to my bedside in the middle of the night, and they stood around me with their white, bloodless faces staring down at me, and one of them said, "What should we have done, Patty? Did we do wrong? Did we act stupidly, precipitously? Should we have taken another direction with our lives?" [*Turns from one imaginary guest to another.*] I know what I would say to him. I would say . . . [*Finger to lips.*] "Shhh. It's over. It doesn't matter anymore. But for the sake of conversation . . . You should have done as the others did. As we did. Those of us who survived. Hang back. Drag your feet. Don't look directly at them. Look behind you. Look to the side of you. Look down at your shoes. But not at them, in their uniforms and ribbons, in their well-tailored clothes. Fight them. Fight them so as not to fight. Complain of illness, backache, flatfoot, perversity, maladjustment, dependency, principle, whatever comes to mind, whatever the cost in face or status. Do not go. Wave a flag. Cry Jesus, Hare Krishna, Holy Moses. Cross the border. Fly to Patagonia. Do not go. It will all be forgotten. Amends will be made. Brotherhood affirmed. Economic benefits derived. Do not go. It will all be forgotten. As you have been forgotten." [*Turns to stare at* DONALD.]

DONALD: This is not what we planned. This is not what we said we'd do. I demand, as a matter of courtesy, equal time! [*He turns at once to guests.*] My esteemed and honored guests. Permit me to go on record as saying that I am categorically in disagreement with Patricia. [*Turns to her.*] My second wife. [*Back to guests.*] The indisputable truth is that we won the war. We were

DONALD: [*Cont'd.*] victorious. We triumphed over the forces of despotism and tyranny. Patricia dismisses or chooses to ignore what was at stake when we went to war. If we as a nation had not responded with military might, if we as Americans had not put our lives on the line, everything we valued would have been taken away from us. Everything! We fought so that we could live as a free people. Imagine what it would have been like if we lost the war! If this country of ours was occupied by the forces of despotism and tyranny! Is there any doubt in anyone's mind that we would have been totally dominated and enslaved by a foreign government? We had no choice but to do what we did. Fight. Defend ourselves. Participate in a world struggle for decency and dignity! Who died and who lived was in the hands of the Almighty. It is... the essence of humankind to protect the young, the infirm, the helpless, to sacrifice life if need be for an ideal that goes beyond survival. Therein lies our glory and our redemption. Without it we are nothing. We are less than nothing. We are shadows on the wall of a cave. [*A beat.*] My esteemed and honored guests, we won the war. We were victorious. That unparalleled achievement is ingrained in our national consciousness and will never be forgotten, but it will always be a source to us for strength, for pride, and for eternal gratitude to those who made the ultimate sacrifice.

PATRICIA: Donald? [*He turns to her.*] What does that mean, we won the war?

DONALD: [*More in desperation than conviction.*] We won: We were victorious! We triumphed: We raised the flag on Iwo Jima! We bombed the oppressors to smithereens! We brought the fascists and the imperialists down to their knees and stuck their snouts into the muck of their own rotting corpses! No small achievement, my dear! Nothing to be maligned or demeaned or casually dismissed!

PATRICIA: But what does it add up to? What have we won? What has changed? Where are we today, fifty years later? Are we really victorious?

DONALD: [*Losing it.*] I'm not going to quarrel with you, Patricia! That's enough! It's enough! I don't want to hear another

DONALD: [*Cont'd.*] word...! [*He breathes heavily, staring at her, an anguished expression.*] I am sorry. I am so sorry.

PATRICIA: [*Anguished as well.*] Oh, why? why? why?

DONALD: I love you.

PATRICIA: I love you.

DONALD: My biggest fear is to lose you.

PATRICIA: I won't let it happen. I swear. I promise.
[*They are a distance apart; they do not move towards each other.*]

DONALD: Happy anniversary, my dear, sweet, lovely wife.

PATRICIA: I bless the day I met you.

DONALD: Do we begin our party now?

PATRICIA: Yes, yes, we mustn't be rude to our guests! [*Turns.*] Happy, happy anniversary, everyone! Please, eat, drink, ask if you want anything, need anything... [*Fills two glasses with champagne.*] This is a day of celebration! [*Looks about.*] Where's Harry? Did Harry leave? [*Listens a beat.*] He's in the ping-pong room? With Betty Grable? Ahh, that is wonderful. I knew there'd be a reconciliation. I knew it all along.
[DONALD *has put on the cassette player. We now hear Benny Goodman's "Sing, Sing, Sing," or some similar tune.*]

DONALD: [*Approaching* PATRICIA.] Mrs. Lumley?

PATRICIA: Yes, Mr. Lumley?

DONALD: May I have this dance?

PATRICIA: This one and the next one and the one after that, too.
[*And they start dancing the Lindy, as it was done at the Palladium fifty years ago.*
Lights congeal on them dancing in the empty room.
A shaft of light isolates them in a sea of darkness.
Lights and music fade out.]

Lanford Wilson

YOUR EVERYDAY GHOST STORY

Lanford Wilson

Lanford Wilson received the 1980 Pulitzer Prize for Drama and the New York Drama Critics Circle Award for *Talley's Folly*. He is a founding member of the Circle Repertory Company in New York and was a resident playwright for the company from 1969 to 1995.

His work at Circle Rep includes: *The Family Continues* (1972), *The HOT L Baltimore* (1973), *The Mound Builders* (1975), *Serenading Louie* (1976), *5th of July* (1978), *Talley's Folly* (1980), *A Tale Told* (1981), *Angels Fall* (1982), *Burn This* (1987), and *Redwood Curtain* (1992), all directed by Marshall Mason.

His other plays include *The Gingham Dog* (1966), *The Rimers of Eldritch* (1967), *Lemon Sky* (1969), and some twenty produced one-acts, such as *Brontosaurus* (1977) and *Thymus Vulgaris* (1982). He has also written the libretto for Lee Hoiby's opera of Tennessee Williams' *Summer and Smoke*, and two television plays, *Taxi!* and *The Migrants* (based on a short story by Tennessee Williams).

Other awards include the New York Critics' Award, the Outer Critics Circle Award and an Obie for *The HOT L Baltimore*, an Obie for *The Mound Builders*, a Drama-Logue Award for *5th of July* and *Talley's Folly*, the Vernon Rice award for *The Rimers of Eldritch*, and Tony Award nominations for *Talley's Folly*, *5th of July*, and *Angels Fall*. He is the recipient of the Brandeis University Creative Arts Award in Theatre Arts and the Institute of Arts and Letters Award.

He makes his home in Sag Harbor, New York.

CHARACTERS

KEVIN

LANCE

Just a bench, wrought iron and wood, but I don't see this as a bench play. I think they stand or lean and walk around most of the time, except at the beginning and end.

KEVIN *and* LANCE *are reasonably attractive young men in their early 30s.* KEVIN *talks a lot; that's partly just him and partly anxiety.* LANCE *is uneasy at times but not unsympathetic.*

The scene is bathed in an exaggerated golden sunset of a late autumn afternoon. Dark shadows upstage.

LANCE *is sitting on the bench, looking out. He is either unconcerned about his dress or thinks a writer should dress shabbily.*

KEVIN (**Offstage.**): [*Calling.*] Lance!

[LANCE *didn't want to see this guy but he covers it well. He stands as* KEVIN *enters. Kevin dresses smartly.*]

LANCE: Oh. Hi, Kevin — God, you look great!

KEVIN: Are you kidding, I've got cancer!

LANCE: [*Taken aback, recovering.*] No! Kevin! [*Very awkward.*] That's terrible. Are you sure?

KEVIN: You knew or you wouldn't have said I looked great.

LANCE: No, you do look great. You look great.

KEVIN: Yeah, but you expected me to look like shit.

LANCE: Somebody told me.

KEVIN: So I suppose they also told you I have AIDS.

LANCE: [*Fakes surprise.*] Oh, no. That's — [*Gives up.*] No, yeah, I heard. I think it sucks. They said you were in the hospital, I'm glad you're out.

KEVIN: [*Ironically.*] And you were only pretending you didn't know so you wouldn't embarrass me, or remind me. That's kind.

LANCE: I thought maybe you didn't want people to know.

KEVIN: Everybody and his fucking cat knows. It makes it real interesting walking down the street.

LANCE: What are they doing for you?

KEVIN: They're fucking killing me. I've got chemo and radiation four times a week. They're taking things out of my lungs and my ass, my liver. I've had biopsies on glands I haven't used in years.

LANCE: Oh, God.

KEVIN: They've got radiation machines big as a house, well, I don't know, I close my eyes. They can't *find* any more veins, I don't *have* any more veins. My legs, my arms, are black and blue all over, I'm doing a reverse Michael Jackson, it's horrifying.

LANCE: What's making your arms black and — ?

[KEVIN *makes a shoving motion into the veins of his arm.*]

KEVIN: Bruises. From the chemo.

LANCE: Oh, Christ, it's intravenous?

KEVIN: You didn't know that? And you call yourself a writer. You're getting very pale, you aren't going to faint, are you?

LANCE: No, I'm fine, but —

KEVIN: [*He can be a little malicious.*] Yeah, I'm learning a lot of shit no one should have to know. On top of everything else they made me stop smoking. Well, I was coughing up my guts. Which I used to think was only an expression. I'm sorry, I hope you haven't just eaten or anything.

LANCE: No, I —

KEVIN: Also it makes you stink.

LANCE: What does?

KEVIN: The chemo. Nobody tells you that part. It makes you smell like... Death.

LANCE: Oh.

KEVIN: Well, I'm sorry, but that's what it smells like. [*Beat.*] They fired me. From that fucking display studio. They said I was

KEVIN: [*Cont'd.*] becoming irrational. Who would be rational. Of course I'm becoming irrational! Assholes!

LANCE: They can't fire you, it's illegal.

KEVIN: It's *Philadelphia* all over again. Write a movie. Make a fortune. Call it Patchogue, New York. [*Note: pronounced PATCH-hog.*]

LANCE: It doesn't scan.

KEVIN: I know, but that's where the bastards' studio is.

LANCE: I can't write movies, the proper misogynistic tone keeps eluding me.

KEVIN: And you don't write unfunny gay characters.

LANCE: That was *Philadelphia*, it's been done.

[LANCE *is trying to wind up the conversation.*]

KEVIN: I know, you've got to go finish the last chapter of the Great American Novel. Look at you. Trying to make your escape. You always do that. You did it to me.

LANCE: No, really. I'll call you —

KEVIN: You will not. Everyone knows you run from hospitals and sick people like the plague. Well, in this case it is the plague so you have every right.

LANCE: I'm sorry, I just —

KEVIN: "Sorry" doesn't cut it. God save us from your fucking artistic temperament. All the novels and stories and TV shit, none of your gay characters have a care in the world.

LANCE: They have cares, Kevin. Only I do write people who are toilet trained. They're not pawing around in their own feces.

KEVIN: Oh, that's attractive. I happen to think pawing around in feces is where good writing comes from. That's just a lay opinion, you understand.

LANCE: If you want stories about how mom and pop and the boy next door hated us, read someone else.

KEVIN: The boy next door did not hate me. [*Beat.*] Do you avoid

KEVIN: [*Cont'd.*] just *everything* that's a little messy? Messy is what life is largely about. There are enough writers avoiding messy, we don't need you doing it.

LANCE: What is this? Nobody needs another one of your every-damn-day ghost stories either.

KEVIN: You are the weirdest combination of self-destruction and denial. You just don't want to go there, do you? Is it the monstrosity, the face-to-face with it, the loss? —

LANCE: — I have a very tenuous grip on reality, here, Kevin —

KEVIN: —Does all this rotting death just remind you of your own? That's the same for everyone, honey. "It is Margaret you mourn for" and don't forget it.

LANCE: Come on, you look weak but you're very strong. I look strong and everything scares the shit out of me.

KEVIN: Well, it damn well should; with the way you drink it won't be pleasant. I mean you're healthy now, but: liver transplants, kidney failure, bypasses. Isn't there a history of emphysema in your family? Can you smell it? Smell my hands.

LANCE: — Come on. It's the whole fucking set-up —

KEVIN: — Even in your work, you dodge and glance, finesse, waft your point across the night air —

LANCE: — I've been told —

KEVIN: — Feint, parry. What are you afraid of? Going down there and getting lost? Drowning, feeling, losing it?

LANCE: *People should not die!*

KEVIN: Oh. Well. I don't know. *Some* people shouldn't die, other people probably should but they never do. *One* should not die. One's friends shouldn't die. One's assistant shouldn't die. I heard about Fred. I'm sorry.

LANCE: I know. I still can't believe it.

KEVIN: Who's going to edit all your stuff?

LANCE: I don't know. I can't think about it. Someone at the publishing house. I can't think about it.

KEVIN: How was he?

LANCE: I was going to see him, a couple of us called the hospital —

KEVIN: — He worshipped you for Christsake —

LANCE: — We were going to go! They said he was scheduled for another operation —

KEVIN: I don't believe you. Jesus!

LANCE: — so we didn't go that day.

KEVIN: And he died. They do that. Poor you. He'd been in and out of the hospital five months; you had plenty of opportunity.

LANCE: I know. Fuck you. Fred was weird; he never told anyone. You don't know what people want.

KEVIN: Acknowledgment! Friendship! Jesus! What good is all your famous compassion if you deny everyone's pain?

LANCE: I feel bad enough without your —

KEVIN: [*Overlapping completely.*] — Please, please, please, you have to live with it, I don't have to live with it. Can you smell it?

LANCE: Come on. Yes. I don't even know you that well.

KEVIN: Isn't that always the way? And I thought we were close. I always tell people I know you.

LANCE: And it's just as well that they fired you; you didn't belong at that display house anyway.

KEVIN: It's called a *job*, darling.

LANCE: You're an interior designer, not a window display — person.

KEVIN: Sure. Christ, if they don't find a cure for this there won't be a window display left in America.

LANCE: I liked your shop.

KEVIN: Oh please. Never did two faggots crash and burn so spectacularly as Peter and I did with that shop. Forget the shop. The world can turn without another pouffe.

LANCE: I thought it was wonderful. The places you'd seen.

KEVIN: Tell it to the buying public. Nobody was interested in

KEVIN: [*Cont'd.*] "exotic" that year, and you only get one crack; it's like fashion. Ten thousand yards of gorgeous, for want of a better word, "ethnic" fabric, all I got from it was a spectacular Halloween gown.

LANCE: Very spectacular.

KEVIN: What was important was learning so much about the people, the artisans, all over the world; that was important. Finding a really deep artistic integrity and originality in some 90-year-old Chilean woman; their appreciation and pride.

That was rare: Two faggots with a great eye drifting through Malaysia, India, South America, Africa.

[*Not dreamy.*] Poling down mud rivers, passing grass huts, we get to a village of about 200, you've never seen silks like that, the colors alone — fuck it, nobody wanted it. Major miscalculation. Everything went *chintz* that year. Our whole shop looked like a sixties holdover. What a disaster. We sold three pillows and one chair that the bitch wanted re-upholstered. Four years in the planning, almost two years traveling, and the shop was only open two months; we didn't even make it through the summer. Three years later the guy who bought it for *11 cents on the dollar!* made a fucking killing. No lie, over a million and a half. You can't think about it.

LANCE: But the people, that was important.

KEVIN: And the memory of all that will go with us. Poof! It never happened. "Quick, grab the ruby slippers."

LANCE: I think it'd made a terrific movie. The two of you eating with the nomads and villagers, screaming over some puce cotton.

KEVIN: You can't use it unless it comes out funny.

LANCE: Kevin. Think about it. It's funny.

KEVIN: But with great depth and sensitivity.

LANCE: Poignant and funny. That's my trademark. Sort of a gay Around the World. Go everywhere from Mauritania to Timbuktu.

KEVIN: You're sweet and condescending as shit, but you're stupid.

KEVIN: [*Cont'd.*] Why don't Americans know geography? And you call yourself a writer.

LANCE: Not lately. What?

KEVIN: Mauritania and Timbuktu, honey, are about 50 miles apart. Timbuktu is in Mali.

LANCE: Mali is in Africa? I thought it was in Asia.

KEVIN: Northwest Africa. *Way* up the Niger river. And we didn't go there; nobody goes there; there's nothing there. It's only famous because it must have rhymed with something.

LANCE: Call it *Kevin and Peter*.

KEVIN: Hmmm. Peter's been a brick, of course, Peter's been a saint. Peter's been a brick saint. A brick saint barber. "Stylist," he prefers.

LANCE: Peter is a saint.

KEVIN: Try being married to a saint. I've been giving him hell. I'm not being cool with this at all.

LANCE: I could tell. I had a trim yesterday, he must have known I knew; he didn't say a word. Well, neither did I. Peter's always so positive.

KEVIN: Yes, well, darling, now he really is. If you catch my drift.

LANCE: He always has been — Oh, God, no. Not him too.

KEVIN: He has a constitution of iron. I'm hoping he'll hold on till they find that mythological cure. In Valhalla. That great hall where all those who died in battle go. Thank God it turns out he's a fabulous hair-cutter. *Stars*, darling. Movie, TV, rock stars! Flocking to our little garage salon. Mercedes, Range Rovers and Jaguars lining the driveway. Who knew. Well, he's gorgeous and, as it turns out, majorly talented. We don't know how much longer he'll be able to work. He hasn't been sick at all, but who knows what will happen if word gets out... Still, we hope. But time is not our friend.

LANCE: Time is nobody's friend.

KEVIN: Tell me about it.

[*A reverie for a moment. No change other than that. Except:*]

LANCE: The memorial was beautiful. I mean, trust Peter. It was one of the only really spiritual experiences I've had at that sort of thing. It was out of town on this farm.

KEVIN: A farm?

LANCE: Well, a country place. There must have been over a hundred people. A big white house and a beautiful garden and then this meadow with a huge pond with trees around it.

KEVIN: That's Jim and Judy's place. It's beautiful out there.

LANCE: They had the memorial service in the garden. You know, the usual stories. Peter talked about living with you and all your travels and asked other people if they had anything to say. That was a little weird—we all just stood there, I guess everyone with his own thoughts. Then the girl whose place it was, Judy, started talking, and then one by one everyone began telling stories. It wasn't heavy, it was kind of light. Well, you're light.

KEVIN: [*Seeing it.*] In Kentucky we used to call that testifying. [*Beat. Then wary.*] What kind of "stories"?

LANCE: Anecdotes. Stories. Amusing things. You know.

KEVIN: Ummm.

LANCE: Then we all went through the gate and Peter had had them set up this huge —

KEVIN: — Excuse me, like what kind of "amusing things"?

LANCE: I can't remember exactly what anyone said, it was just —

KEVIN: You have a memory like a rat cage. I've heard you tell the complete scenario scene by scene of movies you saw when you were ten. What kind of amusing stories?

LANCE: Oh . . . Well, a lot of people just read postcards you had sent them from all over the world. [*Beat.*] OK. I said my most vivid memory was seeing you and Peter out at The Millstone one Halloween, you were both in total high drag —

KEVIN: That was my spectacular gown. And the one and only time I've gone out in drag.

LANCE: —And my date ditched me, so I caught a ride with you and Peter in your pickup. And you'd never driven in heels before but you refused to take them off because you said it was vulgar.

KEVIN: I remember it vividly. I did refuse and it is vulgar. [*Beat.*] And you all "went through this gate ... ?"

LANCE: When we left the garden we went through the gate into the meadow overlooking the pond and they had set up this gigantic tent with a catered dinner. I had no idea. I think we all thought the last thing in the world we could do was eat, then we all discovered we were starving. Every seat had one of your silk pillows on it — incredible colors, a little piece of paper pinned to it with where it came from — that we took home as a kind of party favor.

KEVIN: Morbid. Thank God he found a use for those. They've been in storage for years.

LANCE: So we had a fabulous dinner as the sun set, with a string quartet yet, and after dinner we all took a glass of champagne and walked out around the pond, completely circled the pond, the damn thing is more like a lake. And Peter said, "To Kevin!" And we all yelled across the lake, "To Kevin!" and drank a toast to you.

KEVIN: And threw your glasses in the water.

LANCE: We did not. They were rented.

KEVIN: What ever happened to the grand gesture?

LANCE: Then we went back to the tent, about twenty of us, and got totally smashed. I couldn't get out of bed the next day. I have no memory of how I got home.

KEVIN: The kid knows how to throw a party. I told him I didn't want a memorial, just have a bunch of people over for dinner.

LANCE: He did. It was very moving, I still don't know why. I didn't describe it well, it was better than that.

KEVIN: You did OK. I mean, not for a writer, but I can imagine.

KEVIN: [*Cont'd.*] And God knows I know Peter's style. Aren't we all just crawling with style. Not you, of course. I bet you think there's something honest about dirty jeans. You can bet he planned every moment. You want to be sure, in your life, that they get one thing right.

LANCE: They got it right.

[KEVIN *gets up from the bench. In a moment he'll walk away.*]

KEVIN: Well . . .

LANCE: It doesn't work, you know. It just makes it worse.

KEVIN: How's that?

LANCE: The memorials and tributes and — If it's designed to let you go. To help us get on with our lives, or accept the loss. It doesn't work.

KEVIN: Oh. No. That isn't want we want, I don't think. I think we're more selfish than that. [*Calling back.*] I think we want very badly for you to remember. [*Beat.*] I'll be back.

[KEVIN *has walked into the dark shadows and is gone.* LANCE *sits on the bench, as at the top, looking out, lost in thought. The lights fade to black.*]

THE END

Doug Wright

WILDWOOD PARK

Doug Wright

Doug Wright's other works include *The Stonewater Rapture*, *Interrogating the Nude*, *Dinosaurs*, *Lot 13: The Bone Violin*, *Watbanaland*, and a musical, *Buzzsaw Berkeley*, with songs by Michael John LaChiusa. His play *QUILLS*, based on the life and writing of the Marquis de Sade, received the 1995 Kesselring Prize for Best New American Play from the National Arts Club, and a Village Voice Obie Award for Outstanding Achievement in Playwriting. His work has been performed at New York Theater Workshop, the WPA Theater, the Yale Repertory Theater, Lincoln Center, the Wooly Mammoth Theater in Washington D.C., the McCarter Theater in New Jersey, the Cleveland Public Theater, the Geffen Theater in Los Angeles. He has been published by Dramatists Play Service, Heinemann Books' *New American Plays* anthology, *The Paris Review*, and now three times in the Applause Theatre Books' *Best American Short Plays* series. Wright's television scripts include pilot projects for producer Norman Lear, and his film credits include screenplays for Fine Line Features, Fox Searchlight, Talking Wall Pictures, and Dreamworks SKG. He was named a McKnight Fellow for 1995-6 by the Playwrights Center in Minneapolis, and is a past recipient of the William L. Bradley Fellowship at Yale University, the Charles MacArthur Fellowship at the Eugene O'Neill Theater Center, an HBO Fellowship in playwriting, and the Alfred Hodder Fellowship at Princeton University.

CHARACTERS

MS. HAVILAND A realtor. She is middle-aged, a working mother. She wears an attractive quilted jacket, a navy skirt, and cloissonné jewelry. Her shoes are sensible, for walking.

DR. SIMIAN A prospective buyer. He is of indeterminate age, and wears an expensive suit. He is disarmingly handsome.

TIME: *Now.*

SETTING: *The stage is bare. The architecture, the furnishings and the props of the play are all invisible, and indicated by the actors through gesture—not in an overly-demonstrative or "mime" fashion, but simply and clearly, with minimal movement. Even when specific mention is made in the text of night stands, vanities, or fireplaces, these things are not seen; they are created through inference and the power of suggestion.*

A stark, sunny day. Both MS. HAVILAND *and* DR. SIMIAN *wear dark glasses, to shield their eyes from the offending light. They stand side-by-side, in front of the "house," gazing up at its exterior.*

DR. SIMIAN: The neighborhood. It exceeds my expectations. The trees are symmetrical. The mail-boxes have tiny flags. Along the alley, the trash cans all have matching lids.

MS. HAVILAND: It's well-tended.

DR. SIMIAN: It's almost perfection, isn't it?

[DR. SIMIAN *smiles at* MS. HAVILAND. *She does not return the gesture. There is a stiff pause.*]

MS. HAVILAND: How did you hear about this listing?

DR. SIMIAN: The newspaper.

MS. HAVILAND: The Real Estate section?

DR. SIMIAN: Yes.

MS. HAVILAND: That's not possible. Boulevard Realty . . . in the

MS. HAVILAND: [*Cont'd.*] interest of discretion...in the interest of taste...opted not to publish this particular address. So when you called, when you called with your *specific* request...

DR. SIMIAN: The...ah...front page, Ms. Haviland. That is how I knew. I realized...I *surmised*...the house would be for sale.

MS. HAVILAND: Did you?

DR. SIMIAN: And your firm...your size, your reputation...what other firm, I asked myself...

MS. HAVILAND: Well. What other firm *in this area*...

DR. SIMIAN: Surely I am not alone. You must admit, public preoccupation with...*this house*...I am not the first prospective buyer whose interest was initially piqued by reports of an altogether different nature....

MS. HAVILAND: No. You're not. *You most certainly are not.*

[*A tense pause.*]

Where have you been living?

DR. SIMIAN: Glen Ridge.

MS. HAVILAND: I'm not familiar with Glen Ridge.

DR. SIMIAN: No?

MS. HAVILAND: I have never even heard of Glen Ridge.

DR. SIMIAN: Beyond Ridge Falls. Near Beacon Ridge. Before Ridge Dale.

MS. HAVILAND: Suddenly you've decided to move?

DR. SIMIAN: Yes.

MS. HAVILAND: More room? Better schools? A sound investment strategy?

DR. SIMIAN: It's *time*.

MS. HAVILAND: Why *now*?

DR. SIMIAN: I've weathered a change in status.

MS. HAVILAND: Marital? Professional?

DR. SIMIAN: Both.

MS. HAVILAND: I hope it works out. For the best.

DR. SIMIAN: I hope.

[*Another stilted pause.*]

MS. HAVILAND: I'd like to point out some of the exterior features of the house, if I may. It's a Colonial, of course. The portico dates back to the Revolutionary War. Wildwood Park's own *Monticello*. Of course, the drainage system, the storm windows, the pool, the car port—that's all contemporary.

DR. SIMIAN: Conservative, isn't it?

MS. HAVILAND: Classic. Beyond faddish. A constant. [MS. HAVILAND *points.*]

MS. HAVILAND: Notice the weathercock.

DR. SIMIAN: Where? I don't see...I can't quite...

MS. HAVILAND: The rooster.

DR. SIMIAN: The glare ...

MS. HAVILAND: The *silhouette*.

DR. SIMIAN: The sun's so *white*...

MS. HAVILAND: Left of the chimney.

[DR. SIMIAN *uses his hands like a visor, shielding his eyes. He spots the weather vane.*]

DR. SIMIAN: Ah! Yes!

MS. HAVILAND: It wasn't bought; it was commissioned.

DR. SIMIAN: Impressive.

MS. HAVILAND: This house belongs on the dollar bill.

[*Another pause.*]

What sort of work do you do?

DR. SIMIAN: Medical.

MS. HAVILAND: You're not a journalist?

DR. SIMIAN: Should I be?

[MS. HAVILAND *glances from left to right. She speaks in a low, confidential tone.*]

MS. HAVILAND: I have to ask...

DR. SIMIAN: Yes?

MS. HAVILAND: You're not *undercover*, are you?

DR. SIMIAN: Under what?

MS. HAVILAND: You're not *wearing a wire*?

DR. SIMIAN: Excuse me?

MS. HAVILAND: You are not an *opportunist*, are you?

DR. SIMIAN: I rather expected I'd be asking the questions this afternoon.

MS. HAVILAND: I've learned the hard way, Dr. Simian. I can't be too careful. A few weeks ago, a man came, requesting to see the house. He brought a camcorder. He told me that his wife was back home, in Terre Haute, and that he intended to mail the tape back to her, before deciding. Well. You can imagine my surprise, when a few days later, I turned on the television, one of those alarmist news programs, and there it was. Edited. With an ominous soundtrack.

DR. SIMIAN: He'd sold the tape?

MS. HAVILAND: So forgive me if I exert caution.

DR. SIMIAN: My sole interest, Ms. Haviland, is in purchasing a home.

MS. HAVILAND: Thank goodness.

DR. SIMIAN: I am far more invested in a firm foundation, a basement which does not leak, a patio for summer parties than I am in... the unsavory.

MS. HAVILAND: Count yourself among a rarefied few.

DR. SIMIAN: If you distrust my *sincerity*...

MS. HAVILAND: I didn't say that.

DR. SIMIAN: I am *eager* to relocate. I have an *approved loan*. My intentions could not be more *serious*.

MS. HAVILAND: I am *relieved.*

DR. SIMIAN: Would you care to see my correspondence with the bank? A copy of my current mortgage?

MS. HAVILAND: Please. I—

DR. SIMIAN: Proof positive. The listing for my own home in *The Town Tattler.*

MS. HAVILAND: That isn't necessary. [DR. SIMIAN *pulls a folded newspaper from his inner breast pocket.*]

DR. SIMIAN: [*Reading.*] "Glen Ridge Charmer: Raised ranch, designed with family in mind. Three bedroom, two and a half bath, breakfast nook with skylight, basement rec room—"

MS. HAVILAND: I *apologize.*

[DR. SIMIAN *slaps the paper against his hand twice, to flatten it. He re-folds it, and returns it to his pocket. Another short pause.*]

DR. SIMIAN: I would be less than honest—

MS. HAVILAND: [*Quickly.*] Yes?

DR. SIMIAN: — if I didn't confess to an ulterior motive.

MS. HAVILAND: I suspected as much.

DR. SIMIAN: The reason I chose this house ... this *particular* house ... with its rather ... notorious ... history ...

MS. HAVILAND: Mm-hm?

DR. SIMIAN: I am ... I am ... I am a *bargain hunter.*

MS. HAVILAND: Oh. Well.

DR. SIMIAN: Correct me if I'm wrong, but I would assume, by-and-large, your average buyer would have, well ... *trepidation.* A fear that the house had somehow been ... *besmirched.* That it had absorbed its own history, and that it had somehow become ... *a hard sell.* But I am not a superstitious person. Karma, aura. These things mean nothing to me.

MS. HAVILAND: [*With significance.*] I have an unhappy surprise for you, Doctor.

[MS. HAVILAND *makes a thumbs-up gesture, which suggests that the asking price has soared.*]

DR. SIMIAN: No.

MS. HAVILAND: [*Nodding.*] *Oh yes.*

DR. SIMIAN: That's shocking.

MS. HAVILAND: Through the roof.

DR. SIMIAN: Is that the culture? The culture-at-large? Is that what we've become?

MS. HAVILAND: [*As a vulture.*] "Caaw! Caaw!"

DR. SIMIAN: You'll make me a cynical man, Ms. Haviland.

MS. HAVILAND: 1120 Sycamore Avenue has made me a cynical woman.

DR. SIMIAN: And the property values. In the neighborhood. They are—

MS. HAVILAND: Holding their own.

DR. SIMIAN: My, my.

MS. HAVILAND: Wildwood Park has not changed. It is the same enclave it always was. The traffic, of course, is heavier.

DR. SIMIAN: People ignore the blockades.

MS. HAVILAND: It's a constant battle.

DR. SIMIAN: License plates from Iowa. From California.

MS. HAVILAND: The furor will die down. By the time you're ready to take occupancy...should you decide to pursue the house... the traffic will taper, I assure you...

DR. SIMIAN: Naturally.

MS. HAVILAND: We still boast excellent schools. And I don't have to tell you, Doctor, the shopping in our little town is world-class. We have our own library. Our own post office. Our own women's auxiliary, and our own police force.

DR. SIMIAN: I couldn't help noticing. At the curb. The squad car.

MS. HAVILAND: A precaution against vandalism. A few weeks ago—
a rock, some spray paint. *Eggs.*

DR. SIMIAN: I see.

MS. HAVILAND: An isolated incident.

DR. SIMIAN: It's to be expected.

MS. HAVILAND: It gives me great civic pride, Dr. Simian, to tell you
that—for weeks—the front porch was teeming with candles.
Bouquets. My own daughter made a wreath from sapling twigs.
I was moved.

[*A pause.*]

   Shall we go inside?

DR. SIMIAN: Please.

[MS. HAVILAND *begins the complicated process of opening the door.*]

MS. HAVILAND: You'll notice there are two double-bolt locks, with
pick proof cylinders. In addition, the house has a twenty-four
hour, fully computerized security system with built-in alarm,
automatic police and fire notification, and an electronic fence.
Oh, and the lights. They're on timers.

DR. SIMIAN: These precautions. They are . . . recent?

MS. HAVILAND: Yes. They are *new.* They were not here *before.*
[*Another brief pause.*]

   Shall we?

[*They "enter" the house.*]

[*As* MS. HAVILAND *and* DR. SIMIAN *move from room to room
throughout the house, they follow the markings on the blueprint beneath them. It's as though they are tokens on a board game, moving through implied three-dimensional space.*]

MS. HAVILAND: Eight thousand square feet, Doctor. Five bedrooms,
four and a half baths.

[MS. HAVILAND *makes an extravagant gesture, indicating the vast
expanse of the front hall.*]

   Notice the upward sweep of the foyer. The walls rise the

MS. HAVILAND: [*Cont'd.*] full height of the house. The candelabra; that's brass. And look at the sunlight streaming down. We're flooded, aren't we? We're drowning in light.

[MS. HAVILAND *removes her sunglasses.*]

 Dr. Simian. Your glasses. The color scheme.

DR. SIMIAN: Safe now, isn't it?

[DR. SIMIAN *removes his glasses, and slips them into his breast pocket.*]

 Well, well. Isn't that strange. A cryptogram of some sort, isn't it?

MS. HAVILAND: Where?

DR. SIMIAN: Above the arch.

MS. HAVILAND: Ah, yes. *That*. It's Pennsylvania Dutch. A touch of *whimsy*.

DR. SIMIAN: What is it?

MS. HAVILAND: *Oh, dear.*

DR. SIMIAN: You're blushing.

MS. HAVILAND: It's a hex sign. *That is a hex sign.*

DR. SIMIAN: No.

MS. HAVILAND: For *good* luck.

DR. SIMIAN: One can't help thinking—

MS. HAVILAND: Please. Don't.

[DR. SIMIAN *wanders ahead.*]

DR. SIMIAN: Is this the living room?

MS. HAVILAND: I must ask you, *don't barrel through*.

DR. SIMIAN: Forgive me.

MS. HAVILAND: I am conducting the tour.

DR. SIMIAN: Of course.

MS. HAVILAND: "Follow the Leader." *Indulge me.* Watch your step.

DR. SIMIAN: Thank you.

[*They "enter" the living room.*]

MS. HAVILAND: An exquisite space, Doctor. Floor-length windows. On the ceiling, rosettes. And the fireplace. You'll note its size. Its grandeur. Quarried marble. Venetian, I think.

[DR. SIMIAN *runs his hand along the mantelpiece.*]

DR. SIMIAN: A substantial mantel.

MS. HAVILAND: Yes.

DR. SIMIAN: Can it support sculpture? Can it support *objets d'art*?

MS. HAVILAND: [*Curtly:*] I think you can *gauge*, Doctor.

DR. SIMIAN: The house is still furnished.

MS. HAVILAND: Not for long.

DR. SIMIAN: It looks... *inhabited*.

MS. HAVILAND: Things happened so quickly. The house was placed on the market so soon.

DR. SIMIAN: This room reminds me, Ms. Haviland, of an exhibit in a museum. The stillness. Its past hanging heavy in the air, unspoken.

MS. HAVILAND: There was of course, a will, provisions were naturally made, but in the absence of any... *beneficiaries*... the furniture will be sold at auction.

DR. SIMIAN: Aha.

MS. HAVILAND: The proceeds will benefit the Children's Legal Defense Fund.

DR. SIMIAN: An appropriate gesture.

MS. HAVILAND: If... *when* it is recovered... after its release from evidence... the Nubian statuette is expected to fetch a startling sum.

DR. SIMIAN: Surprise, surprise.

MS. HAVILAND: "Who," I ask myself. "Who would buy—"

DR. SIMIAN: Our society is predatory.

MS. HAVILAND: I'd almost bid on it myself. So I could take it home.

MS. HAVILAND: [*Cont'd.*] So I could take it home with me, and with my husband's hammer—

DR. SIMIAN: Yes.

MS. HAVILAND: I'd pay a hefty sum, just for the pleasure of seeing it *destroyed.*

DR. SIMIAN: Do you know, Ms. Haviland, the totems of our time?

MS. HAVILAND: The "totems"?

DR. SIMIAN: In Milwaukee, a stock pot on the stove. In Beverly Hills, an errant glove.

MS. HAVILAND: And among them ....

DR. SIMIAN: ... yes ...

MS. HAVILAND: ... in Wildwood Park ...

DR. SIMIAN: ... exactly ...

MS. HAVILAND: A Nubian statuette.

[*They "enter" the dining room.*]

You'll notice how the living room segues into the dining room. Dignified, isn't it? Vintage. You can comfortably seat up to twenty-four. Those sconces are from a tavern in the Hudson River Valley, circa 1890. You'd never guess ...

[MS. HAVILAND *toys with a light switch.*]

... they're on a dimmer.

DR. SIMIAN: The kitchen can't be far behind.

MS. HAVILAND: Careful; that door swings.

[*They "enter" the kitchen.*]

A rustic look, but with every modern convenience. An electric oven, an industrial range, a microwave, and—for "old world" effect, a touch of antique romance—a wood-burning stove. Charming, yes? The cabinets are cherry wood, and the counter tops are Mexican tile. And you'll note, there's an island ... cherry, too, with a granite top, pull-out shelves below, and of course ... a ... you see it, there ... with a ... a ... *oh, dear* ...

DR. SIMIAN: A what?

MS. HAVILAND: *A block.*

DR. SIMIAN: A block?

MS. HAVILAND: A *butcher* block.

[MS. HAVILAND *smiles a guilty smile.*]

DR. SIMIAN: Why, Ms. Haviland.

MS. HAVILAND: I'm horrible.

DR. SIMIAN: You've made a pun.

MS. HAVILAND: I'm a monster.

DR. SIMIAN: A pun, that's all.

MS. HAVILAND: I should have my tongue *cut out.*

[MS. HAVILAND *suppresses a giggle.*]

Oh, there. I've done it again.

DR. SIMIAN: You're giddy.

MS. HAVILAND: Shame on me. Shame on us both.

DR. SIMIAN: Humor, Ms. Haviland, fortifies.

[MS. HAVILAND *wipes tears from her eyes, composing herself.*]

MS. HAVILAND: This house, all day, every day. Dodging past the news vans. Those rapacious tourists. I fight my way past. *I have business here.* If it's made me loopy, Doctor, then I have every right to be.

DR. SIMIAN: Bravo.

MS. HAVILAND: My husband says it's nerves. My husband says all those infernal shutter-bugs, all those flash-bulbs, they've *seared* my *brain.*

DR. SIMIAN: A fanciful thought, Ms. Haviland.

MS. HAVILAND: My husband tells me that I take things to *heart.* That I should go on *automatic.* That is easy, Doctor, for *my* husband to say. It is, after all, his *forte.*

[MS. HAVILAND *snorts a laugh, a little bark, which afterwards makes her cheeks burn red.*]

DR. SIMIAN: I'd like to see the master bedroom.

MS. HAVILAND: [*Sadly.*] I'm exhausted. Frayed. That's the truth.

DR. SIMIAN: The bedroom, please.

MS. HAVILAND: But you haven't seen the den. You haven't seen the home office, the play room, the maid's suite—

[DR. SIMIAN *leaves the kitchen.* MS. HAVILAND *follows, suddenly strident.*]

MS. HAVILAND: *Don't charge ahead!*

DR. SIMIAN: I'm overeager.

MS. HAVILAND: I can't have people *wander*. I can't have people *traipsing through*.

DR. SIMIAN: I might go nosing in the linen cupboards.

MS. HAVILAND: Don't be absurd; it's not that.

DR. SIMIAN: I might empty the medicine chest.

MS. HAVILAND: *It's not that at all.*

DR. SIMIAN: I might pirate away knick-knacks, and open a souvenir stand on the corner.

MS. HAVILAND: I am responsible for the house, and its contents. I have *police* on my back. There are *attorneys*. A *battalion* of *lawyers*. Under the circumstances, it is an *overwhelming* duty.

DR. SIMIAN: I was insensitive.

MS. HAVILAND: My psychiatrist is *worried*. She *fears* for my *safety*. I am on *tranquilizers*.

DR. SIMIAN: It must be a strain.

[*They "enter" the master bedroom.*]

MS. HAVILAND: There are ceiling fans in all the bedrooms. You'll find that saves a fortune in cooling costs during the summer. A walk-in closet, which I dare say is larger than my living room.

DR. SIMIAN: Poignant, isn't it?

MS. HAVILAND: What?

DR. SIMIAN: There. On the floor, by the bed.

[DR. SIMIAN *points:*]

Empty shoes.

[*A palpable chill descends in the room.*]

This is where it began, yes?

MS. HAVILAND: [*Alarmed.*] *I beg your pardon?*

[*The following dialogue is rapid-fire, accelerating in speed, a crescendo.*]

DR. SIMIAN: The balcony doors.

MS. HAVILAND: I'd rather not.

DR. SIMIAN: They were left ajar? They were pried open?

MS. HAVILAND: You know I don't *approve* . . . I don't *appreciate* . . .

DR. SIMIAN: Around the lock, scuffs. Gouges.

MS. HAVILAND: I'm here to show the house. I'm not a *detective*. I am not a *talk show host*.

DR. SIMIAN: Forgive me. But I couldn't help noticing—there—on the wainscoting—

MS. HAVILAND: The paint has been retouched.

DR. SIMIAN: Along the molding—

MS. HAVILAND: The carpets have all been shampooed.

DR. SIMIAN: Traces exist.

MS. HAVILAND: No. Where?

DR. SIMIAN: Splotches.

MS. HAVILAND: *There is nothing to notice.*

DR. SIMIAN: There. On the edge. Rimming the baseboards . . .

MS. HAVILAND: *I don't see a thing.*

DR. SIMIAN: The electrical outlets. Where are they?

MS. HAVILAND: [*Frightened.*] *What?*

DR. SIMIAN: It's a fair question.

MS. HAVILAND: It's a *taunt*. It's a *jibe*.

DR. SIMIAN: For *lamps*. For *clock-radios*. A *laptop*. These things require *voltage*.

MS. HAVILAND: All sorts of *appliances* require voltage, Dr. Simian. ALL SORTS.

DR. SIMIAN: A heating pad, perhaps! An electric blanket! Nothing menacing, nothing *pneumatic*.

MS. HAVILAND: Don't be *facetious*, Doctor.

DR. SIMIAN: SHOW ME.

MS. HAVILAND: Please!

DR. SIMIAN: *WHERE?*

MS. HAVILAND: Behind the headboard. And there. Under the vanity.

[*A short rest.* DR. SIMIAN *goes to the vanity table. He gets down on his hands and knees, and looks beneath it.*]

DR. SIMIAN: The wall plate. It's scorched.

MS. HAVILAND: What did you expect? It was *overburdened*, it was profoundly misused.

DR. SIMIAN: Hidden down here. Out of sight, out of mind?

MS. HAVILAND: There are still a few details...

DR. SIMIAN: A few *vestiges?*

MS. HAVILAND: A few REPAIRS.

[DR. SIMIAN *stands up. He looks in the mirror of the vanity, back at* MS. HAVILAND's *reflection.*]

DR. SIMIAN: She was a singer for a while, wasn't she? She was on television in New York.

MS. HAVILAND: Dr. Simian, if you have inquiries about the house, about its *architecture*, its *design*, its *upkeep*—

DR. SIMIAN: She sold thigh cream, and overcame personal problems. And he made a fortune in junk bonds.

MS. HAVILAND: I'm sure I don't know.

DR. SIMIAN: Of course you know. *Everybody knows.*

MS. HAVILAND: I'm not *interested.*

DR. SIMIAN: You can't flip on the radio, you can't watch the news—

MS. HAVILAND: I *mute,* Doctor.

DR. SIMIAN: Even pick up a paper—

MS. HAVILAND: Because of my *professional obligations* . . . my *necessary involvement* . . . there are certain things I'd rather *not* know . . .

[DR. SIMIAN *notices something on the wall. He points:*]

DR. SIMIAN: The little one. The youngest. The girl.

MS. HAVILAND: I have recommended to my employer that we remove these photographs. They're unnerving. Prospective buyers are unhinged.

[DR. SIMIAN *traces the shape of the frame on the wall, with his finger.*]

DR. SIMIAN: Freckles. A gap tooth.

MS. HAVILAND: Their eyes follow you. No matter where you turn.

DR. SIMIAN: What was her name?

MS. HAVILAND: All day, every day, they stare me down. Here at work. In *this* room. Outside, too. In line at the grocery store, the tabloids. On *T-shirts,* for God's sake, they've even been silkscreened . . .

[DR. SIMIAN *notices another picture, this one on the night stand. He approaches it, and picks it up.*]

DR. SIMIAN: Here she is again, in a pageant of some kind.

MS. HAVILAND: *Put that down!*

DR. SIMIAN: Look at her. She's dressed as a radish. She's singing.

MS. HAVILAND: *You're not supposed to touch things!*

DR. SIMIAN: Oh, and look. Washing the family dog.

[DR. SIMIAN *puts the picture back in its place.*]

    Is it true? *Even the dog?*

MS. HAVILAND: *You are disturbing things . . . me . . .*

DR. SIMIAN: The police posit that, sometime after three, she . . . the girl . . . heard a sound. If only she'd opted to hide under the bed, they said, if only she'd run out the back door, they said, if only her little legs—

[MS. HAVILAND *relents, and cuts him off.*]

MS. HAVILAND: *Heather*.

[*A pause.*]

    Her name was Heather.

DR. SIMIAN: Take me to the nursery.

[*Another pause.*]

MS. HAVILAND: Do you have *children*, Dr. Simian?

DR. SIMIAN: More questions, Ms. Haviland?

MS. HAVILAND: Because if you don't have children . . . if you don't have *young* children . . . then the nursery is *irrelevant*.

DR. SIMIAN: Surely you are not offering the house on a room-by-room basis.

MS. HAVILAND: Don't insult me, Doctor.

DR. SIMIAN: I am interested in the entire structure. Not a portion thereof.

MS. HAVILAND: It's just, you've hardly inspected the house. The living room, the kitchen, the dining room, and nary a remark. "He's bound to have questions about the plumbing," I say to myself, "and radon, and chimney flues. He'll want to know about the new roof, about winter insulation." *But no!*

DR. SIMIAN: Ms. Haviland, I—

MS. HAVILAND: *Oh, no!* With you it's all . . . hex signs . . . and hollow shoes . . . and *little girls*.

DR. SIMIAN: There are still whole rooms—

MS. HAVILAND: The tour is over.

DR. SIMIAN: *Entire wings*—

MS. HAVILAND: It's half-past-five.

DR. SIMIAN: The backyard. The guest house.

MS. HAVILAND: The work day has come to a close.

DR. SIMIAN: I've driven a great distance—

MS. HAVILAND: Please leave.

DR. SIMIAN: I can't readily arrange a second visit—

MS. HAVILAND: Wildwood Park is a private community. A discreet community. It is not some sordid *theme park*, Doctor. It is not a *freak show*, with its tent flaps spread—no, *torn*—open for the nation's *amusement*. It is not some *dime store, penny-dreadful, Stephen King*—

DR. SIMIAN: A daughter, six, and a son, eight.

[*A pause.* MS. HAVILAND *blushes. Slowly and definitively—like a lawyer giving a summation of evidence—*DR. SIMIAN *continues.*]

DR. SIMIAN: [*Cont'd.*] My daughter's name is Sarah. She has a widow's peak, hazel eyes, and what at first might seem like an extra appendage but which, upon closer examination, reveals itself to be a very old, very odorous stuffed bear, a veteran of her bouts with the flu, the washing machine, and even a long, torturous night spent, abandoned, in the supermarket. He has one eye, and leaves an unmistakable trail of fleece wherever he goes. His name, should you require it for the record, is Mister Pete. My son is Joshua. Because he was slow to walk, he was misdiagnosed with cerebral palsy, and it gave us quite a scare. Now he is graceful and long of limb. He is obsessed with choo-choo trains. The court—at the recommendation of my wife's psychologist—has granted custody solely to me.

[*A long pause.* MS. HAVILAND *swallows, hard. Her face is pinched. Finally.*]

MS. HAVILAND: It's upstairs.

[*They climb in silence up a flight of stairs to the nursery.*]

The wallpaper is a pale green candy-stripe, suitable for a boy or girl. The border is Beatrix Potter. Window guards, of course. An intercom, so wherever you are in the house, you never feel far away. The children have their own bath. The basin is low, and the tub has a rail. As you can see, the emphasis here...the design insures...*attempts* to insure...a child's *safety*.

[MS. HAVILAND *sighs, heavily*.]

I want *desperately* to sell this house. I do not like being a

MS. HAVILAND: [*Cont'd.*] *sentinel*. I do not like standing by quietly as people *gape* and *mock* and *jeer*. It's a disease, Doctor, and it is contagious, and some days, it's true, I fear *I am catching it*. This is not a *movie*. This is not *television*.

[MS. HAVILAND *cries, softly*.]

What I do is necessary. Houses are bought and sold. But sometimes...what I do here feels like *desecration*. Walking in their tracks. Sifting through their things. *Oh, God, forgive me*.

DR. SIMIAN: Did you know the victims, Ms. Haviland?

MS. HAVILAND: No.

DR. SIMIAN: Even a passing acquaintance?

MS. HAVILAND: No.

DR. SIMIAN: Then permit me to suggest...this unfortunate event wields far greater power over you than perhaps it should.

MS. HAVILAND: *It's all I think about*. I have my own husband, my own children, we're remodeling our place on the Eastern shore, my mother has *cancer*—these things, they are *the substance of my life*—and now they are merely *distractions* to keep me from *obsessing*...to drive the endless litany of questions from my head. *Why that night? Why those children? The parents, were they spared the sight, were they taken first, or were they forced to witness...And ...this, Doctor, haunts me the most...what sort of man...what kind of brute creature...*

DR. SIMIAN: Anyone, I suppose, would wonder.

MS. HAVILAND: It's worse than *wondering*. Far more *extreme*.

[MS. HAVILAND *cannot continue. She musters strength, and then:*]

Once...a canceled appointment...I barricaded the front door...reset the alarm....drew the blinds... from her closet, a robe, blue with pink piping...and I sat in the study...

swathed in her smell...poring through family albums.
Birthdays. Christmases. The first day at school, afternoons at
the Fair, anniversary notes, private, still perfumed...They
were not mine, but they *could've* been mine, they might as well
have been mine...I am such a *hypocrite*, Doctor.

DR. SIMIAN: It's all right.

MS. HAVILAND: I sat, alone in this house, with the lights out, and I
waited.

DR. SIMIAN: For what?

MS. HAVILAND: The balcony door to open. The soft, almost noise-
less crunch of rubber soles on white shag...

DR. SIMIAN: Why?

MS. HAVILAND: *If God gave me the chance to see evil, Doctor, then I
would look. And that's a terrible thing to know about oneself.*

[MS. HAVILAND *looks at* DR. SIMIAN, *pleadingly. He responds in a
tender voice.*]

DR. SIMIAN: You are...

MS. HAVILAND: Go ahead. Say it.

DR. SIMIAN: You are a *very bad* little monkey.

MS. HAVILAND: I want my own life *back*. My own *concerns*.

[DR. SIMIAN *takes her hand*. MS. HAVILAND *takes a moment to
calm herself.*]

MR. SIMIAN: Take a breath. We don't have to move. Remember, Ms.
Haviland, that you have your *own* home. Your *own* retreat.

MS. HAVILAND: A new family. Here. That would be nice. An *anti-
dote*, yes, Doctor? Isn't that the word? I hope that you will con-
template this house. I hope that with all my heart.

DR. SIMIAN: I intend to.

MS. HAVILAND: I would like...I would like to be free of this. And I
would like you...

DR. SIMIAN: Yes?

MS. HAVILAND: You...and your children...a fresh start.

DR. SIMIAN: Remember, Ms. Haviland that you have your *own* home. Your own *retreat*.

MS. HAVILAND: [*Consoled.*] Yes.

[DR. SIMIAN *slips his dark glasses out of his pocket. He puts them back on.*]

DR. SIMIAN: Would you see me to the porch?

MS. HAVILAND: My pleasure, Doctor.

[*Again, they back-track in silence, this time without any obvious tension. They leave the house, and step outside onto the porch.*]

I'm embarrassed. My employer.

DR. SIMIAN: The robe, the snapshots.

MS. HAVILAND: If they knew...

DR. SIMIAN: Not a word.

MS. HAVILAND: Here's my card. If you have any questions, don't hesitate.

DR. SIMIAN: [*Taking the card:*] I won't.

MS. HAVILAND: I'm sorry. My *display*.

DR. SIMIAN: Don't mention it.

MS. HAVILAND: I've shown you quite an afternoon, haven't I?

DR. SIMIAN: Quite.

MS. HAVILAND: You. A stranger.

DR. SIMIAN: I did wonder—

MS. HAVILAND: Yes?

DR. SIMIAN: A musing. A curiosity. Nothing pragmatic. Nothing "nuts and bolts."

MS. HAVILAND: Please.

DR. SIMIAN: One thing concerns me.

MS. HAVILAND: Oh?

DR. SIMIAN: No arrest. No conviction.

MS. HAVILAND: Sadly enough.

DR. SIMIAN: No substantive leads.

MS. HAVILAND: Every day, we pray.

DR. SIMIAN: As you suggest . . . there exists the possibility of . . . well, the perpetrator . . . he might return.

MS. HAVILAND: I see my paranoia has spread.

DR. SIMIAN: No, no. Your *prescience*. It's often been documented. Many a criminal—in spite of the immense risk—will return to the scene of the crime.

MS. HAVILAND: I can't *imagine* . . .

DR. SIMIAN: Regardless of the alarms. The reversible bolts. The electronic fences. Even the squad car at the curb.

MS. HAVILAND: But why?

DR. SIMIAN: All in pursuit of the covert thrill that comes with the successful commission of a wrongful act.

MS. HAVILAND: Is that *true*? Is that what they *say*?

DR. SIMIAN: It would not shock me to learn, Ms. Haviland, that you yourself had escorted the culprit through these halls.

MS. HAVILAND: It is a good thing that I am so thorough, Doctor. So vigilant.

DR. SIMIAN: He feigns interest in the housing market. Comes well-armed, perhaps, with the classifieds. You interrogate him, and for every question, he has a ready quip. He is from an obscure town. He is a banker. No. A lawyer. No. A doctor.

[MS. HAVILAND *freezes. Her whole body seems to clench.* DR. SIMIAN *takes a step closer to her.*]

MS. HAVILAND: Yes.

[DR. SIMIAN *takes another step, even closer.*]

DR. SIMIAN: He is newly married. No. Expecting a baby.

MS. HAVILAND: No. Separated.

[*And another step closer.*]

DR. SIMIAN: He has grown daughters. No. Adopted sons. No—

[DR. SIMIAN *is so near, she can feel his breath.*]

MS. HAVILAND: *A boy and a girl. One of each. She has a toy . . . it's plush . . . Mister Somebody . . . .*

[DR. SIMIAN *cocks an eyebrow, and waits for* MS. HAVILAND *to finish.*]

I can't . . . . I don't . . . . oh, God . . . .

[DR. SIMIAN *reaches down, and takes her hand. He separates her fingers with his own, and intertwines them. He speaks in a sensuous, hypnotic tone.*]

[*Deep within* MS. HAVILAND, *continental plates begin to shift.*]

DR. SIMIAN: You usher him over the threshold. As you patter on—stucco and mini-blinds and Formica and chintz—with each step he's reliving, with a kind of salacious glee, the very night he thwarted every fragile notion of civilized behavior. The very night he let loose the constraints of his own base nature, and made the very darkest kind of history.

[*With his free hand, gently,* DR. SIMIAN *takes* MS. HAVILAND *by the chin. He raises her face to meet his.*]

[*They stare at one another.*]

Tell me. *Do you ever consider that possibility?*

MS. HAVILAND: No. I do not.

DR. SIMIAN: Perhaps you should.

MS. HAVILAND: *I emphatically do not.* I can't . . . *afford* . . . to entertain such . . . *notions.* It would render my job untenable.

DR. SIMIAN: Yes.

MS. HAVILAND: It would induce paralysis. It would hold me captive.

DR. SIMIAN: Precisely.

MS. HAVILAND: *I cannot live my life that way.*

DR. SIMIAN: You're a wise woman.

[MS. HAVILAND *speaks with a very slight, almost imperceptible tremor.*]

MS. HAVILAND: I hope that you will consider this house. I hope that you are in the market, and I hope that you will buy.

[DR. SIMIAN *nods in the direction of the squad car.*]

DR. SIMIAN: Perhaps, when I leave, you'll offer the policeman a cup of coffee.

MS. HAVILAND: No.

DR. SIMIAN: Perhaps you'll have a conversation.

MS. HAVILAND: We've never met. I see him every morning, but we've never met.

DR. SIMIAN: Perhaps today is the day.

MS. HAVILAND: I do not know him.

DR. SIMIAN: That doesn't preclude a polite introduction.

MS. HAVILAND: I know *you*, Doctor.

DR. SIMIAN: Thank you.

MS. HAVILAND: You are the man whom I know.

DR. SIMIAN: Thank you *so much*.

[DR. SIMIAN *lets her hand go. He takes a step back.*]

[MS. HAVILAND *wavers, starts to melt into him. She holds herself back.*]

It's been a lovely afternoon. And the house. The house is beautiful.

[DR. SIMIAN *turns to leave.* MS. HAVILAND *calls him back.*]

MS. HAVILAND: You're interested, then?

DR. SIMIAN: Yes.

[*Again,* DR. SIMIAN *turns to go. Again,* MS. HAVILAND *stops him.*]

MS. HAVILAND: [*Impulsively.*] Dr. Simian?

DR. SIMIAN: Ms. Haviland?

MS. HAVILAND: [*Darkly; almost seductively.*] You *are* interested?

[DR. SIMIAN *smiles an enigmatic smile. He holds up* MS. HAVI-

LAND's *business card. With deliberate slowness, he slips it into his breast pocket. He pats his heart, three times.*]

[*They stare at one another a long time. Finally,* DR. SIMIAN *leaves.*]

[MS. HAVILAND *lingers after him for a moment. Slowly, she turns back, to gaze at the house.*]

[*Slow fade.*]

END OF PLAY